A KIND OF GRACE

A TREASURY OF SPORTSWRITING BY WOMEN

EDITED BY RON RAPOPORT

WITH AN AFTERWORD BY MARY GARBER

ZENOBIA PRESS
A DIVISION OF RDR BOOKS
BERKELEY, CALIFORNIA

First Zenobia Press Edition, May 1994

Published in the United States of America by Zenobia Press, a division of RDR Books.

ISBN 1-57143-013-X

Library of Congress Catalog Card Number: 94-60001

Grateful acknowledgement is made to the following writers and publications for permission to reprint the articles contained in this book:
"Life on the Fly" by Laura Vecsey: © The *Times Union*, Albany, NY.
"Out of Bosnia: 'Our Tennis Courts Are Now a Graveyard'" by Karen Rosen; "A Gift For Vivian Stringer" by Ailene Voisin: © The *Atlanta Journal-Constitution*.
"Battle with Bulimia Tarnishes Cohen's Golden World" by Suzanne Halliburton: © The *Austin American-Statesman*.
"Richly Rewarded" by Barbara Barker: © The *Record*, Bergen, NJ.
"Driving Force" by Jackie MacMullan: © The *Boston Globe*.
"The Pride Of East St. Louis" by Toni Ginnetti: © The *Chicago Sun-Times*.
"Pam Minick: Inexorably Tied To Roping" by Cathy Harasta; "Jennifer Capriati's Helping Hands" by Kelly Carter: © 1992, The *Dallas Morning News*.
"The Lady Buffs Are Finally Getting Their Due" by Donna Carter: © The *Denver Post*.
"Memories of Iowa's Cherished Six-Girl Game" by Jane Burns; "Cross Country To Memory's Finish Line" by Rachel Blount: © The *Des Moines Register and Tribune Company*.
"Tonya Harding: Skating On The Edge" by Michelle Kaufman: © The *Detroit Free Press*.
"Runner's Story: Why Did Kathy Ormsby Jump Off That Bridge?" By Sharon Robb: © The *Fort Lauderdale Sun-Sentinel*.
"Trying Out" by Michele Himmelberg: © The *Fort Myers News-Press*.
"Team Player" by Patricia Rodriguez: © 1993, The *Fort Worth Star-Telegram*.
"The Fight Of Heather Farr's Life" by Betty Cuniberti; "The Most Intimidating Game Of All" by Lesley Visser: © *Golf Digest*.
"For John and Debbie Lucas, The Demons Never Far Away" by Helen Ross: © The *News & Record*, Greensboro, NC.
"The Lady Who Rode Like A Man" by Maryjean Wall: © The *Horsemen's Journal*.
"AWOL Tackle Puts Family First" by Melanie Hauser: © 1993, The *Houston Post*.
"Lynette Woodard: From Blacktop To Desktop" by Jo-Ann Barnas: © The *Kansas City Star*.
"I've Seen More Flesh On The M1 Roadworks!" by Liz Kahn: © *The Mail On Sunday*, London, England.
"Mike Boyd's Field Of Dreamers" by Elizabeth M. Cosin: © The Los Angeles *Daily News*.
"Oh, No! Not Another Boring Interview With Steve Carlton" by Diane K. Shah: © The *Los Angeles Herald-Examiner*.
"Zola Budd: On The Run No More" by Julie Cart; "Angels' Jackie Autry Increasingly Taking Reins from Cowboy" by Robyn Norwood; "Why Aren't Women Racing At Indy? Janet Guthrie Knows" by Tracy Dodds; "A.C. Green And The Abstinence Rap" by Helene Elliott; "The Cannon Is Quiet" by Maryann Hudson: © The *Los Angeles Times*.
"An Emotional Goodbye To Chucky" by Lynn Zinser: © The *Commercial-Appeal*, Memphis, TN.

Cover Photograph by David Madison
Cover Design: Bonnie Smetts
Book Design: Richard Harris

The publisher acknowledges the generous assistance of Deborah Dunn, Calvin Goodman, Elizabeth Kelly, Wendy Ann Logsdon, Li Suk Woon and the Association For Women In Sports Media.

Zenobia Press, P.O. Box 5212, Berkeley, CA 94705

Printed in Hong Kong by Twin Age Limited.

FOR JOAN, REBECCA AND JULIE
—WHO FIGURED ONE IN THE FAMILY WAS ENOUGH.

ACKNOWLEDGMENTS

One of the many gratifications of assembling this book was the enthusiasm with which it was greeted by so many of the best sportswriters I know. I am indebted to all of them for searching their files and their memories for the articles that appear here.

In addition, I am grateful to a number of people for valuable advice, ideas and suggestions. Among them are Jayne Custred, Mike Downey, Michael Farber, John Fried, Ken and Yetta Goodman, Dave Kindred, Lisa Nehus-Saxon and George Vecsey. Michele Himmelberg, Mary Schmitt and Lynn Zinser of the Association For Women In Sports Media repaid my membership dues to that organization many times over.

Thanks also to Bob Burdick, the editor of the Los Angeles *Daily News*, for his encouragement and assistance, and to Margaret Douglas, the *Daily News*'s chief librarian, for her wizardry at locating many of the articles via computer. Wendy Ann Logsdon and Deborah Dunn of RDR Books deserve special thanks for their work in bringing this book to publication.

I DON'T THINK BEING AN ATHLETE IS UNFEMININE.
I THINK OF IT AS A KIND OF GRACE

—Jackie Joyner-Kersee
(Quoted by Tom Callahan
in *Time*, Sept. 19, 1988)

TABLE OF CONTENTS

INTRODUCTION

by Ron Rapoport

I KNEW I WANTED TO BE A SPORTSWRITER WHEN I WAS 14 YEARS OLD.
I had discovered Mark Harris's *Bang The Drum Slowly* in the library and Doc Greene's sports columns in the *Detroit News* and I never had a second thought.

The idea that you could spend your life going to ball games, talking about sports and being around athletes without *being* an athlete was an amazing discovery. You mean all you had to do was *write?* Why, anybody could write. That was something, as Indiana University basketball coach Bobby Knight has said in dismissing sportswriters, we all learn in the second grade.

It never occurred to me back then that there might be any 14-year-old girls who wanted to be sportswriters. I certainly didn't know any, nor did I encounter any women sportswriters when I went to college or in my first years on the job. But that has all changed, as the 66 women who have contributed to this book demonstrate.

It is no accident that with only a few lonely exceptions women's bylines began appearing in the sports section in the early 1970s. Sport is a metaphor for life in more ways than one and the women's movement is no exception. Billie Jean King's tennis match with Bobby Riggs in 1973 is occasionally cited as one of the great symbolic events of women's liberation. What is often overlooked is how few women were there to cover it.

In those days, women sportswriters were so rare that even athletes who were not offended by their presence found it hard to take them seriously. When Lesley Visser was a sportswriter for the *Boston Globe*, she once stood outside the Pittsburgh Steelers' locker room—there was no question of her actually entering it—waiting to interview quarterback Terry Bradshaw. When he finally emerged and saw her holding a notebook, Bradshaw did the natural thing: He took it from her and signed it.

But today, the revolution is complete. Visser and Bradshaw went on to cover football for the same television network and women in great numbers write for the nation's sports pages. Nor do they cover only women athletes or write innocuous features that fit some sports editor's idea of a subject that would benefit from "a woman's touch." Today, women cover baseball, football, basketball, hockey and college sports of every description. They write about horse racing, tennis and golf. They do investigative reporting and write columns. A few have even overcome their sports editors' outmoded assignment notions by becoming sports editors themselves.

But if women sportswriters no longer face the problem of standing out in a crowd—a serious problem indeed in a trade where going unnoticed can be essential—they are still not able to relax completely. They may have won every battle of equal access, but not all male athletes or readers (or, alas, sportswriters) have raised the white flag of acceptance.

When Mary Jollimore's weekly sports column appears in the *Toronto Globe and Mail*, she routinely gets a call from an elderly man who says she ought to get married, stay home and please her husband. Julie Vader, a columnist for *The Oregonian*, was once told by a male colleague that women could never be good sportswriters because they hadn't played baseball and football when they were children. "The more worked up he got, the more I wanted to tell him not to worry his pretty little head about it, and that he was beautiful when he was mad," Vader says.

But these naysayers no longer matter much. They have been overwhelmed by sheer numbers, and by the fact that a second generation of women sportswriters, one that took its cue from the first, is now on the job.

When Jo-Ann Barnas of the *Kansas City Star* was a teen-ager, her family took a trip to Washington, DC, where they saw most of the usual sights. None of them moved her as much as finding a story in the *Washington Post* about the Redskins written by Betty Cuniberti. Later, when Barnas went to Michigan State, she was anxious to meet another role model, Lynn Henning, who covered Big Ten sports for the *Detroit News*. They became friends, but only after Barnas got over the disappointment of discovering Henning was a young man, incipient bald spot and all.

One of the major differences between male and female sportswriters is that the women are often better athletes. Most of us, who couldn't hit a curveball and cringed at the thought of being tackled, came to enjoy sports by watching. Many of them, in a manner lovingly described in an article by Mariah Burton Nelson in *Ms.*, did so by playing.

Of the contributors to this book, Donna Carter, Jackie MacMullan, Michele Himmelberg and Nelson were college basketball players. Karen Crouse was a varsity swimmer. Julie Cart was a scholarship athlete who threw the discus well enough to make the U.S. Olympic trials. Mary Jean Wall is an accomplished horsewoman. Christine Brennan played tennis, field hockey and basketball and was her high school's Senior Athlete of the Year. Lesley Visser was captain of her high school's field hockey and basketball teams. Others, like

Karen Rosen and Sally Ann Michalov, developed their interest through their fathers who were coaches.

Another point of entry for women into sportswriting has been watching their fathers go to work. The wild humor found in Dan Jenkins's magazine articles about golf and football—and in his novels—has convinced many readers he must be having an awfully good time writing about sports. Sally Jenkins, now a senior writer at *Sports Illustrated*, was among them. "I get to recreate for a living like he did," Jenkins says. "What he taught me was it's not a bad thing going to football games and to cover sports in Europe. He always said it beats heavy lifting."

Nor did the *New York Times*'s Jane Gross, whose late father Milton was a columnist for the *New York Post* for many years, object to taking time off from school during the winter to attend spring training in Florida. She also practiced her high school cheerleading routines outside the press room at Madison Square Garden.

Then there is Laura Vecsey, who writes a sports column for the Albany *Times Union* and is part of the most extended sportswriting family I know. Her grandfather was the sports editor of the *Long Island Press*—where he met her grandmother, who was the society editor. Her father writes a sports column for the *New York Times*. Her uncle is the professional basketball columnist for the *New York Post*. Her younger brother is a sportswriter for the Peoria *Star-Journal*.

"Pretty good genes," says Vecsey, whose training began early. At the age of seven, while waiting at Yankee Stadium for her father to finish a story, she asked Thurman Munson for an autograph. The Yankee catcher complied and then added, in a manner common to ballplayers, "Come back and see me in 10 years." Those words became a staple of Vecsey family humor until the day she called her father in tears because the date could not be kept. Munson had died in a plane crash. It was nine and one-half years later.

The question naturally arises as to whether women write differently about sports than men do. The answer is yes. And no. The singular Mary Garber, whose rousing speech to an audience of her peers about her five decades as a sportswriter closes this anthology, once presented several articles to a seminar of sports editors and asked them to identify the authors by sex. No one could.

But this does not take into account the *kind* of stories women often write. The changes they have brought to the sports pages often reflect experiences and perceptions men cannot share.

When Betty Cuniberti wrote about the late Heather Farr's harrowing battle with breast cancer for *Golf Digest*, she brought to her assignment the passion of a survivor of that disease. When Linda Robertson told *Miami Herald* readers how the best American women college basketball players must leave the country to pursue professional careers, she addressed a topic that would not have occurred to many male sportswriters. Karen Crouse's article in the *Orange County Register* about women athletes who are stalked by obsessive men—it appeared, almost clairvoyantly, shortly before Monica Seles was stabbed on a tennis court in Germany—did the same.

Jane Gross has observed that when ballplayers live together for months at a time they become "more exuberant and loving toward each other than women." This is a judgement no man is qualified to make. Sonja Steptoe's withering critique in *Sports Illustrated* of the defense strategy used in the Mike Tyson rape trial and Kristin Huckshorn's painful coming to terms with her inadequate response to sexual harassment when she was a sportswriter for the *San Jose Mercury News* likewise spring from their own experiences. As for Julie Vader's hilarious take on the *Sports Illustrated* swimsuit issue, only a woman who worked at that magazine could have seen things quite that way.

Beyond this, it is clear that athletes tend to react differently to being questioned by women than by men. Often, they seem to view female reporters as sisters in whom they can easily confide. And in the case of women athletes, there can be a frankness, a sense of camaraderie, that is absent when they speak to men.

Talking to the *Orlando Sentinel*'s Melissa Isaacson, Gussie Moran told how startled she was to find herself an international sex symbol simply because her lace-trimmed shorts were occasionally visible while she played tennis. "You know," Moran said, "I was really never anything to write home about. I was a plain girl." This is not, I believe, something Moran would have said to a man.

Jane Leavy, whose article in the *Washington Post* on Sarajevo's preparations for the 1984 Winter Olympics is chilling to read in the present context, sums up the difference between male and female sportswriters this way: A man will ask the batter who hit the game-winning home run what kind of pitch he hit; a woman will ask how he felt when he hit it.

As a member of a generation of sportswriters labeled the chipmunks—for our habit of chattering impertinent questions—I do not entirely accept that analysis. My male colleagues and I have practiced a fair amount of psychiatry without a license ourselves over the years, and there are some women whose knowledge of the nickel defense and the infield fly rule I would not care to test against my own. But there is no doubt that women sportswriters have proliferated at a time when the boundaries have expanded for all of us.

In a way, this book is not representative of the work women are doing today. Michael Jordan, Pete Rose and Joe Montana do not appear in these pages. Rather, the emphasis is on articles depicting women athletes and, in many cases, the problems they have faced in their rise to prominence. These are articles that give some sense of the changes in conscience and consciousness the growing number of women writers has helped bring about. Even the articles about male athletes, I believe, give some indication of this.

In the midst of this celebration, several cautionary notes should be struck. One is that while women sportswriters are now taken for granted in many areas of the country—California in particular has proven to be the land of opportunity—some pockets of resistance still remain. When Lynn Zinser went to Memphis, Tennessee, in 1988, she was the first woman to write about sports there. When she left in 1993 to work in Charlotte, North Carolina, she was still waiting for the second one.

Nor is sportswriting a line of work women seem comfortable growing old in. Melanie Hauser of the *Houston Post* notes that though she is in her early 40s she may be the senior woman in the country writing about sports on a regular basis.

"I look at the women I came into the business with in 1975 and the majority of them are gone," Hauser says. "But the men are still there. People are going to kill me for saying this, but I think women feel a little differently about it. It can be thrilling for a while, but I think women reach a point where they need more of a balance to their lives. You wake up and realize you're spending your life in a locker room with 50 professional football players. Like it or not, it's still an all-boys network. You still are dealing every day with boys covering boys."

Many of the women sportswriters of Hauser's generation have gone on to jobs—often elsewhere in journalism—with more sensible hours, less frequent travel and saner deadlines. A few, like Diane K. Shah and Jane Leavy, have written novels. Others have left to raise families. It is one thing to say true equality awaits a time when women will feel as comfortable as men in telling their young children they are leaving on another 10-day road trip. It is something else to say it to the women sportswriters who have chosen not to do so.

One way to achieve, if not a solution to this problem, at least some sympathy, is for sportswriters to join forces. Lesley Visser's husband is CBS sportscaster Dick Stockton. Joan Ryan of the *San Francisco Examiner* is married to broadcaster Barry Tompkins. New York horse racing writer Jenny Kellner is married to Rich Rosenblatt, an editor at the Associated Press.

Lisa Dillman and her husband, Mike Penner, write sports for the *Los Angeles Times* while Janis Carr and Randy Franz are both sportswriters for the *Orange County Register* where they once worked together on the same investigative project. ("I was surprised how well it went," she says.) When they decide to have children, Carr may be the one who continues writing sports while Franz moves on to something else. "He's not as enamored with the business as I am," she says. Michelle Kaufman of the *Detroit Free Press* is married to a sportswriter for a competing newspaper, *Detroit News* columnist Terry Foster. So far, Kaufman says, their papers have resisted the temptation to assign them to the same event in order to save the cost of a hotel room.

Cindy Martinez Rhodes, of the *Riverside* (CA) *Press-Enterprise*, is married to Jim Rhodes, a sportswriter for the *Antelope Valley Press*. With staggered shifts and a doting grandmother they have so far been able to accommodate the needs of 2-year-old Paige. "We do *not* plan on her going into the family business," Rhodes says, although she fears she may be fighting a losing battle. "You know how 2-year-olds always mimic? Well, Paige will get out her crayons and coloring book and say, 'I'm going to write a feature now.'"

As for the future, I thought I might have caught a glimpse of it after the 1990 British Open at St. Andrew's when Jayne Custred of the *Houston Chronicle* and I drove together to Edinburgh so we could catch our respective planes the next morning. I was off to Barcelona to meet my family for a pre-Olympics look-around while she was returning home to complete a different assignment—the final three months of her first pregnancy.

At a golf tournament a year later, I stood outside the press tent as Custred was handing off her infant son to her husband before setting out for the course. I wondered if, early in the 21st century, somebody would ask young Nicholas Custred what he wanted to be when he grew up. And I wondered if he would reply, without a second thought, that he was going to be a sportswriter like his mom.

ONE

CROSSING THE LINE

PIONEERS

by J.E. Vader
The National

HOW DO THINGS CHANGE? WE THINK OF VIDEO CLIPS ON THE EVENING NEWS, OF banners held high amid chanting throngs, of charismatic leaders speaking out. We think of mass movements, forces of history, swelling orchestral music.

On a chilly April morning 25 years ago, Roberta Gibb crouched in the bushes in Hopkinton, Massachusetts, and waited for scores of runners to pass her before she stood and blended in with the pack. She wore a hooded sweatshirt to disguise her hair and face. This was the way she had to start the 1966 Boston Marathon, the first marathon run by a woman. Gibb knew something that few people thought possible—that women can indeed run long distances. It was a shocking idea, so scandalous that some of the people who *knew* that women could not run long distances would naturally prove their point by stopping her before she ran 10 feet.

But the fact that she could run more than 26 miles was about all Gibb knew about distance running. The four days before the Boston races she blithely spent traveling on a bus from San Diego, sleeping in her seat, eating at the bus stops. The night before the race she feasted on pot roast, and then had cheese for breakfast, foods she would carry in her stomach, undigested throughout the race. She thought it was a mistake to drink fluids while exercising, and she wore brand new running shoes (made for boys). "I did everything wrong," Gibb says.

Diane Crump was sure of one thing: She didn't have a chance. She had never seen the horse before, or the trainer. "They told me: He's not much horse," Crump says. "He probably doesn't belong in here, but do the best you can. Those were my orders: Do the best you can."

At Hialeah Park in February 1969, Crump became the first woman to ride in a parimutuel race. She was 19 years old, and passionately obsessed with horses. In the starting gate she hunched in the saddle on her bay horse, Bridle 'N Bit, and waited for the bell to ring and the doors to slam open. "I really wasn't that nervous," she says. Crump was a veteran exercise rider; she knew what she was doing. She was ready to go. The jockey in the next stall, Craig Perret, looked over, looked her up and down. He reminded her to put her goggles on.

Maria Pepe didn't have the faintest idea she was doing something significant. She just wanted to play baseball. Over and over again, before, during and after the furor, she kept repeating it like a mantra. Baseball, baseball, baseball. What do 11-year-old kids know from history, from politics? Maria was a nice Catholic girl. She was just playing a game, like always, with the kids in her neighborhood in Hoboken, New Jersey. Only this time they were all wearing real uniforms, and there were real umpires, real coaches—all the trappings of Little League.

Of course, in 1972 girls were not supposed to play organized baseball, but nobody on her team was going to make a big deal out of it. They didn't know then, as others would declare, that their very manhood was at stake. Maria's brown, curly hair was cut short under her baseball cap. In the local paper, Maria is in the background of the traditional picture of the mayor of Hoboken at the Little League opening ceremonies. The mayor takes his traditional awkward swing, and the caption notes: ". . . While Naria Pepe waits his turn at bat."

"Naria?" the editor must have thought as the caption was typed. "What an odd name for a boy."

How quaint it all seems, how distant. Of course women can run farther than a mile and a half. Of course women can ride racehorses, and the world does not fall apart when little girls play baseball with little boys. How could anyone think anything else?

The amazing thing is that this was all so recent. It is startling to look at the faces of these women—these pioneers—and realize that they are not ancient curiosities. They are *young*. Each, in her way, helped change sports forever, and each of their lives was changed by sports. They became famous, publicly celebrated and reviled. And now they are mostly forgotten.

Maria Pepe, 30, still has short, dark curly hair. She still lives in Hoboken. But she isn't stuck in the past. She is a young executive, a controller for a large teaching hospital in Hackensack. She teaches night classes in accounting and is working toward an MBA in corporate finance at Fairleigh Dickinson. She plays third base for the medical center's co-ed softball team. She seems amused to be talking, again, about her Little League days. And she does mean days.

"The one thing I really wanted to do was play," she says. "And I really didn't get to play—just three games. I still feel bad about that."

Pepe grew up playing with the boys in her neighborhood. "There were no activities for girls at the time," she says. "It was unusual to even see women wearing sneakers."

When the other kids in the neighborhood went to sign up for Little League, Pepe held back. "I guess I knew there wasn't ever a girl who played," she said. James Farima, a member of the Young Democrats club, which sponsored the team, asked her why she didn't register. "I guess he thought I was a boy," she says, laughing. But Farima encouraged her, and after three games, and with interest in the "Little League Libber" mounting, Little League headquarters threatened to revoke insurance for the entire Hoboken league and suspend its charter—all for allowing a girl to play. Farima went to Maria's house and told her she had to give back the uniform, but she would be allowed to keep score.

Off the team, the now-famous kid would read her name in the papers looking for only one thing. "I would read until I came to a part that would say whether they were going to allow me to play or not," Pepe says. Then she would toss the paper aside in disgust.

"Look at this," she says, and reads from a yellowed clipping: 'A 12-year-old curly haired girl who broke the sex barrier on the Little League team has been dropped from the roster because she is physiologically and medically unfit.' Can you imagine? Here I am a 12-year-old. You could grow up with a serious complex reading this stuff!"

A letter to the editor of the *Jersey Journal*: "It would be unfair to the boys to inflict a lower class of play that would surely result from playing at the girl's level. The whole purpose of Little League, aside from recreation, is to take boys and give them purpose and direction, strengthen character and prepare them for manhood."

Maria's purpose and direction was that she loved baseball and wanted to play with her friends. In the meantime, her character was strengthened by having camera crews film her walking home from school. She became skilled at ducking reporters, just like a big-time athlete.

"As a kid I always went to church and talked to God and said, 'If I'm a girl and I'm not supposed to play, then why did you give me the ability?' I could never reconcile that in my own mind. I figured I should have been a boy or something."

It was two years before Maria felt at peace; that's how long it took for Little League to cave in and allow little girls to play—only after a string of protests and lawsuits, spearheaded by one filed on Maria's behalf by the National Organization of Women. By then, of course, time had run out for Maria; she was too old to play.

"Of all the people that have contacted me," she says, "there is still one entity that has never called. I'll give you one guess."

But then, why would Little League Baseball Inc. get in touch, give her credit or even apologize? The organization thwarted a kid's wish to play baseball by threatening to take the game away from all children in her town. And since then it has also, literally, rewritten history.

The official 50th anniversary book for Little League Baseball, *Growing Up At Bat*, was published last year. The book quotes Little League official

John Lindemuth: "It wasn't that anyone had anything against girls. It was just that throughout most of the years of the program the issue never came up. Discrimination of any kind has always been frowned on by Little League Baseball." There is no mention of the threats to revoke charters and withhold insurance. No mention of the official Little League rule specifically forbidding girls.

Can Pepe ever foresee the day when women will play in the major leagues? She frowns. "I don't know what the restrictions are," she says. For one who learned early that success is not based on merit alone, the first thought is not of physical limitations, but of man-made barriers.

She wanted to be an athlete, not a historical footnote. Asked if she would rather have been born ten years later, she answers: "Yes!" with surprising force. "I would have gotten to play four full seasons." She would eagerly trade in the scrapbook of clippings, the day in the Yankee dugout, the appearance on "To Tell the Truth" ("Only Kitty Carlisle guessed it was me"), the chapter about her in a children's book written by Geraldo Rivera, all this minor celebrity, this footnote in history stuff, for a few more anonymous swings at bat.

Diane Crump has to really stretch to brush the filly's back, but there is never any doubt she is going to get the brush there. Crump, not surprisingly, is short—but she is by no means slight. The former jockey moves with brisk determination, speaks loudly and clearly. Every movement has a purpose—roll bandages, paint a hoof, comb the tail. Horses are too much work to allow superfluous action.

Crump is in the first year of her trainer's license. She rents ten stalls in a barn in the rolling hills of Virginia's horse country, running her horses at Charlestown or other small tracks. The neat buildings, the manicured hills, the iron entrance gates all connote money—but Crump is just a commuter. "The farther west you go, the less expensive it is," she says. She lives an hour's drive west, in Browntown, in a house with her parents and her 11-year-old daughter. She is divorced after a 17-year marriage, and her family has suffered some financial setbacks. "I'm over 40 now," she says with a sigh, "and right back where I was when I was 17."

Times are not easy. Two years ago, Crump was exercising a big, skittish, stupid thoroughbred named Proof Positive, who reared and fell over backward. Crump's left leg was crushed; the doctors removed her fibula, and replaced it with a steel rod. Under the eight-inch-long scar on her calf are a half dozen screws, and her knee is a metal plate. The wound still weeps. But it doesn't stop Crump from getting back on horses; she says she wouldn't train them if she couldn't ride them.

Crump may be newly licensed to train, but she's been handling horses ever since she was a horse-crazy kid. Her family moved to Tampa when she was 12, and she kept her first horse, an ornery gelding called Buckshot, just two miles from Florida Downs. From the first time she rode Buckshot to the race, she was hooked. At age 13 she started working for a nearby thoroughbred farm, helping break yearlings, then dropped out of school to follow the racing string to the big Miami tracks.

"I never wanted to be a jockey because it was something you just didn't think about," she says. "There were no women riders. Of course, I wanted to gallop on the track, I wanted to do everything everyone else did even though there were only one or two other women galloping and one or two ponying."

She became the first woman jockey almost by default. Kathy Kusner, an Olympic equestrian, applied for and was granted a jockey's license. Other women followed suit and, on the last day of the Churchill Downs meet in 1968, Penny Ann Early was scheduled to ride in a race—which caused the male jockeys to boycott. A few weeks later, at Tropical Park in Florida, jockeys boycotted a race in which Barbara Jo Rubin was named to ride a horse.

By the time the circuit moved to Hialeah, officials there made it clear they would not tolerate a boycott. Catherine Calumet, wife of trainer Tom, felt sorry for women who were trying to ride and she had her husband name Crump to a horse. That was how she found herself on 48-1 Bridle 'N Bit. The race went off without incident, and she finished 10th in a 12-horse field. The following day a headline read: SHE BEAT ONLY 2 HORSES IN HER HISTORIC RIDE.

Crump's scrapbook bulges with clippings with the word "jockette" in the headlines—including this popper: TAMPAN CRACKS JOCKETTE BARRI-ER.

What the jockette looked like, of course, was vital. The Associated Press report leads with it: "Miami, Fla., Feb. 7 (AP)—Pretty Diane Crump became the first woman today to ride in an American parimutuel horse race. . . ." Crump's light brown hair apparently offered a challenge to reporters' skills—it was described as blond, brunette, red, rust-colored, golden—and several stories duly noted her "doll-like blue eyes." A picture of Crump wiping mud off her face was captioned "Much in need of a powder puff . . ."

Although the press may have been amused, there was a hard core of resentment at the track.

"I thought change would come faster than it did," she says. "I thought people's attitudes would change. But they didn't. It took ten years to make any difference at all."

Those ten years, when Crump was at her physical peak, she was out on the backstretch, every day, trying to get work. Even when she proved she was good, she didn't get mounts.

"I never had the chance to ride that many horses," she says. "I rode on a regular basis for 17 years, and in the last five or six, I think I rode my best races. But it took so many years to get the experience. At that point, I was as good a rider as there was."

She remembers a night at Latonia (Kentucky) racetrack, when jockey Steve Cauthen came in to ride as part of a special promotion. "In the feature we came down the stretch, neck and neck," Crump says. "We were on horses of equal ability—and I outfinished him! Well, I shouldn't say I outfinished him, but let's put it this way—I won."

Crump refuses to admit that her best is behind her. She grooms her big filly—a $5,000 claimer called Heavenly Wish—and thinks about building a stable of contenders. Then, after her leg has fully healed, she can start race riding again. This time, if she gets a good one, there's no telling how far she can go. "I don't care how old I get," she says. "I don't want to give up my dream."

Roberta Gibb makes tea in her cluttered kitchen, a room of pleasant disarray, filled with her clay sculptures of runners and presidents and with fur from white angora cats. Her home is an 18th century house in Rockport, Massachusetts, just north of Boston.

Gibb started to run when she was a student at Tufts in suburban Boston, after she met her boyfriend, a cross-country runner. "I had never even heard of something like running five miles," she says, softly. "I thought, 'How can you keep going?'" She started to run "for the joy of it—I had a feeling of joy and the only way I could express it was running."

When she first heard of the Boston Marathon, "I didn't believe it," she says. "I thought, 'It's not humanly possible to run 26 miles.' I was running about five miles at that point. Then I went to see the 1964 Boston Marathon and that was it. It was a gut level decision." She knew at that moment she would enter the race. She didn't notice that everyone she saw going by was male.

Gibb began to train with no notion of how to train. She simply ran as far and fast as she could. In the autumn of 1965 she went to Woodstock, Vermont, and ran beside horses and riders competing in an equine endurance contest. The first day she ran 40 miles over rugged terrain; the next day she ran 25 miles before her knees gave out. She felt she was ready for the marathon and, in February 1966, sent away for an application.

"I received a curt reply that women were not physiologically able to run such distances. I was stunned. I assumed the marathon was open to every person in the world." And that is how she found herself hiding in the bushes in Hopkinton.

She not only finished the race—with painful blisters on her feet from her new shoes—she ran it in 3:21, placing her 135th out of more than 600 runners. It was a stunning achievement. Although Japanese runners had swept the first four spots, the story of the first woman marathoner was the news—although, of course, the word "woman" rarely appeared in the copy.

The Boston papers:

BLONDE WIFE, 23, RUNS MARATHON

GIRL SHOWS MARATHON'S BEST FORM

LADY RUNNER NO CRUSADER

WOMEN RUN HOME, ISN'T THAT ENOUGH?

Gibb laughs at the clippings. The front page of the *Record American* shows her cooking fudge after the race–"I guess to show that I was normal," Gibb says. "Can you imagine a headline: BLONDE HUSBAND RUNS MARATHON?" But at the time the press didn't seem strange to Gibb at all. "That was just the '60s." she says, laughing again.

Gibb thought, when she started all this, that change would be easy. "I thought once I showed that women could run, everything would just automatically open up," she says. "That's how naive I was. I thought: Well, they didn't believe women could run, but now they'll see they made a mistake. I didn't realize it was a lot more subtle than that."

Gibb assumed women would be allowed to compete not only in future Boston Marathons, but also in the Olympics, and she dreamed of running in the Games herself. But, of course, women did not have an Olympic long-distance race for another 18 years—in 1984, in Los Angeles—and only after hardball politicking.

Gibb also found her history rewritten. The year after that first Boston Marathon another woman, Katherine Switzer, entered the race under the name K.V. She apparently had a friend take the physical exam, and she started the race with an official number. When marathon official Jock Sample saw her running with the number he became enraged and tried to rip it off her shirt in mid-stride. News photographers were right there and the series of pictures—a short burly man attacking a woman runner—were published everywhere. Switzer finished the race and faced a media bonanza. Gibb, running in her second straight race without incident, finished virtually unnoticed more than an hour ahead of Switzer.

Somehow, in the years that followed, the perception grew that Switzer was the first woman marathoner—a notion that Switzer, who now works as a television sports commentator, did little to dispel.

"I would watch interviews where she would be introduced as the first woman to run the Boston Marathon and she would say, '"Yes, thank you,"' Gibb says. "She was making her living off this. I would write letters, and call her and say if you keep doing this I'll be forced to sue you."

Switzer has gotten better about it, Gibb says, explaining that her resentment is not based solely on being denied her due credit. "She had her boyfriend take the physical and then she lied about it," Gibb says. "It really put women's running in a bad light. Plus, she took more than four hours to finish the race." The Switzer-Semple incident put running right on a men vs. women course—exactly what Gibb wanted to avoid.

She sees running as simple, natural, healthful—and doesn't "compete" in the conventional sense, although she would like to know just how good she could have been. "If I regret anything it's that after the first race, I didn't find a coach. I did continue to run marathons, but I got stuck in other aspects of life—getting married and having children and getting through law school. And of course it wasn't possible then to make a living as a woman runner."

Her husband left her 15 years ago, five days after her son was born, and she had to go to work as a real estate lawyer. She still ran, and continues to run almost every day, but not at the top level of competition. Now 48, with her son away at school, she finds she is restless for change.

"Maybe I'm going through a mid-life crisis," she says. "If I was radicalized by running I was even more radicalized by having a baby. I never realized what women were going through. I didn't feel anything running the marathon compared to that."

Gibb smiles and sips her tea. She is stretching her mind to places far beyond sports. If only she could demonstrate her beliefs as easily as she ran a marathon 25 years ago.

"I don't know if I would have come to all this consciousness without the marathon," she says. "And it has made me much more aware of how social change comes about. One person sees one little thing and does something about it. They never do get the credit. That's what makes ordinary people special."

(January 9, 1991)

J.E. Vader is a sports columnist for The Oregonian *in Portland. A graduate of the University of Michigan, she started her career as a temporary secretary, then spent nine years at* Sports Illustrated *before becoming a staff writer for* The National, *an all-sports newspaper that lasted less than two years.*

WOMEN'S OLD IMAGES FADING RAPIDLY

By Jane Gross
New York Times

WHEN WOMEN RUN THEIR FIRST OLYMPIC MARATHON IN 1984, KATHRINE Switzer will be beaming like a proud parent. Miss Switzer ran in the Boston Marathon eight times—the first in 1967. That year, however, she was an uninvited, unwelcome guest because women were barred from the event. To Miss Switzer, the inclusion of the 26-mile-385-yard race in the Olympics is "not just another event" for women. It is, instead, a symbol of the strides women have made in the last decade, when they have broken through psychological, sociological, physical, financial and legal limits to improve their performances dramatically and shatter long-held perceptions about the roles of women in sports.

"The thing that excites me the most is the lack of a sense of limitations," said Miss Switzer, who is 35 years old. "When I was first running marathons, we were sailing on a flat earth. We were afraid we'd get big legs, grow mustaches, not get boyfriends, not be able to have babies. Women thought that something would happen to them, that they'd break down or turn into men, something shadowy, when they were only limited by their own and society's sense of limitations.

"Now, all those myths surrounding women athletes are going by the board in the face of knowledge and opportunities. Now, women realize they can do anything they put their minds to doing. That's in every aspect of life. The marathon, to me, is the pinnacle of that breakdown of limitations. For centuries, it was said to be the most arduous distance and that only the strongest hearts could do it. We've shown that women have the capability of doing that. And, if we
are capable of doing that, we're capable of doing anything."

"The acceptance is the huge difference," said Eva Auchincloss, executive director of the nine-year-old Women's Sports Foundation. Mrs. Auchincloss often tours the country lecturing on the gains made by female athletes.

Those gains, she tells her audiences, can be measured in many ways, including these:

—The sharply improved performance of women in various events as sophisticated training and coaching methods have become available.

—The increased participation of female athletes at the high school and college level, aided by the passage of Title IX legislation that forbids sex discrimination in educational institutions receiving federal funds. Ten years ago, 7 percent of the interscholastic athletes and 2 percent of the intercollegiate athletes in America were women as compared with 35 percent of the high school athletes and 30 percent of the college athletes today.

—The growing corporate sponsorship of women's events that has contributed to the dramatic increase in prize money. The women's golf tour, for example had a total purse of $6.4 million in 1982 as compared with $1.2 million in 1975.

"Women are taking minutes off, while men are taking seconds off," Mrs. Auchincloss said about the improvement in performances, pointing to Allison Roe's record-breaking time of 2 hours 25 minutes 9 seconds in the 1981 New York City Marathon, which was better than the men's gold medal winner at every Olympics until 1952. "Those are the kinds of things I think are proof positive that women's sports are here to stay," said Mrs. Auchincloss.

Both Miss Switzer and Mrs. Auchincloss referred as they spoke to the August 30th issue of *Time* magazine, which featured a cover story about "the new ideal of beauty" that depends on a taut, fit body. "The athletic woman is now considered sexy," Miss Switzer said, recalling the taunts directed at so-called tomboys during her childhood.

That memory is shared by most female athletes. Cathy Rigby, a gymnast on the 1972 Olympic team, says her sport gained early popularity because "it was lumped together with ballet and tap as a good thing for little girls to be interested in" and because "gymnasts were usually small and feminine looking." Sheila Young Ochowitz, an Olympic champion speed skater and world-champion cyclist, recalls telling people she was visiting friends rather than competing when she went out of town on weekends because she didn't want to be labeled as someone who wore "ugly black skates and unattractive costumes" rather than the more traditionally feminine garb of the figure skater.

Carol Blazejowski, a member of the 1980 basketball team that missed the Olympics because of the United States boycott, said "it was always a hassle" to play with the boys, and Pam Shriver, the tennis professional, shudders at the memory of being a self-conscious 6-foot teenager. Carol Mann, a Hall of Fame professional golfer, used to "make up stories or sort of clam up" when seatmates on airplanes asked what she did for a living.

"There really existed very stereotypical ideas of what a female athlete was like," said Merrily Dean Baker, the director of women's athletics at the University of Minnesota. "Those prevalent attitudes changed drastically in the 1970s. The whole focus on women in the '70s was to do and be what you chose to, in all areas, and that spilled over into sports."

Before, a guy who competed and won proved his masculinity, where a woman who did the same thing had to prove her femininity," said Dr. Letha

Hunter, an orthopedic surgeon and sports medicine specialist in Atlanta. "Once if you were a 6-foot girl you were an oddball, you hunkered down. Now you're looked on with admiration and offered a scholarship. That's a psychological adaptation and it had to come first."

Donna Lopiano, the director of women's athletics at the University of Texas, says she has seen a different kind of female athlete in the last few years because of the decline of the old stereotypes. "I've never seen women as strong, as well developed," she said. "They have a long, lean, confident look. They arrive here outgoing, confident, with a good self-image. It's beginning in their hometowns, where athletic scholarships have become status symbols. They're not hiding in their rooms with people saying, 'Oh, those phys-ed majors.' They're like male athletes. They're revered."

They are also afforded the benefits of more sophisticated coaching and training. Miss Lopiano points to women gaining access to the weight rooms that were once an all-male province. Lindsey Beaven, a former tennis pro and the tour director of the Women's Tennis Association, points to the former players who have turned to coaching. Theresa Shank Grentz, the woman's basketball coach at Rutgers and a member of the Immaculata College team that won the national championship in 1972-74, points to summer camps that teach skills and college scholarships that provide goals.

"Ten years from now," Miss Lopiano said, "we'll look at today's records and say, 'Is that all?' Female athletes are not halfway to where they'll be even though they're already impressive human beings, like a new generation of women."

Some people see dangers in the regimen this new generation of women is subjecting itself to, citing the injury history of tennis players like Tracy Austin and Andrea Jaeger, who have had full competition schedules since their childhoods and the hard lives of professionals since their early teens. "These kids are all injured and injured badly," said Miss Beaven, author of a book for players, parents and coaches called *Getting Started*.

"I myself am very concerned about it," said Miss Beaven.

So is Ted Tinling, an observer of women's tennis since he umpired Suzanne Lenglen's matches six decades ago. Tinling argues that today's teenage tennis players are the first real athletes in their sport "in the proper sense of the word" because they participate in weight-training programs and "do everything athletes do.

"They think being conditioned means they'll get better," Tinling said, "but it's not necessarily true. I think they've overdone it. The sporting medicos preach strength and all that jazz and that may be good in moderation. As a generalization I'd say they've gone mad over being athletes. Tracy and Andrea have probably overindulged in playing tennis. I know I used to

absolutely resent sunset when I was that age. One doesn't want to stop playing when one is 13 or 14, but someone has to tell you to stop like they have
to tell you that you can't eat a whole chocolate cake."

Miss Rigby added: "Parents who push their kids to succeed are often
blind to these kinds of abuses."

Despite the progress since the enactment of the Title IX legislation, there is
concern among some female officials and athletes over the uneven enforce-
ment of the law and a series of conflicting court interpretations of the law's
intent. "They are dragging their feet," Mrs. Auchincloss said about the
Office of Civil Rights, which supervises the implementation of Title IX.

Nonetheless, many observers of women's sports say the legislation seems
to have a momentum of its own. "Women now expect more from institutions in terms of coaching, equipment and facilities," said Mrs. Baker, "and
they are demanding on the college level that those expectations be met.
Women are becoming increasingly vocal about their rights under Title IX."

"There is a demand," said Mrs. Auchincloss. "Athletes are asking for it.
Parents are asking for it. The bottom line is the pressure is on."

Miss Blazejowski knows better than most the fate of a woman's athletic
venture that has neither credibility nor viability because she was a member of
the New Jersey Gems in November 1981 when the Women's Basketball
League went out of operation. Owners of franchises in the defunct professional league, among them Ed Reisdorf of the New York Stars, argue that the
league failed because of insufficient fan and news media support. Miss
Blazejowski, and other women with a stake in such professional opportunities, view the situation differently.

"The WBL was too much too fast," Miss Blazejowski said. "Rather than
playing in regions, we traveled coast to coast and tried to play in places like
the Superdome and Madison Square Garden where the overhead is tremendous. It's the natural course for a sports league to take a while to catch on.
We started and folded, and we'll probably start and fold again. But one of
these times, we are going to catch on and hold on. That I am sure of."

"Professional opportunity is limited and that's unfortunate," Miss
Lopiano said. "But that will change, I'd say, in another five years. As the
economy goes, so goes professional sports. In this kind of economy, you
don't see people entering into risk areas."

While professional opportunities for women in team sports are virtually
non-existent, such athletes are finding an increase in other kinds of jobs. "If
you had told me 10 years ago that I could make a very comfortable living as
a head basketball coach, I wouldn't have believed you," said Mrs. Grentz,
who graduated six seniors from her team last season, four of whom are now
employed as assistant coaches.

The economy, however, poses risks to high school and college programs as well as to professional ventures like the WBL. "We can't lose sight that women's sports are still relatively non-revenue producing," Miss Lopiano said. "When the economy goes down, non-revenue sports—men's and women's—have to fight for their lives. There can be considerable backsliding in a bad economy."

"It's just a very bad coincidence that we as a nation are experiencing economic constraints we never felt before," said Mrs. Baker. "Even though economic hardships affect men as well, they don't have the prior deprivation to surmount."

Miss Switzer, from her vantage point as the director of sports programming for Avon Products, refuses to feel daunted by the remaining obstacles to the athletic advancement of women. "Once you have that sense of accomplishment, of being somebody, you never go back," she said. "You'd have to be a pea-brain not to realize that women's sports is here to stay. It is not like the hula hoop."

(October 29, 1982)
Jane Gross, the San Francisco bureau chief for the New York Times, *covers earthquakes, fires, riots and just about anything else that happens in California except sports. She previously wrote sports for the* Times *and* Newsday, *where her beats were professional basketball, baseball and tennis.*

FEMALE SPORTSWRITER FINALLY ROCKS THE BOAT

by Kristin Huckshorn
San Jose Mercury News

The commissioner of the National Football League has ordered an investigation of Boston Herald *reporter Lisa Olson's charge that New England Patriots players sexually harassed her in the locker room on Sept. 17. On Tuesday, the NFL also announced that Cincinnati coach Sam Wyche will be heavily fined for barring a woman reporter from the Bengals' locker room after Monday night's game.* Mercury News *staff writer Kristin Huckshorn, who has reported from team locker rooms, has her own opinions on the issue.*

WHY DOESN'T LISA OLSON SHUT UP?

I admit it. That is what I have been thinking ever since Olson, a Boston sportswriter, began publicly explaining how she was sexually harassed by five New England Patriots in their locker room last month.

That is what I thought again Tuesday, when I heard that another sportswriter, Denise Tom of *USA Today*, had been denied access to the Cincinnati Bengals' locker room after their loss Monday night to the Seahawks.

Denise and I became sportswriters more than a decade ago (I switched to news three years ago.) And knowing that she was a member of the old guard, I knew what answer I could expect from her Tuesday.

"I'm referring calls to my sports editor," she said. "I'm not the focus of the story."

Right answer. Dignified. Succinct. Within the unwritten code that governs female sportswriters when they venture through the locker room door.

Rule No. 1: Maintain eye contact.

Rule No. 2: Carry a big notebook.

Rule No. 3: Don't rock the boat.

Lisa Olson rocked the boat. I wish she would shut up.

Feeling this way is difficult to admit. After all, I am cofounder of the Association for Women in Sports Media, the national organization of female sportswriters that was formed four years ago.

Nor do I question Olson's story. What happened to Olson on Sept. 17—and Patriots' owner Victor Kiam's chauvinistic response—was the worst incident of locker room sexual harassment yet.

Worse than an incident several years ago in which *San Francisco Examiner* columnist Joan Ryan, then with the *Orlando Sentinel*, reported that a football player had run a razor up her leg.

Worse than an incident in 1986 when Dave Kingman of the A's played postman and sent a rat in a pink box with a ribbon to *Sacramento Bee* sportswriter Susan Fornoff.

Worse than an incident this summer when Detroit Tigers pitcher Jack Morris told a female intern from the *Detroit Free Press*, "I don't talk to people when I am naked, especially women, unless they are on top of me or I am on top of them."

Nor should anyone question Olson's presence in the locker room. Whatever you think about that, it is not at issue here. Female sportswriters have been interviewing athletes inside locker rooms for almost 15 years. Every professional league (and many intercollegiate teams) have policies guaranteeing equal access. Virtually every major daily newspaper has a female sportswriter on its staff. The *Mercury News* has three.

Women are in the locker room to stay. The NFL underlined that Tuesday by fining Bengals Coach Sam Wyche for refusing Denise Tom equal access.

So what bothers me about Olson's reaction?

She is vocal. She hasn't asked anyone to speak for her. She hasn't ducked reporters and network news cameras. She's appeared on "Entertainment Tonight," for heaven's sake. She has become the story and, in doing that, she has broken the rules.

Reporters work best as flies on the wall. We are observers, not participants. Supporting cast, not leading ladies.

Female sportswriters know we have two strikes against us from the start. We can't enter a locker room and blend in. So we strive for perfect comportment. A cross between Miss Manners and Mary Richards. We develop peripheral vision (the better to see when a player has his pants on). We develop a thick skin. We develop a sense of humor.

Female sportswriters routinely laugh off comments that should be reported. They accept treatment that should be fined. They keep quiet, figuring silence is the price of admission for doing the job. That is why I wish Lisa Olson would shut up. I wish she would shut up because I was one of those women who kept quiet.

I remember being reduced to tears by Indiana University basketball coach Bobby Knight. I didn't complain. I might never again have been assigned to cover the team.

I remember being hit with jockstraps, dirty socks, wads of tape, obscenities. I didn't snitch. Players might avoid me.

I remember standing toe-to-toe with a 6-foot-7 football player, demanding that he stop verbally harassing another female sportswriter. I never asked the players, and male reporters, why they didn't come to our defense.

I never rocked the boat.

And I wasn't alone. For every Lisa Olson, there are 100 locker room incidents that are dealt with quietly or not at all.

Ann Killion of the *Mercury News* recently was verbally harassed by Charles Haley, a defensive lineman for the 49ers. Haley later apologized. Killion said Tuesday she has accepted his apology and doesn't want to talk about the incident.

"I have to go back in there," she said.

Women who are sportswriters value their jobs. They value their relationships with players. Most have worked hard to be accepted. They know that if they become the story—like Olson—all they have worked for is lost.

By speaking out, Lisa Olson is destroying the fragile status quo. She is bringing an old and dreaded issue back to the forefront. She is reminding us that the battle is not yet won. She is rocking the boat.

She makes me wonder: If I had spoken up all along, would this still be happening now?

I wish she would shut up.

She makes me wish that I hadn't.

(October 3, 1990)

Kristin Huckshorn is a national reporter for the San Jose Mercury News *based in Washington, DC. She covered sports at the paper for 10 years, including the NFL and the 1988 and 1992 Olympics. In her current assignment, she has covered the conflicts in Bosnia and Somalia.*

DONNA LOPIANO AND THE ART OF REFORM

by Johnette Howard
The National

ONE OF THE GREATEST DISTAFF REFORMERS IN COLLEGE ATHLETICS RISES AT 3 a.m. to begin her 18-hour workdays, constantly lugs her portable computer around as if it's a purse, and has been overheard chiding the office copy machine because its slow pace wastes her time. She serves on a breathtaking array of national panels and symposiums, writes prolifically, and has been called before Congress to contribute her opinions on Civil Rights legislation. She barnstorms the country 50 weeks a year, delivering an average of three speeches a week from a live file of 102 titles.

When she is home in Austin, Texas, she enjoys dragging friends out to golf—though it's understood she may cover all 18 holes in about three hours, even if that requires revving up her golf cart to breakneck speed and leaning out the driver's side to hack at the ball as if she's playing polo.

Donna Lopiano fell out of the cart once playing golf that way, leaving her basketball coach stuck in the passenger seat as the runaway vehicle bounced crazily off the fairway and crashed into the woods.

"Well, I was unhurt anyway," Jody Conradt sighs.

The fact that Lopiano ever landed as women's athletic director at the University of Texas is another marvel. Friends joke that her ability to avoid getting fired within two years in such an ultra-conservative setting approaches miracle status, too.

"She scared us witless," said Betty Thompson, head of the 1975 search committee that twice recommended Lopiano to then-president Lorene Rogers, and twice was told to look for another candidate before coming back with Lopiano's name again.

"My first impression? I thought she was a pushy Yankee," laughs Conradt, a strictly raised Baptist from Goldwaithe, Texas, whose mother didn't approve of Lopiano's directness when they first got together over lunch. Lopiano had already been relentless while prying Conradt away from a good situation at UT-Arlington and, well . . . the way Lopiano tells it: "I remember being quoted in the newspaper here as saying 'damn' or 'what the hell.' For the east coast, that's normal talk. But to many people in Texas, that's terrible. I think I said something like 'Jeez.' Jody's mother thought I took the Lord's name in vain. She was putting sugar in her coffee and I noticed she grew quiet and her hand started shaking. Sugar went everywhere."

Lopiano is used to eliciting such reactions. No high-profile woman in athletics save Billie Jean King has rivaled Lopiano's effectiveness as a dauntless advocate and protector of equal opportunity for women in sports.

In her remarkable 15-year tenure at Texas, Lopiano has whipcracked and cajoled the eight-sport women's program from intramural quality to national eminence. In women's collegiate sports, only Tennessee and Iowa come close to Texas's across-the-board success. Texas has won 17 NCAA championships since 1982 and graduates 93 percent of its players. For sheer size, Lopiano's program is the undisputed frontrunner with a $3.7 million budget and staff of 36 people—including a full-time marketing manager, business manager and events manager.

Conradt's basketball team, now the gaudy money-making jewel of the program, was still wearing demure little kilts for uniforms and stuck with an attendance record of 75 when Lopiano arrived. With Conradt as coach, the Lady Longhorns perennially contend for the national title (winning it in 1986), averaged 7,525 fans a game last year, and have approached sellouts at the 16,231-capacity Frank Erwin Center. (This is a phenomenon that surely made a good ol' boy like Erwin do 360s in his grave, especially during those two seasons when the women's basketball team outdrew the men.)

"If it's do-able here, then it's do-able anywhere," Lopiano insists.

Such success doesn't just happen, of course. And Lopiano's peculiar combination of idealism, vision, and daffy workaholic enthusiasm has led to some memorable strategies. Of course, not all of them have worked.

"She wants you to disagree with her," says Rhonda Lands, the staffer who handles Lopiano's roiling schedule, "but if there's a point she wants to win you over on, she'll bombard you with paper. She's something with the written word. She just condensed our policy manual from 13 chapters to 16."

At various times, Lopiano has personally helped drum up interest by taking a cannonball leap from a three-story-high diving tower, shambling out to midfield at a football game to kiss the school mascot, Bevo the Longhorn steer, and threatening to start a kazoo band when the real Texas pep band balked at showing up for women's basketball games.

Conradt says she used to be "continually nervous" over what Lopiano might think of next—especially in those early years. "Somehow I still just can't imagine the people we have at Texas warming up to their alma mater as played by a bunch of kazoos," Conradt groans.

Currently, Conradt is having trouble with another Lopiano brainstorm: being wired for sound at home basketball games and distributing transistor radios to fans who can hear everything the wildly popular coach says—live and uncensored.

"Why?" Conradt repeats incredulously. "Money! She thought maybe she could rent these radios for something like $5 a pop. Then they could hear everything we say on the bench. I said, 'Donna? No.'"

Lopiano's lobbying and emphasis on fundraising has increased the women's athletic budget by 600 percent since she arrived. About $65,000 comes from the two annual fundraisers the department stages itself—a spring walkathon, and a classy tennis-golf gala that includes a silent auction of memorabilia confiscated from just about every Olympian and star athlete the University of Texas has produced.

"When we get 'name' people in, we just strip them and sell everything they wear—sweatsuits, shoes, swimsuits, you name it," laughs Lynn Wheeler, Lopiano's head of internal operations. "And if they go on to the Olympics? We're like customs when they come back. We intercept them, take their suitcases and say, 'Thank you. You can go now. That's all we want.'"

At the most recent silent auction in October, Lopiano's usual donation—a home-cooked Italian dinner for 10 with "La Prima Donna"— pulled down $375, easily beating the $175 fetched by an autographed baseball from some guy named Nolan Ryan. But that just goes to show Lopiano has a gift for making people warm up to her and her message.

Knowing Longhorns football fanatics were afraid their men's athletic program would lose revenues to the women's, Lopiano embarked on a community public relations campaign not long after she arrived to address the fears head on with speeches like, "Does Women's Athletics Mean Trouble for (then-football coach) Darrell Royal?"

Lopiano, in another speech, says she has a theory about insecure people. "When they're feeling threatened, they try to exert their power instead of taking valium" like they should. She's enough of an ex-jock to regard eye makeup as "combat warpaint . . . sort of like eye black" and high heels as "power shoes," but she admits both hateful necessities make a good first impression in her business dealings. She also coined a term for men who think their knowledge of sports is genetically superior to women's: "Testicular knowledge," Lopiano says proudly, as if she's considering taking out a patent on the phrase.

Lopiano unwittingly offended Royal during her job interview by saying she liked Austin fine, but found the inescapable country and western music "terrible." Since Royal has been known to dine with Willie Nelson three times a week and ranks country music second only to the sounds put out by God's seraphim and cherubim, it's a wonder his Longhorn-ness didn't send Lopiano back to her alma mater, Brooklyn College, with the sheet music to that old country standard, "The Only Shoulder I Had to Cry on Was The Shoulder of the Road."

* * *

As much as Lopiano writes and speaks, it's not hard to find out what she believes in. Her talks range from the rhapsodic "Difference Between Good and Great" to the serious "Requiem for the Women's Movement" to the delightfully wicked "How to Survive in Predominantly Male Organizations," a 10-point primer for women in the workplace that teaches subversion with a smile. As important as Lopiano's message is, though, and as eloquent as she can be, it surprises some people that she's so funny.

Donna Lopiano has been jolting them for years with her sense of humor and her shrewd insights. But the reason she stays in a university setting and keeps up the whirlwind pace has remained the same.

"It would be real easy—there's no doubt in my mind—to go into some commercial industry and make $250,000 or $300,000 a year, especially if you're a workaholic, a perfectionist, and can get along with people like I can," she says. "But at the bottom line there would be money. Here it's people. And I think education is a very rewarding thing. The brightest people in the world are in universities and you're talking about having something to do with people growing up, developing, building, becoming more competent than they otherwise might have been. I don't think everyone can do education and I happen to do sports in education because that's what I grew up doing. Maybe it would have been different if I played the violin. But by playing sports, I got to grow up with an appreciation of what it is to feel really good at something and that's a million-dollar feeling. That's something every human being should get to have."

Lopiano was a great fast-pitch softball player. She decided to devote her life to sports at age 10, after making her local Little League team in Stamford, Connecticut, and being turned away the day uniforms were distributed. The problem: She was a girl. It's no coincidence a lot of her career has been devoted to protecting opportunities for women and "trying to do everything here at Texas that everybody said we would never be able to do."

As president of the female-run AIAW, which governed women's intercollegiate athletics until 1981, Lopiano led a dogged but unsuccessful battle against the NCAA's takeover of women's national championships. Once the fight for self-determination was lost, however, she didn't pout or stay out in the cold.

Lopiano moved within the NCAA to effect change—"You have to understand the rules of guerrilla warfare," she jokes—and now, eight years later, her voluminous work on ethics in sports has been applauded as a groundbreaking contribution to the cleanup movement sweeping the NCAA.

When the NCAA annual convention meets this January, Lopiano proposals like cutting back the hours in an athlete's work week will hit the floor for debate. Wilford Bailey, president of Auburn University, has called Lopiano's contribution to the rewriting of the NCAA rulebook nothing short of "genius." Among Lopiano's many collaborators, the words "integrity," "visionary," and "brilliant administrator" come up a lot too. But one theme dignifies her work: "She will tell you she doesn't even want to be in the room with somebody if they don't have the students at heart," says Big East assistant director Chris Plonsky.

To say Lopiano is "just" a women's advocate misses the point. Her consuming ambition is creating a model for all college athletic programs where academic and athletic goals are compatible. Breaking NCAA rules, for example, would be regarded no differently than falsifying research data. The traditional athletic department practice of awarding teams resources based on the money they make would also end if they created inequities.

"Few people stop to think that the primary mission of the university is the pursuit of truth—learning," Lopiano writes. "If we held to the theory that only the money-makers should exist, then our education system would be in sad shape. Should Germanic languages be eliminated because the business school makes more money? Liberal arts is as important as chemistry despite the fact it does not produce revenues. The same principle should be applicable in athletics programs. We—coaches, athletic directors, and in some cases, university presidents—have told the public more money means more winning.

"There is nothing wrong with being damn good at football or chemistry or art or English. Whenever an educational institution produces such excellence, there will be a public demand to consume it. There is also nothing wrong with the commercialization of sport or academia, as long as that revenue production does not exploit human beings or exclude qualified individuals . . . (and) as long as it does not come at the expense of higher education's larger responsibility, which is to seek the truth . . . to lead society."

Richard Lapchick, director of The Center for Study of Sport in Society, says such a model "could be the salvation of intercollegiate athletics." And if it sounds melodramatic or outrageous to suggest the person who can save college sports is a woman, Lapchick says, "Aw, be melodramatic. Go ahead."

Men's college athletic programs went wrong for the same reasons women and minorities were shunted aside—the perpetuation of the lucrative sports' status quo. Now the idealists are having their say. And Lopiano has not been caught unprepared. She likes to smile and tell people she's been keeping a file all these years called "Ideas Whose Time Has Not Yet Come."

"These are ideas that I file away," Lopiano says, "until they become the ideas of men. And then they get done."

* * *

Lopiano has little use for euphemisms. She is not a blind apologist for women. She doesn't hoist a clenched fist for every cause that comes along. She doesn't launch personal attacks on someone who disagrees with her, either—she much prefers the temperature that cool reason gives her arguments. Nor has she been accused much of veering too close to feminism's I-Hate-Men axis. Lopiano does give money to some radical groups, but even that makes sense. As she says with a laugh: "They make me seem reasonable."

"It still always surprises me when people say, 'Oh, Lopiano, I could never work for you—you're a radical feminist,'" Lopiano says. "I see myself as a rational feminist. Rational describes everything I do."

That includes tweaking women in athletics for their shortcomings. Lopiano has been critical in the past of administrators who aren't willing to do what it takes to make their women's programs successful. The message it sends, she says, is "The success of our daughters is not as important as the success of our sons." She once confessed she found "a lot of women's basketball is boring"—then hastened to add that didn't include Conradt's fast-breaking, fundamentally schooled teams. She also says women shouldn't be afraid to hire more women when they become bosses.

"Women are hearing if they're married, they won't have time for the job and they'll want to have children. If they're not married, they're hearing that they must be homosexual," Lopiano says. "My advice is that everyone get married, then divorced. I've observed many women are in this mode and loving it today."

Lopiano raised eyebrows among some fellow women's administrators at the 1987 NCAA special convention too. By forging an alliance with football coaches, Lopiano helped defeat a scholarship reduction measure that preserved football's preposterous allotment of 95 grants-in-aid. But there was a logic to Lopiano's madness: She knew women's programs would bear a disproportionately large share of any cuts, since women have less to cut from.

Lopiano demands plenty from her staff. Unlike some other college athletic administrators, Lopiano doesn't mince words about who is ultimately responsible for athletes' conduct. "We should hold coaches responsible—they hold the carrot of participation," Lopiano says. "But we also need to make sure we tell coaches beforehand exactly what is expected of them. Coaches are experts at adapting to the rules of any game they play."

Lopiano has taken flak for stipulating in contracts that her coaches should annually field Top-10 ranked teams. But she brushes aside the criticism, saying: "There is nothing wrong with firing a coach, or any master teacher, for incompetence in their field. I would do that. Sure. I would have to look at all the factors not just one alone. But the absence of any one of our stipulations is enough to get fired."

Her other three stipulations are meeting graduation rate goals of 90 percent or better, adherence to NCAA rules and department policy, and professional conduct by the coaches and their students. Her formula at Texas is simple: Hire the best coaches, offer the maximum number of scholarships allowed to attract the best athletes, play the most competitive schedule, and challenge athletes to do their best in the classroom and on the playing field.

"We've pretty much got the competitive side and academic side of things where we want them," Lopiano says, "What's taken me 15 years to do here, I could now do in five somewhere else. But the third part—this performance team idea, and how much we can help these kiddos realize their full human potential—well . . . that's going to take me another 10 years to figure out."

Lopiano likes to point out to would-be activists that "longevity equals power." As she told members of the Association For Women In Sports Media earlier this year:

"Notice that organizations usually change one of three ways—either by a lawsuit, bad press or you becoming the boss. So it's important once you get in a business, you stay in. Most of the enemies I've had in this business are gone. Some of them are retired and some of them"—here Lopiano paused theatrically—"some of them are dead."

Johnette Howard *is a sportswriter and weekly columnist for the* Washington Post. *She previously worked at the* Detroit Free Press *and* The National, *which ceased publication shortly before this story was to run. It appears here for the first time.*

Real Trouble with Sports Illustrated's Swimsuit Issue Is Not the Photos

by J.E. Vader
The Oregonian

When they brought out the giant inflatable penis, I thought they had missed the point.

The thing is, when you work at *Sports Illustrated* as a journalist, you have nothing to do with the annual swimsuit issue, which appears once again this week. It is separate from the "real" magazine, as remote to most editors and writers as is the advertising. It just emerges, makes a pile of money, and is gone.

Of course, the magazine's readers see it as a whole. So everyone on the staff gets those annoying wink-wink, drool-drool questions about the swimsuit issue, as if scantily clad models were hanging out by the Xerox machine and arguing the designated-hitter rule in the cafeteria. This, naturally, is an affront to serious journalists who are busy trying to figure out yet another way to whine about fighting in the NHL or mispredict the Super Bowl.

SI staffers also are pestered by people who think pictures of women in swimsuits are immoral, or by those who think the feature degrades women by treating them as sexual objects. A few years ago, one women's group held a swimsuit-issue protest in front of the magazine's New York office and brought along a giant inflatable penis (used as an attention-getting device, much like the first sentence of this column which, if you've read this far to see what the heck I was talking about, worked).

In my almost nine years at the magazine, I had to defend the swimsuit issue many, many times. It is, after all, a fashion layout, virtually indistinguishable from the stuff in *Elle, Glamour* or *Vogue*, and I love fashion magazines. And there is, after all, nothing inherently sexist about an attractive photograph of a good-looking person on a beach. Besides, I was worried about a far more serious issue—my own career.

Sports Illustrated is a very tough place for journalists who happen to be women. Female editors are invariable slotted into "soft" beats—that is, sports that include women, animals or a lot of foreigners. For editors, the hard sports, which comprise most of the magazine's coverage, are no-woman's land. Currently there are three female writers, but in the past year their bylines have been as rare as flaws on a swimsuit model. And the masthead does list one female photographer. Of course, this pioneer got her position not by working her way up at the magazine, or by proving herself at another publication, but through close, personal

44

friendship with a former SI managing editor. (You may think this is an unfairly easy way for a rank amateur to get ahead, but if you could see her wizened, hunchbacked boyfriend you'd realize she did it the hard way.)

SI is a very competitive place for young reporters, and we all complained that we didn't get enough assignments from editors. But I can't complain I didn't get enough attention. While working on an important, breaking story, I was slapped on the butt by an unattractive, married editor who told me to "loosen up." On an Olympic junket, a powerful editor invited me to engage in close, personal friendship activities, which might have been tempting if he were not also unattractive and married. And a particularly unattractive editor, who later became the top editor, sent me flowers and inappropriately affectionate notes, which stopped after I suggested he might want to develop a more close personal friendship with his actual wife.

Assignments from these editors then became as rare as fat on a swimsuit model. On the other hand, I felt fully prepared should I ever decide to pursue a career in Washington, DC.

So you can see why all the huff and puff about the "sexist" swimsuit issue seemed paltry to me. Besides, there was such an obvious, easy fix for the whole controversy, and I was sure they would implement it every year: Use a few male models. Fashion magazines do it all the time—it makes the pictures sexy and fun. The departure from the tradition would generate massive amounts of positive publicity and more people, especially women (who already account for a huge chunk of newsstand sales for the swimsuit issue) would buy the thing, which would attract more advertisers, and generate more money. Everybody would be happy. It's a no-brainer.

But don't expect the current managing editor to make such a smart move. Because although there is nothing inherently sexist in a swimsuit issue, the men behind it are as sexist as they come. When these guys look out their windows in the Time-Life Building and see a giant inflatable penis, they are no doubt thinking two things: "Good, more airtime on the 6 o'clock news," and "Yeah, that's about right."

(February 16, 1993)

THE GREAT OLYMPICS GENDER BENDER HUNT

by Mary Jollimore
Toronto Globe and Mail

THE DECISION BY THE INTERNATIONAL AMATEUR ATHLETIC FEDERATION TO abandon gender testing because it is unscientific prompts one to ask why it was introduced in the first place.

The notion that male athletes have masqueraded to snatch gold medals away from real women is absurd. Or is it?

Olympic history books note a few "questionable" gender cases, but evidence is far from conclusive.

Suspicious case No. 1: Polish-born sprinter Stanislawa Walasiewicz, later known as Stella Walsh. At the 1932 Olympics, she won the 100-meter gold medal over Canadian Hilda Strike.

In David Wallechinsky's *Complete Book of the Olympics*, a Canadian official described Walasiewicz's "long, woman-like strides." Walasiewicz won the 1936 Olympic silver medal behind American Helen Stephens. A Polish journalist accused Stephens of being a man. Officials promptly did a visual sex check and pronounced Stephens a genuine woman. In 1980, when Walasiewicz died, an autopsy revealed male sex organs. History books now include an asterisk after Walasiewicz's 11 world records denoting: "controversial gender status."

Suspicious case No. 2: German Dora Ratjen, fourth in the 1936 Olympic high jump. She turned out to be a hermaphrodite, with both male and female sex organs.

Suspicious cases Nos. 3 and 4: The Soviet Union's Press sisters, competitors at the 1960 and 1964 Olympics. They set 26 track-and-field world records, won five Olympic gold medals and one silver. Tamara and Irina Press quit track with the advent of sex tests. Last month they appeared on a TV documentary on amateur sports. Each wore a dress. Who knows?

Suspicious case No. 5: Poland's Ewa Klobukowska, 100-meter Olympic bronze medalist in 1964. In 1967, she failed the sex chromosome test, but "passed" visual inspection. The IAAF, world governing body for track and field, disqualified her and deleted her records in 1970.

To sum up: Walasiewicz had "controversial gender status." Ratjen was a hermaphrodite. The Press sisters were never proven anything but women. Klobukowska flunked the chromosome test invented to nab imposters, but "appeared" to be a woman.

So why was gender testing in the form of a check for the female XX-chromosome introduced in 1967?

"The process was a vestige of the 1960s when there was a great advance in women's performances," said Abby Hoffman, who ran for Canada at four Olympics from 1964 to 1976 and is a member of the IAAF women's committee. "There was a big change in the number of Eastern European women who were far better trained than their Western counterparts. People in the West saw these competitors, who were not influenced by the hoo-ha about femininity, and (thought) women don't get muscles. There was a suggestion they weren't females."

The silly notion women athletes must appear "feminine" and not athletic is not antiquated. It was only in 1984 women ran an Olympic marathon for the first time. Until then, Olympic fathers believed women mustn't run that far. There is a more logical explanation for "masculine" women athletes in the 1960s.

"Others, beside myself, say these may have been crude attempts at doping," Hoffman said. "The use of steroids has a masculinizing affect on some women. When people saw facial hair and increased muscles they assumed these have got to be males rather than women who were on drugs or just women who were well-trained and had big muscles."

Hoffman said at the 1966 Commonwealth Games and 1967 Pan-American Games—before chromosome tests—female athletes lined up for a physical exam and "coped with this by treating it as a big joke. It was just plain dumb. I remember at the 1966 Commonwealth Games some athletes tarted themselves up. Some wore long nightdresses. It was professionally handled by a gynecologist and another doctor. We went in one by one. You were undressed, they examined your breasts, they may have laid a hand on the genital area to make sure there were no hidden genitals."

Last month, the IAAF deemed gender testing by chromosome analysis scientifically flawed. They're through with bad science. The gender test does not take into consideration chromosomal abnormalities in genitally appropriate females. At future IAAF meets women will undergo a visual inspection only if chosen to provide a urine sample.

Yet the IOC, which runs the Olympics, will use the chromosome test at the Barcelona Games. Even though it's seen as unscientific and even though it was introduced only to explain why women athletes were performing so well.

"I'm totally opposed to gender testing," Hoffman said. "The notion that no purported female could be successful athletically is the most insulting and denigrating part of the whole process."

Indeed, if the IOC is concerned about female athletes who surpass what it considers a believable performance level, then perhaps it would be best to concentrate efforts on drug testing and not gender testing.

(June 15, 1992)

Mary Jollimore writes a sports column for the Toronto Globe and Mail. *She began as a news reporter and has worked for United Press International, CTV Television, the Canadian Press and Reuters. She would like opportunities for male and female athletes to be more equitable so "men, too, can experience the absurdity of synchronized swimming."*

TWO

PAYING THE PRICE

A Delicate Balance

by Linda Robertson
Miami Herald

SUSIE KINCAID IS HARDLY WIDER THAN THE GAP BETWEEN HER FRONT TEETH, but she is counting calories at age 12. To maintain her matchstick size, she tries not to go above 1,500 a day, and during workouts, she wears an elastic "tummy band" to remind her to keep her stomach flat or, better yet, concave.

Her hands are still small, so the skin rips and blisters when she hurls her 85-pound body around the uneven bars. She holds up her palms to show streaks of blood coagulating in the chalky powder. She grins at her badges of courage.

Susie Kincaid is not your typical little girl. She wants to be an Olympic gymnast. School and a 30-hour-a-week training regimen in a Pompano Beach gym take up most of her time. But two weeks ago she spent precious hours in front of the TV, mesmerized by girls not much older than herself, basking in the white light of global love and admiration in Barcelona. As she watched, a thought ran through her mind like a mantra: In four years, everyone could be watching me.

Watching the American girls bow their heads to be draped with Olympic medals made Susie all the more determined to face the countless practices that lie ahead.

Sometimes her feet ache from landing with a thump on the four-inch-wide balance beam. According to Susie, the beam is her scariest event. When she's nervous, she can feel it trembling beneath her. It's four feet off the ground, which means it comes up to Susie's chin.

"When I was 7, I saw a girl fall off and hurt her leg," Susie says. "It was gross. It bent the wrong way."

Susie is working on a vaulting maneuver no one has ever done before—a handspring with $2\frac{1}{2}$ twists. If she succeeds, it will be called "The Kincaid."

There are moments when all the effort catches up with her. She talks about weariness with an adult's sigh. "Some days I go home after a workout and tell my mom I feel like I got run over by a truck."

Susie is a smart, articulate girl, with a cute smile that puffs out her cheeks. Her brown hair is pulled back by a ribbon that matches her leotard. Her life is no different from that of thousands of other dedicated girls who aspire to be on TV someday, waving to the crowd from the medal platform, cradling a bouquet.

* * *

In the Summer Olympics, women's gymnastics takes center stage, much as figure skating does during the Winter Olympics. The men's version of the sport takes a back seat. It's the girls people want to see: leotards and lipstick, spins and smiles, perfect girlish bodies and perfect 10s. There is muscle involved, but beauty, too. Some routines, with certain kinds of music, require flirtatious, Lolita looks from the girls. Brandy Johnson, a former Olympian from Altamonte Springs, Florida, used Donna Summer's "Hot Stuff" in one of her routines. At the same time, the 15-year-old carried a white teddy bear in her gym bag.

Consistently high TV ratings prove viewers love to watch the breathtaking mix of strength, grace and sex appeal. But the folks at home don't see the pain behind the ponytails, the humiliation that comes before the hugs.

"People think it's a glamour sport," Johnson says. "But it's really kind of disturbing. A lot of these girls walk away with a lot of problems."

Athletes, artists, business people—all know the painful equation behind success: Sacrifice plus hard work equals triumph. The end justifies the means. Becoming the best is often a Faustian trade-off. German composer Robert Schumann built a contraption above his piano that pulled up his ring finger with a piece of string. The ring finger is the weakest of the five because of the natural construction of the hand. But Schumann wanted to make it more agile. In the process he injured the finger, and had to give up on his goal of becoming a concert pianist.

Athletes routinely push their bodies to the breaking point. At a track meet in May, long jumper Llewelyn Starks' shin bone snapped with an audible crack as he launched from the takeoff board. Larry Bird has to lie on the floor during basketball games to rest his battered back. Runners have been known to hallucinate during the final miles of ultramarathons.

What price glory? It is a question all athletes must ask. But female gymnasts are the only athletes who must grapple with the rise and fall of their careers during the years when other children are finding it difficult enough simply to grow up.

Many people in the sport say girls who master gymnastics are gaining more than they give up—lifelong discipline and the conviction that dreams can come true.

"They are athletes with an unusual integrity," says Bela Karolyi, one of the most successful gymnastics coaches in the world. "They grow up to be strong, sturdy people."

Others—those who have fallen victim to eating disorders, broken bones, burnout, or the short end of sport's politics—say they would never let their daughters put on a leotard.

Fort Lauderdale's Wendy Bruce, 19—frequently referred to as the "old lady" of the 1992 Olympic team—has suffered illness, injury and loneliness in pursuit of the sport she loves. She has been living away from her parents' home since she was 14.

"People see the overall impression, the tricks, the pretty music," she says. "They don't realize how hard we work, how much pressure we're under, how much we give up of a normal life."

One man has set the tone for women's gymnastics in this country: Bela Karolyi. Karolyi defected from Romania in 1981 during a trip to New York, five years after revolutionizing the sport with star pupil Nadia Comaneci, who, at the 1976 Olympics in Montreal, scored the first perfect 10.

Karolyi, a national hero in Romania, ran afoul of the Romanian government—then in the orbit of the Soviet Union—when he attacked what he perceived as favoritism toward the Soviets in international gymnastics competition. When he defected on a team trip to the United States, he had only a few dollars in his pocket. He worked as a dishwasher, janitor and dock hand. He learned to speak English by watching "Sesame Street." He now owns three gyms, the base of a gymnastics kingdom that in the last eight years has produced the United States' top gymnasts—Mary Lou Retton, Phoebe Mills, and Kim Zmeskal, the first American to win a world championship, and a favorite to win the all-around gold medal in Barcelona until she stepped out of bounds in the floor exercise event.

Since coaching Retton to gold in 1984, Karolyi has become an Olympic fixture, a tall man with a bushy mustache and heavy accent, wearing a sweat suit and giving bear hugs to his petite prodigies on international TV.

Karolyi, 49, sleeps from 1 to 5 a.m., and spends 16 to 18 hours a day in the gym. Occasionally, he heads to his 53-acre ranch in the Texas countryside, where he raises horses and cattle, and goes rabbit-hunting. He lives by a simple philosophy: Whoever works hardest reaps the most rewards. The hours—the years—of work pay off in those fleeting moments at meets when the gymnast nails a beautiful routine, gets the Bela hug and steps onto the medal platform.

Karolyi has 500 girls at his gyms. But only the top six—"Karolyi's six-pack" or "Karolyi's kids"—work directly with Bela and his wife, Martha, a former Romanian gymnast considered the world's top balance beam coach. This year's seven-member Olympic team included three Karolyi gymnasts—Zmeskal, Betty Okino and Kerri Strug—and one ex-Karolyi kid—Michelle Campi, who now trains with a former Karolyi assistant in Sacramento. They were good enough to win the team bronze, the only Olympic team medal for American women since 1948, besides the team silver of 1980, when the Soviets boycotted the Olympics.

Karolyi imported the training regimen that has made the former communist-bloc countries the dominant force in women's gymnastics. And now, 11 years later, those methods are beginning to pay off in Olympic gold.

Training for Karolyi's hand-picked six is conducted in a boot-camp atmosphere. The girls—who range in age from 14 to 17—train eight to 10 hours a day, six days a week. They get off Sundays, July 4th, and three days at Christmas.

"Gymnastics is not for fun," Karolyi says. "It is not golf. I believe everything worthwhile is hard. Mildness is not the proper approach. You always have to be demanding, always asking for more. As long as you want to create something better, you have to be hard. If you want to be the best, you have to get the most out of every minute." Brandy Johnson, now an aspiring actress who does stunt work in Orlando, described a typical day when she was training with Karolyi prior to the 1988 Olympics:

"From 7 to 10:30 a.m. we worked on compulsories. Nobody was late and nobody missed workout, even if you were sick. I had chicken pox once, and Bela said he didn't know what that was. [She practiced.] From noon to 3 p.m. we had dance lessons. And from 4 to 9 p.m. we worked on our optional routines. We were supposed to get out at 9, but he always noticed some mistake so he could keep us until 10."

And in their spare time?

"We mainly slept. I'd get up at 6, and get dressed to make sure I was ready, and then go back to sleep from 6:15 to 6:45. We ate just a little. In gymnastics you don't eat much. Mainly we ran off of our nervous energy, which makes it difficult for your body to recuperate when you're injured."

Some of the girls had tutors at a nearby private school. Others learned through correspondence courses. Johnson remembers teaching herself geometry at odd hours. But there was no question where their primary responsibility lay.

"Studying was not high on Bela's priority list," says Phoebe Mills, Johnson's teammate at the 1988 Olympics and now a diver for the University of Miami. Mills, like many of her gymnastics peers, is a straight-A student, but all the time devoted to preparing for the Olympics meant she fell behind a year in school.

Karolyi is tired of the criticism of his single-minded training methods. On the night the Americans won the bronze medal, he announced that he would go into semi-retirement. Of course, Karolyi has threatened to quit before, then changed his mind. Even if he does stop coaching, his influence will continue to dominate the sport for years.

* * *

Karolyi and the gymnasts loyal to him say his record speaks for itself.

"My goal is to make them sturdy and aggressive girls," he says. "Each child has their own parent. I cannot be responsible for everything in their lives outside the gym."

There are issues inside Karolyi's gym as well. All his gymnasts say he berates them in practice about imperfections in their routines and in their appearance.

"Everybody gets called an idiot," Mills says. "The first time he called me an idiot I phoned my mother after a workout, crying. I never let him see me cry, and you never talked back."

In fact, his former gymnasts say, there is no talking, period, during workouts, except for Karolyi's voice, yelling out his pet phrases: "You look like an overstuffed Christmas turkey. You look like a donkey. You look like a dead frog. You look like a pregnant goat. You look like you're in the Special Olympics. You are an embarrassment. What are you doing, making fun of gymnastics?"

"I hope they don't feel blame," Karolyi says about his name-calling. "It is only to make them stronger. Competition is tough. Holy cat! Life is tough. They know not to take it personally."

It is survival of the fittest. Karolyi sees himself in the girls he chooses, girls with talent but also girls who have a hunger for 10s, and who always will, even in endeavors beyond gymnastics. The resilient ones develop calluses on their nerves, become unflappable competitors. The sensitive ones drop out or move to a different gym. Even the ones who stay with him seem to have mixed feelings.

"You want to impress him," Brandy Johnson says. "You want the bear hug. You don't want him to grab you by the back of the neck, which is what he does when you screw up."

Some of his gymnasts say that Karolyi has an irascible affection for them. Lighter moments mix with the marathon of intensity. Occasionally, he takes the girls out to his ranch and they stay overnight in the cabins. Johnson once celebrated a birthday there.

"There was a big birthday cake, and we were all eyeing it but trying to ignore it, and Martha said, 'Go ahead, girls, eat some cake,'" Johnson says.

Karolyi's favorite stunt was to let his herd of bulls out and have the girls round them up.

"We were scared of them, but he'd yell, 'Girls, keep running,'" Johnson says, imitating Karolyi's accent. After that, he invited them to play a game of basketball, first to 21, then, when the girls were ready to rest, to 50.

"And there was a railing at the gate where he'd make us do pull-ups," Phoebe Mills says, laughing. "Whatever he could find, he'd use to make another workout."

Nadia Comaneci remembers Karolyi's reaction after she scored the first 10 at the Olympics on the uneven bars. When she walked off the mat to the crowd's roar, he was right there to greet her. The commentators said something about the deep bond between them. But he wasn't whispering words of affection: "He was very gruff: 'Okay, now you get ready for beam.'"

Comaneci's boyfriend, Bart Conner, who won a gold medal in gymnastics in 1984, says Karolyi's methods would not be controversial if he was coaching boys. "People wouldn't give it a second thought," Conner says. "But because it's cute little girls, they're appalled. He treats them like champions. We would never have had a Nadia without that type of training."

Says Comaneci, winner of four gold medals: "He was like a father to me. I spent more time with him than with my parents. He's tough, but he's the only one if you want to be the best."

Chelle Stack, 19, a Karolyi gymnast who left the Romanian's gym shortly after she was in the 1988 Olympics:

"Without him I wouldn't have made the Olympic team. But after the Olympics, as I got older, he was driving me crazy. He's very cruel. He ruins your self-esteem. I had to go through therapy sessions to get over some emotional problems I was having."

Survey the whole spectrum of sports. Anyone can play a friendly game of touch football, swat a ball casually around a tennis court, toss a baseball, hack at a golf ball. But most people do not have the slightest idea how to attempt a back handspring, let alone three in a row.

"You see Michael Jordan flying through the air, but he can't fly through the air and do what these girls do," says physical therapist Andy Vogel, who works with athletes from all sports. In his eyes, no sport is harder than gymnastics, which requires a rare combination of skill, strength, grace and tolerance for pain. Flexibility is essential for contorting the body into unnatural positions. Gymnasts can bend their backs like a bow and raise and lower their legs like the blade of a pocketknife.

Add to the physical challenges the mental pressure of being judged, on a scale of one to 10, while you're out there all alone, doing flips on the beam. Not only do you have to hit the flips without a bobble, but the judges have to like the way you look, your "lines"—the shape of your body. In international competition, gymnasts are so closely matched that the difference between winning and losing can be one one-thousandth of a point—a toe not pointed, or an ounce of fat in the wrong place.

Weight control is as important for gymnasts as it is for models. Except that gymnasts are usually five feet or shorter, meaning the pounds show more. And gymnasts reach their prime as teenagers, when the body is growing—in all the wrong places if you want judges to see your "lines" rather than your curves. Weight also shifts a young girl's center of gravity, makes injury more likely, and makes those lightning-quick twists and flips harder to execute. Height makes tumbling more difficult.

Karolyi says the ideal size for a gymnast today is 4-foot-7 to 4-foot-10, 75 to 85 pounds. "You look at the parents, especially the mamas, and you can tell who will be small," he says.

Gymnasts find themselves racing against a biological clock. They are butterflies flitting through a small window of opportunity: One Olympiad. By the time they're 17, 18, 19, they're getting old. As they grow more beautiful, less board-like, their gymnastics careers shrivel.

Susan Stokes, mother of one-time Olympic hopeful Erica Stokes, is relieved to see her daughter retired at age 16. Erica trained with Karolyi for three years before suffering foot and shoulder injuries. She was demoted from the elite six. She and her family moved to Oklahoma City, where there was another top-flight gym, in an attempt to come back in time to make the Olympic team. Erica is tall for a gymnast, 5-foot-2, and while she was injured, she'd put on weight.

Last December, Susan Stokes came downstairs at 2 a.m. and found her daughter in the bathroom, throwing up.

"She had bought chocolates as Christmas presents for the other girls, and had eaten them all," Susan says. "She broke down and told me she had been bulimic for over a year. It started when she was first injured. She figured that no matter how well she did her routines, unless she could somehow get down to 90 pounds, she'd never make it. She'd be a 'pregnant goat' instead of a maturing young woman.

"I decided then and there that the price we were paying was too high. We gave it up. We moved back home with our emotional scars."

Erica, 16, has been seeing a psychologist. She's better now, as a 120-pound cheerleader for her high school.

"But she's still very concerned about her body," Susan Stokes says. "One day she'll panic about overeating and the next day she'll fast."

Kristie Phillips was on "The Tonight Show" at age 14, being touted as the next Mary Lou Retton. She never even made the 1988 Olympic team. While at Karolyi's, she said she took laxatives and diuretics to maintain what she considered the ideal weight of 92 pounds at the twice-weekly weigh-ins.

"I was called an overstuffed Christmas turkey," says Phillips, now a Louisiana State cheerleader. "I felt like a failure because I was fat. These are things that stay with you, maybe forever."

Karolyi denies that he forces girls into eating disorders. He says nutrition is stressed. "I do not make their menus," he says. "Yes, body style is important. But I am not there making their meals for them."

More than 200,000 girls participate in gymnastics in the U.S. For most of them, and for most young athletes, sport is a confidence-building, healthy experience. But Mike Donahue, president of the United States Gymnastics Federation, says he is aware of the problems at the world-class level. The USGF has started a coaches' education program so "you don't just put a girl on a scale; you learn how to watch for signs of anorexia, you know something about child psychology."

Still, Donahue says, not all of the criticism at the elite level is deserved. Jealousy is at the root of it, he says.

"It's ironic that the kids and coaches who didn't make the Olympic team are the ones with bad things to say," he says. "The good things about gymnastics—the joy of competition, of making friends, of accomplishing goals—outweigh the bad things." With some exceptions, Karolyi's stringent methods are emulated among coaches producing serious Olympic contenders.

One of those exceptions is Tim Rand, who, with his wife, Toni Rand, runs the American Twisters Gymnastics Academy in Pompano Beach. "In this country we have a problem always telling people what they did wrong instead of telling them how to do it right," Rand says. "I have no objection to hard work. But with these kids, who are as eager to please as puppies, I think positive reinforcement is more effective. At some gyms, they're not bringing up children, they're producing machines."

Rand says that unlike most serious coaches, he takes pride in blending success with fun.

But even Rand is not above using invective to motivate little girls. The difference is: "I know whom I can call Shamu, and whom I can't."

Rand consistently develops top-level gymnasts, and the gym is filled with trophies almost as tall as the athletes. But he has yet to coach an Olympian. Two girls who went to Barcelona—Wendy Bruce and Michelle Campi—are South Florida natives. When they began to show Olympic potential, their parents shipped them off to more prestigious gyms.

Michelle's mother, Celi Campi, explains why her daughter switched coaches: "There are the 'fun' gymnastics coaches. That's the American way. But it won't make us competitive with the Russians. I'm not saying Michelle never has fun, but if you ask her the best part about gymnastics, she won't say it's all the fun that she has."

*   *   *

Whether achieved through shouted epithets, or encouraging words, training for Olympic-level gymnastics can lead to trouble. The strenuous exercise and emphasis on low body fat can actually delay the onset of puberty and disrupt menstrual cycles. Brandy Johnson, for instance, says she had no periods while she trained at Karolyi's. Kathy Johnson, a 1984 Olympian, did not start menstruating until age 25. Recent studies show amenorrhea—irregular or nonexistent menstrual periods—can cause long-term bone damage or the early onset of osteoporosis. The eating disorders that often accompany amenorrhea can cause thyroid problems, anemia, fatigue and, in extreme cases, cardiac arrest.

"Amenorrhea leads to low estrogen levels and low bone mass," says Dr. Barbara Drinkwater, of the American College of Sports Medicine. "This is occurring at a time when these girls should be maximizing their bone mass. We don't know if they'll catch up, and we won't know until they're in their 40s and 50s."

Says Susan Stokes: "Since these girls don't menstruate, they don't develop until after they quit training. Look at Kim Zmeskal and Betty Okino. They have no chests. My daughter wonders where her hips and breasts are."

The trend in gymnastics is toward compact and powerful bodies—like Zmeskal's—and away from tall and elegant bodies—like that of retiring Soviet star Svetlana Boguinskaia, "the Byelorussian swan," who is 19 and a womanly five-foot-four. Despite her striking beauty and grace, Boguinskaia finished a disappointed fifth in the overall competition, behind the younger, smaller competitors.

Unified Team Coach Alexsandr Alexsandrov calls the new crop of competitors "midgets," and hopes it represents a temporary phenomenon. But Karolyi says the shorter, stockier gymnasts have the laws of physics on their side.

"It's not really women's gymnastics anymore," says Phoebe Mills, a bronze medalist on the beam in 1988. "It's children's gymnastics. You don't see as much grace and beauty anymore, but more of who can do the hardest tricks. It's lost some of the aesthetics. I think that's kind of sad."

Says Johnson: "They're getting younger and younger. I see girls peaking at age 11."

There is another reason gymnasts don't last much beyond 17.

"As they get older, they get minds of their own," says Coach Rita Brown of Brown's Gymnastics in Altamonte Springs.

Johnson and Mills remember lying in bed at night, talking dreamily about discovering a normal life after the Olympics. "We talked about going home, going to school, having dates, going to the prom," Johnson says.

But when the girls do return to the mainstream, the transition can be rough, like someone going to a cocktail party after years on a desert island.

"As a rule, gymnasts are very intelligent girls," says Susan Stokes, whose Houston household was always filled with boarding gymnasts who trained at Karolyi's. "These kids can make international plane connections, make overseas phone calls, talk to the press. But they're socially stunted. They're not thrown in with the normal teen population."

Michelle Campi's mother has heard the criticism about gymnasts' lost childhood, and doesn't buy it. She moved her daughter from Broward to train in Houston at age 12.

"When you're on the road up, you get a lot of raised eyebrows," Celi Campi says. "You hear the comments, 'Your daughter doesn't get to go to high school football games.' Frankly, when I go to a mall and I see kids sitting around smoking cigarettes with their hair teased up to here, I know Michelle hasn't missed out on anything.

"There's no comparison. She's 15 and has already been around the world."

Michelle Campi had the horrible misfortune of dislocating her elbow just two days before June's Olympic trials.

"She was doing a floor routine and it looked like she stumbled and landed on her arm," Celi Campi says. "The bone popped out."

Michelle was taken into surgery at a Baltimore hospital and a pin was inserted in the elbow. That might have been the end of her Olympic hopes, but her mother knew that Olympian Shannon Miller—who would go on to win a silver medal in the all-around competition—had recovered from a similar injury. Besides, Michelle had broken an arm and an ankle at age 10 and come back to make the national team.

The doctors said it would take "something short of a miracle" for Michelle to recover in time for the trials camp in Altamonte Springs a month later.

But Celi wasn't ready to give up. She and Miller's coach gave Michelle a bedside pep talk. She was lying there, wan and woozy, with IVs in her arm, throwing up every ten minutes because of the morphine.

"You've devoted 90 percent of your life to this!" Celi Campi told Michelle. "It might seem difficult now, but you don't want to regret it five or 10 years from now."

When Michelle got out of the hospital, Celi put her on a macrobiotic diet of carrot juice and alfalfa sprouts to speed the healing process. There was one frustrating workout when mother and daughter retreated to a bathroom for a good cry. "Then Michelle splashed water on her face and went back out there like she was going to show everybody," Celi says.

Michelle's elbow did not buckle. She made the team.

But she didn't compete in the Olympics. Once she was in Barcelona, it became increasingly clear that the elbow was not completely healed. That leaves her only the hope of 1996. But by then Michelle will be 19, practically an old lady.

In gymnastics, the real question is not if an injury will occur, but *when*.

For Brandy Johnson, it was age ten—a dislocated kneecap and broken finger. By the time she retired at 17, she had broken her ankles three times each, all the toes on her size-3 feet, and her collarbone. She has a metal screw in one big toe. She has three different hip problems, including stretched ligaments that allow the ball to slip out of the socket.

"After a while, warning lights were going on all over my body," she says.

Phoebe Mills's worst injury was a cracked heel. She had been trying an innovative move on the uneven bars and kept swinging around and hitting her heel on the bar, over and over, for weeks, until it finally broke. She's also suffered "a broken wrist, a few broken fingers, a toe or two," she says.

Wendy Bruce's career was waylaid for almost a year because of an array of injuries that included a dislocated shoulder, hyperextended arm, torn foot muscles, chipped bones in the ankle and torn knee cartilage, for which she's had two operations.

Olympian Betty Okino missed 10 months of competition because of a stress fracture in her spine, which sometimes made it uncomfortable to sit.

"A dismount from the beam generates force equal to six times these girls' body weight," says Dr. Lyle Micheli, a pediatric orthopedist at Harvard Medical School. "You can have long-term wrist problems; it becomes painful to turn a key in a lock. You can have stress fractures in the lower back, and if they're not discovered early, you could need surgery.

"In terms of injuries, gymnastics is right up there with pro football. As sports become more sophisticated and our training becomes more intense, we're flying blind on the aftereffects. We train and train a kid until she gets hurt or until she stops improving."

Wendy Bruce has lived with six different families since she left her own at age 14. She didn't always get along with her surrogate parents or siblings in Altamonte Springs, so she moved a lot, from one awkward situation to the next.

Wendy's parents, Virginia and Fred, sent Wendy upstate so she could train at "a club with clout."

They thought they could visit their homesick daughter every weekend. They put 26,000 miles on their car the first year and often slept on the floor of the bedroom where Wendy was living. As the number of visits dwindled it "became every two weeks." Then even less than that. It was hard on the family, but, Virginia points out, not as hard as it might have been. She counts off on her fingers the families she knows where mothers followed daughters to different cities and the marriages ended in divorce. She needs both hands.

Then there are the kids who go so far from home their parents can afford to visit only a few times a year. Or parents who uproot themselves, find new jobs in the cities where their daughter trains, only to have her not make it.

Virginia considers her family lucky because they never had to move to find that extra edge for their daughter. But there were plenty of other sacrifices.

To make Wendy an Olympian, the Bruces took out two $5,000 loans; got three second $30,000 mortgages on their modest Fort Lauderdale house; acquired eight credit cards and routinely used each to its $5,000 limit; paid families $300 a month to board Wendy; spent $10,000 to $15,000 a year on gymnastics. Their sacrifice is not unusual.

"We couldn't paint our house until now, while all the neighbors are on the second paint job," Fred Bruce says. "We had a smashed-in car door for years. We have only one car between us. The Barcelona trip was our first vacation in the 23 years since our honeymoon. With Wendy it was like a snowball going downhill, and you just get sucked along."

Was it worth it? Yes, say the Bruces: They got to see their daughter win a team bronze medal in the USA uniform at Barcelona.

But what are the chances that all this investment will pay off in endorsements? Not very good. Unless you are Mary Lou Retton, who not only won the all-around gold medal in 1984, but captured the public's imagination with her dynamic personality and the first American perfect 10, you don't wind up on a Wheaties box.

"Mary Lou was a once-in-a-lifetime phenomenon," says Nova Lanktree, a director of Burns Sports Celebrity Service in Chicago. "Gymnastics stars are adorable, they're amazing, but they don't have big appeal in advertising because they are only in the public eye a short time. Come September we'll forget most of these names."

Brandy Johnson and Phoebe Mills have taken divergent paths since the nights they sat up late fantasizing about going to the prom. They look back on their gymnastics careers with fondness and few regrets, but they're glad they have moved on to other things.

The two former teammates live four hours apart now, but don't keep in close touch. Their lives are a long long way from the circumscribed world they knew at Bela's.

A year after the 1988 Olympics, Mills got the Epstein-Barr virus, which causes chronic fatigue: "My six years in Houston caught up with me." She said goodbye to Bela at the age of 16, and went home to Chicago and high school. She soon got restless and took up diving. By her senior year she was gone again, this time to Boca Raton, training with Greg Louganis' old coach, Ron O'Brien, and his son Tim. She's now on scholarship at the University of Miami, excelling as a platform diver. The 1996 Olympics beckon.

Johnson's gymnastics career ended at a meet in Belgium, when she was suddenly terrified of doing her usual routines on bars and beam. She knew it was time to quit.

"As you get older you see the consequences of things," Johnson said. "My brain was telling me to stop."

Johnson moved back home to Altamonte Springs and became engaged to Bill Scharpf, a professional water skier and stunt man. She has done stunt work at Disney World and Universal Studios, had bit parts in a couple of movies and TV shows, performed "elastic gymnastics" on a bungee cord with a traveling troupe, and coached at gymnastics clinics. In one movie, a hijacking thriller, she and her fiancee ride around in a Ferris wheel as a crashing plane flies toward them. They didn't have to do anything more difficult than scream.

She still has the dimples and blond hair that made her one of gymnastics' most charismatic stars, and she wants to parlay her gymnastics career into acting and TV commentating. "A lot of girls are lost after gymnastics," Johnson says. "They've spent their whole life doing something they can't use anymore."

Phoebe Mills is not the type to be interested in underwear endorsements, aerobics tours or circus gymnastics.

Mills is back into the competitive grind because, she says, it's the only way she knows. She has diving practice almost every day. Still, it's less time-consuming than gymnastics. She has time to be a college student, socialize with her friends. She's out in the sun instead of in a gym, her brown hair bleached blond. Her relationship with her coaches is more "friend to friend rather than teacher to student."

"If I didn't pursue a sport, I'd be bored," she says. "That's why I got along with Bela, because we were both hard workers."

Soon she'll be 20, and her growing-up years will recede, like the hours on the balance beam, into scrapbook nostalgia. But something carries over from those days when 9.9s flashed above the judges' table.

After gymnastics, diving. After diving, what? What is Phoebe Mills searching for?

"Perfection," she says.

* * *

As Susie Kincaid watches her heroes perform on television, questions about life after gymnastics don't occur to her. For the young Broward gymnast her perfect timing is more relevant: She was born in 1980, which means she'll be 16 in 1996, the ideal age for an Olympic gymnast. Of course, she can't afford to grow much over the next four years.

"I want to be maybe five feet tall," says Susie, who is 4 feet 10. "If you stay about the same weight and you grow, you look thinner. It stretches your muscles."

Susie has muscle definition you don't normally see on a girl. Her biceps and quadriceps make her look like a miniature bodybuilder. She knows she'll have to get even stronger if she wants to contend for the Olympic team. She may have to spend even more than 30 hours a week in the gym.

She hopes she can keep living at home in Lighthouse Point so she won't be separated from her family, but she could end up in Houston or Oklahoma City, training with big-name coaches.

"My friends are like, 'How can you practice so much?'" Susie says. "Most people would probably quit. It's too hard.

"Sometimes I think about all the hours I have to put in, all the years left. You have to give up going to the movies with your friends, or going to the beach.

"But when I walk into my room, and I see all the trophies, that makes me feel good. At the end, when you finally make it, it's all worth it."

(August 16, 1992)

Linda Robertson covers college basketball and writes sports features for the Miami Herald. *A native of Midland, Michigan, and a graduate of the University of North Carolina, she has covered general news and such sports assignments as the Olympics in Barcelona and Lillehammer, the Final Four and the 1991 Pan-American Games in Cuba.*

MARY BACON LOSES HER FINAL RACE

by Joan Ryan
San Francisco Examiner

NINE YEARS BEFORE JOCKEY MARY BACON PUT A BULLET IN HER HEAD AT A Motel 6 in Fort Worth, Texas, she had already begun to die. It was the fifth race on June 9, 1982, at Golden Gate Fields. Bacon's horse clipped the heels of another horse on the backstretch. She crashed to the ground and a trailing horse stumbled over her. When the ambulance attendant reached her, she was motionless, bleeding from her skull, nose and mouth. He thought she was dead.

Bacon was in a coma for 11 days, in intensive care for 23.

When doctors told her the blows to her head were so severe she would never regain the balance she would need to ride again, she found new doctors. She had come back from worse spills than this, she said. Once she was clinically dead for three minutes after a fall in 1973. Another time a horse pinned her against a barn wall, crushing her pelvis and rib cage and rupturing her spleen. She once spent four days paralyzed from the waist down. By the early 1970s, when Bacon was still in her mid-20s, she figured she already had broken 39 bones in all.

Nothing had ever kept Mary Bacon from riding. She was abducted at knifepoint in 1969 by a crazed stablehand at Pennsylvania's Pocono Downs, escaped and raced three horses that night. She rode when she was seven months pregnant. She rode a week after giving birth. When it became clear that tracks would enforce a rule (now rescinded) prohibiting spouses to ride against each other, she divorced her first husband.

"I want to ride," Bacon once said. "That's all that matters. Riding is living."

Bacon was one of the first notable female jockeys. She came to prominence in the late 1960s at the New York tracks, drawing attention as much for her private life as for her riding. She was beautiful, cocky and tough as a new saddle. She modeled for Revlon cosmetics and posed nude for Playboy. When her fellow female jockeys criticized her cheesecake image, Bacon retorted, "They're just jealous. Most of them couldn't tie a knot in my reins."

Publicity was Bacon's constant companion. In 1975, she was taped by two television stations in Walker, Louisiana, speaking at a Ku Klux Klan rally. Later, she said she went to the rally out of curiosity after seeing the movie *The Klansman.* But it cost her the Revlon contract and a TV campaign for

65

Dutch Masters cigars. Not long afterward, she stirred up another controversy when, without presenting any evidence, she accused tracks in Louisiana of drugging and mistreating thoroughbreds.

"We used to say she had one tap too many on the head," said Phyllis Wuerth, who was a nurse at Golden Gate Fields when Bacon rode there. "But she was as tough as they come. No one put anything over on Mary. No one, no one, no one."

Ten months after the Golden Gate Fields spill, Bacon still had not received medical clearance to ride. "To say she is depressed is an understatement," her second husband, jockey Jeff Anderson, told reporters as he prepared to ride Billy Ball in the 1983 Cal Derby. "She's not complete unless she's on a horse."

For five years, Bacon traveled from state to state and track to track searching for a doctor who would give her an okay. Anderson describes those years as "living with a wildcat." Finally, in 1987, a doctor at the fairgrounds near New Orleans gave her the all-clear. Bacon rode a few races there, but trainers were reluctant to give her mounts. Why hire a 40-year-old woman when they could get a 20-year-old man?

So Bacon kept moving, looking for rides. She found her way to Texas, to what racing people call "the bushes." Jockeys work horses in the morning for the opportunity to race them in the afternoon. The purses were almost nothing. Bacon didn't care.

"Mary ended up winning a race in September of 1989," Anderson said by phone the other day from Kansas City. "It was the biggest race of her life. She had the biggest smile I ever saw. It didn't matter to her that this wasn't Belmont. She was so happy just to be riding again. She'd ride anything with hair."

A month later, Bacon was diagnosed with cervical cancer. It wasn't terminal, but the radiation treatments left her too weak to race. Traveling with Anderson, who was by then a jockeys' agent, she got jobs exercising horses. Anderson could see she was struggling to control the horses. He kept telling her to give it up, but she refused. Predictably, a horse threw her last year, breaking her arm in three places.

"Finally, she came to the conclusion she couldn't ride any more," Anderson said. "The truth is, she never fully recovered from the accident at Golden Gate Fields. She was never the same after that."

Anderson and Bacon spent the past winter in Hot Springs, Arkansas, then moved on to The Woodlands Track in Kansas City. While Anderson went to the track, Bacon spent her time grocery shopping, cooking, jogging. She was miserable.

"She won most of her battles early in her life, but in this battle there were very few winners," Anderson said. "How much can a person take?"

On Wednesday, June 5, Bacon told her husband she was going to Trinity Meadows near Fort Worth. She had heard there might be opportunities there. She packed the car and drove off. She checked in to the Motel 6 off Interstate 35 on Thursday. At about 11:30 Friday morning, a maintenance worker saw Bacon walk to her car, retrieve a small-caliber revolver and walk back to her room. She had bought the gun when she arrived in Texas, and, Anderson later guessed, must have had someone else load it for her. "She didn't know anything about guns," he said. Thirty minutes later, a maid found her on the floor with a bullet in her head. She was still alive.

When Anderson got the call from the hospital, his first reaction was, "I wanted to beat the crap out of her." He flew down and was at her side when she died at 1:45 the next morning. She was 43.

"I went through her things at the hotel room and I never came across her saddle or her helmet or any of her jockey clothes," Anderson said. "She went down there to die.

"Mary had so many battles in her life and she just got tired of fighting them. She went to the place she loved more than any place to end her life."

There will be a memorial for Bacon in the winner's circle at Belmont Park in New York Monday. Her ashes will be scattered near the grave of Ruffian, one of her favorite horses.

A few years back, Anderson was in the hospital recovering from a fall, and Bacon was visiting him. A reporter surveyed the toll racing had taken on them, the broken bones, broken backs, pinched nerves, blood clots, concussions, ruptured organs. What, they were asked, would it take to make them quit riding?

"Death," Anderson said.

"That's right," Bacon said. "I'd have to be dead."

(June 23, 1991)

Joan Ryan, *a columnist for the* San Francisco Examiner, *has covered the Super Bowl, World Series, many heavyweight championship fights and Wimbledon. A graduate of the University of Florida, she previously worked at the* Orlando Sentinel *and is completing a book on the pressures faced by young female athletes.*

THE FIGHT OF HEATHER FARR'S LIFE

by Betty Cuniberti
Golf Digest

LIKE MOST NEWLY ENGAGED YOUNG WOMEN, HEATHER FARR DOVE INTO HER wedding plans in a state of frantic delirium. She immediately ordered her gown, a simple white cotton brocade, and selected bridesmaid dresses—dreamy Laura Ashley designs with scalloped V-necks, puffed sleeves and sprays of pink, periwinkle and white flowers on a lemony background. Along with the dresses, the food, the flowers, the enormous guest list and the honeymoon, there was another detail to be taken care of. Unlike most newly engaged young women, Farr had to make sure the man proposing to her understood something she refers to as "the big risk." She is battling a monstrous cancer. So former NFL kicker Goran Lingmerth, a native of Sweden who Farr had known less than three months, was given a written chronology of the dark side of Farr's life. "You should know all this," she told him. "I won't marry you if you don't know all this."

Farr was diagnosed with breast cancer three years ago when she was 24 and a rising LPGA Tour star. The lesion was a large, late-stage tumor that spread to her lymph nodes and bones, a condition that kills 84 percent of women within five years.

To beat those bleak odds, Farr has waged a war that almost defies comprehension, surviving a mastectomy, 13-hour back surgery, a bone-marrow transplant, skull surgery and several rounds of the strongest chemotherapy and radiation that could possibly be prescribed. She has sued longtime family physicians for initially ignoring the troublesome lump in her breast for seven critical months. She has had to wonder if growing up near a toxic waste site led her to these gates of hell. She has had to fight for, and ultimately lose, her health insurance. She's had to accept the charity of other golfers, caddies and strangers to help pay her enormous medical bills. She has lost all her hair three times. She has vomited for months, cried in despair and screamed in pain so intense she thought it might kill her. But mostly she has amazed those around her with her unrelenting spirit.

Many women in Farr's situation get their affairs in order and wait for death to come knocking. But she has taken on cancer the way she approaches a golf course: Attack. Hit one shot at a time. Never give up.

This spring, when tests revealed two previously undetected cancerous lesions on her skull and pelvis, Farr reacted in her typical fashion. She put

68

her wedding date on hold, made an appointment to start radiation therapy, and decided to investigate further treatment at the National Institute of Health. Three days later she, her family and Lingmerth set off in the early morning for Old Hickory, Tennessee, and the Sara Lee Classic, where Farr competed in a six-hole skins game. She's still determined to return to the LPGA Tour to play a shortened schedule next year. And she's not planning to just play. She's planning to win. Farr is going to go for it all—whatever all that may be—on and off the golf course.

"People live for years and years fighting little spots here and there," Farr said shortly after the latest diagnosis. "Truly only God knows what's going to happen. I'm not going to quit today because something might happen tomorrow."

There is a tendency to perceive courageous cancer patients as utterly fearless. But just the opposite is true. True bravery involves facing the deepest of fears. "It's human nature to be terrified." Farr says. "Jesus was afraid on the cross. If He is, no one is better than Him. No one can tell you they'd go through something like this and not be afraid."

On a glorious April morning capping a month of dreary rain, Farr enjoyed a pancake breakfast at the Stonecreek Golf Club near her Phoenix home and told her story. Occasionally she shifted a little stiffly in her chair to relieve the constant pain in her back, where a seven-inch rod shaped like a paper clip holds her spine together. Her dark curly hair gracefully framed her green eyes. She is pretty, even if she looks older than her 27 years. A few half-inch scars dot her neck where chemotherapy catheter tubes had been set for months. At 108 pounds she is a petite version of the athletic young woman who bounced along the fairways carrying her bag, her long ponytail whipping happily in the wind. She talked about her decision to get married.

"You could sit and say, well, I'll wait five years to make sure I'm okay," Farr says. "But then in five years and two days you could find something wrong with you, and then where do you sit? You've lost five years of your life that could have been wonderful with someone. We take one day at a time and we've got each other for today and that's what matters."

What brought Heather this far was her abiding Catholicism, her golf friends and the heroic support of her parents, Sharon and Jerry, and sister, Missy. It was her father who unintentionally taught her how to deal with cancer when he suffered a malignancy of the kidney in 1983. Nine days after his kidney was removed, he insisted on leaving the hospital so he could watch 18-year-old Heather play her first U.S. Open—in 110-degree Tulsa heat. It took him 45 minutes to walk one hole.

Falling in love has done no harm to Farr's attitude, either. Lingmerth has grasped as well as anyone can what Farr has been through, but he does not treat her like a fragile doll. He knows that the high-dose chemotherapy she received with the bone-marrow transplant probably has sterilized her reproductive system. When the new cancer showed up in April, "he didn't run off," Farr says. He knows they may not grow old together.

"It takes a very strong person to accept all that and realize the risk involved, because there still is a risk," Farr says. "A big risk. A friend of ours died in a car accident a couple of weeks ago and she was only 30 years old. Just because I've had cancer doesn't mean I'm in any worse situation than anybody walking down the street."

Farr's nightmare began in one of life's supremely happy moments. She had just bought her first house, and was sleeping peacefully on a mattress on the bedroom floor. Farr had been the youngest woman ever, at age 20, to qualify for the LPGA Tour. Now it was December 1988, and she had just wrapped up her best year yet, winning more than $75,000. Around her stood a Spanish-style patio home with windows galore, a garden big enough for her beloved roses and a cheery kitchen where she could create her specialties: spaghetti or stroganoff from scratch. There was not much furniture yet, but already visions were dancing in her head of greenery dripping from the skylights to the floor, golf and baseball memorabilia on walls and shelves, the blue-flowered sofa and curtains. She rolled over in the middle of the night and was jolted by a pain in her breast. Quickly, her fingers searched and found a lump. From that moment on, her life would never be the same.

She made an appointment to see her longtime family gynecologist, who told her not to worry. Twenty-four-year-old women don't get breast cancer. Only one of five breast biopsies proves to be malignant, and doctors are under intense pressure from insurance companies and consumer groups to cut back on so-called unnecessary surgeries. Heather and her mother "had to plead, push and scream" at two local doctors before finally—seven months after Farr first felt the lump—a biopsy was scheduled over the July 4th weekend of 1989. Ten minutes before the procedure, Sharon Farr thanked the doctor for breaking up his holiday weekend. She recalls him replying, "You know, it's overprotective mothers like you who screw up our lives half the time anyhow." That was one of the last things Heather heard before being administered anesthesia. The next words she heard from him, as she regained consciousness, were "Heather, it doesn't look good."

Farr was so young to be stricken that she and her mother are haunted by the question of whether Heather's disease, as well as Jerry Farr's kidney cancer, was caused by toxic pollution of their drinking water and soil. Breast cancer in a very young woman is believed to be associated with strong genetic factors. Yet there is no history of breast cancer—or kidney cancer—in the Farr family. When Sharon Farr also learned from doctors that breast cancer has no genetic connection to kidney cancer in a parent, then she really began to wonder. "That's like lightning hitting the same house twice," she says.

For more than 20 years the Farrs have lived less than a mile from a Motorola Semiconductor plant, where heavy groundwater and soil contamination has resulted from 200,000 gallons of chlorinated solvents seeping into the ground. The area was declared a Superfund site in 1989, meaning that it has been targeted by the Government for special pollution cleanup funding. Farr grew up playing golf at a course next door to a Motorola plant.

Early data from the Department of Health Services indicate that cancer mortality rates and childhood cancer incidence in the area are not elevated, and that the drinking water is safe. But last December a group of more than 500 local residents filed a $1 billion lawsuit against Motorola, alleging the company has endangered their health and property values. Motorola has spent more than $10 million in cleanup and response costs but denies that health and property values have been damaged. The Farrs are not plaintiffs in that suit. But Sharon Farr says that in her block alone, she has discovered at least five cases of cancer.

The day of the biopsy, the whole family cried. Heather decided she'd had enough of Phoenix doctors. She called then commissioner of the LPGA, Bill Blue, in Los Angeles and asked for help. Through him she found two top-notch surgeons at Cedars Sinai Hospital in Los Angeles to perform the modified radical mastectomy (removing the breast and underarm lymph nodes) and immediate plastic reconstruction with a silicone implant. The tumor, measuring three centimeters square, was too big for a lumpectomy, a procedure in which the cancerous tissue is removed but the breast is left intact.

"The hardest time was the morning that they took her to surgery for her mastectomy," says Heather's mother. "She looked fine, she still had her long hair, she looked healthy. And I knew when she went in that door she was not going to come out the same way she was. I'll never forget, they came and took her in a wheelchair. And just before she got to the double doors where she couldn't go past, she slumped over and was crying. Just for a couple seconds. And then all of a sudden she sat up and said, 'Let's go get this over with.' Had I known what was ahead of us I probably *really* would have lost my mind."

The mastectomy revealed more bad news. There was cancer in 11 of Farr's 16 lymph nodes. Farr's oncologist, Edward Wolin of Los Angeles, said he would be surprised if the tumor had existed more than a year. This enraged the family when they recalled how much time had been wasted after Heather first felt the lump.

Heather usually stresses that she has no time for anger over her fate, but when she thinks of the two Phoenix doctors who put off her concerns for seven months, "Of course I'm angry," she says. "I'm fried beyond words at these people." The anger has gone well beyond words, into the Arizona court system where a malpractice suit was filed by the Farrs last summer.

After her diagnosis Farr told her oncologist she wanted the most aggressive treatment available. He spent two hours on his computer researching adjuvant therapies currently in use all around the nation and came up with a protocol from Johns Hopkins University Hospital in Baltimore, a harsh regimen of nine days on chemotherapy and five days off, continuing for four months. "When she had the mastectomy, we thought that was the worst part of it," Sharon Farr says. "We realized very quickly that was nothing. Her first round of chemo was very intense, it made her very, very ill, so we thought that was the worst thing."

But what lay ahead was unimaginably worse. Just a few months after Farr completed the chemotherapy, tests in December 1990 showed tumors on the back of her skull and on an upper thoracic vertebra. At that point, her best shot at survival was an autologous bone marrow transplant (ABMT).

Farr underwent three weeks of chemotherapy to shrink the tumors in preparation for the transplant. But before she could go forward with the ABMT, the tumor on her back progressed to a stage where it had destroyed her vertebrae and was in danger of reaching the spinal cord and paralyzing her. It would have to be removed before the transplant. While she had her chemotherapy and then spent five weeks recovering, she had to wear a bulky back brace. During those two months, "she could have stepped off the curb and become paralyzed," Sharon Farr says. Heather was taking steroids for the pain, which gave her a fatty dowager's hump on her back and an appetite like a starved wild animal. Her waist swelled as wide as her shoulders.

She was also bald from the chemotherapy, the greatest emotional strain of her entire ordeal. She tried wearing wigs but found them itchy, painful and fake-looking. During one of her chemotherapy programs, a car rental agent looked at Farr's driver's license, picturing her with long hair. Then he glanced up at her barely fuzzy head and remarked, "Nice haircut."

Farr chewed him out, one of only two times she's blown up at ignorant strangers.

The back surgery, performed in Denver, sounds like something no human could survive. Three surgical teams—thoracic, neurological and orthopedic—spent almost 14 hours making the gruesome and delicate repair. A thoracic surgical unit cut her open in back and front and closed down her left lung to make work room. Her left shoulder also had to be separated and pulled open for eight hours. The neurological team carved the tumor from the spine, an exacting procedure that can paralyze a patient if something goes wrong. An orthopedic team then removed an entire rib and pieces of Farr's pelvic bone to form a bone graft replacing the destroyed vertebrae. A seven-inch oval rod, as thick as a large pen, was inserted in Farr's spine for stability.

After the operation Farr's eyes were swollen shut. She could only hear what was going on around her—someone scooting in a chair closer and closer—and she was terrified. Her fingers were so swollen she could not push the button on her pain-medication pump, and her face was too puffed up to talk, so she couldn't tell anyone. One time a catheter that led into Heather's heart exploded and sent blood spurting all over the room. "When that thing blew, it was like somebody got shot," Heather recalls.

It was the worst week of Heather Farr's life, when she suffered indescribable agony. It was the only time she considered bailing out of treatment. "I thought I was going to die right then," she says. "I mean, I thought I couldn't take any more."

The regimen Farr underwent at the University of Colorado Cancer Center in April 1991 included a relatively new process. Farr's bone marrow was purged of cancer cells before it was injected back into her body. Dr. Scott Bearman, clinical director of the Colorado bone-marrow transplant program, says his team tells patients with metastatic breast cancer, like Farr has, that "in the best circumstances," about 25 percent of them will be cured—meaning free of disease on a long-term basis (compared with about 3 per cent cured on standard chemotherapy). More than half of the patients with this late-stage disease are expected to die within five years of the transplant.

This bone marrow transplant (ABMT) is costly (about $160,000) and rigorous. The bone marrow is removed through a needle in the lower back so the patient can receive chemotherapy in doses three to ten times stronger than normal—amounts that would destroy the bone marrow and kill the patient if the marrow was left in. During an approximately five-day period without bone marrow, as well as the first few weeks it is back in and reconstituting, the body has no immune system and suffers infection after infection. The patient must be kept in isolation, seeing only medical personnel and family members who first don gowns in an airlock chamber.

Farr was in isolation for some 38 days. She slept with a white teddy bear sent by LPGA Hall of Famer Patty Berg, a cancer survivor now in her 70s. During the time when the body has no immunities, "you're living on constant blood transfusions, platelet transfusions and antibiotics," says Sharon Farr. Gallons of blood were needed, and the Colorado Women's Golf Association conducted a drive that collected all Heather required. "[Heather] has a lot of golfers' blood in her," her mother notes in a lighter moment.

A small percentage of patients die of complications brought on by ABMT. The transplant makes both women and men (who undergo ABMT for leukemia or lymphoma) sterile. Insurance companies often fight paying for transplants, labeling them experimental. Considering all the pros and cons, ABMT is an option that very few breast cancer patients choose.

With her entire adult life ahead of her, Farr did not find it a difficult choice. It was slim chance or no chance. "It surprises me sometimes when people say, 'You've been so courageous,'" she says. "I sometimes think just the opposite. To me the other choice was so terrifying, I was so afraid of the other option, I didn't want to find out."

To be admitted to the Colorado transplant program, patients have to promise to pay for it. Farr's insurance company balked at covering her expenses, using the experimental treatment exclusion. So the Farrs agreed to be personally responsible for the six-figure bill.

When her situation was publicized, money poured in from everywhere. The LPGA Tour players donated their 1991 pro-am prize money, about $2,000 a week. Raffles were held, and caddies put on bowling tournaments and sold "Conquer the Mountain" caps—a salute to Sharon Farr's labeling the upcoming transplant "just another mountain to climb." Strangers would send $5.

Amid the public outpouring of support, Farr's insurance company relented and paid for most of the transplant. But in the meantime her policy changed underwriters, and the new group did not pick her up. She continued paying for her ongoing tests and treatment from money that has been donated.

Compared with back surgery the ABMT wasn't quite as horrible—even though the five-day high-dose chemotherapy was so toxic Farr lost some of her hearing and continued vomiting for two months after she returned home. Some eight weeks after the transplant, tests showed the tumor on her skull was still there. It was surgically removed June 11, 1991. When

Farr awoke in intensive care, her mother handed her two dozen long-stemmed roses. "These are from Ben Hogan," Sharon told her. The next day Heather thought it had been a hallucination.

Three months later, last September, tests revealed a spot on her hip that probably was cancerous but not removable. It was treated with radiation therapy. Five months after that, in February 1992, Heather Farr announced she would attempt to return to the LPGA Tour in 1993.

Throughout her ordeal, Farr received a steady shower of correspondence and gifts from everywhere, especially the LPGA. Berg wrote 95 cards. Even Nancy Reagan, the former First Lady and breast-cancer survivor, sent her a handwritten, two-page letter. "I always had little things show up at about the time I would think I couldn't handle it anymore," Heather says. The Amana company gave her a microwave when she had to live in a Los Angeles hotel room for two months while receiving treatment. Farr's tour sponsor, Sara Lee, turned down her offer to dissolve their contract and later signed her on for three more years. "Because of them, I've been able to keep my house and pay my bills," she says. "I will forever, ever, owe them."

Inspiration also came from Darrell Gwynn, a race-car driver who was paralyzed in an accident. They met at a pro-am tournament in Florida benefiting both of them. "You see something like that, and you think, what does *he* deal with every day?" Farr says. "He can't feed himself. *That's* courageous. There's always somebody worse off than you. I feel lucky. And I'm sure he feels lucky."

Helping other women avoid her fate has become Farr's cause. She has shared her story in candid detail and encouraged women to watch for symptoms and demand action on possible malignancies.

In her activist role, Farr argues about the need for increased government funding for breast-cancer research. The estimated figures for President Bush's fiscal-year 1993 budget include $160 million for breast-cancer research, a woefully inadequate amount, she argues, when compared with the $873 million earmarked for AIDS research. Death figures for the 12-month period ending October 1991: 45,220 from breast cancer; 28,260 from AIDS.

When Farr was racked with illness, her mind protected her and told her she did not miss golf. But as soon as she gained some mobility and strength, the urge to play gushed fast and furious. She is still hampered by pain and fatigue, her legs are weak, her left shoulder slides around and she cannot putt for long before the muscles in her neck, severed in the brain surgery, cause intolerable pain in her upper back.

To resume a career as a professional athlete in this condition is something almost no one would attempt. But almost no one has the fighting spirit of Heather Farr. It's like the bone-marrow transplant: Even if there's just a slim chance of success, she'll take that chance.

"I don't know if I can get back and play golf," she admits. To warm up for the April skins event, she played nine holes and shot a 42. "But, gosh," she says, looking at the golf course stretching around her, "we're sitting here in a place where I look out and see perfect grass, I see blue sky and you can hear the birds. That's what I love. Golf is my life. I love my job. I want that back."

(July, 1992)

Betty Cuniberti *was a sportswriter for the* San Francisco Chronicle, *the* Washington Post *and* Star *and then a political writer for the* Los Angeles Times. *After a successful battle with breast cancer, she is a now full-time mother and part-time writer for* Golf Digest. *Heather Farr died November 20, 1993.*

VICTIMS OF OBSESSION

by Karen Crouse
Orange County Register

ON THAT FIRST NIGHT IN HER APARTMENT IN 1989, THE PHONE CALLS WERE more a source of amusement than anything else.

The caller, who had introduced himself to UCLA volleyball player Laurie Jones after a match earlier in the day, rambled on about volleyball, Disneyland and anything else that popped into his head.

Not wishing to be rude, Jones patiently hung on the line.

When she finally managed to hang up, it was only a matter of minutes before the phone rang again. And again.

Jones' roommates eventually came to her rescue. Stifling giggles, they answered each successive call from the man with the greeting, "Domino's Pizza."

Jones was less amused the next day when the man showed up at a UCLA match against Loyola Marymount and stuck to her like gum on her sneaker.

That night, back in her apartment, Jones turned off the ringer on the phone and switched on the answering machine. In the morning, the red light was flashing. The messages, all left well after midnight, paralyzed her with fear.

Beep.

"I think we should go steady . . . I think you're perfect for me."

Beep.

"If that big, blond guy you were with . . . is your boyfriend then I'm going to kill the son of a bitch."

Stalking long has been a hazard of Hollywood—witness the much-publicized attack in 1984 on actress Theresa Saldana, and the fatal shooting five years later of actress Rebecca Schaeffer, both by obsessed fans.

Now come unsettling stories from the sporting arena, involving accomplished athletes such as Jones, Olympic swimmers Janet Evans and Summer Sanders, tennis player Steffi Graf and figure skater Katarina Witt.

Victors and victims all. "Weirdness is on the rise," said Dr. Park Dietz, a forensic psychiatrist from San Diego who has devoted the past 10 years to the study of stalking behavior.

In such a climate, to feel safe is to risk being sorry. Los Angeles police Detective Greg Boles is the supervisor in charge of the LAPD Threat Management Unit, which tracks and arrests stalkers.

Said Boles: "My guess is that 40-50 percent of the cases we deal with involve what we call ordinary citizens. Maybe another 17-18 percent involve highly recognized celebrities."

Athletes can fall under either category.

Celebrities have the visibility that makes them easy targets; ordinary people have the accessibility. Athletes generally have both, and therein lies the danger.

"The athlete cases I've seen range from a serial bomber stalking female high school basketball players to the homicide of a famous male athlete by a romantic stalker," Dietz said.

Isolated incidents or a terrifying trend?

"I think it's inevitable that as women's athletics becomes more popular and the athletes become more familiar to the public, the chances of weirdos getting obsessed with them increases," said Donna Lopiano, executive director of the Women's Sports Foundation.

She paused.

"How else can you explain things like this?"

Item: An elderly man from Ohio lavished Evans, 22, with letters, the content of which she described as "more religious than sexual." Intent on meeting the object of his attentions, he showed up at her family's home in Placentia last November. The Evanses called the police and the man left without incident. He continues to write letters to Evans, which she forwards unopened to the police.

Evans, a two-time Olympian, is no stranger to weird correspondence. In 1989, shortly after she enrolled at Stanford, a man living in Michigan began sending her untoward letters. Evans said they stopped after he was threatened with a restraining order.

Item: Michael Salata, 38, was arrested and charged with trespassing in December at the gated community in Boca Raton, Florida, where Graf lives. He ignored repeated warnings to stay clear of the development. In his report, Palm Beach County Sheriff's Deputy Mark Ray wrote of Salata, "He wanted to harm Miss Graf."

It was the second time Graf was harassed at her home; in 1988 a Montreal man was arrested after he made repeated attempts to meet the tennis star.

Item: Mason Crist, 37, was arrested on New Year's Eve for "peeking and loitering" at the home of Sanders's father outside Sacramento. He had made several attempts to contact the swimmer at her family's home and at Stanford, where Sanders is a junior.

When Watsonville police searched Crist's apartment, they found letters to Sanders, actresses Priscilla Presley and Elizabeth Taylor and tennis player Andre Agassi.

Crist, who pleaded guilty to a misdemeanor charge of trespassing, spent

16 days in Placer County jail and will return to court next month for a probation hearing. The district attorney handling the case told reporters last month she believes Crist "has learned his lesson."

Item: Harry Veltman III, 47, of Westminister, was sentenced to 37 months in prison last June after he was convicted of sending Witt obscene and threatening mail, including one letter that read in part, "Please don't be afraid when God allows me to pull you out of your body to hold you tight! Then you'll know there is life beyond the flesh."

"The sad truth is a certain percentage of the population has major mental disorders, and public figures, because of their visibility, are at a greater risk of being incorporated into the fantasies of these people," said William Vicary, an assistant professor of clinical psychiatry at USC.

"Some way or another, the victim gets swept up in the person's delusions."

Chronic mental illness can be hard enough to define, much less explain. But Dietz said all stalkers regardless of the circumstances behind their delusions, "share some characteristics."

"They send letters, leave gifts, make telephone calls, make inappropriate visits and do at least one of these repeatedly before the first attack," Dietz said.

"They have in common an inability to listen to reason and respond in a rational manner," he said. "So sending letters back unopened, having a lawyer send a letter telling them to stop, that's generally not going to help. Any response at all will be taken as encouragement."

Jones, a fifth-year senior, is wiser, warier, now. But before the start of her sophomore year at UCLA, the Huntington Beach High graduate embraced the world. At 18, who's not to trust, what's not to like?

Then David Carlsberg's path crossed hers, and before long, many of her illusions about life began to crumble under his gaze.

His attentiveness made her nervous, but Jones tried to act polite yet disinterested.

"Why worry?" she thought. At 5-8 and 145, Carlsberg, in his 20s, hardly cut an imposing figure. Often clad in jeans, a polo shirt and a brown corduroy jacket, he looked . . . average, she thought. Jones would later describe him as harmless, non-threatening.

Still, "something about him just gave me the willies," said Jones, a lithe, 6-1 blonde. "But we've been told to treat our fans nice. I didn't want to make anybody mad."

Besides, she added, "I'm not a confrontational person. I'm really bad at telling people to buzz off. Though I've gotten better since this."

Jones finally did confide to coach Andy Banachowski and his assistants, telling them offhandedly, "This guy's following me and he's kind of strange. I think he's got a screw loose."

Banachowski, a soft-spoken man, has been the Bruins coach for 5 years and a father for 21. Or is that 26?

Sometimes, Banachowski acknowledges, it's hard to distinguish where the coaching stops and the fathering begins.

"I've always felt that I do have a very strong responsibility to look out for the welfare of my players," Banachowski said. "Society tends to think boys can take care of themselves. I think any coach of a women's team tends to be a little protective of his athletes."

Stalking victims come from all walks of life, but athletes tend to be particularly vulnerable, if only because so much of their lives are played out in public.

On college campuses, they are easy to spot and easier to find, owing to daily schedules that are regimented and generally well-publicized.

Practices usually are held at the same time and place. And the times and locations of competitions are there for the scrutinizing on posters and wallet cards.

"It was just so easy for him to find out where I was and what I was doing," Jones said of Carlsberg, who lived with his parents in nearby Bel-Air.

The UCLA athletic department has a policy for anyone trying to contact an athlete by mail or telephone: Leave your number with a coach and it will be passed along; send your letter to the athletic department and it will be delivered.

"Even before (Jones's ordeal), we've tried to alert our coaches and athletes to (the potential for) any untoward fan behavior," said Judith Holland, UCLA's senior associate athletic director.

"When it happens, and I can only think of three or four cases in the 18 years I've been here, we don't attempt to make a distinction as to whether they're harmless or not," Holland added. "We take whatever steps we feel necessary to protect our athletes."

Beginning in September 1989, Holland thought it judicious to enlist a police escort for Jones at every home match.

The officer sat in the first row behind the UCLA bench. Jones, too, did a lot of sitting. She was redshirted after six matches because of shoulder and ankle injuries. Despite the obvious distractions, the Bruins compiled a record of 30-3, went undefeated in the Pac-10 and finished third nationally.

"It definitely got scary," Banachowski said. "Everybody became a little paranoid, not for themselves but for Laurie."

After a match in September, three weeks after Jones's initial encounter with Carlsberg, Jones's father discovered him lurking in the underground garage where his daughter's car was parked.

He warned Carlsberg to stay away from Jones. Undeterred, the man was spotted only minutes later peering into the window of a room where the volleyball team was holding a reception.

Campus police were summoned and Carlsberg was arrested for trespassing, cited and released.

In October 1989, Jones filed for a restraining order. After listening to a few of the messages Carlsberg had left on Jones's answering machine, Superior Court Judge Robert Altman ordered him not to come within 500 yards of Jones for three years.

The relief felt by Jones's parents, James and Joanne, was shortlived.

In April 1991, Carlsberg tried to approach Jones after a practice. Teammates summoned campus police while Jones hid behind some bushes. Carlsberg was arrested, slapped with a year of probation and sentenced to 40 hours of community service.

In early July, Carlsberg called Jones's parents and left a message on their answering machine.

"I'm just calling to say hello and that . . . things in regard to women are still very difficult for me . . ." he said. "The women thing is just very, very tough for me . . ."

Three weeks later, Carlsberg showed up at Loyola Marymount during a U.S. Olympic Festival match involving Jones's team.

She was not playing because of an injury but she was in the stands. Recalling the incident not quite two years later, Jones is fuzzy on the particulars of the match.

But what she experienced afterward—from her sweaty palms and pounding heart down to her frozen legs—as she watched him walk toward her, left an indelible impression.

"That feeling of being trapped, of being so helpless. I'll never forget it," Jones said.

Carlsberg was arrested and sentenced to 10 days in LA County jail—he served two before being released. He also was ordered to enroll in a psychiatric counseling program, and the restraining order, due to expire in June of last year, was extended through June 27 of this year, coinciding with Jones's graduation from UCLA.

Jones has not seen Carlsberg since. Peter Linnett, executive director of the Life Adjustment Team in Culver City, where Carlsberg is undergoing treatment for an obsessive-compulsive disorder, said he is making steady progress.

"One of David's main problems is that he has poor impulse control," Linnett wrote in a letter to the presiding judge at Carlsberg's court hearing in July 1991. "David is learning to redirect his inappropriate behavior and solve problems in areas that have been poorly controlled in the past."

The Joneses can only hope Linnett is right.

"It really hasn't ended," said Joanne Jones who, like her husband, developed an ulcer during the three-year ordeal. "We know David's still in the area."

Jones does, too, of course. But she doesn't dwell on the thought.

"I'm a little more standoffish now around people I don't know," said Jones, a history major who plans to pursue a teaching credential as well as a professional beach volleyball career after graduating.

"I mean, who's to say it won't happen again?" she said. "I realize now you never know when someone like that is going to step over the line and do something. People like that are like a time bomb ticking."

(February 21, 1993)

Karen Crouse is a general assignment sports reporter for the Orange County Register. *A former varsity swimmer at the University of Southern California where she earned a journalism degree, she previously worked at the* Los Angeles Herald-Examiner, *the* Riverside Press-Enterprise *and the* Savannah *(GA)* News-Press.

Zola Budd: On the Run No More

by Julie Cart
Los Angeles Times

IF EVER THERE WAS A PLACE WHERE A PERSON COULD GO TO HIDE FROM THE REST of the world, this would be it. Now, in the high summer, there is something desolate and scorched about it, lying dead in the center of southern Africa. It's as if Nature had been here once, but left in a hurry.

It might be the richest region in South Africa. Far under the earth lie fields of diamonds and vast veins of gold. The mining operations in the Orange Free State are the country's most extensive, with shafts running both vertically and horizontally. It is possible to imagine the ground under your feet as being hollow and your footsteps echoing in the ears of miners laboring below.

This is where many Afrikaners found haven in the 19th Century—driven north from the Cape Colony and the hated British. These Dutch-descended white settlers halted here, put down their Calvinist roots and set about the business of producing children who would become South Africa's ruling elite.

Bloemfontein is the capital of the Orange Free State—the most conservative, most insular of South Africa's four provinces. It is the home of the Afrikaners, the stubborn, hardy and proud people who view their province as a kind of oasis in a sea of madness.

An enduring symbol of the Afrikaner is the laager, or protective circle of wagons, an effective method of defense while under attack. The image of the laager, if not the fact of it, lingers.

Today, as then, Afrikaans is spoken here. It is the language that begat the word apartheid, or separateness. In the thick Afrikaans accent, the word is pronounced, APART-hate.

This is where Zola Budd ran to when she could no longer run. Budd, one of the world's most reviled athletes, came home when, at last, she wanted no one to find her. The Free State swallowed her, and she was lost to the world.

This is where she found herself again.

The directions were clear, but quite wrong. Take the Kimberly Road for about one kilometer to Tarrel Road, then right. Look for the animal kennel on the corner. Follow the dirt road to the third house on the right, on Van Vuuren Laan. No address.

There is no Tarrel Road exit off the N1. Every scrubby gravel street looks the same. All the low-slung ranch-style houses look identical. A check of the directions didn't help. They are clearly the product of a person to whom street names had less navigational value than local landmarks, much as a rural resident might helpfully explain, "Turn left down at the Miller place, by the old elm tree."

Finally, the animals give it away. Ducks, dogs, ostriches, cats, a menagerie roaming peacefully around the front yard. This is the home of Zola Budd Pieterse. A guest might not find this place easily, but the visitor is not unwelcome once here.

Sitting in a sunny living room, two cats on her lap, Budd tries to reconstruct the blocks of her life since she left England hurriedly in May of 1988, suffering from nervous exhaustion. At the time, Budd said she was retiring from international competition.

Since returning to her home in Bloemfontein, Budd has watched the disintegration of her family, gotten married, resumed her running career and finally broken her long silence and denounced apartheid.

And when attention had begun to wane, Budd was in the news again. Her father, Frank Budd, was found murdered last September, killed with his own shotgun. The killer told police that Budd, 56, had made homosexual advances toward him.

Frank Budd, who had engineered his daughter's career and withheld huge sums of money from her, left specific instructions in his will that Zola be barred from his funeral. Further, he forbade her burial in the family plot.

Despite all this and sporadic international curiosity, Budd, 23, says she is the most relaxed and happy she has ever been. She is at peace.

"I finally feel settled," she said. "At the end of the day, I feel satisfied with what I've done. I don't feel I could have done more. I really enjoy just a normal life. It's nice to be normal. Being here is a relief from the pressure and attention from the press. It's a relief."

Only months after her controversial collision with Mary Decker Slaney in the 3,000 meters at the L.A. Olympics in 1984, in which she competed as a British citizen, Budd was once again the target of the international anti-apartheid lobby. Budd had returned to South Africa to seek treatment for a persistent leg injury.

The International Amateur Athletic Federation, which governs track and field, discovered that while she was in South Africa, Budd had attended two road races. The IAAF found this to be in violation of its rule that forbids "participation" in competition in South Africa. After hearings in London, the IAAF recommended to the British track authorities that Budd be suspended for a year.

Something in her snapped. Running was the only thing that brought her happiness, and now she wouldn't be allowed to have that. Budd's London physician later reported that she was experiencing depression and long bouts of crying. He prescribed complete rest. He advised her to go home—to South Africa.

As Budd explained in her autobiography, *Zola*, written last year with South African sportswriter Hugh Eley, "It came to a choice between running and life; I chose life."

The life she came back to was much as it had been in the simple days of her youth. Budd grew up on a farm surrounded by animals. Today, she and her husband, wealthy liquor store owner Mike Pieterse, live in a modern but modest rural home with six dogs and three cats.

Budd is doing what she has always wanted to do but was not allowed to do. Coming out of high school, she wanted to go to a technical college. Her domineering coach, Pieter Labauschagne, told her she was going to a university. Today, Budd is studying computer programming at a nearby technical college.

Even her marriage was a kind of rebellion. Budd had met Pieterse casually in 1986. Then, after she returned to South Africa, her sister Estelle arranged a dinner where the two would be together.

"I think it was a set-up," Budd said.

The relationship grew steadily, but Budd was troubled. Having been betrayed in the past, she sought a commitment from Pieterse—she proposed.

"Feminism hasn't hit the Free State yet," she joked. "But Mike is very different from other men. I don't think it was a shock to him. I wouldn't have asked if I wasn't sure he would say yes.

"I just felt I had to have some security. In past relationships with people, some have been intimidated by my success. But with him, it was quite the opposite. I came back and I wasn't running well. It didn't matter to him if I was running well. He's very patient and much better with people than I am. He takes life much easier than I do. I've met a lot of new people and made new friends through Mike, and that is quite nice.

"It's just another environment. When you do athletics, all the people you know are other athletes. Sometimes it gets really boring. It's nice not to just talk about athletics. I think that's one of the things that really attracted me to him. Athletics was one of the subjects we never discussed."

The wedding was April 15, 1989. Her mother, Tossie, her sisters and her brother, Quintus, were there. Frank Budd was not. Still estranged from her father, Zola had asked Quintus to give her away. But Frank Budd threatened to disinherit his son if that happened. In the end, Zola's father-in-law gave her away.

The wedding generated enormous attention. For South Africans, the marriage of shy little Zola to "Mike, the big teddy bear," was the same as if the nation's youngest sister were getting married. The church was mobbed.

Frank Budd did not attend and was quoted as saying, "I no longer have a daughter called Zola."

Budd has still not worked out her complex relationship with her father.

Frank Budd ran a print shop, worked long hours and was seldom at home. One of Zola's warmest memories of her father was her tiny hand in his as he proudly marched her around after she had won a race in elementary school.

Frank and Tossie Budd frequently quarreled. Frank, who spoke English, and Tossie, who spoke Afrikaans, would have each of their six children speak to them only in English. The Budds didn't share similar philosophical outlooks, either. Frank was liberal and outgoing, Tossie was conservative and retiring. They divorced in 1986 after 33 years of marriage.

When Budd broke Mary Decker's world record at 5,000 meters by more than six seconds on Jan. 4, 1984—because she was a South African, Budd's time was not recognized as a record—Frank Budd conceived, constructed and got behind the wheel of the great lumbering beast that was to become the Buddwagon. It made him rich.

Within weeks after Zola's amazing race, in which she ran barefoot in the wind at altitude, Frank Budd and Zola's coach, Labauschagne, negotiated with representatives of the British tabloid, the *Daily Mail*. Because her paternal grandfather had been born in London—and with the help of the *Mail*—Budd was granted British citizenship in 13 days, receiving her passport on April 6, 1984, only three months before the L.A. Olympics.

The furor in England and abroad was immediate. Budd was criticized because of her "passport of convenience" and her status as a South African brought the anti-apartheid lobby into her life.

Budd, then 17, hated her new life in England, away from her home and her animals. She begged to go back, but the adults around her—with the exception of her mother, who also hated England—told her she must see this thing through.

At work were her father and coach. From her book: "Together with the *Daily Mail*, which arranged the cloak-and-dagger operation to get me to England in what was, for it, a massive and highly successful publicity stunt, they turned me into some kind of circus animal. I was expected to perform, and perform well, every time I put a foot on the track."

The deal Frank Budd had negotiated was for 100,000 pounds, and it broke down this way: 20,000 in a trust fund for Zola, 20,000 for Pieter Labauschagne, 5,000 each to Budd's brother and two of her sisters, and, notably, 45,000 for Frank Budd. Additionally, Frank Budd acted as his daughter's agent, taking 35 percent of the gross.

Looking back, Budd realizes she relied almost totally on the advice of her father and others and therein made critical mistakes. She also found that the Buddwagon was a cynical and cruel way to extort money from her.

Budd made the gradual discovery that it was her running—not her—that was so loved by her father and coach. She says now that as a result she lost her ability to trust anyone for years. Budd has tried to work this out, but she has kept the pain as a souvenir. There are some lessons she doesn't want to forget.

"When I ran well and everything was going well, they were interested," she said. "I think that was the main reason they were interested in me. I don't think it was a personal matter, or that they wanted to be involved with me as a person. It was the athletics. When that didn't fulfill all the potential they wanted, they just disappeared.

"It was painful, especially with my coach, because we spent a lot of time together, seven years together. It was very difficult for me to handle that."

Budd said she became aware that Labauschagne's loyalty was contingent on her performance when she ran poorly in England in 1986 and returned to South Africa with an injury. Labauschagne told Budd she was faking the injury and told her to get back to Europe and run.

"That's when I decided he was not interested in me," she said. "The point is, you need a coach when you are running well, but when you really need a coach is when you are not running well. That's the time when you need people."

Budd's estrangement from her father was slow to build but exploded suddenly. They had a fight and she moved out of the house. She rarely spoke to him after that. Problems with her father put a strain on Budd's relationship with her brother, Quintus. He never understood what had happened between Budd and her father while she was living in England. He never knew about the problems with Zola's missing money.

"Even now, it's very difficult for my brother to understand," Budd said. "I think, in a way, he still blames me for things that have happened between my mother and my father. Relations between us aren't as bad as they were between me and my father. He's still upset about everything. He's taking it very badly."

The "it" Budd referred to was their father's murder and the subsequent allegations of his homosexuality.

"I wasn't seeing him before his death," she said. "It was quite hard for me to accept. I always hoped that one day we would have a reconciliation. It is a terrible thing not to have said, 'I love you.'"

Budd learned from her sister the provisions in Frank Budd's will. She didn't attend the reading of the will. She did not attend the trial of Christian Johannes Botha Barnard, the 24-year-old who worked on Frank Budd's farm, "The Hope," near Bloemfontein.

Barnard was charged with shooting Budd twice with Budd's shotgun, then stealing Budd's truck and checkbook. Barnard testified that Budd had made derogatory remarks about the younger man's girlfriend and had, on the night of Sept. 30, made sexual advances toward him.

Barnard faced the death penalty, but the judge, citing "extenuating circumstances," sentenced Barnard to 12 years in prison.

Asked how she felt toward her father's killer, Budd said she had "sort of a neutral feeling."

In January, Budd did something many people had wanted her to do for a long time. On a BBC television program, she gave her views about apartheid. She told the audience that she could never accept a political system that entrenches the superiority of one race over another. She said that, as a Christian, she believed that all people were created equal. Her country's system of apartheid was wrong, she said.

The statement was astonishing not in that she held those beliefs, but in that she actually voiced them. For six years, ever since she had become a world-class runner, Budd had been asked her views on apartheid. For six years she had steadfastly refused to share her views, saying she was an athlete, not a politician.

For her silence and because she failed to sever her ties to South Africa, Budd was made Public Enemy No. 1 by the world's anti-apartheid groups. She was picketed every time she ran, and the British team was threatened with boycotts at meets in which she took part. There was a simple way to defuse all this—denounce apartheid. Budd refused. It was a revealing decision, for it showed her stubbornness and her willingness to fight, even in a battle she had little chance to win.

"I've been quiet for so long, I just spoke my mind," Budd recalled, "In a way, it was a relief. I could finally say what I thought. But I still felt it was unfair for people to expect me to talk about politics. I have opinions, but they are private.

"I felt I didn't want to be forced into making political statements just because they wanted it. In a way, the whole time I was just a bit stubborn, because I didn't want to give in to their demands. I don't think you can ever win against the people who were as fanatical as the people I was up against, or even with the press."

Budd said that the reaction to her views in South Africa was mixed. She said she received hate mail from "the conservative elements," as she had previously been threatened by anti-apartheid groups. Nevertheless, she is not sorry she spoke her mind, especially given the political changes recently.

"I think South Africa had to change," she said. "The time is right. I just hope people accept the changes and work together. I just hope South Africa survives as a country. You can expect violence from both sides, but I think it is time for people to accept what is happening, to accept what the opinion of the whole world is.

"It's hard here because it's been going on for so long. I'm 23 years old and I know nothing else. I've never seen an international running team in South Africa. So, from a practical side, it will be difficult for South Africa to adapt to the change.

"To look back on it, the anti-apartheid people have been very—not stupid, but I think if they had allowed (South African) blacks to compete overseas and not the whites, it would have been much harder for people here. Changes would have come much quicker."

Budd recently began to compete here, at a low-key level. She understands that by doing that, under the present rules, she has made herself ineligible to compete internationally, even though she still holds a British passport. But she won't miss it.

"No, I think I have seen it all and been through it all," she said. "I realize now how artificial everything was. Running, although it is a sport, is very artificial. You run well today and tomorrow is the next day and you have to perform well all over again. When I look back on three years of running, I don't really feel I have achieved a lot, especially not as a person.

"It's all right, running well. But at the end of the day you have to satisfy your own needs. Looking back on it, it was a very boring time. I got overwhelmed by just doing athletics.

"If something reckless happened, and South Africa was allowed back into the Olympics tomorrow, and the opportunity arose for me to run a few meetings, I might do it. But on the other hand, I would be very careful not to let athletics take over again. Not to run because I have to but because I enjoy it. There is always the balance.

"Running is something that is a part of my life. In the past, it was the only thing and I had to do it well. So it's really nice now, if I don't run well today I'll come home and just forget about it. I don't want running to take over my life as it once did. There are so many other things to do now."

Budd might have accepted this, but the people of South Africa yearn for their Zola to beat the world again, so that, through her, they become winners. Budd tells them to look elsewhere for a symbol.

"People seem to take it for granted that I am going to run well again and that I am going to achieve," she said, sighing. "It's something I'll just have to cope with. When people ask me what my future plans are, I reply that I just don't know. I'll take it as it comes."

The road that leads away from Zola Budd's home is easier to find than the one that leads to it. There is an airport close by and the town. There is a world beyond Bloemfontein and the Orange Free State and even beyond the borders of this isolated country.

Zola Budd has seen what lies beyond. And that is what has driven her back here. You get the impression that after losing herself out there, she has found herself again here, and that she doesn't ever want to leave again.

(May 7, 1990)

Julie Cart, a sportswriter at the Los Angeles Times *since 1983, was born in Eunice, LA, was a scholarship track athlete at Arizona State University and has a graduate degree from the University of the West Indies in Kingston, Jamaica.*

FIGHTING THE WHISPERS

by Ann Killion
San Jose Mercury News

JENNIFER SELF HAD HEARD THE RUMORS. SHE FIRST HEARD THEM WHEN RIVAL recruiters tried to dissuade her from playing basketball at the University of California. They told Self that Cal was "one of those" schools. They said that women's sports there had a reputation for lesbianism. They implied that if she went there she would be tainted.

Self was concerned. Her parents were concerned. So she asked about the issue on a recruiting visit to Berkeley.

The twist was that Self knew that she was a lesbian.

"So here I am thinking, 'I know I'm gay, I know I'm gay,' but I'm asking if there's a problem with lesbianism," said Self, who finished her final year of eligibility at Cal last season. "There's a lot of pressure."

And a lot of fear. Homophobia is a powerful and insidious force in women's sports. The mere threat of being labeled a lesbian is enough to turn women—both gay and straight—away from a particular program or from sports altogether.

"The lesbian label is used even if you're not one," said Pat Griffin, a physical education professor at the University of Massachusetts and an expert on homophobia. "It's a control to keep women's sports off balance. The issue isn't lesbianism. The issue is homophobia and discrimination."

Self chose Cal for academic reasons and found the rumors to be unfounded; she said she was the only gay member of the Cal basketball team last season.

Concerns about homosexuality kept Stanford junior Martha Richards out of certain schools. Richards, who played basketball and now plays golf, said she ruled out several programs because of the lesbian issue.

"When you have the background I have, it's definitely something you're scared of," said Richards, who is from Hudson, Wisconsin. "When I was choosing a school, I didn't want to have to deal with it if I didn't have to."

Homophobia also exists at the high school level.

"It's very strong there," said Michelle Wagner, a three-sport star at Lynbrook High. "Especially in certain sports there's a lot of stereotyping. I think it's turned girls away from athletics, and that's too bad."

Mitzi Zenger, a San Jose State softball player, knows her sport is considered by many a lesbian sport. Zenger, who dates an SJS football player, said she is often called a "dyke" by fraternity members during softball practice.

91

"I think it's hurt the sport a lot," said Zenger, who was told by recruiters of SJS' alleged reputation. "A lot of parents don't want their girls to be exposed to it."

Said Christine Grant, women's athletic director at the University of Iowa: "It's like McCarthyism in the 1950s. The fear is paralyzing."

A 1988-89 NCAA study on perceived barriers in women's intercollegiate athletic careers surveyed female administrators and athletes at 180 randomly selected institutions.

The study found that 75 percent of administrators felt stereotypes were barriers in their careers and 54.4 percent of that group specifically said that their involvement in sports led others to assume they were homosexuals. The findings held true for female coaches and athletes.

"It affects all women and everybody who works in women's sports," Griffin said. "The really obvious effects are discrimination in hiring and firing, or being kicked off teams. But it ranges from the blatant to the subtle. Young girls are terrorized. There's a climate of fear."

Griffin led a mandatory workshop on homophobia at Penn State, where women's basketball coach Rene Portland had banned homosexuality on her team, threatening to revoke scholarships of gay players.

"That kind of thing goes on at other places," Griffin said. "She was the one who got caught."

Richards was recruited by Portland. Richards said the Penn State coach told her, "I don't have any lesbians on my team and I don't want any. If that's an issue, we can end this right here." Richards said that statement kept Penn State in the running.

Cal player Self prides herself on her openness, but said she wouldn't know what to do if she had played at Penn State.

"Coaches can hang your scholarship over your head and that's a big pressure—that's too much to give up," Self said.

The implication of homosexuality—real or false—also can affect jobs.

"I have friends who are straight as can be who have gotten out of coaching because of the label," said Mary Zimmerman, former SJS associate athletic director.

Griffin said that athletic directors call each other to check out a job candidate's sexuality.

"The best thing you can be as a job candidate is divorced with no children," said Donna Lopiano, executive director of the Women's Sports Foundation. That status, she said, implies heterosexuality without family burdens.

Homophobia also affects commercial opportunities.

"It absolutely does," said former tennis star Billie Jean King, who was sued for palimony by a former secretary in 1981. "All you have to do is ask Martina (Navratilova) and Chris Evert what they make in endorsements. It's not even close."

Evert, who projected an All-American image on court, is retired but will earn $7 million in endorsements this year, according to the *Sports Marketing Letter*. Navratilova—whose homosexual relationships have become public—still is playing but earns far less in endorsements. "I've been able to get very, very few," she told the *Washington Post*. Her agent, International Marketing Group, refused to release details.

"It's all perception," King said. "Everyone is supposed to be the girl next door."

(June 22, 1992)
Ann Killion *is a columnist and a feature writer for the* San Jose Mercury News. *A native of San Francisco, she graduated summa cum laude from UCLA and earned a master's degree in journalism from Columbia University. Prior to joining the* Mercury News, *she worked at the* Los Angeles Times.

Battle with Bulimia Tarnishes Cohen's Golden World

by Suzanne Halliburton
Austin American-Statesman

Life and swimming embraced Tiffany Cohen during a golden Olympic summer in Los Angeles.

It was 1984 and the lean, ecstatic teen-ager was one of the few swimmers capable of beating the East Germans who dominated the sport. And with her chief competitors at home because of a boycott, she coasted to two gold medals.

That fall, Cohen came to the University of Texas, one of swimming coach Richard Quick's two recruits off the U.S. Olympic team. In the spring, she won two NCAA titles and was voted the Southwest Conference female athlete of the year.

But winning Olympic gold had fueled an obsession with weight and appearance, starting a long slide that finally put her in St. David's Hospital in Austin for nine weeks last fall.

"I had planned to talk about this when I got out of the hospital," she said recently, pausing for several seconds. "I hope someone can learn from this. I want so many people to know that there's more to life than just their sport."

Cohen, now living in El Toro, California, outside Los Angeles, told the story of her battle with eating disorders. It began with excessive exercise before the Olympics.

"I would come home and do 400 situps and all kinds of pushups—and this was on top of workouts," Cohen recalled. "I was obsessed. All I ever thought about was winning a gold medal."

Her parents had divorced when she was a sophomore in high school, but her Olympic quest pushed that out of her mind. After winning the gold and moving on to Texas, Cohen had time to remember the heartbreak. And there was even more pressure. She had classes to attend, homework every night and daily challenges at the Texas Swim Center, where the elite of college swimming came to compete.

"At Texas, it was all-out quality. The girls were quality swimmers," she said. "With all the quality here, they were competing even in workouts. I never was a workout swimmer, and they would come out and say they beat Tiffany. I always did well in meets. But this got to me more than I thought it did. There was always pressure."

An even more crushing burden came in the form of her coach's weight goal. Cohen came to Texas seven pounds above her Olympic weight. Quick decided she needed to lose 10 pounds to be at her best.

She struggled for three years. Her weight gradually increased, then drastically decreased, then began a slow climb. To an athlete who had never had a weight problem, the constant battle with the scales was frightening.

"Richard was very much into weight," Cohen said. "He was hard on me, and I was hard on myself. In high school I was always underweight. In college, I started gaining. There was always the pressure of college, and eating was such a social thing. You stayed up late studying and you'd order pizza. You'd come in the next morning, and you would have gained some weight.

"It bothered me because I am a perfectionist. Richard knew that, and he knew who (weight) really affected. He played on that; he played on people's neuroses. He really bothered me."

Many athletes who swam for Quick describe him as almost a god, as someone they always wanted to please. Cohen was no different. She did not want to come into workouts overweight, so she started resorting to drastic measures.

Her swimming began to falter, so she would try to forget her sorrows by indulging in food. But that meant more of the drastic measures necessary to keep the pounds off. Soon she was trapped in the bulimic cycle of binges and purges. A person with bulimia will overeat and then induce vomiting or use other artificial means such as laxatives or diuretics to purge the digestive system.

"I did everything, something once a day," she said. "It wasn't even like I wanted to do it. The urge just came over you. You couldn't help it. I didn't know what was going on. But I knew if I had overeaten, I had to get rid of it."

Cohen thought no one knew how she was losing weight, but she unknowingly was leaving a trail of clues each time the numbers changed on the scale.

Then she confessed her problem to her roommate, Tracey McFarlane.

"I tried to help, but they do it so secretively," McFarlane said. "I lived with her for an entire year before I ever knew anything. Then I lived with her again for a year. I knew, but after she told me, she did it kind of secretively. Then she finally realized she had a problem. She'd feel bad and tell me when she did it. She'd tell me maybe once a week, 'I did it again.'"

Cohen injured her shoulder during her junior year, and that and the eating disorder caused her swimming to suffer. Quick left her in Austin when the rest of the team went to Indianapolis and won its fourth consecutive NCAA title in 1987.

Cohen said she told Quick about her problem that spring but he did not direct her toward treatment.

"It was so hard for me to tell him," she said. "He said, 'You have to take care of it.' That was it. He never brought it up again. It was still real hard. I still felt pressure. And he would say to me, 'Work on your weight.'"

Quick said he didn't recall when he first learned of Cohen's problem.

"I wasn't aware of her problem while she was swimming, until toward the end," he said. "I can't remember specifically."

Cohen left for home after the 1987 NCAA championships and surprised most of her teammates by swimming well that summer. They figured the problem couldn't be that severe if it wasn't showing in the water.

Cohen said her new coach—Flip Darr of Irvine, California—didn't bother her about weight. Her shoulder injury prevented her from swimming distance races, but she was the top qualifier in the 400 at the U.S. Championships and placed second to Janet Evans.

"It amazed me that I swam really well that summer," she said. "I decided weight wasn't the factor. I had no pressure from my coaches. I mean, the pressure was there, but it wasn't like it was here (in Austin). Nobody bothered me there. I still had the problem, but it wasn't anything like it was here."

Cohen returned to Austin after the championships, under pressure to swim until the 1988 Olympics. In her mind, she had retired, but at age 20, it appeared logical for her to try for the U.S. team, or at least finish out her senior year.

But the eating disorder returned as soon as she got back to Austin. After telling her teammates she needed treatment, she left again.

"I was under so much pressure to swim in 1988 and to stay at Texas," she said. "But then I thought: Was all this worth my life? Did I want to end my career swimming a race and having a heart attack?

"My intention was to get better, but I still really wanted to lose a lot of weight."

Cohen said Quick still was not helpful.

"He knew I had the problem, but he told me I could go home if I worked on my weight," she said.

Cohen said Donna Lopiano, Texas's women's athletic director, told her when she left in the fall of 1987 that if she needed help, "to come talk to me. I really want to help you."

In California, Cohen went through an outpatient treatment program, and it helped her until she decided to return to Texas to get her degree. Once in Austin, the pressure returned, and so did the bulimia.

"I got better, but I still had the problem," she said. "But the world caved in for me. It was just too hard. A lot of people knew. I just got worse when I got back to school.

"I was growing heavier and heavier because I wasn't swimming," she said. "I was so obsessed. I actually had a normal person's body, but then I just couldn't imagine having a normal person's body." She talked with Kelley Davies, another Texas swimmer who went through treatment for eating disorders. Davies recommended the program at St. David's Hospital. Cohen entered the hospital and completed the program nine weeks later. Afterward, she returned to El Toro, where she is studying to be a nurse. She says she has learned to control her eating. But more important, she has learned that if she does overeat, it's not a reason to worry. A few pounds aren't a good reason to put her life in jeopardy.

(July 30, 1989)

Suzanne Halliburton covers *University of Texas sports and does investigative reporting for the* Austin American-Statesman. *A Texas graduate, she previously worked at the* Beaumont Enterprise *and has won awards from the Associated Press Sports Editors, the Women's Sports Foundation and the Center for the Study of Sports in Society.*

SARAJEVO: HEARTS OF GOLD IN A SEA OF GRAY

by Jane Leavy
Washington Post

HIGH ABOVE THE CITY ON SVET MARKOVICA, A YOUNG MAN STOOD OUTSIDE HIS house shoveling snow with a dustpan. There was not an Olympic poster in sight. Vucko, the mascot of the XIV Winter Olympics, was nowhere to be found.

Two strangers, refugees from the hustle and bustle of the daily Olympic grind, asked the man, Edib Babic, what the Games mean to him. He spoke little English, so with his finger he traced a heart in the grime on the wall of 29 Street Markovica.

Sarajevo is a city painted in shades of gray, ranging from drab to dreary. The color is in the faces of the people, in their ever-present smiles, in their diversity.

Cultures have clashed here for 2,000 years. On one corner in the city, there is a mosque, a cathedral and a synagogue. From the minaret the crier summons Moslems to prayer and is drowned out by Michael Jackson's "Beat It."

Sarajevo has resisted invasions by the Romans, the Turks, the Austro-Hungarians and the Nazis. Now comes an invasion it welcomes—the Olympics.

This transient occupation force has been greeted with warmth in many forms, including a plum brandy bomb called slivovica. One traveler was met at the airport by a man with a neatly trimmed mustache and open arms. "You quality people," he said, beaming.

Cab drivers in a city where the average annual income is $670 return tips they think are too large.

The militia men, in their brand-new powder-blue uniforms, do their best to seem benign. "Loaded?" someone said to a soldier, gesturing toward his Soviet-made weapon. Yes, he murmured sweetly. "Real bullets?" He nodded again, almost embarrassed, and offered a handshake.

An American, Daniel Nebel, here for the Games, asked a Yugoslavian friend if the militia is always so friendly. "He said, 'No,'" Nebel said. "It's like, 'Don't bother anybody if they're having a good time.'"

The Olympics are a form of advocacy. The Nazis used them in 1936 to claim innate superiority of Aryans. The Soviets used the 1980 Olympics in Moscow as a showcase for socialist efficiency. The organizers of the 1984

Summer Games in Los Angeles brag about being the first capitalist, free-enter-prise Games.

Yugoslavia's ambitions are more modest: establish a ski resort and fix Sarajevo as something grander than the site of Gavrilo Princip's assassination of Archduke Ferdinand in 1914.

"The world does not know where Yugoslavia is before this Olympics," said Marina Borak, 25, an English teacher working in a duty-free shop here. "In Argentina, a friend asked me, 'Yugoslavia, is that in Africa?' I said, 'No, Australia.'"

The Sarajevo of this week is not the Sarajevo of six months ago. A group of American Field Service students stopped reporters in the street of the old section of town, just to speak English. "I've been dying to tell somebody this," said Beth Wilson of Newtown, Conn. "Usually, they don't have much fruit. I hadn't seen a banana until two months ago. My host brought home bananas for us, two small, brown, bruised bananas. I thought, 'Is this supposed to be special?' This hostess went into ecstasy over these bananas she hadn't seen in two years. I ate one to be polite. I probably should have given it to her."

Ilija Sisovski, an economics student from Strumica, said, "I heard the girl before say we have no bananas. Some 10 years ago, it was full of such things, but we were importing. Now we must pay back."

When Yugoslavia was awarded these Games in 1978, the inflation rate was 50 percent; the country owed $20 billion to the World Bank, and unemployment ran to 30 percent in some parts of the country.

"Because of the Olympics, food is much better," Sisovski said. "You can buy everything."

A group of American military personnel had come from Germany on a one-week package deal that included tickets to six events, room, and bus transportation for $330. The Americans stayed in the homes of Yugoslavs who moved out for the duration but came back every morning to clean—and bring them presents. At the Yugoslavian border, the German superhighway turned into "a one-lane road with potholes all the way," said Iris Zimmerman of Miami Beach. "It hits you like a brick wall. I thought, 'My God, what kind of country is this?' Then you get to Sarajevo and it's like Sarajevo is their oasis. You don't feel like you're in an Eastern bloc country."

Unless you do something the authorities consider suspicious. Just over the border, Charles Statham, Chief of the Defense Department Toxicology Lab in Germany, stopped to take pictures of a bird feeder. Guards detained him 35 minutes. They were very polite. But still, he said, "It is a communist country and you worry a little bit."

Sarajevo knows about worry. To learn that, drive to Vraca, an 86-year-old fortress on a hill at the edge of the city.

On the walls in two snow-filled courtyards of Vraca are the names of 11,000 people killed by the Nazis. The names, in alphabetical order, are chiseled from stone and raised up in memorium. There are hundreds of Altaracs—Moishe and Avram, Ester and Klara and Aaron, all Altaracs.

A museum documents Sarajevo's loss: 8,106 went to concentration camps, 4,000 of them Jews; 597 went to firing squads; 400 went unfound. It is only a three-mile drive from Vraca to 29 Svet Markovica. It is a long way.

(February 12, 1984)

Jane Leavy is the author of Squeeze Play, *a novel inspired by her career as a sportswriter at the* Washington Post. *A movie based on the novel is planned by Paramount Pictures. She is currently finishing her second novel,* Fugazi, *about a radical anti-war protester who lives as a fugitive for 25 years.*

OUT OF BOSNIA: 'OUR TENNIS COURTS ARE NOW A GRAVEYARD'

by Karen Rosen
Atlanta Journal-Constitution

SAFE AMONG PALM TREES, SUN-BAKED TENNIS COURTS AND CHEESEBURGERS FOR lunch, Igor Jekauc has found peace. His true refuge, however, is hard work.

He doesn't want to think, Jekauc told his new coaches at the Palmer Tennis Academy. He is very sad all the time.

Jekauc, a 14-year-old with sleepy eyes, is Bosnian.

When tennis fails to occupy his mind, he thinks only of the endless war in Bosnia-Herzogovina and his mother still in Sarajevo.

Jekauc and three other Bosnian players arrived two weeks ago at the Palmer Tennis Academy as part of the "Save the Athletes of Bosnia" program. The United States is one of 12 countries hosting 240 athletes in 15 sports during the next few months.

Here, the only shots fired are forehands and backhands and the occasional rocket serve.

The four athletes are appreciative, polite and conscientious, never demanding. They want to fit in and make something of themselves. They study English in the morning, then play tennis. Coaches praise their solid fundamentals and on-court intensity. Maybe, if they work hard enough, they'll be so exhausted they can fall asleep quickly at night.

And if sleep doesn't come . . .

"That is the worst moment," Jekauc, Bosnian champion in the 14-and-under division last year, said in near-fluent English.

"When I go to sleep, I think about my family," said Aljosa Piric, 16. "All night."

They are grateful tennis has removed them from the war but they also feel uncomfortable with their good fortune when others were left behind. Piric once came within 20 meters of an exploding grenade.

"Yes, but what can I do?" asked Piric. "I'm lucky."

He doesn't watch television news. It's better not to always be reminded of the fighting. "I just watch MTV," he said.

Edin Terzimehic, 15, now has an American nickname.

"They call me Eddie, like Eddie Murphy, the actor," he says.

And he has giggling fits, egged on by his new friends.

But, he said, "If I have a choice, to be with my family in Sarajevo, or come here alone, I would go to Sarajevo."

Why? He smiled. "It's my family."

Most of their families don't even know they are in the United States.

Alma Damadzic, 19, "third best girl in Bosnia," is from Tuzla, about 80 miles from Sarajevo, and hasn't seen her mother, father or brother in more than a year. She can't contact them now. "No letters, no telephone."

Damadzic, Jekauc and Piric were plucked out of the war-torn area by Bosnian officials and spent several months at a tennis camp in Umag, Croatia.

"I must go because in my town is war and I can't stay there," said Damadzic, who also shows creativity as an artist. "It's not possible to play tennis. Every day, grenades. I can't go to school, nothing. I can't live normal."

A tear runs down her usually cheerful face as she recalls the five months she stayed in her house, forbidden by her father to go outside. "It's very dangerous for us," she said.

Terzimehic went to a camp, too, but the one he was sent to was for refugees in Croatia. He and his mother shared a tiny room. His father, an engineer who taught him to play tennis, is in the army. "I never beat him. Never."

In a halting voice, Terzimehic said he couldn't play tennis for three months while he was at the camp, but kept his rackets with him. "I must," he said.

Terzimehic spent 10 days amid the fighting, which began April 6, 1992. That was long enough. "I saw what happened. The Serbs," he said, making a circle with his hands, "surround Sarajevo. People in Sarajevo have just guns. Serbs are . . ." he held his hands high. "They have bombs. It was terrible. The shelling."

The fighting obliterated the Sarajevo he knew. He recalled attending the Winter Olympics in 1984, watching the skiing and the bobsled events. "All gone," he said. "Our tennis courts are now a graveyard. I'm very lucky. Many of my friends, they are on the front. I heard one of my friends is killed. He was 16. We grew up together."

Terzimehic is Muslim. "Now in Croatia, it's not good to be Muslim," he said, then stopped. "I don't want to talk about politics. Somebody will be angry at me."

Asked her religion, Damadzic said assertively, "I am a Bosnian."

She wants to compete in the Atlanta Olympics, representing the country she loves. "It is a new country, a beautiful country. Now it's not beautiful because there is war."

Most of the other 38 students at the Palmer Tennis Academy and adjoining Palmer Preparatory School cannot comprehend the horror of battle.

They come from places as diverse as South Carolina, Madagascar, France and Brazil. Sen. Strom Thurmond's son Paul is here. One who can sympathize is Kristian Capalik, a Bosnian who has been here since December. His parents are refugees in Holland. They owned casinos in Sarajevo, "now destroyed." One of his uncles was killed by a sniper.

Capalik, 14, who is already Americanized, briefed the new arrivals. He said they don't ask about the lifestyle, only the tennis.

Norman Palmer and his staff set up a 90-day program, intended, he said, "to make a significant impact on their development as tennis players and give them things they can take away and continue to work on. The interesting question is: Where does this lead for them?

"Home," Damadzic hopes. But first to a U.S. tournament, and of course, she wants to go to Disney World.

In the meantime, they play tennis. If Piric could send a message back home, he would say, "I'm good. But I want the war stopped. Fast as you can."

(September 26, 1993)
Karen Rosen *covers Olympic sports for the* Atlanta Journal-Constitution. *She has also covered college football and basketball, tennis, TV-radio and the occasional drag race. A love for the Olympics runs in her family: Her father, Mel, coached the 1992 U.S. men's track team.*

Prospects Warned About the Dangers of Life

by Claire Smith
New York Times

STEVE PALERMO AND DR. LONISE BIAS WOULD NOT SEEM TO HAVE A LOT IN common, one being a major league umpire, arguably the best in his profession, the second being a doctor of religion, blessed with the evangelical passion and fervor of a Martin Luther King.

But both, in a sense, are victims and survivors of sociopaths who have had the humanity stomped out of them, of a society that often sends such confusing messages that morality and ethics, the sense of right and wrong, are the first but not the last casualties.

And both have, in their way, carried their messages about the dangers and blessings of life to youths, especially to the strong, the seemingly invincible, who populate the heady world of professional sports.

"Excuse the pun, but one thing I know more than ever, now, is that no one is bullet-proof," said Palermo, who was shot in the back last summer while trying to break up an armed robbery and suffered a spinal injury that left him partly paralyzed.

Bias has also suffered grievous wounds in her life, having lost two sons, one to a drug overdose, one to murderous gunplay.

"We are in trouble," Bias said, "because we are in danger of losing our greatest natural resource. In this land of plenty, the United States is the poorest when it comes to our children. Our dear children are so poor because they have a lot of critics, but not a lot of role models. Every time they see an athlete, they're on a beer commercial or doing something negative on or off the field."

Do you know, Bias will ask any athlete who will listen, that such behavior reaches the four- and five- and six- year-olds who already know sports figures as heroes? "You can no longer go and just do what you want to do," Bias said to a group of 75 baseball prospects last weekend in Dallas.

Speaking with an open cry from a mother's heart, in a voice straight from an evangelist's revival tent, she hammered home the point that every athlete, every celebrity should hear. Like the burden of public life or not, it's there. It's not all about you and what you want. No matter how much one wants to think that it is so, it's not.

104

* * *

Len Bias, Bias's talented basketball player son who died of a drug overdose on the eve of a professional career with the Boston Celtics, learned that
the hard way. Wrong choices sometimes lead to consequences from which
there is no escape. And for all the riches achieved, for all the dreams unful-
filled, the reality that claimed Len Bias was as stark as there was.

So her message is grim, but poignant, hopefully touching a nerve within
anyone who can still feel and has the time to make a difference. It is why
she speaks to athletes in the National Basketball Association, in colleges,
and most recently, to major league rookies who gathered in Dallas last
weekend.

"My question to you beautiful, precious young men is, 'If something
were to happen to one of you all today, whose life would be changed for the
better?'" she asked the ballplayers on the verge of making at least a name, if
not a difference. "You have a responsibility on the earth. It's not all about
you and baseball and following your dream. It's about you being the best
that you can be and reaching back and helping someone else.

"Will you cause other young men to be a curse on this earth or will you
cause them to be a blessing? For, you see, good advice with poor example is
very confusing. If you want to help young men today, you have to live as
something. If you tell your little brother, your little nephew, your little
cousin, 'Don't do this and don't do that,' then go and do something else,
you mean absolutely nothing.

"You are educators, whether you want to be or not. You will influence
the decision of someone sitting at the table with you or someone who will
be sitting at a baseball park looking at you. You will influence the decision.
Either you will lead a life of prosperity or death and destruction and you
have a responsibility to be the best that you can be."

Palermo, having put the correct value back into words such as bravery
and heroism, acted as unselfishly and responsibly as any society has a right
to ask. Yet, it is not something that he immediately counsels everyone to do,
to jump in front of a bullet in defense of fellow human beings.

Indeed, it's a moment that Palermo admittedly lives time and again,
searching for another choice. He cannot conjure one, not for Steve Palermo,
anyway, so he too lives with the consequences. The difference is, Steve
Palermo can always look in the mirror and like what he sees. Now he wishes the same for the umpires, the players who come along behind him.

Palermo does not speak in brave or heroic terms. He does not flaunt any
meritorious decorations other than the two canes and a leg brace. What
Palermo did do is, in simple but wise words, speak the language of a veter-

an. "You have to listen," Palermo said. "When I came up in 1977, there was nothing I needed to hear because I already knew everything. But I soon realized that the more I learned, the less I knew back then."

And so Palermo imparts what he has learned. Bias imparts what she has felt. And they share, having learned all too clearly that situations can and do interrupt life, the body can be so fragile and no one, from the most gifted athlete to the most avid couch-potato sports fan, can afford to take anything for granted. Not their legs, their arms, their strength, their agility, nor their lives.

(January 30, 1992)

Claire Smith *is the national baseball reporter for the* New York Times. *She previously worked at the* Hartford Courant, *the* Philadelphia Bulletin *and the* Bucks County Courier Times. *A graduate of Temple University, she is co-author of* Nothing But the Truth: A Baseball Life, *the autobiography of Don Baylor.*

Runner's Story: Why Did Kathy Ormsby Jump off that Bridge?

by Sharon Robb
Fort Lauderdale Sun-Sentinel

On the surface, Kathy Ormsby had it all. The adoration of her hometown, a straight-A average in pre-med and the respect of her peers as one of the premier female distance runners.

But something must have been torturing Kathy Ormsby. On the evening of June 4 in Indianapolis, she dropped out of a race, ran to a bridge and jumped, an apparent suicide attempt. Today she lies in the Duke University Medical Center, paralyzed from the waist down. There is little hope she will walk again.

Only Ormsby knows why she jumped. And for now, friends, relatives and teammates are trying to figure out why the 21-year-old record-setting junior from North Carolina State, who seemed to have everything, would want to throw it all away.

"It's going to take a while for me to get a handle on this," said N.C. State women's track coach Rollie Geiger, who found Ormsby crumpled in the grassy field below the bridge. "How can I tell you what I felt when I found her? I love her. We all do. She was—still is—a very caring and loving person. She was a true reflection of our program.

"If I were going to pick an athlete to be in our program, it would be Kathy. If I were going to pick an individual to be my daughter, it would be Kathy."

"I will never accept that it was a suicide attempt in the classical sense," said Ralph Robertson, principal of Richmond County Senior High School, where Ormsby was valedictorian and a hero to the townspeople. "I don't think she was Kathy Ormsby at that point—not the Kathy Ormsby we know. I am convinced she made no conscious decision to do this."

In Rockingham, Ormsby won friends with her selfless devotion, but at the same time worried them with her drive for perfection.

"You get a Kathy Ormsby but once in a lifetime," Robertson said. "She was the classic overachiever, doing nothing but the best. Track just seemed to be a sidelight from her studies, we thought."

On the night of June 4, Ormsby was competing in the 10,000 meters of the NCAA Outdoor Track and Field Championships at Indiana University's stadium. She was in fourth place and within a step of third with 3,500 meters to go in the race when she broke away from the pack.

Said Harley Lewis, NCAA track rules committee member and former Oregon track coach: "She was in a position where she could have won the race. She apparently just felt she was no longer able to continue at that pace and quit. Usually when they quit, they drop off to the inside of the track and walk. She didn't. She walked to the outside and disappeared."

Ormsby slowed her pace to duck under a railing and ran past Wisconsin coach Peter Tegen. She picked up speed again and ran up a set of steps into the stands and vanished. Geiger had seen Ormsby leave the race and had gone outside to look for her.

According to witnesses, she ran across a softball field, scaled a 7-foot chain-link fence and then ran west for two blocks alongside New York Street, a main thoroughfare, toward the bridge.

When she reached the steel bridge over the White River, she apparently climbed a four-foot guard rail and jumped. Instead of landing in the water, she fell onto a hard field beside the river.

Geiger went looking for her. About 10 minutes after she ran off the track, Geiger spotted Ormsby on the river bank, flagged down a motorist to call an ambulance and then climbed down the bank to her side and waited for help.

When a campus policeman, Bill Abston, questioned the coach, Geiger replied, "She said she jumped."

Police called it a suicide attempt.

The cost of success is sometimes a price runners are too willing to pay. In Ormsby's case, the price was too high. Ormsby probably never realized the social and psychological aspects of her growing period were sometimes more strenuous than the endless workouts that she demanded of herself.

She earned a partial track scholarship to North Carolina State and enrolled in a pre-med program with hopes of becoming a medical missionary. Although she made the dean's list every semester, running came first. She found herself on a team full of high school champions. Overcome by anxiety to do well, Ormsby started blacking out and dropping out of big races. At Geiger's suggestion, she started seeing a sports psychologist a month ago.

Ormsby blacked out her freshman year in a meet at Lehigh and again last fall in Milwaukee at the NCAA cross country championships. She would faint during the race and after a minute or two get up on her own and take herself out of the race. Most other times she ran well.

She was becoming a star collegiate runner her junior year. She set a U.S. collegiate women's record for 10,000 meters (32:36.2) at the Penn Relays April 24. In her first 10,000-meter race on the track, she broke another record.

"It was great," Geiger said. "We had just wanted to find out how fast she could run the event."

"That's why she ran so well, she was relaxed," said teammate and close friend Connie Jo Robinson. "It was her first time running the distance and she was an unknown. No one expected her to win."

After her Penn Relays performance, Ormsby told *Track and Field News*, "One thing that has helped me is not placing so much importance on my performances and trying to please other people. I just have to learn to do my best for myself and for God, and to turn everything over to Him. It seems like I have been able to do that better this track season than ever."

She was selected a track All-American.

A week after the Penn Relays, at the Twilight Track Invitational in Raleigh, she blacked out again. "She was seeing a sports psychologist. But who knows if she opened up to him?" Robinson said.

Stanford's Brooks Johnson, 1984 U.S. Olympic Women's track coach, cited the fine line between pressure, impulse and chemical imbalance when dealing with runners, especially women. He said the pressure at national athletic championships leads runners to levels of frustration and identity crises beyond the norm.

"I think what people have to realize is what happened to Kathy Ormsby could have happened to any runner," Johnson said. "She was operating in a state of diminished capacity. The heat conditions were severe. The mind could no longer control what was going on. She was pushed to the brink.

"She was embarrassed because she thought she wasn't doing well. She was hurt and distraught when she ran off the track. The bridge happened to be there. How many times have you and I thought about committing suicide but never did because the opportunity wasn't there? Well, this time the opportunity presented itself. The impulse was there, and so was the bridge. Here was a girl who always needed to overcompensate in athletics. People just don't realize how much pressure these runners put on themselves."

For Geiger and his runners, the agonizing began the day after the tragedy.

"I feel like I missed something along the way, but I had no indication whatsoever something like this would happen," Geiger said. "When we talked just before the race, she seemed to be looking forward to it—not only that race, but other things this summer."

Robert Phillips, a Charlotte sports psychologist, said athletes tend to define their whole reality around that one thing they do and "When you combine total mental, emotional and physical involvement, it's not hard to define your world as being totally good or bad at that moment.

"When you're running in that race, you don't look ahead to next week or back at last week. There is potential for distortion of reality to a high degree.

During the running experience, with chemical reactions going on and with natural opiates released causing a high, inhibitions are greatly reduced. Seeds of depression or stress could come out."

Geiger was unprepared for what happened: "Either I missed the signs or there were no signs. Maybe it was something that had been building up through the years. All I know is, if you were to walk into that hospital room, meet and talk with her, you wouldn't know what to write. She's the sweetest person you'd ever want to know."

Robinson said there were no signals that she would do anything so drastic. "She never mentioned the pressure. She believed her record was a gift from God," she said. "A lot of new things were happening to her. She had stepped up from being a 5:02 high school miler. She was elite. She was on TV and in the newspapers. Anytime a person excels the way she did, there's obviously a lot more pressure. When you get better, you are expected to do more, and there's just no way out. I don't think she saw a way out."

"Running and school are her life," said teammate Wendy McLees. "She's always been a pusher, very dedicated to both."

Kathy Love Ormsby, born Nov. 1, 1964, grew up in Rockingham, a textile town of 8,284, a quiet place of sandy hills that was the perfect training ground for a long-distance runner.

She was a shy, Baptist girl with little time for socializing, an overachiever whose motivation was not to glorify herself but God. She loved to win, but was embarrassed by the adulation. She loved to run, but at times would become so lost in her exhilaration at workouts that her coach would have to hold her back.

She was dedicated to making good grades: She brought her notes to track practice and studied in the car on trips to track meets. She ran at 5 a.m. Sunday mornings so she could get back in time for services at the First Baptist Church, where she was a youth co-pastor and sang in the choir.

She lived with her parents in a two-story colonial brick house on tree-lined Curtis Street in a middle-class neighborhood. There were no tragic overtones to her background.

"Even though she's been a high achiever most of her life, you would never know it because she is so unassuming," said First Baptist's pastor, William W. Leathers.

Ormsby began running in junior high. She ran the 100- and 200-yard dashes. Those who saw her race the first few times knew she was special.

"You don't have to know her very long to know she is a very conscientious and dedicated person," said Rockingham Junior High track coach Charlie Bishop, who converted her from sprinting to distance running.

The rewards were many for the state high school champion middle-distance runner. Her sophomore year she won the state championship in the 1,600 meters. Her senior year she set state high school records at 800, 1,600 and 3,200 meters. Her only disappointing race was a cross country championship her junior year when she finished second. After the race, her coach found out she had run with a stress fracture in one leg.

She was as brilliant in the classroom as on the track: No. 1 in her high school class of 600, never making below an A. She was the only student honored by the 12-year-old school with her own day, Kathy Ormsby Day, May 26, 1983. There was an assembly in her honor and a proclamation to hang on her bedroom wall.

Although pro athletes Franklin Stubbs of the Los Angeles Dodgers, Mike Quick of the Philadelphia Eagles and Perry Williams of the New York Giants graduated from Richmond County Senior High, only Ormsby had her jersey retired.

She was under great pressure to succeed, not from her parents, coaches or teammates but from within, according to her high school track coach, Pete Pittman.

"During the three years she ran here, she never once left practice without saying, 'Coach, is there anything else I need to do?'" Pittman said. "She was that way in the classroom, too. She kept her mind on business."

There is a clearly defined peak for the academic perfectionist—a perfect score of 100 or straight A's. But for the runner, there is no ultimate time.

"As far as who worked hard to be better than anybody else, I've never seen anybody like her," said Richmond Athletic Director George Whitfield.

Kathy's mother, Sallie, 49, a nurse at Richmond Memorial Hospital, once told a training mate of Kathy's, Rockingham marathoner Jackie Tanner, that she wished her daughter would relax a little—ease up.

Her father, Dale, 58, a Burlington Industries Inc. textile plant manager in Cordova, said his daughter was under great pressure to succeed.

"Kathy has always tended to be an overachiever and puts a tremendous amount of pressure on herself," Dale Ormsby said. "I believe it had something to do with the pressure put on young people to succeed.

"It's a question of pressure, pressure to succeed. It was physical, and maybe it was mental, and it blotted out the ability to think rationally. I know she wanted to do well, it was important to her."

Ormsby told her father she doesn't remember exactly what happened. According to a team of physicians, she probably will have significant lapses in her memory for some time.

Her parents have kept a prayerful vigil by her bedside. Only her two brothers, Dale Jr. and John, sister Donna Freshwater, and close friends have been allowed to visit her, first at the Wishard Memorial Hospital in Indianapolis and now at Duke, where she was moved to be closer to home.

Robinson said the hardest part of the ordeal was seeing her in the hospital, on a respirator, unable to talk. "I told her I loved her and that God would love her," Robinson said. Ormsby squeezed her hand.

Johnson said it is ironic one of Geiger's runners would attempt suicide. Geiger is nationally respected and known for sensitivity toward his athletes.

Ormsby wasn't the first runner Geiger dealt with who had a personal crisis. In 1981, former Hollywood McArthur High state champion Sue Overbey Molloy had a 15-month struggle with anorexia nervosa, a psychological disorder characterized by self-starvation. At one point, she dropped to 86 pounds, having lost 29. After coming to grips with her problems, she recovered. Today the newlywed is an electrician's apprentice, lives in Lake Worth and no longer races competitively.

"His kind of program is not one that lends itself to that kind of thing," Johnson said.

Upgraded from serious to stable condition June 9, Ormsby underwent an operation June 19 to stabilize the spine. A second operation will remove fragments from the spinal canal—before her six-week rehabilitation period begins and she can go home.

She suffered a broken rib, a collapsed lung and a fractured vertebra, which injured her spinal cord in her middle back. The paralysis has been diagnosed as permanent. She has complete use of her arms.

"About everybody who goes through this will experience some depression, usually a few weeks down the road," said Dr. Peter Hall, chief of neurosurgery, who supervised her treatment at Wishard Memorial.

"Kathy has been told this and has kind of accepted it, and so have her mother and I," Dale Ormsby said. "We can only hope that something good will come out of it."

Kathy Ormsby's day of reckoning may have been inevitable; she had lived on the fringes for some time.

World-class runner Mary Decker Slaney said she "can't see running becoming an obsession—not to the point of hurting yourself or taking your life." But she cites the fine line between dedication and obsession.

One of Ormsby's closest friends, Alex Wallace, said he often wanted to tell her she worked too hard. He said when they last talked, two weeks before Ormsby jumped, she seemed happy.

"I can't imagine what was going through her mind," said Wallace, who went to high school with her and is on a baseball scholarship at N.C. State.

"To me, everybody looked up to her. She was my hero, even though she was my peer."

Missouri women's track coach Rick McGuire, who has a doctorate in sports psychology, has been working with elite athletes, preparing them for the Olympics. McGuire was going to see Ormsby, but scheduling conflicts set it back.

"We assume it was a sports-related crisis, and it may not be that at all," McGuire said. "Maybe things had happened so that she couldn't handle a highly visible failure."

None of her teammates had to ask why.

"They didn't need to know why," Robinson said. "They know why. We're all in the same boat. We feel the same pressure."

Honors student and national age-group and high school state champion Mary Wazeter of Wilkes-Barre, Pennsylvania, felt the same pressure when she tried to kill herself by leaping from a bridge in February 1982. Wazeter, 22, now a paraplegic living with her parents and writing a book, said their stories are similar.

"You think you're going to find happiness in setting goals, and you think if you win this race, you'll be happy," Wazeter said. "So you try to compensate for that with achievement and please people by winning.

"I would like to talk with Kathy someday. The most important word of encouragement I could offer is to be patient with herself and learn not to be driven and not to be hard on herself. You can't expect to be superhuman."

(June 29, 1986)

Sharon Robb, *who has been at the* Fort Lauderdale Sun-Sentinel *since 1982, has covered three Olympics as well as college football, basketball and numerous other sports. A three-time winner of awards from the Florida Sportswriters Association, she previously worked for the* Hollywood Sun-Tattler.

Tonya Harding: Skating on the Edge

by Michelle Kaufman
Detroit Free Press

HER FATHER BOUGHT HER A .22 RIFLE WHEN SHE WAS IN KINDERGARTEN AND chopped off the stock so it would fit her tiny hands. Her mother has been married seven times. A drunk half-brother once tried to kiss her; she retaliated by burning him on the neck with a curling iron. Twice in the past two years, she filed for divorce and sought restraining orders against her hot-headed husband.

Three months ago, police seized a handgun from her after it went off during an argument.

Less than a month before the Winter Olympics, Tonya Harding faces the toughest chapter of her tough life: allegations that her husband and bodyguard conspired to injure her chief rival. Harding's background contradicts every image associated with figure skating. She isn't rich. She isn't spoiled. And there isn't a dainty bone in her 5-foot-1, 105-pound frame.

The newly crowned U.S. champion enjoys drag racing, rebuilding engines, playing pool, hunting and fishing. She smokes cigarettes, despite a serious asthmatic condition.

While other skaters choose classical music, Harding has skated to such tunes as "Wild Thing" and "Funky Cold Medina." Harding's skating dresses are a far cry from the designer beauties worn by former U.S. champions Nancy Kerrigan, Kristi Yamaguchi and Jill Trenary. In fact, Harding's most recent purple outfit wouldn't have had beads on it had a Portland, Oregon, costume shop not donated the costly decorations.

"I wasn't born with a silver spoon in my mouth," Harding, 23, has said. "I am a skater who has had to overcome obstacles. That's why a lot of people like me."

The FBI and Detroit police are investigating allegations that Harding's husband of three years, Jeff Gillooly, and her bodyguard, Shawn Eric Eckardt, hired an Arizona man to injure Kerrigan last week during the U.S. Championships in Detroit.

On Thursday, Eckardt and Derrick Brian Smith of Phoenix were arrested in Portland and charged with conspiracy in the attack on Kerrigan. There was no reason to believe Harding had knowledge of the alleged plot, and she made no comment.

Harding won the U.S. title Saturday, earning a spot on the U.S. Olympic team that will compete Feb. 12-27 in Lillehammer, Norway. Kerrigan also was selected to the team.

Although Harding said she was thrilled with her most recent victory, she said her title wouldn't be complete until she "beat Nancy's butt" at the Olympics. The two skaters have been in the spotlight since Yamaguchi's retirement in 1992, and have an excellent shot at the Olympic gold medal.

Harding, perhaps the most athletically gifted female skater in U.S. history, is one of only two women in the world who has landed a triple Axel in competition. Kerrigan had emerged as a gold-medal favorite by combining grace and five triple jumps.

An Olympic victory could translate to $5 million to $10 million in endorsements and appearance fees for a female figure skater, according to several sports agents. The high-profile title is something Harding craves. "I'm not coming home with anything less than the gold," Harding said last week. "I'm going there to win."

It's a wonder Harding has gotten this far, considering her beginnings. The diminutive blond was the only child born to LaVona Harding, then a waitress, and her fifth husband, Al, who struggled to keep a steady job. The family lived in Portland. Money was scarce and the Hardings did all they could to keep their talented daughter in figure skating lessons. LaVona sewed Harding's dresses and school clothes. "They were pure polyester blends, and the other kids made fun of them," Harding told *Sports Illustrated* in 1991.

"My first day of high school, my mother made me wear these forest-green pants with white polka dots. We had a big fight over that, and she won."

To this day, Harding complains about her wardrobe. She told reporters before the Skate America competition in October that she was ashamed by her lack of costumes.

"It's kind of embarrassing to keep wearing the same thing over and over," she said. "I haven't bought new clothes in two years." What she lacked in costumes, she made up for in guts.

Harding landed her first triple loop at age 9 and began working on her triple Axel at 14. At 17, she placed fifth in the national championships.

The ice rink was Harding's place to escape from her troubled teen-age years. She dropped out of school briefly in eighth grade, re-enrolled and then dropped out for good in the 10th grade. It was about that time that Harding's half-brother, Chris Davison, tried to kiss her. After she burned him, he threatened her life and spent some time in jail. Five years ago, he was killed by a hit-and-run driver.

Harding's mother left Tonya and her father in 1986, about the time Harding began dating Gillooly. Harding's parents didn't approve of Gillooly, and her mother tried to discourage Harding from marrying him in March 1990.

"I knew Jeff had a violent streak," Harding's mother told *Sports Illustrated*. "Once when Tonya was living with me and my new husband, he tried to break down the door because he thought she had gone out with another boy."

Fifteen months after their wedding, Harding filed for divorce and was granted a restraining order to keep Gillooly away. At the time, she said Gillooly had pulled her hair, shoved her and hurt her arm. She said she feared for her life. The divorce was supposed to be finalized in November 1991, but the couple reconciled. Also in 1991, Harding had a well-publicized skirmish with another driver at an intersection near her practice rink. Police found her brandishing a baseball bat at a woman. No arrests were made.

Harding filed for divorce again in the summer of 1993 and again sought a restraining order. Again, they got back together. On the evening of Oct. 2, police were called when a gunshot was heard in the parking lot of Harding's apartment complex. Harding and Gillooly were in their pickup when police arrived and insisted the gun went off accidentally. Police seized the weapon.

The marriage seemed to be on an upswing in recent months. Harding bragged about how Gillooly was taking real estate classes and selling T-shirts for her fan club. She said they were working together to make ends meet.

Although Harding isn't popular with the skating establishment, she has one of the largest fan clubs in the sport, with members from 21 states and four countries. The latest edition of the fan club newsletter listed eight donors who contributed more than $500. New York Yankees owner George Steinbrenner has made significant donations.

Harding's boisterous fans donned bright yellow "Team Tonya" T-shirts at last week's championships. There is little question Harding is talented enough to be an Olympic champion, but her career has been filled with on-ice mishaps. She had to stop midway through a program at the 1993 nationals when a shoulder strap on her outfit broke. Ten months later, at Skate America in Dallas, Harding quit during a program, saying a skate blade came loose. She withdrew from the 1993 Northwest Pacific Regionals after receiving a death threat.

"If anything would stop me from winning this year, it would be lack of money," she said in October. "But I will do whatever I can to make sure I make it to the Olympics. I want to prove that I am No. 1."

(January 13, 1994)

Michelle Kaufman is the Olympics beat writer for the Detroit Free Press. *A graduate of the University of Miami, she previously worked at the* St. Petersburg Times, *where she covered the Tampa Bay Buccaneers.*

CROSS COUNTRY TO MEMORY'S FINISH LINE

by Rachel Blount
Des Moines Register

THE TREE DIED LAST SUMMER. FOR MORE THAN TWO YEARS IT HAD HELD ON, blackened and gouged at the base where the 30-inch-thick oak had been struck by a light plane on an icy night in 1985. Now, on the spot where three members of the Iowa State women's cross-country team were killed with their coaches, trainer and pilot, leaves blow freely and nothing shelters the grass.

About the same time the tree died, seven saplings were coming into full foliage at the Veenker Memorial Golf Course in Ames. Planted near the starting line of the path that cross-country runners follow there, one tree lives for each of those who died.

One day, as those trees near the size of the oak that stood on Country Club Boulevard in Des Moines, they will shelter a nearby boulder and its memorial plaque. As that day approaches, fewer will remember the crash. Those who will never forget will have moved on, running away from the empty places and toward the things that grow.

"I think it'll always be in people's memories," said Dick Lee, who was hired as women's track and cross-country coach in the summer of 1986 and charged with rebuilding the program. "As we have fewer people here that were around at that time, the strength of the memories will gradually diminish.

"But they were very close, and you don't work that closely with someone without always having memories of the tragedy. We were forced to learn a lot of things about ourselves and about others that year. Most importantly, we learned that we have to look forward. We have to control our own destinies."

Men's cross-country coach Bill Bergan coached the women's program for six months following the accident. "This year is the first I've seen them make a real recovery, both emotionally and team-wise," he said. "I don't think it will ever be completely behind us. Those memories will always be as clear as yesterday. But they're getting it behind them; it's been a struggle for a lot of athletes."

The championships have been the last thing to return to the program since the crash turned it upside down on Nov. 25, 1985. In the two seasons that followed, the Cyclones failed to win a bid to the national championship meet, something they'd done regularly in years past. In 1986, they finished fifth in both the Big Eight Conference meet and the NCAA regional meet, a year later they were fourth in both meets. Only one runner, All-American Suzanne Youngberg in 1986, qualified to run at the national meet during that time.

This year, the team finished a surprising third at the Big Eight meet after being picked to place fifth—and went on to place third at the regional. Two runners, junior Maria Akraka of Sweden and senior Jill Slettedahl of Granite Falls, Minnesota, finished in the top 10 at the regional, and Akraka will run at the NCAA championships Monday at Jester Park in Granger.

And for the first time since 1985, when the twin-engine Rockwell Aerocommander crashed into a yard while bringing the team home from its second-place finish at the NCAA championships in Milwaukee, Iowa State came within a shoelace of making the national rankings.

"It felt so good to be running well again and reaching some of the goals we'd set," said Slettedahl, one of three runners who have been with the team since the crash. "Finally, we were getting close to what we wanted to do: getting to the nationals, getting ranked. I think we proved a lot to ourselves this year. I think we'll be back."

The road back began Nov. 26, 1985, when the impact of what had happened settled in. Flying to Des Moines through a haze of freezing drizzle, the tiny airplane veered off course over a west-side neighborhood and rapidly dropped into the trees, crashing into the oak and bursting into flames.

Killed were Ron Renko, the team's coach for seven years; assistant coach Pat Moynihan; trainer Stephanie Streit; pilot Burton Watkins; and team members Sheryl Maahs, Julie Rose and Susan Baxter. After 20 months of investigations, the crash was blamed on ice that had formed on the plane.

The surviving team members, who arrived safely at the airport in a pair of small planes shortly before the crash, were devastated. They had lost their teammates, training partners, best friends. For months, they grieved with the entire ISU community. No one knew what else to do.

"There was so much uncertainty that followed," said Bergan, who was named the interim coach 12 days later. "The program had always been first in our lives; then, we didn't know what was first anymore. No matter what we did the rest of that year, it was always on our minds."

In Waverly, another track coach was grieving. Lee, then the men's coach at Wartburg, had earlier served five years as an assistant to Renko at Iowa State. Later that spring, he was asked to rejoin the program in the most trying of times.

He came to Ames in the summer to find a team still unsure of how to go on. For some of them, the accident marked the first time someone close to them had died; for many, it marked the first time running had brought pain instead of pleasure. With Lee, who felt about Renko as they did, they had someone who understood how difficult the recovery would be.

"We did a lot of talking that year," Lee said. "We tried not to dwell on what happened. It was nothing psychoanalytical, but we tried not to let the tragedy take away the good feelings we had. There was a big enough hole there already. We had to remember that they'd all been a big part of our lives, a happy part.

"It was a difficult, difficult year. After it was over, I began thinking we could've approached some things differently, but there was no predicting what we would feel and how we would deal with it. We couldn't sit down for one hour and work out all the tensions we were feeling. There were so many diversions it was hard to keep our minds on our work."

That first year was filled with obstacles. Some team members struggled with themselves, trying to decide where running—the most important part of many of their lives—fit into a new sense of priorities. On the first plane trip of the season, they held hands, and some prayed. Wherever they went, coaches and teams offered their condolences, keeping the memory fresh.

The team struggled through the season, ending it with a poor performance that was far below its ability at the regional meet. Although Lee shared the team's feelings, there was only so much help he could lend; because a runner's motivation comes from within, the recovery had to come from within as well.

"I finally realized it was just going to take time," Lee said. "They needed to get their lives back to where they felt good about the things they felt good about before—including running. It was quite a while before they felt that just because running was involved with this, it doesn't mean it has to bring up painful memories.

"That first year, we talked about what we had to do to qualify for the nationals. But there were still so many painful memories that the feeling was, 'If we don't go to nationals, that's something we don't have to deal with.' Looking back. I don't think they were ready to face going back to the nationals yet."

After the season, Lee began thinking about recruiting. Although most runners he recruited knew of the accident, it seemed to have no effect on their decisions. The bigger problem was in dealing with the returning runners.

Because Iowa State had built a reputation as a strong women's cross-country program, it depended heavily on upperclassmen to provide leadership. But many of them were still healing emotionally. They were troubled by the idea of replacing the runners that died in the crash; it seemed so cold, so insensitive.

They also were still coming to terms with what it meant to be a member of a team. Three of them had died without warning; how could they fill that void with new faces and avoid losing their team's identity?

"Recruiting that year was not a top priority," Lee said. "It was more important that we deal with the people on the team. We looked at them as a very important part of Iowa State, and we wanted to take care of their needs. We didn't want the girls to feel like we were bringing in people to replace those that were lost; we wanted them to feel like the team was being rebuilt.

"Eventually, we came to the conclusion that we are not the Iowa State Team. We are caretakers here for a short time to do our best. It's our responsibility to care for and nurture the team, to give it all we have while we're here, and to turn it over to others when we're done. The people who passed away had a very instrumental role in the program. They were caretakers, just like we are."

With so many barriers crossed, the 1987 season went much more smoothly. The women welcomed several new runners into the program, and they ran much better, improving on their 1986 showing in both the conference and regional meets. Lee was meeting his goals of recruiting runners who excelled in sports and in school, and the university was supporting him by offering 16 scholarships in women's track and cross-country.

The program received an unexpected boost earlier that year when the NCAA awarded Iowa State the right to host the 1988 national championship, something Bergan and Renko had often talked about.

"One of the reasons we wanted to host the meet was to honor the memory of the staff and athletes," Bergan said. "We felt an obligation to them. When we won this, I thought to myself how excited Ron Renko would have been; it was something he had only dreamed of. He never thought it would happen."

After the team's strong showing this season, Lee said he is confident about its future. Only two of his top seven runners will graduate, leaving him the majority of another close-knit team to work with next year. In addition, the national meet should enhance ISU's reputation as a school devoted to its distance runners.

And with the passing of another year, the focus on what is to come sharpens as the memories of what was fade. For months, Lee and the team saw only the past. Now, they see the future again.

Running still has an important place in my life," Slettedahl said. "The accident changed the way I looked at running, but still, running was a big help in getting all of us through this. And because of the spirit this program has, I think it has a great future.

"We struggled a long time with this. There are still days we struggle with it, and it may always be that way. But one thing I know: if I could go back, knowing all that I know now, I would do it all over again. My experiences here, and the people I've known here, will always be a special part of my life."

(November 20, 1988)

Rachel Blount *covers the NHL and NBA for the* Minneapolis Star-Tribune. *A graduate of Notre Dame with a masters in journalism from Missouri, she previously worked at the* Des Moines Register *and the* Atlanta Journal-Constitution *as a general assignment reporter.*

FOR JOHN AND DEBBIE LUCAS, THE DEMONS ARE NEVER FAR AWAY

by Helen Ross
Greensboro News & Record

LIKE MANY OF US, JOHN LUCAS OCCASIONALLY FORGETS BIRTHDAYS AND anniversaries.

But one date is indelibly etched in his mind. He can't afford to forget it. His life may depend on it.

March 14, 1986.

That was the last day Lucas tasted a drop of alcohol or snorted a line of cocaine. He has even sworn off coffee, aspirin and other over-the-counter medications in the intervening two years, 11 months and 22 days.

For Lucas, a native of Durham, it has taken eight years to achieve sobriety. Since first publicly admitting he was an addict in 1981, the former University of Maryland standout has been in and out of treatment four different times.

The last one appears to have stuck. So far, that is. It is his longest stretch of sobriety in more than a decade.

Trite as it may sound, Lucas, who at 35 is in his 13th season of playing NBA basketball, now takes life one day at a time. So does Debbie Lucas, his wife of 10 years. So do his three children.

"We don't plan ahead now," Debbie Lucas said. "We don't plan for the future. We always live with the fact that it can come back. Even though John has had sobriety for three years, he has to fight his addiction every day of his life. Once you are addicted, your body cells are not the same. Your body constantly craves it. It's like a monkey saying, 'You have to have me. You've got to get me.' And if he does mess up, it's like going right back to day one."

Day One was March 14, 1986.

The previous night, Lucas, who then was playing for the Houston Rockets, had drawn a technical foul in a game against the Boston Celtics. He was angry and frustrated. He went home to have a beer. Then he had another. And another. He doesn't know how many more. Nor does he remember much of what happened that night. Debbie Lucas, as was her custom when John started drinking like that, locked the dead bolts on the doors of their Houston home.

"He never thought to try the windows," she said. "And usually he would just sleep it off."

But this time, she forgot to hide the keys. Lucas found them and went outside. He was dressed in a neatly tailored suit, four pairs of athletic socks and no shoes. But he didn't forget his sunglasses so people wouldn't recognize him. The next day, when the Rockets were practicing in The Summit arena, Lucas was stumbling around the streets of Houston.

Because he had tested positive for cocaine during the previous season, Lucas' contract contained a clause that provided for more tests if there was probable cause. With the missed practice, there was probable cause. He tested positive again, and the Rockets released him.

"I was looking to get caught," Lucas now says. "I had reached the spiritual bottom. I was sick and tired of being sick and tired. I woke up downtown. I remember it like it was yesterday. I can never let any pain get greater than the pain of drinking again. If I do, then I lose everything."

The game he loves to play. The money he has made playing it. Everything. But most of all, Lucas doesn't want to lose a family that has provided him support when he didn't think he deserved it.

"At times, I thought about leaving him," Debbie Lucas said. "And a lot of times, he told me to leave him. Drunk. Sober. But I just couldn't. I said the Lord will know how much I can handle."

Debbie and John Lucas have known each other since they were 8 years old. Debbie's family of 12 lived four blocks away from John's in a middle-class neighborhood in Durham that borders N.C. Central University. They went through junior and senior high together.

But the two didn't start dating until the summer of 1972, after their senior year at Hillside High, just as Lucas was preparing to play for Lefty Driesell at Maryland. Debbie decided to stay closer to home and went to N.C. Central.

Lucas was an extremely popular teenager, talented as both a tennis and basketball player. Girls clamored for his attention. Boys wanted to be his friend.

"He was Mr. Macho back then," his wife said. Now she describes him as a "good-hearted . . . very sensitive . . . and good father."

But when he was using cocaine and alcohol, Debbie Lucas says without hesitation, he was a totally different person.

"The drugs took over his whole life," she said. "They made him become a liar. They made him hide things. It got so bad, I was the one who had to run the household. I had to do the mother *and* the father things."

Debbie Lucas's first indication that her husband might be an addict came early in his career. Lucas's agent handled their finances, and a joint allowance check regularly appeared. Lucas would divide the money and give his wife her share.

"Then it would start to disappear," Debbie said. "If I put it down, he made me think that I had misplaced it. I trusted him. It took me a while to realize he was taking it."

Debbie Lucas doesn't know whether her husband used cocaine at home. She did find it sometimes and promptly flushed it down the commode.

"And, sure, a lot of times, I was scared," she said. "I didn't know if he had gotten it on credit and not paid or what. From what I know about drugs, a little man sells it to you and then there's a bigger man down the line. If he doesn't get what he wants, then he goes back to the little man to get revenge."

Finally one night Debbie, who had seen the monster in her husband's eyes, pushed their children into a car and followed John. Spotting his wife and children in his rear-view mirror, Lucas deliberately pulled out fast into traffic and lost them.

"I realized then that I couldn't protect him anymore," she said. "Sometimes you have to love them and let them go as far as dying goes. You can't be with them all the time. You have to think about what addiction is. Most times it starts with drinking. Then you look for something that gives you a higher high and that leads to cocaine. Both are terrible. John just happened to be blessed that he got away from it before he got deeper and deeper into it with needles."

Debbie Lucas wasn't the only one in the family who was aware of her husband's addiction. Tarvia, now 9, and young John, 6, both were introduced early to a darker side of life by their father. Only Jai, who was born Dec. 5, has been spared. Perhaps that's why Lucas currently is so involved with young people through his organization STAND—Students Taking Action Not Drugs.

When Tarvia was still a toddler, her mother found her trying to sniff some cigarette ashes—as her father did with cocaine. And once little John was found stuffing small bottles of apple juice into his warm-ups prior to a junior league basketball game. When his father asked what he was doing, John replied, "I'm stashing my brews like you used to."

Debbie Lucas said, "It really hurt me. My kids idolize their father. But little kids . . . they know what is going on. You know how you're supposed to comfort your kids? Well, when John would come home (drunk or high), John-John would get in bed and hold him. He'd get in bed and put his arms around his dad like he was going to protect him.

"And my little girl, she'd tell me, 'Dad's going to be all right, Mom. Dad's going to be all right,' A lot of times, I'd want to walk out, but he was so pitiful."

Sometimes Lucas would become verbally abusive to all of them. But physical violence was never involved, so Debbie Lucas continued to stick it out.

And besides, when he wasn't drunk or high, Lucas became the same man with whom she'd fallen in love.

"When he talked ugly, I took it as the drugs talking," Debbie said. "When he was sober, he did everything possible to make up for what he'd done. He'd take the kids to the toy store or something like that. I have a closet full of toys here that have never been opened."

Lucas himself had little time for toys as he was growing up.

He began playing tennis in the fifth grade, winning a Durham city junior tournament a month later. The winner of 92 straight matches in high school, he later became an All-American in tennis at Maryland. He also played the sport professionally in the World Team Tennis League with transsexual Renee Richards as his doubles partner, a pairing that drew the nickname "The Odd Couple."

Basketball was another sport in which he excelled. A member of the first freshman class that was eligible for NCAA competition in more than a decade, he made nine of his first 10 shots in his first game at Maryland. He started all four years, earned All-America honors and was the first player chosen in the 1976 NBA draft.

But sports was by no means the sole focus of Lucas's existence. His parents, John Sr. and Blondola, have recently retired after long terms of service as public school educators in Durham. Their son was the valedictorian of his class at Hillside High.

"A lot of people say that we must have encouraged him," Lucas's mother said. "But we didn't have to. Sports was self-motivating for him. We never had to say, 'John, go practice.' We had to go to practice to get him, but we never had to tell him to practice."

Somewhere along the way, though, Lucas found enough time to have a drink. He had his first beer at the age of 15. Both his mother and wife think the availability of alcohol on the tennis circuit may have contributed to the problem.

"If you go to tennis matches, there's nothing but beer . . . kegs of beer all over, and it's all free," Debbie Lucas said.

In fact, the first time his mother was aware of her son's drinking was at one of those tournaments while he was still in college. "We were sitting together in the stands and a little guy brought John a beer," she said. "He rolled his eyes like he'd been caught."

Actually Lucas wasn't caught until much later. After graduating from Maryland in 1976, he signed with the Houston Rockets for $1.6 million over five years. Two years later, he was traded to the Golden State Warriors. It was during his three years in the San Francisco area that Lucas's behavior first became erratic—especially in the 1980-81 season. He missed six games and more than 12 practices that year. Rumors of his drug and alcohol abuse pursued him around the league.

The Warriors finally had enough. After missing a game with Houston in March, his sixth such absence, Lucas was suspended for the remaining eight games of the 1981 season and later traded to Washington. When his suspension was announced over the public address system at the Oakland Coliseum, most of the 12,237 Warrior fans cheered.

Golden State Coach Al Attles took considerable heat for his support of Lucas. He was baffled by his player's behavior. He even went so far as to talk to a doctor about signs that would indicate drug abuse—only to find that there were no easy answers.

"I was kind of naive to the situation," Attles said. "Like so many people, I find it difficult to think that an intellectual person would do something so detrimental to his body, especially when his body is his life."

Several factors may have contributed to Lucas's problems. A paternity suit was settled out of court for roughly $120,000 the previous summer. Then his high school coach, Carl Easterling, and his maternal grandmother, Alice Powell, died within a month of each other.

"Those were the first two people close to me who had ever died," Lucas once said. "I was out in California alone with nobody to check on me, and it made a big difference."

Another problem surfaced on the court. Just before that season, the Warriors had acquired World B. Free, who brought a high-profile presence and hefty scoring average to compete with Lucas in the backcourt. He also was named the team captain after sharing the title with Lucas during pre-season training.

As Lucas would later describe another low point, he was suffering from the poor-mes . . . "Poor me, this. Poor me, that. Pour me another drink."

Peer pressure also played a part in Lucas' addiction. Debbie Lucas says her husband was always trying to fit in, even as far back as their childhood. Lefty Driesell, who noticed a similar penchant when he coached Lucas at Maryland, agrees.

"John is such an outgoing person," he said. "He likes to be liked, and I think maybe he just got hanging around the wrong people. If he was at a party and someone said, 'Do this or do that,' then he might have. But when I read it in the paper, it shocked me, to tell you the truth. I talked to him about it several times. I told him it was like he had a disease. Like a cancer. But he knows he has a problem now, and he's intelligent enough to know it can kill him."

Tom Nissalke was Lucas's first pro coach at Houston. He has his own theory about what he calls the "nit-wit" element, the hangers-on who fawn after pro athletes. In a 1981 *Sports Illustrated* article, Nissalke spoke of a weakness he perceived in Lucas.

"On the court, he's got charisma, leadership, whatever you want to call it," he said. "But off the court, he will let himself be led."

If Lucas let himself be led, then it probably was because he no longer found excitement in the games he'd played since childhood.

"I got involved with drugs because I was bored with basketball," he said. "I had accomplished just about everything I could. I had devoted a lot of my life to basketball and tennis. But there was still a lonesomeness to John Lucas. When things were going really well for me, I needed to find another outlet. More challenges."

Some prevailing theories about addiction center around a low feeling of self-esteem. But Attles feels in the case of a professional athlete, the opposite might apply.

"The ego of an athlete tells him he's a little different," Attles said. "So I'm not sure it's low self-esteem—it might be the opposite. Their egos are such that they don't think it can hurt them."

But drugs and alcohol did hurt John Lucas.

"His game didn't sink to such a low point that I definitely could say, 'You've got a problem,'" Attles said. "He still had the ability to do many things. He had bad games, then he'd have games so good that you didn't think anything was wrong. The first indication I really had, though, was that I saw changes in his body over a summer. He seemed to lose the definition in his legs."

Lucas regards lost weight, sleepless nights and irritability as the primary physical manifestations of his addiction.

"It didn't tarnish my skills as much as it tarnished me," Lucas said. "I wasn't a hard-core user. I was a finely tuned athlete. But what it really cost me was *me*. I spiritually lost John Lucas."

He didn't find himself in Washington, either. In fact, Lucas maintained the same pattern of missed games and practices that had marked his latter years at Golden State. He totalled the family car twice within a month but escaped with only a cut over his eye.

Finally, he checked himself into a treatment center, the first of three such visits, for six weeks. But after a third missed practice, the Bullets released him in January 1983. Seven months later, Lucas failed a tryout with the Cleveland Cavaliers. But he was signed by San Antonio in December, played in 63 games and averaged 10.9 points per game.

The following year, the Spurs traded Lucas to Houston for forward James

Bailey. The Rockets needed a proven point guard like him to get the ball to the "Twin Towers," Ralph Sampson and Akeem Olajuwon. While in Houston the second time, Lucas failed two drug tests for cocaine. He was waived after the first, then re-signed two months later. He played more than a year before failing the second drug test March 14, 1986. Although the relapses were extremely distressing, once the problem was out in the open, Lucas's friends and family could take steps to deal with it.

"To have him say, 'I need help' took a lot of courage," his mother said. "I loved John before all this happened, but this is a different level of love. It's all right to love your child when he's lovable. But you have to go to a different level of love when he's not. All in all, this has been a strengthening experience that we might not have expected. Some might think it's been a killing experience, but actually, it's been uplifting."

Ten months would pass before Lucas resurfaced in the NBA, this time at Milwaukee, where he would spend the next two years. He was sober. He was clean. And by all accounts, he has stayed that way. Lucas now plays with the Seattle SuperSonics, a grizzled veteran of 35 on a team of youngsters challenging for a berth in the NBA playoffs. He is the backup point guard and averages about 5 points and 13 minutes per game.

"I had no qualms about picking him up," said Sonics coach Bernie Bickerstaff, who saw some of Lucas's worst behavior as an assistant coach at Washington. "Even in Washington, he was always good for the basketball team because of his fidelity and his enthusiasm. We needed someone to give our young guys some direction. And that's where his value increases—if we are fortunate enough to get to the playoffs—because John is a winner."

Win or lose, Lucas hopes to continue playing pro basketball until he is 40.

"But my motives today are different," he said. "I want people to know that recovering people can make it. I want people to realize that dependency is a disease."

Bickerstaff, for one, wouldn't be surprised to see Lucas reach that goal.

"Some guys are just survivors," he said. "And Luke is one of them. John will outlast us all. Some people just have that ability to survive."

(March 6, 1989)

Helen Ross, a 1975 graduate of the University of North Carolina, has worked at the Greensboro News & Record, *her hometown paper, for the past 15 years, covering golf and Atlantic Coast Conference football and basketball. She spent many weekends watching games on television with her father, who was the first to suggest sportswriting as a career.*

THREE

RUSHING THE NET:
TENNIS FROM LENGLEN TO CAPRIATI

THE LADY IN THE WHITE SILK DRESS

by Sarah Ballard
Sports Illustrated

WHEN HER CONTEMPORARIES RAN OUT OF WORDS TO DESCRIBE SUZANNE Lenglen they always fell back on "incomparable." On that and that alone they could all agree. Everything else about her was cause for furious debate on both sides of the Atlantic. Was she heroine or harridan? Was she courageous or corrupt? Was her infamous temperament a byproduct of genius or just the manipulation of an overweening *arriviste*? Did she purposely keep Queen Mary waiting at Wimbledon? Did she quit rather than lose to Molla Mallory at Forest Hills? Could she have survived a third set against Helen Wills at Cannes? Was she rich? Was she broke? Was she in love, engaged, about to be married? Was it cognac in the little silver flask from which she drank at the changeovers? And by the way, between us, exactly what *did* she wear beneath those silk tennis dresses of hers?

No matter where she went or what she did, controversy, scandal, gossip and rumor buzzed about Lenglen's bandeaued head like a swarm of benevolent bees, and she, who understood better than even the best sports promoters the uses of fame, did nothing to quiet any of it. This delightful, outrageous and quintessentially French woman was the unrivaled queen of tennis from 1919 to 1926. In that span she won the Wimbledon singles title six times, the French title six times and the world hard-court championship four times, as well as two gold medals at the 1920 Olympics in Antwerp. But most impressive of all, in those seven years she lost only *one* match, a highly controversial (of course) default to the U.S. champion, Mallory in 1921. *One* loss in *seven* years. And she didn't just beat her opponents, she demolished them. They measured their successes against Lenglen in points. A game was a triumph. A set was historic. In 1925, her greatest year as a player, she won the Wimbledon singles title after losing a total of only five games to her seven opponents and the French championship after losing just four. In 1926 her fame transcended not only tennis but also all of sport. In an era of living legends like Babe Ruth, Red Grange, Jack Dempsey, Gertrude Ederle and Bill Tilden, she was the best-known athlete in the world, the one whose private life was hot news and whose personal style was a yardstick by which contemporary sophistication was measured.

In that year, she did what no other tennis player had ever done: She became a playing professional. When she announced her intention, the world was stunned.

131

The elaborate pretense that tennis was an amateur sport, the same charade that was doggedly maintained until 1968, already was fully institutionalized by the mid-1920s. Lenglen and other notable players of the day were rewarded for their efforts in wondrously devious ways. It was rumored, for instance, that Wimbledon officials once guaranteed Lenglen's appearance by betting her father, Charles, a considerable sum that she would not show. When of course she did, Papa Lenglen collected.

As long as an athlete toed the line as it was laid down by his national or local tennis federation, he or she was reasonably well looked after, and in the case of a star such as Lenglen, lavishly indulged.

Deviation from the rules, however, brought swift punishment. The capital crime was uncamouflaged professionalism, even straightforward teaching professionalism, and its penalty was that most terrifying fate of all, banishment. At Wimbledon it was understood that a player, even a former champion, who had become a teaching professional was no longer even entitled to sit in the friends' box with those who had not. In 1932, when Lenglen, then in retirement, returned to Wimbledon as a spectator, she and Dorothea Lambert Chambers, with 13 Wimbledon singles titles between them, were seated together, far from the center of social action. Chambers's transgression had been to become a teaching pro.

Lenglen was nothing if not daring. Her disdain for convention was a large part of her allure during the period of social tumult that followed World War I. She was continually doing in broad daylight what most people only dreamed of in the dark night. She drank, she danced, she smoked, she swore, she wore her skirts short and her arms bare and she had lovers—lots of them. She was a Gallic elaboration on the postwar silent movie siren, The Vamp, adding to that sullen stereotype her own elements of wit and charm.

As a tennis player, Lenglen was her father's creation. As a public figure, a star, she invented herself. She would appear at a strategic moment, dressed with care and surrounded by courtiers, often handsome young tennis players, all of them chattering and laughing at what, one imagined, was something terrifically witty, utterly sophisticated, terribly chic and, above all, deliciously French. She was far from beautiful, but she was glamorous to her painted fingernails, and there were few sacrifices she was unwilling to make for her breathless audiences. Regardless of the climate, she appeared for tennis clad in fur, or fur-trimmed, coats with large collars that framed her pale, powdered face, with its gray-green eyes and dark red lips. When she posed for photographers she stood with her rackets in the crook of her left arm and her right hand on her hip, holding her coat so as to reveal the tennis costume underneath—a white silk dress, knee length and pleated, and a brightly colored sweater which exactly matched the two yards of silk chiffon wound around her bobbed black hair, the celebrated "Lenglen Bandeau" that was copied by millions of women, whether or not they had ever held a racket. Beneath the silk dress she wore silk stockings rolled just above the knee, and who knew what else. Certainly not a petticoat. Tennis had had its beautiful women before Lenglen—the French champion Marguerite Broquedis was one—but it is nevertheless safe to say that Lenglen, in the liberated style of her play—full of acrobatic, even balletic leaps and lunges—her dress and her life, introduced sex to tennis, and vice versa.

When Lenglen went onto the court, however, the glamour show was over. Her smiling mask was set aside and the tense, drawn and, at times, haggard face of a driven, sleepless, unrelenting perfectionist was revealed, a face that looked decades older than the lithe, graceful body below it. Lenglen's face was not her fortune, but it told the story of her brief but brilliant life.

By the time she turned 15, Suzanne Lenglen was already established in continental tennis circles as an amazing prodigy. Her teacher, guide, business agent and hard-driving taskmaster was her beloved Papa, Charles Lenglen, a retired businessman of moderate means who moved his family—wife Anais and small daughter—from Compiegne in the north of France, where Suzanne was born on May 24, 1899, to Nice on the Riviera. Within three months of being given a tennis racket, Suzanne, then 11, played before her first gallery.

By special dispensation, she was allowed to play Thursdays and Sundays at the Nice Tennis Club. Charles, who served as club secretary, arranged matches for her with winter visitors, many of whom happened also to be among the world's most talented players. She was an appealing little girl, small for her age, with long dark curls down her back. She was not pretty even then, but the vivacity that was the foundation of her charm throughout her life emanates from the old photographs.

Charles spent many hours each day at the Nice club studying the better players. He later wrote in an American newspaper: "The play of the English ladies consisted mostly of long rapid drives placed accurately along the lines and impressed me by its great regularity and calm, reasoned placing." But it was the superior play of the men that impressed him even more. He wrote, "Why then, I asked myself, should not women accept the masculine method. Is there any good reason why they do not do so, or is it merely a matter of custom and precedent?"

Thus Suzanne became the first woman player to train with men. Ted Tinling, who in his youth lived for several years on the Riviera, reports in his memoir, *Love and Faults*, that *"Voulez-vous jouer avec ma fille?"*

became a familiar phrase at the courts along the Cote d'Azur. As time passed, however, and Suzanne's successes mounted, the number of notable players not only willing but also eager to play with Charles Lenglen's little girl grew rapidly.

In May 1914, while she was still 14, Suzanne won the world hard-court championship in Paris. In the light of that success it was thought she might make her Wimbledon debut that summer, but Charles was far too clever to risk his rising star on a foreign surface (grass) in a foreign country. So Suzanne didn't enter Wimbledon in 1914 and, as it turned out, in 1915, '16, '17 and '18 as well, because the tournament was not held during World War I. But in 1919, with Europe at peace again, Lenglen was 20 years old and ready.

Until 1922 Wimbledon was a tournament to decide who would challenge the defending champion. Lenglen won that honor in 1919, losing only 17 games and no sets in the process. The defender that year was Chambers, 40, the greatest player of her day and the ladies' singles title-holder for the previous seven years.

The two, separated by two decades and a chasm of experience, went at it for three sets—Chambers, the proper Edwardian in her ankle-length tennis costume, and Lenglen, the child-woman at the dawn of an era, short-skirted, brazenly bare-armed, consuming cognac-soaked sugar lumps tossed to her from the grandstand by her father. As King George V and Queen Mary looked on, Lenglen won 10-8, 4-6, 9-7 in a tremendous upset. The new queen of tennis was crowned and the tone of her long reign set when, after the match, she received congratulations while in her bath.

For the rest of her life, Lenglen maintained that the Chambers match had been her most difficult and most rewarding. But Mrs. Chambers viewed it as tragic for the Frenchwoman. Years later she confided in Tinling her belief that the match had given Lenglen "a taste of invincibility and a subsequent compulsion for it," which eventually caused her great unhappiness.

From then on Lenglen had everything—fame, adulation, and all the trappings, if not the substance, of wealth. The city of Nice provided the Lenglens a large, comfortable house, the Villa Ariem, just across the street from the entrance to the tennis club. Her clothes were designed by Patou, the celebrated Parisian couturier. Her friends were beautiful or rich or titled or all three; her lovers were legion if not always suitable. Before she was 22 she had already broken off an affair with the French tennis player Pierre Albarran, a married man. Her mother, a dumpy little woman whom Suzanne sometimes called "*ma poule*," was her daughter's sympathetic chaperon. Tinling, who as a youth of 14 and 15 had umpired many of Lenglen's matches on the Riviera, recalls Anais and Charles Lenglen seated below him, wrapped in rugs against the chill, arguing loudly and reproving their daughter for her slightest errors.

America's first glimpse of Lenglen came in August 1921. Against Charles's wishes, Suzanne agreed to play a series of exhibitions in the U.S. for the benefit of "the [war] devastated villages of France." Once in New York, she further agreed to play in the U.S. women's championship, being held that year for the first time at Forest Hills after 34 years in Philadelphia. Charles, back home in Nice too ill to travel, told his friends that Suzanne had made the biggest mistake of her life.

Everything went wrong from the start. First she caught a bad cold and had to postpone her departure twice. Then, aboard the liner *France*, she declined to use the deck tennis court that had been set up for her and issued a news bulletin declaring that "the fox-trot and the shimmy were excellent training for tennis." In New York her reception by the press was effusive (MLLE. LENGLEN'S PETIT FEET AMAZE ON ARRIVAL), but she soon learned that her fate in the draw at Forest Hills was to play No. 5-ranked Eleanor Goss in the first round and, probably, the five-time U.S. champion, Mallory, in the second. The seeding of players according to ability to pre- vent just such an undesirable pairing had not yet been instituted. Even worse, on the day of Lenglen's scheduled first-round match, Goss defaulted and Lenglen, who had had one day's rest and one day's practice, was ordered to play Mallory instead so as not to disappoint the crowd that had gathered at Forest Hills Stadium to see her.

New surface, new ball, new climate and, for her first opponent, the best female player in America. All this without Papa by her side. Lenglen's nerves showed signs of fraying even before her match began. Once it was under way, her strokes lacked power and she coughed intermittently. Mallory, for her part, was at the top of her form. Allison Danzig, who was then a reporter for the *Brooklyn Eagle* and later became the tennis writer for the *New York Times* for 45 years, recalls, "Molla had a hell of a fore- hand. She didn't have a backhand. She had the weakest service I have ever seen. But what a forehand!"

Mallory put her forehand to good use in the first set, winning it 6-2 while Lenglen coughed more frequently. Lenglen had beaten Mallory badly in France the previous year. Now Mallory, backed enthusiastically by her good friend Bill Tilden, who disliked Lenglen intensely because her fame over- shadowed his, was about to take her revenge. With the score 0-15 in the first game of the second set, Lenglen, serving, double-faulted and then for- feited the match, saying she was too ill to continue. Holding a towel to her mouth as some spectators booed, she was led sobbing from the court.

"Cough and Quit" became Lenglen's middle name in America, and that view of her prevailed until she returned to the U.S. as a pro in 1926 and set the record straight.

On later occasions Lenglen withdrew from tournaments for reasons of strategy or ill health or both, but she never again lost a match and she never again ignored her father's advice.

A spectator at the Lenglen-Mallory match that day was 15-year-old Helen Wills from Berkeley, California, who was in New York to play in the National Junior championships. As Lenglen's successor, Helen Wills Moody was to win eight Wimbledon singles titles. In her book, *Fifteen-Thirty*, which was published in 1937, Moody recalled her first sighting of Lenglen on the clubhouse veranda at Forest Hills: "She wore a yellow organdie dress, a large hat and a white lapin coat described as ermine by the newspapers. The fur coat on a hot day made me ask why. I was told that she had a cold . . . I was impressed, and later even more so when she came out to practice with six racquets."

In December 1925 Wills (she did not marry Frederick Moody until 1929) was a 20-year-old who had won the American championship three times and stood at the brink of what was to become a great career. Lenglen at that time was 26 and at the peak of her powers. She had won Wimbledon, the unofficial world championship, for the sixth time, and the most enjoyable season of her tennis year was about to begin—the "spring circuit" on the Riviera, a series of weekly tournaments from Christmas to Easter. Her midday matches would be a fixture in the daily round of pleasure-seeking and hostesses would schedule their parties to avoid conflict with them. She was La Belle Lenglen, queen of the Cote d'Azur. Sportswriter Al Laney, in his book *Covering the Court*, described her in her prime: "She was far from beautiful. In fact, her face was homely in repose, with a long, crooked nose, irregular teeth, sallow complexion, and eyes that were so neutral that their color could hardly be determined. It was a face on which hardly anything was right. And yet, in a drawing room this homely girl could dominate everything, taking the attention away from dozens of women far prettier . . ."

When it was learned that month that Wills was coming to France in the expectation of playing Lenglen, it was thought to be a bold, impertinent, but very exciting, challenge to Lenglen's total domination of the game. From the moment Wills and her mother landed at Le Havre in mid-January, a fever of anticipation took hold in the sporting press. Tennis regulars such as John Tunis of the *Boston Globe* and Wallis Myers of London's *Daily Telegraph*, writers who often played in the same weekly Riviera tournaments they reported, were joined by an international press corps large enough to cover a medium-sized war. Grantland Rice arrived. So did James Thurber. So did the eminent Spanish novelist Vincent Blasco Ibáñez, who had never so much as seen a tennis match.

The longer the meeting of Lenglen and Wills was postponed—one would enter a tournament, the other would withdraw—the larger became the army of journalists camped out from San Remo to Cannes. Bookmakers who had at first made Lenglen a 1-10 favorite, dropped their odds to 1-4 when Suzanne appeared to be ducking the confrontation for fear of losing. In the midst of growing hysteria, only Wills remained calm. She recalls today, at her home in Carmel, California, her first glimpse of Lenglen at Villa Ariem. "It's like a picture in my mind," she says. "She lived across the street, or very near, to the tennis courts. My mother and I went to the courts by taxi and when I got out, I saw her in an upstairs window. It was a wide French window, and she waved to me. She wore a bright yellow sweater. I can still see the palm trees around her house. It's like a postcard in my mind."

Ultimately, the day arrived. Feb. 16, 1926, the singles final of the Carlton Club tournament in Cannes. Lenglen, always tightly strung at the best of times, was "empty, exhausted and frightened," according to her friend Florence Gould, wife of Frank Jay Gould, son of financier Jay Gould. With nothing to gain and her near-perfect seven-year record at stake, Lenglen was about to risk all over the challenge of a "little country girl," as a Nice newspaper referred to Wills.

Lenglen's lifelong friend, the French playboy Coco Gentien, would later write in his memoirs of Lenglen's apprehension about the match, brought on by the pressure to win: "For Suzanne every day was a torture . . . She hardly ate or slept. A few friends and I never left her side. Every day she seemed thinner. Her small face was drawn, and all you could see were two big eyes filled with dread."

Lenglen won the first set 6-3 but she was clearly not herself. Papa Lenglen was ill again, but Anais was present to shout to her daughter when things were going badly, "Oh, you're playing miserably, my dear!" To which her daughter sharply replied, *"Merde, Maman!"* Between games Lenglen resorted to her restorative silver flask, and dramatically underlined her exhaustion by placing one hand on her hip, the other over her eyes.

In the second set Wills warmed to the contest. "A thing that surprised me," she wrote in *Fifteen-Thirty*, "was that I found her balls not unusually difficult to hit, nor did they carry as much speed as the balls of several other of the leading women players whom I had met in matches. But her balls kept coming back, coming back, and each time to a spot on the court which was a little more difficult to get to."

Lenglen lost a long game at 3-all, but then, heartened by a bad call that went in her favor, evened the score 4-4. In the 12th game, at 40-15, match point, there was another long rally, and Wills sent a hard, fast forehand to Lenglen's forehand corner. A voice called "Out!" Lenglen trotted to the net smiling, her hand outstretched. Spectators poured onto the court. Baskets of flowers appeared as if out of the air. In the midst of this pandemonium a linesman, Lord Charles Hope, almost unnoticed, approached the umpire's chair to say that the ball had been good, that he had not called it out.

The umpire, one Commander George Hillyard, changed the score to 40-30. In a few minutes the court was cleared and the players returned to their positions, one drained, the other revivified. Lenglen lost the next three points and the game to make the score 6-all, but 10 minutes later she was again at match point—7-6, 40-15. At that crucial moment she double-faulted, she who was said to have double-faulted only six times in seven years! The game went to deuce. But then, from deep within her well of experience, Lenglen drew two winners in a row and the match was hers, for the second time.

Lenglen sank onto a bench, exhausted, and later, when she was led by friends to a small office near the dressing rooms, she collapsed onto a desk that was covered with neat stacks of bank notes, the proceeds from the sale of tickets. Hysterical now, she began to tear them into little pieces.

As Tunis wrote in the *Globe* of Lenglen's having to replay match point: "Without a word, without a murmur, without any protest visible or otherwise, she returned to her task . . . There was the real champion of champions."

Unwittingly, Tunis was writing Lenglen's epitaph. To the world at large the Wills match was Lenglen's greatest triumph, but a few observers, like Tunis, looking past the bouquets to the shattered figure and then over to her taller opponent in the sun visor standing unnoticed and unperturbed amid the confusion, sensed the truth, that at long last Suzanne's successor had appeared. Lenglen surely knew it too.

About a year before the match in Cannes, a crass but inventive American sports promoter named Charles C. (Cash and Carry) Pyle, who had dollar signs spinning where his eyes should have been, stepped onto Lenglen's stage. Pyle who has been described as "P.T. Barnum with a short attention span," knew nothing whatever about tennis, but he knew box office when he saw it. He had already made his reputation by signing the University of Illinois' Red Grange to a professional football contract. Now Pyle wanted a class act. Pyle offered Lenglen $50,000 on the spot and possibly more later, depending on the gate, for a four-month tour of the U.S. For months, Papa

Lenglen and Suzanne vigorously denied rumors that she was to be paid, but the facts were that Charles's health was poor and her funds were running low. If ever there was a time to cash in on Suzanne's celebrity, this was it, while she remained unbeaten and her fame undiminished. Still, becoming a professional was a daring idea. Perhaps Suzanne felt that her status made her unique, that the tennis establishment, which had deferred to her for so many years, would not dare to ostracize her now. Or perhaps the unfortunate events at Wimbledon in 1926 made up her mind for her.

There, because of a scheduling change about which Lenglen claimed not to have been informed, Queen Mary, who had come one afternoon especially to see Lenglen play, sat gazing from the Royal Box at an empty court for half an hour. Overnight, British fans and the press, insulted in behalf of their queen, were transformed from Lenglen's adoring subjects into raving chauvinists ready to take up arms against her in defense of crown and country. She played one more match at Wimbledon, a mixed doubles with Jean Borotra, and then withdrew from the tournament.

On Aug. 2, 1926, Pyle held a press conference in Paris to announce that Lenglen had signed with him. He did not mention money; he knew enough to leave that to the imagination of the reporters. Predictably, a New York newspaper headline read: SUZANNE LENGLEN BECOMES A PROFESSIONAL; IS COMING HERE NEXT MONTH FOR $200,000 TOUR.

There was a furor. The French federation, for which Lenglen had earned hundreds of thousands of francs, called her action deplorable, refused her permission to play exhibitions at its member clubs and asked the Nice Tennis Club to expel her, which it did not do. The All England Club, however, revoked her honorary membership.

On Aug. 10 Suzanne was interviewed by Thomas Topping of the Associated Press, who observed that she looked five years younger, carefree and happy. "Some seem to believe I am tied up hands and feet by becoming a professional," she told him. "To me it is an escape from bondage and slavery. No one can order me about any longer to play tournaments for the benefit of club owners. I got great fun out of tennis for a few years after the war, but lately it had become too exacting . . . I have done my bit to build up the tennis of France and of the world. It's about time tennis did something for me."

The most urgent question on both sides of the Atlantic was whom would she play in both singles and mixed doubles. There were few women who could give her a game, and none of those was a professional. An amateur would automatically lose his or her amateur status by competing against her. Lenglen's first choice for a mixed doubles partner was her current lover, an Italian Davis Cupper named Placido Gaslini. But Gaslini's father, a

Milanese banker, would not permit it. In Gaslini's place, Paul Feret, the fourth-ranked French player, was picked and accepted. Feret at the time was disconsolate over the death of his 19-year-old wife and ready for a change of surroundings. (When Feret returned to France after the tour, he applied for reinstatement as an amateur, pleading tennis's version of temporary insanity. The federation accepted his plea, accompanied by a check representing his professional earnings, and anointed him an amateur again.)

When Lenglen and Feret sailed for New York on the liner *Paris* they had no idea who their opponents might be, but en route, when the *Paris*'s sister ship, the *France*, was sighted steaming in the opposite direction, they got their first news. Aboard the *France* were the Four Musketeers: Borotra, Rene Lacoste, Henri Cochet and Toto Brugnon. During a ship-to-ship radio conversation Lenglen learned that Pyle had signed a former U.S. champion, Mary K. Browne, to be her singles opponent. Although 35 and past her playing prime, Browne was well-known, having won the American women's title in 1912, '13 and '14.

But Pyle had saved his real stunner for the landing of the *Paris* in New York. When the liner docked on Sept. 30 he announced to a glittering assemblage in the ship's ballroom that he had acquired the services of "the greatest male tennis player in the world . . . Vincent Richards is now a professional!"

Richards was then 23 and about to be awarded the No. 1 U.S. ranking, dislodging Bill Tilden from that spot for the first time in six years. His decision to turn professional at the very peak of his amateur career was almost as startling as Lenglen's.

The United States Lawn Tennis Association took its revenge on Richards just as the French federation did on Lenglen. Both were stripped of their No. 1 rankings and thereafter dealt with as nonpersons.

Pyle filled out his troupe with two Californians: Howard Kinsey of San Francisco, who was ranked No. 6 in the U.S., and Harvey Snodgrass, a Southern Californian who had been ranked No. 6 in 1924 and subsequently had become a teaching pro in Los Angeles.

Again Charles was too ill to travel, but for company Suzanne had her mother, a personal maid, Helene, an Irish masseur named William T. O'Brien and Ann Kinsolving, 19, cub reporter for the *Baltimore News*, now Mrs. John Nicholas Brown of Newport and Providence.

"When Suzanne was introduced to me, she stared at my fur-lined cloak as though she were studying its texture," Ann Kinsolving Brown told Italian journalist Gianni Clerici. "I seemed to pass her test, and she quietly said to me, 'You're the person I'm looking for. I need someone who understands me and will know how to speak about me.'" So Kinsolving signed on as tennis's first personal press agent, for $6,000.

* * *

Opening night, Oct. 9, 1926, at Madison Square Garden, was preceded by intense publicity. Lenglen's name was everywhere, endorsing French perfume, French girdles and French gowns. She was reported seen in the audience of a Broadway musical, at a Mary Pickford movie and at a World Series game at Yankee Stadium.

Just as Pyle had planned, the hype produced an opening night crowd of 13,000 well-heeled New Yorkers attired in black tie and evening gowns, including Governor Al Smith, Mayor Jimmy Walker, golfers Walter Hagen and Glenna Collett, assorted Astors, Pells and Vanderbilts, even Bill Tilden, who was introduced in the manner of a former champion at a prize fight. It was probably, though not provably, the largest crowd ever to watch tennis in the U.S. up to that time and the first to attend a professional tennis exhibition anywhere.

The preliminary, so to speak, was Richards vs. Feret. Richards won 6-3, 6-4. Then Lenglen entered the arena as a spotlight played on her and the band struck up the "Marseillaise." While the crowd did not sit on its hands, neither did it give her a standing ovation. After all, New York's last sight of Lenglen had been of a coughing, sobbing quitter being led off the court at Forest Hills. But this night, as she beat Browne 6-1, 6-1 in 39 minutes, Lenglen won them over.

The second night at the Garden, 6,000 fans watched Lenglen beat Browne 6-2, 6-2, and Ring Lardner wrote, "It is obvious to everyone, even the experts, that Miss Wills would never beat Miss Lenglen if they were ever to meet in years to come."

Late that night the troupe, 14 people in all, including two baseball clowns, Al Schacht and Nick Altrock, who enlivened the intervals between matches with their buffoonery, set off for Toronto by train. In the baggage car was a 2,000-pound collapsible tennis court made of cork and rubber and covered with green painted canvas, which would be laid down in arenas, armories and auditoriums in 40 cities in the next four months.

As long as the tour remained in the Northeast, the audiences, which ranged from 8,000 in Cleveland to 1,500 in Buffalo, were made up, for the most part, of those who had at least a nodding acquaintance with tennis.

"It was a strenuous tour," says Ann Kinsolving Brown. "We always traveled by train, often at night. There were no proper sleeping cars in the European style, only Pullman berths, each separated from the next by tightly drawn curtains. There was only one real compartment at the end of the carriage with proper washing facilities. This was reserved for Suzanne. She suffered from insomnia. One night she decided to switch all the pairs of shoes that had been put outside the couchettes for cleaning. Next morning there was pandemonium."

In Toronto, Lenglen's visit was a social extravaganza. Her every waking moment was taken up with wining, dining and tea dancing. Her skin was compared in print to Eleanora Duse's, her mouth to Pola Negri's, her personality to Sarah Bernhardt's, her artistry to Fritz Kreisler's, her greatness to—get this—Edmund Burke's!

In Baltimore, 5,000 people were at the Fifth Regiment Armory to watch Lenglen wipe the floor with Browne, 6-0, 6-0. Billy Jacobs, now 71, who was the head ball boy for the matches, recalls, "It was very cold. In those days they didn't have too much in the way of proper heat, and she came out on the court with a white fur coat and she asked me to help her off with it . . . It was a nice crowd. Any people who were interested in tennis at the time would be very happy to brave any bad weather to see it." However, Felix Morley, writing in the *Baltimore Sun*, saw things in a different light: "There is nothing monotonous about Suzanne but there will soon be distinct monotony to her massacres of Mary Browne . . . Suzanne is far too good for her, or any other woman player."

Browne, who died in 1971, once told a reporter, "Time after time I have run games up to 4-0, but try as I would, I never could get the set over. She would just run me ragged while I was accumulating that lead and then, when I no longer had the stamina for court covering, her deadly accuracy in placing the ball finally began to tell and the points began to mount up for her."

Meanwhile, Lenglen was charming the socks off the press wherever she went. Her interviews were frequently conducted over breakfast in her hotel suite, where her costume ranged from black silk pajamas to a white satin negligee.

In private, among the other members of the troupe, however, she was less than sunny. Snodgrass, who's now 86 and lives in Sun City, Arizona, says, "She was really a contradiction. Her game was grace and speed, soft shots well-placed; she was a very well-conditioned athlete. But she was always upset, flaring mad. Sometimes it was hard to understand how the two could be connected. She had the worst temper I've ever seen. She was always threatening to bolt and go home. Off the court the other players on the tour didn't want to have anything to do with her."

But Lenglen, with her retinue, did not lack for company. "She took her meals in her bedroom, as she found American food inedible," says Ann Kinsolving Brown. "She drank French wines and made great salads, with beetroot, green peppers and Gruyere cheese. At breakfast, late in the morning, her bed became the center of a sort of royal levee. She would be massaged by O'Brien in front of anybody. Her telephone was by her bed. Once she answered a friend's call, 'I'm in the hands of an Irishman.'"

As always, she was unpredictable. One time, in the middle of a match, she told Pyle that she was not feeling well. She had had her period, she said. She wanted a break. Pyle replied that all the women *he'd* ever known complained when they *didn't* have their periods. Lenglen's response was to burst out laughing and carry on with the match.

In Philadelphia, Lenglen told a reporter, "I'm so happy. It is fun being a pro—no worry, no terrorizing fright because I might lose a game, no harrowing criticism. Oh, it's much better!" Yet privately she flared with anger when the detested Tilden showed up for the matches at the Sesqui Auditorium in Philadelphia, where the court was laid over a hockey rink and the temperatures were polar. "*Ce pederaste* comes especially to see me in this igloo!" she growled to Kinsolving.

As the troupe headed farther west, public apathy grew and ticket sales declined. Los Angeles, a tennis hotbed, was supposed to have been the last stop on a triumphant tour, but as gate receipts dwindled, Pyle kept signing up more cities. In spite of the disappointing returns on his investment, he treated the Lenglen entourage to a 10-day holiday at the Hotel del Coronado in San Diego in December. Suzanne was photographed shaking hands with Jockey Tod Sloan at the nearby Caliente race track and doing calisthenics on the beach at Coronado, clad in "a black wool tank suit of meager proportions." Carefully excluded from the photographs but often included in Suzanne's excursions around San Diego was a tall, tanned and very rich California playboy, one Baldwin M. Baldwin, known as the Sheik. Grandson of E.J. (Lucky) Baldwin, who had made an enormous fortune during the California gold rush and who later owned the tract in Arcadia, California, where the Santa Anita race track now stands, young Baldwin became her constant companion, as constant, that is, as his position of husband, father and scion allowed. Two years later there was open talk of divorce and marriage, but in 1926 the Sheik was a somewhat shadowy figure. He joined the tour in its last weeks and occasionally was referred to in newspaper accounts as Lenglen's business manager.

On Dec. 28 at the Olympic Auditorium in Los Angeles, before a knowledgeable crowd of 7,000, the Pyle troupe went through its paces again. Much fuss had been made in the preceding weeks over Browne's great improvement. Browne was a Southern Californian, and hopes ran high that she would win her first match from Lenglen on home ground. Alas, Magnificent Mary reverted to form and lost 6-0, 6-1.

By late fall 1926, Pyle had started paying more attention to his pro football investments—he started the American Football League that year—and following the L.A. engagement, he handed the management of the troupe to Richards, who led the players east through Texas to New Orleans, Miami and Havana, then north to Newark, Hartford and finally, in February, to Providence and an audience of approximately 2,500.

Pyle, rejoining the players in New York when the tour had ended, boasted to the press, "Mlle. Lenglen had played to capacity or near-capacity throngs in every city she visited" and "the venture has been a financial success far beyond our expectations." But the amateur tennis establishment knew better and it rejoiced.

It would be gratifyingly tidy but historically inaccurate to say that Lenglen's professional tour was a courageous act of pioneering that led by a direct route to today's tennis-playing millionaires, but the open-tennis revolution was so long in coming that the Lenglen tour seems to have no connection with it.

In February 1927, Lenglen went back to France with her mother. They returned to America only once after that, in December 1928, when they went to visit Baldwin's mother, Mrs. Anita Baldwin, in Arcadia, California. Baldwin was still wed, but rumors of his imminent marriage to Lenglen persisted.

The social call turned into a donnybrook, however. On Jan. 15 the following four-tiered headline appeared in the *Los Angeles Times*: LENGLEN LEAVES HOSTESS' HOME; BOTH DENY ROW; TENNIS PLAYER'S WHEREABOUTS UNKNOWN—HAD TICKETS FOR EAST; MRS. ANITA BALDWIN IN COLLAPSE, REPORT SON, FRENCH WOMAN'S MANAGER, ALSO QUITS CALIFORNIA HOUSE.

Back to Europe Suzanne went, this time for good, with the Sheik in tow. As the party left New York, Baldwin's lawyer announced to the press that he would seek a divorce for his client in Paris.

The divorce never came about, nor did the marriage, but the affair lasted four more years. By 1930 Lenglen was at work selling sports clothes in a Parisian dress house, which was distinguished by a vest-pocket tennis court on the premises. Some society page observers exulted in print over what they saw as Lenglen's descent from queen to shopgirl, although no one seemed sure whether financial need was involved. In fact, it probably was. The family had lost the use of the villa in Nice, and Charles Lenglen had succumbed at last to failing health, in 1929, dying at age 70.

When the French tennis federation reinstated Feret in 1933, it was expected that Lenglen, who had also applied to regain her amateur status, would be next, but that never happened. Her movements were still news, though, and her public appearances in informal tennis matches always attracted attention.

Five-time U.S. champion Helen Jacobs recalled in her book, *Gallery of Champions*, a practice match she played with Lenglen in 1933 during the French championships at Roland Garros Stadium: "Jean Borotra was playing on the stadium court and the stands were filled to capacity. The court to which Suzanne and I walked was behind the stadium, but visible from its rim. A spectator must have passed the word that 'Lenglen was playing,' for in a matter of minutes we were being followed by a procession of people far more eager to watch Suzanne than any of the tournament aspirants."

From 1933 until her sudden death at the age of 39, in 1938, Lenglen was director of a government-backed tennis school in Paris, apparently having given up hope of being readmitted as an amateur.

The one event in her life that she could not stage-manage was her death, of pernicious anemia. On June 29 she was given a transfusion and on July 4 she was dead. The disease by then was no longer considered incurable, but Lenglen's health had never been robust.

Her funeral at Notre Dame de l'Assomption in Paris befitted that of a national heroine. Her old friend King Gustav V of Sweden sent an emissary, as did Premier Edouard Daladier of France. Borotra and Brugnon represented the Musketeers, and floral displays from tennis clubs filled three automobiles in the procession to the cemetery in suburban Saint-Ouen. Suzanne was buried in the family plot, alongside her beloved Papa.

At Wimbledon, Moody, who had just won her eighth singles title, said Lenglen was "the greatest woman player who ever lived." So, at one time or another, did every other prominent player who had ever been her opponent, including Mallory, Chambers and Browne.

But of them all, the one who knew her best was Elizabeth Ryan. Ryan was one of the last players to beat Lenglen at singles, when she was 14. She also gave Suzanne one of her few tough matches at Wimbledon, a three-setter in 1924, after which Lenglen withdrew from the tournament. For six years Ryan was Lenglen's doubles partner, at Wimbledon and elsewhere. As a team they were never beaten.

Ryan died in 1979 at the age of 87, 24 hours before Billie Jean King finally broke her long-standing record of 19 Wimbledon titles. In 1941, when Ryan was a teaching pro at the Royal Hawaiian Hotel in Honolulu, sportswriter Bob Considine sought her out there and asked her the old question—who was the best?

"Why, Suzanne, of course," Ryan replied. "She owned every kind of shot, plus a genius for knowing how and when to use them. She never gave an opponent the same kind of shot to hit twice in a row. She'd make you run miles . . . her game was all placement and deception and steadiness. I had the best drop shot anybody ever had, but she could not only get up to it but was so fast that often she could score a placement off of it. She had a stride a foot and a half longer than any known woman who ever ran, but all those crazy leaps she used to take were done after she hit the ball. Sure, she was a poser, a ham in the theatrical sense. She had been spoiled by tremendous adulation from the time she was a kid . . . But she was the greatest woman player of them all. Never doubt that."

(September 13, 1982)

In her three decades at Sports Illustrated—*as secretary, reporter, writer and editor*—*Sarah Ballard has seen the female athlete rise in editorial esteem from amusing sidebar to front-of-the-book newsmaker. It was a reluctant revolution, she says, but a revolution, nonetheless.*

A Dodo in Name Only

by Jill Lieber
Sports Illustrated

After a thump against a curb, a near miss of a towering palm and a 360 in mid-block, the Pontiac Grand Prix came to a screeching halt in front of a Neighbor-Savor food store in La Jolla. The little old lady from Santa Monica climbed down off her pillow and out from behind the steering wheel.

"Like my hood ornament?" she asked her pals as they piled out of the car. She pointed to a figure of a curvaceous woman holding a tennis racket. "Did it myself. Yanked it off one of my trophies. Then I just screwed it on the hood. Adds a little class, don't you think?"

The little old lady from Santa Monica began waving her arms, orchestrating her troops—left, right, full steam ahead. "Now everybody gets two minutes to go through the store and pick out munchies," she said. "We need sustenance for the poker game."

With that, everyone scattered, returning with potato chips, corn curls, cheese puffs, dips, soda, cheese and crackers. "Let's get two six-packs," she said, watching the mound at the cash register grow. "Oh, oh. It says you've got to show an ID to buy beer." She started rummaging through her purse.

"Will my driver's license do?"

"Ma'am, you look old enough to me," said the teenage cashier with a giggle. The register rang out the damage: $27.45.

"Thank goodness," she said. "Jeepers, the only proof of age I have is gray hair and varicose veins."

Meet Dodo Cheney, mother of three, grandmother of seven, youngest daughter in the First Family of American tennis, neighborhood zucchini queen, abalone fisherman, card shark, creator of secret arthritis remedies and winner of more U.S. national tennis titles—114—than anyone who has ever played the game. Whoa. Run that past again. Dodo Cheney? More national championships than anyone? What about Bill Tilden? Nope. He only had 31. Billie Jean King? She's won 30. How about Chris Evert Lloyd? Just 18. Dodo's nearest pursuer is 68-year-old Gardnar Mulloy, and he's won a mere 55.

So why haven't you heard of her? Well, Dodo never won a title at Wimbledon or Forest Hills—though both her parents did. And while Evert Lloyd *et al.* were typically winning national championships by the time they

147

were 11, Dodo didn't really get started until she was 40, with the U.S. 40-and-over Women's Hard Court singles in 1957. She would win that tournament—in the same age division—every year until she was 53. Now that Dodo has turned 65, she finally has consented to play with people closer to her own age. For the record, her U.S. titles, which have come on all surfaces, break down this way: clay court singles, indoor doubles, hard court doubles, 35-and-over doubles (commonly referred to as 35 doubles, the same being true of other senior age categories), 45 doubles, mother-daughter—one each; 40 singles—17; 40 doubles—14; 50 singles—five; 50 doubles—eight; 55 singles—13; 55 doubles—nine; 60 singles—16; 60 doubles—10; 65 singles—five; 65 doubles—two; senior mixed doubles—nine. Dodo won her most recent national championships just last week, the 65 grass court singles and doubles in Wilmington, Delaware. All this makes her a one woman dynasty, the likes of which the game had never before known.

On the court—and at the poker table—Dodo wraps herself in lace, pleated pastels, puffy caps, pearls, beads, bangles and charm bracelets. "The girls today don't look like girls when they're on the court. They look like men," says Dodo, who cooks up a new outfit for several of the dozen or so tournaments she plays each year. "The players look too tough. For me, there's never too much perfume or lace." But don't let her looks fool you. Dodo is a canny old bird. She relies primarily on a looping Western forehand and chases down just about everything. Then, when her opponent is convinced she has settled in on the baseline, Dodo sneaks up to the net and puts her away with dinks and drops.

Dodo was doing precisely that during a first-round match at the national 60-and-over hard court championships at the La Jolla Beach and Tennis Club in May. "Woo," she cried after a perfect return of an overhead smash, "did I really get that?" A few games later, her opponent drilled a forehand that landed just inside the sideline. "I got it," Dodo yelled as she raced for the shot, her charm bracelets madly jangling, her peach skirt billowing. Without breaking stride, she caught the ball smack in the center of her oversized racket and whacked it back. But what's this? She kept right on running, pretending that she couldn't stop, and zoomed toward the net, narrowly missing the stanchion. Plop. She wound up in the stands, finally run aground by a big-bellied man in the front row. He put his arm around her. "We have to stop meeting like this," said Dodo, laughing.

"Nothing ever amazes me about my mother," says Dodo's daughter, Christie Putnam. "When I was young, every year our family went to La Jolla for a tournament. You know what our schedule used to be? We'd get down there in the late afternoon, and Mom would go out and check to see whether it was high or low tide. If it was high tide, we'd go fishing and have a picnic. Then the kids would go to bed and the adults would play poker until way past midnight. Mom would have us all up about five the next morning, when it was low tide. We'd go out and fish for lobster and abalone. Then we'd play matches all day. You don't think I've always wished I'd had *that* kind of energy?"

Dodo is in a race against time. Too many more bridge parties and poker games. Too many more homegrown zucchinis and cucumbers to give away. Too many more dresses to design, charms to collect and grandchildren to keep track of. Too many more hours of planting, climbing, hoeing, building, painting. Too many more titles to be won.

"A woman asked me the other day where she could find Dodo," says Carol Schneider, national women's senior circuits chairman, as she watched Dodo flit around on and off the court in La Jolla. "And I said, 'When does she play? Three o'clock? Well, look for her at 2:59.' Dodo just has so much going on. I've never seen her watch a tennis match."

After the second round in La Jolla, Dodo and the gang, some locals and a group of fellow competitors, got together to play cards. "What have I gotten myself into?" said Arthur Mace Gwyer, 66, as he watched Dodo scoop up bunches of chips from the middle of the dining room table and stack them in front of her. "Listen, I haven't played poker since World War II. I've only got $45 in cash, but I do have checks. And they are good. After that, I have credit cards."

"Relax, Mace," Dodo said, taking a sip of her milk on the rocks. She says she drinks milk because of an ulcer, but she also likes to keep her mind clear for the task at hand.

"All I did was ask you to go dancing," Gwyer said.

"Relax, Mace," Dodo said. "We'll go over to The Marine Room later and check out the action."

Relax, Mace, it's only money. White chips cost a nickel. Red ones are worth a dime. Blue chips, a quarter.

"We're now playing screw your neighbor," the dealer said, shuffling a fresh deck.

"You have two cards?" Dodo asked.

"I'm chesting them," said Helen Perez, who ranked among the nation's first 10 women in the early 1950s and now is second in the 50-and-over division.

"Keep your cards on the table, girl," said Dodo.

"I like those big cards," said Vilma Gordon, who was ranked 13th in the U.S. in the 50s. "Then I don't have to wear my glasses."

"I'm gonna raise you a dime," the dealer said. "There are all rich people here."

Dodo's blue eyes were clear and ice cold. She wasn't about to give away any secrets. She peered to her right. Hmm. Helen is smirking. Dodo thought. Dodo glanced to her left. Vilma looks shell-shocked.

"Okay," the dealer announced, "here we go."

Up came the cards around the table: ace of hearts, queen of diamonds, 10 of diamonds, queen of diamonds. . . .

"Wait. Something's wrong with this deck," said Dodo, ripping the cards from the dealer's hands.

"All I did was look for a fresh deck," said Helen, innocently holding up a shoe box bursting with at least 30 decks of cards.

"This is a pinochle deck," Dodo said, quite irritated.

"Uh, you never know what'll happen in La Jolla," the guilty party said.

Well, pour some more drinks. Here, have some more peanuts. Grab another deck of cards. The night's still young.

"Dodo used to play this tournament in December," says Schneider. "She'd stay up most of the night playing poker, and she'd win at poker and win her matches. Then, one time a couple of years ago, she lost a match. I said, 'Dodo, you can't stay up so late anymore.' She just smiled."

* * *

Dodo was born Dorthy May Bundy on Sept. 1, 1916 in Santa Monica. Her father, Thomas C. Bundy, won three U.S. doubles championships (1912-14) and was on two Davis Cup teams (1911 and 1914). A real estate mogul, he developed L.A.'s Miracle Mile. He also founded and built the Los Angeles Tennis Club, one of the oldest and most famous bastions of the game in the country.

Her mother was May Sutton, the driven, gutsy pioneer of women's sports in the U.S. The British used to call May "the Pasadena washerwoman," because she was the first female tennis player to push her blouse sleeves up to her elbows. She also wore fewer petticoats than other players because she knew women needed more freedom to move about the court. May won the U.S. women's singles and doubles in 1904, and a year later, at age 17, became the first American to win a singles title at Wimbledon. She won Wimbledon again in 1907, and 14 years later, at 33, was ranked fourth in the U.S. and made the semis at Forest Hills, after having four children.

To know May is to know Dodo. "Mrs. Bundy always walked onto the court looking as if she was in her bedroom," says Pat Henry Yeomans, a childhood friend of Dodo's. "May loved ruffles, lace, feathers and big hats. She was the kind of woman who insisted upon having tea and crumpets before she would begin the third set of any match."

"I remember watching May Sutton and Dodo play a mother-daughter event at a tournament in La Jolla when May was 81," says Ralph Trembley, who was a tournament official. "And her mother would scream at the top of her lungs, 'Dodo, get your ass up to the net.'"

Bill Bundy, Dodo's younger brother, also remembers that tournament. "Mother and Dodo got to the finals," he says. "Mother played net because she still had an extremely quick eye. Well, the net was a little long and part of it was lying flat on the court. Mother poached, and she caught her foot in the net. She fell, and you could hear the crowd cringe. She was bleeding like a stuck pig. We put wet towels on her elbows, arms and knees. Dodo said, 'Mother, we'll default.' And she said, 'We most certainly will not. I've never defaulted in my life.' They didn't win, and Mother couldn't walk the next day, but by God, she didn't default."

Three of May's sisters also were among the best women players in the country. Ethel Sutton Bruce won the Southern California women's championship four times (1906, 1911-13), and Florence Sutton won the title in 1907 and 1914. Violet Sutton Doeg was Southern California champion in 1899, 1904 and 1905. (Her son, John Hope Doeg, won Forest Hills in 1930.) Together, May and her sisters won the Southern California women's title *every* year from 1899 through 1915.

Dodo, who began playing tennis at age 8, learned the basics from Florence. May would have nothing to do with her daughter's tennis career, though by watching her mother, Dodo picked up May's Western forehand—the stroke she made famous—her keen court sense and, most important, her determination.

After a solid but unsensational junior career, Dodo made the Wightman Cup team at age 20 and reached the semifinals at Forest Hills. The next year, 1938, she won the Australian championships. In 1941 Dodo enrolled at Rollins College in Winter Park, Florida, where she and Pauline Betz, who later would win Forest Hills four times, headed what may well be the greatest women's college tennis team of all time. That year Dodo won her first national title, the U.S. Women's Indoor doubles, with Betz. In 1944 Dodo won the singles at the U.S. Clay Courts. From 1936 through 1946 she ranked in the top 10 in the U.S. every year but 1942, climbing as high as No. 3 three times.

Despite her success, Dodo knew she would never be the player May was. Still, she wanted nothing more than to please her mother and carry on the Sutton tradition in the sport. If she wasn't good enough to win major championships, Dodo decided, she would make her mark another way: She would win as many U.S. age-group titles as she could. But first she wanted to settle down and have a family. In 1946 Dodo married Art Cheney, a polo player and pilot for Western Airlines. They had three children, Brian, 34, a former captain of the Arizona tennis team and player/coach of the Phoenix

Racquets of World Team Tennis and now a teaching pro in Phoenix; Christie, 30, in her day a high-ranked junior player in Southern California; and May, 33, who never played much tennis and is now a medical illustrator. Dodo limited her tennis to mixed-cocktail doubles and local tournaments. Also, for 15 years she ran a municipal tennis program for hundreds of kids in Santa Monica that has produced some of the best junior players in the country.

In the late '40s and early '50s, national age-group tournaments for adults were getting popular. "And women were finally realizing it was okay to admit their age," says Dodo. So she grabbed her free Western Airlines pass and set off on the tournament trail. The titles quickly accumulated. Since winning the 40 hard courts in 1957 she has averaged four U.S. titles a year. In 1981 she won 13. The women against whom she had competed when she was younger hadn't kept themselves in as good shape as Dodo had. Nowadays Dodo plays the 50 and 55 doubles and 55, 60 and, occasionally, 65 singles. She doesn't play the 65s often because, as Christie says, "Mom likes to win, but she also likes to know she had to work for the win." Adds Schneider, "Because of Dodo, we've added 70 singles and doubles. But she won't play them. She wouldn't get enough competition."

Which of all the titles means the most to Dodo? "That would be the mother-daughter grass courts in 1976, with Christie," she says. "We had a great time. When I made a stinky shot, she'd say, 'That's okay, Mom.' My mother never would have been that easy on me."

Dodo's physical condition should enable her to keep piling up national titles for a long time. She has only minor arthritic pain in her fingers, but she keeps it under control with a secret homemade remedy. Her worst enemies are nasty calluses that appear on her right hand after marathon gardening sessions. Her eyesight is good—she doesn't need glasses to play—she moves well and her reflexes are sharp. Her serve and backhand, the weakest part of her game when she was young, are now stronger than those of most of her opponents. Her concentration has actually improved with age. Her energy level is at an all-time high. She is rugged and resilient.

Yet beyond all this, something else has kept Dodo puddle-jumping across the U.S.: the last two years, tennis has been a release for her, a way to forget that time doesn't stand still for everyone. "In 1980 my dad had a massive stroke," says Christie. "He was completely immobilized and couldn't talk. We were told he had two weeks to two months to live. My mother made an immediate decision to care for him herself. She felt that a nursing home wasn't what he wanted. He loved their house up in the canyon.

"Well, he ended up living two years. Every two hours, for two years, my mother turned him. She chopped up his favorite foods for every meal because she thought he'd get bored with his formula. When she went to tournaments, friends stayed with him. She never complained. She always thought he had a chance to get better. Think of the devotion there. It wasn't until the last month that he got bedsores."

At 6:30 on a Sunday morning last May, just as she was getting dressed for the finals of the 60 singles and doubles at the National Hard Courts, Dodo got a phone call at the La Jolla Beach and Tennis Club. It was a friend calling to tell her that her husband had died during the night. "Mother and a friend who had recently lost her husband took a long walk on the beach to sort things out," says Brian. "Mother then told the tournament committee something had happened at home and that she had to leave. She said she'd play the doubles because her opponents had traveled so far but she wouldn't play the singles. After she won the doubles, though, she felt great. And she thought, 'Why not?' So she played the singles and won that, too."

Titles No. 110 and 111.

"His death didn't come as a surprise," says Dodo. "Still, you're never quite ready for it when it finally happens. It was just as well that I played in the finals. I would've been a basket case otherwise. It was good therapy. By the time I got home I was in much better shape.

"But I don't know if you should mention that I played two matches after finding out my husband died. I don't know if people will realize why I had to play, why I had to be in La Jolla, why I had to be around tennis. I think too many people will wonder why I didn't go home."

(August 9, 1982)

Jill Lieber is a senior writer at Sports Illustrated *where she specializes in pro football and investigations. A graduate of Stanford, she co-authored* Total Impact, *the best-selling autobiography of star NFL defensive back Ronnie Lott.*

'Gorgeous Gussie' Holds on to Less-than-Glamorous Life

by Melissa Isaacson
Orlando Sentinel

GUSSIE MORAN DOES NOT PLAY TENNIS ANYMORE. WHAT WAS ONCE HER PASsion is now a luxury reserved for others, a game she has neither the time nor inclination to play.

She has long since thrown out the lace panties that created such a fuss at Wimbledon nearly 40 years ago, and she lets out a sarcastic chuckle when asked if anyone still recognizes her.

Adulation is the very least of Moran's worries. At age 64, survival is far more important.

These days, a little more than two years after being evicted from her family's Santa Monica estate, Moran spends the bulk of her time at her place of employment, a souvenir shop just inside the gates of the Los Angeles Zoo, where her co-workers—on this afternoon a teenage boy and girl—know less about her than they think.

"I know she's interested in tennis," the boy said. "We talk about it all the time, because I play. I told her I'd teach her. I'm a pretty good player."

A visitor clued him in that Moran was once a pretty good player herself, one of the best women in this country, in fact. A woman who reached the semifinals at the U.S. Open in singles and the finals at Wimbledon in doubles.

It took a few seconds for the young man to compose himself.

"Oh, my, God," he whispered. "She never told us that. I just got the shivers."

His co-worker nudged him. "Maybe she doesn't want us to know," she said.

Moran, who lives with four cats in a small studio apartment in Los Angeles, hadn't planned on spending her retirement years putting in five shifts a week. She once was a professional athlete, after all, and if that doesn't guarantee you financial security, well, at least it ought to leave you with your dignity.

These days, Gertrude "Gussie" Moran is using most of her energy to find it.

Clocking out after another shift one afternoon last month, Moran made her way past the monkey cage and around to the cookie stand for a cup of coffee. Dressed in brown work pants, an LA Zoo T-shirt, a baggy olive green jacket and pink Reeboks, she walked briskly across the grounds.

"One of the greatest walks ever," British dress designer and tennis observer Ted Tinling said not long ago. "Gussie always carried herself like a dream, like she was walking on a rubber ball."

That's pretty much how everybody knew Moran in the late '40s and early '50s. "Gorgeous Gussie" they called her the year she set Wimbledon on its ear.

It was 1949. Moran was 25, dark-haired and tanned, with a powerful forehand and an eye for fashion. She had heard of Ted Tinling, the man who first gained prominence in the fashion and tennis world with a tennis dress he designed for the great Suzanne Lenglen, and Moran wanted him to do something for her.

"I wrote him a letter prior to Wimbledon, asking him if he would design me something with one sleeve one color, the other sleeve another color and the shirt another color," Moran said. "He wrote back, *'Have you lost your mind?'*"

But Tinling was intrigued by the young American he had been hearing about and decided he would indeed design something unique for her. His idea was to shorten the skirt to just above the knee and trim it in satin. When Moran asked if he could also make her some matching shorts underneath—"We weren't talking Frederick's of Hollywood," Moran said—Tinling agreed.

"The titillation was that you only saw [the panties] about once every three minutes," Tinling said. "No one ever knew what they wore underneath in those days. No one would ever ask. You had photographers, for the first time in history, lying on their backs. Everyone went wild."

Wimbledon officials went mad. And Moran, shocked by the reaction, went into a shell. The first and only time she wore the outfit on court, she walked on with her racket in front of her face.

"I was embarrassed," Moran said, "because they were putting so much adulation on the character, 'Gorgeous Gussie.' You know, I was really never anything to write home about. I was a plain girl. But Life magazine ran a picture calling me Gorgeous Gussie,' [and] the British picked it up and did a real job with it.

"Then people would see me, and I'd hear them say, 'I've seen better looking waitresses at the hot dog stand.' I just went to pieces. Emotionally, I couldn't handle it."

After defeating Shirley Fry at Queens, a tuneup tournament, Moran—distracted by the panties furor—was eliminated early at Wimbledon.

"I really couldn't handle the pressure," she said.

Tinling, who had acted as official Wimbledon host for 23 years, was banned from the event. Not until 1982, 33 years after the Moran incident, was he invited back.

It is not entirely clear whether the incident had a scarring effect on Moran. She dismisses the theory. And yet she describes herself as "still painfully shy," and one can't help but wonder just how much of 1949 she carried with her.

Moran left the tour the year after the incident and turned professional, which essentially amounted to joining the circus. It would, however, be the first time Moran earned money for playing tennis. All tennis players were amateur then, and in order to travel to tournaments such as Wimbledon, Moran had to rely on donations from friends.

In 1950 Moran traveled the country playing exhibitions and making appearances with Pancho Segura, Pauline Betz and Jack Kramer. Bobby Riggs was the promoter of the tour and signed Moran for $87,000, which was funneled back into Riggs' corporation. Moran still won't talk about the details but said she saw only a fraction of that money.

Kramer and Segura were the obvious gate attractions.

"Jack had a huge ego," Moran said. "He was impossible. Segura would jump all over him. As for me, I was completely outclassed. Pauline was one of the biggies of all time."

Moran's highest ranking was fourth in the United States. In her best year, 1948, she defeated another "biggie," Doris Hart, to reach the semifinals at Forest Hills. But as a tennis player, Moran never approached the enormous reputation she had as a sex symbol, a reputation that still makes her uncomfortable.

"All the publicity on the pro tour was about the lace panties," Moran said. "Someone brought me some clippings the other day. They still make me cringe."

It was easy to see, if not understand, why Moran was perceived as a glamour girl, even before Wimbledon. She lived, after all, in Southern California, played tennis at Charlie Chaplin's house and socialized with the likes of Greta Garbo, Olivia de Havilland and Hedy Lamarr.

But even that was misunderstood, Moran said.

"We went there [to Chaplin's] for tea and tennis on Sunday afternoons," Moran said. "He invited many of the young players. It was just a pleasant afternoon. He was a wonderful little man who told wonderful stories. We'd go out for dinner sometimes. Only once did I have dinner with him alone."

The Hollywood image was further fueled when Moran stood in for a friend in three movies.

"I was an extra," Moran said. "I'd go to the studio and be on the set for lighting, but I had to join the Extras Guild, and it looked like I was trying to work my way up the Hollywood ladder and I wasn't. I was just trying to make a little extra money."

Moran's father was a sound technician and electrician at Universal Studios but held no clout when it came to his daughter.

"He was just a worker," she said. "I went on one visit to the studio with him when I was 15 or 16, and I didn't see anybody important."

Her late-teenage years were not a particularly happy time for Moran or for the rest of the country, which was embroiled in World War II. When Moran was 17, her older brother was declared missing- in-action. Devastating as that was, it inspired her to join the war effort and she soon began the graveyard shift at Douglas Aircraft near her home.

"I pulled parts for bolts," she said. "I was a young kid, but I was pretty good."

Soon after, Moran pitched in by touring military bases and hospitals in California with a group of tennis players that the legendary Bill Tilden put together. Moran also joined Johnny Grant's USO Tour, which starred Ann Sheridan. Occasionally, though she wasn't a singer, Moran would perform a duet.

Though she did not necessarily enjoy entertaining, Moran did enjoy being behind a microphone.

In 1951, after her competitive tennis career was over, Moran went to work for Channel 4 in Los Angeles, where she did a 15-minute interview show with the voice of the Rams, Bob Kelly. In 1955 Moran was offered a job at television station WMGM in New York, where she gave the sports news of the day with Marty Glickman for the next six years.

"It was tough," Moran said. "I was one of the first women doing sports and men, particularly, resented it. I got some awful mail and phone calls."

From WMGM, Moran got involved in the garment business, manufacturing and selling her own line of tennis clothes. At about the same time she returned to California, where she served as hostess at a racket club in Palm Springs.

Both jobs lasted a year and a half. Moran and her partner liquidated the business and paid off their creditors the day before John F. Kennedy was assassinated.

Fortunately for Moran, there was another opportunity, this time in television. She was offered a job co-hosting a daily interview show in Hollywood called *Sundown* with Tom Kennedy. But two weeks before the 13-week segment ended, Moran was fired for referring to the Catholic religion as a political party.

From there it was back to tennis and a teaching job at a Lake Encino club started by former tennis star Alice Marble. Moran charged $6 per half hour and taught 2 1/2 years. During her seemingly endless series of jobs, teaching tennis was the one constant.

"I never think I'm going to teach tennis again, then all of a sudden it rears its head again," Moran said.

In the late '60s Moran was offered a job as tennis hostess [that is what they called women pros] at a resort in the Catskills. But upon arriving in New York and renting an apartment, she learned that the job no longer was available. Again, there was a job waiting, this with World Tennis magazine as advertising manager.

In 1970 Moran made another USO tour, this time to Vietnam. During the trip the helicopter Moran was aboard was shot down. Moran is not sure about anything that happened to her after that. She said she was unable to remember a thing until several years after the accident. Later, she was told that she had broken several bones and dislocated several others.

Physically she recovered and returned again to radio in Los Angeles. She resigned from that job when she learned that her duties as sports director included chaperoning cocktail parties and weekend getaways sponsored by the station. During the '70s, Moran free-lanced as a field rep for a fabric manufacturer and as a columnist for Tennis magazine. She worked for Tennis Unlimited, a promotional company involved with tennis camps, clothes and other tennis-related services. She resigned over a business dispute.

But if the early '70s were difficult on Moran, the rest of the decade would be hell.

In 1975, back in her hometown of Santa Monica, Moran attended a centennial celebration. All she can really recall about the afternoon is that Lawrence Welk and his orchestra were there to perform. Her only other memory is talking to two members of the orchestra after they found her lying on the floor backstage. Her feet had been chained to a chair and she had been beaten and raped.

Not until 1982 did Moran remember that day.

"I have a very strange type of memory," Moran says now. "I black out all the very worst memories. It's like something is protecting me from remembering."

In 1977 her mother died [her father had died in 1960] and virtually the only thing remaining of the Moran family's estate was their Santa Monica home, a Victorian structure with a view of the ocean. The house was worth more than $1 million and the taxes alone nearly wiped her out. In 1982 she began a book about tennis in the '40s and early '50s.

"I actually started it in hopes of getting a $5,000 advance for the taxes on my house," she said.

She completed the book, but when it was apparent no one was interested—"They said it wasn't contemporary enough"—Moran mailed a copy of the manuscript to an editor friend and burned the original. "I just wanted to get rid of it," she said.

Teaching tennis to keep afloat, Moran applied for job after job. "I flunked out on every application," she said. "Maybe my age was against me, maybe it was the picture I presented. I don't know."

Borrowing against her mortgage, the money soon ran out, and on April 26, 1986, Moran was on the street, evicted from her home of 22 years.

For five months she lived with friends. Then it was back to teaching tennis, first at the Los Angeles Tennis Club, then, after she found the job at the zoo, on a sporadic basis at whatever court she could find.

"It keeps me fed for a couple of days," Moran said.

Five days a week Moran takes the bus to the zoo, where she works the counter at the souvenir shop. "I'd work seven, but they require two days off a week."

She doesn't mind it, she says, mostly because it keeps her busy, with little time to think about things she'd much rather not think about.

Always adventurous, she started flying lessons not long ago but stopped because she couldn't afford any more.

Moran was married three times, beginning at age 19. That marriage, to a former RAF pilot, was annulled. Two other marriages ended in divorce. She has no children.

Regrets? "I certainly would have had a college education," she said. "But if I carry any emotional scars, it's from emotional rejection from a lover, not something like lace panties."

She hasn't seen Tinling since the late '60s, though he says he has tried to contact her on several occasions. Friends say she finds it difficult to see anyone these days. Once one of the most photographed women in the world, she is now highly self-conscious of her looks and refuses to have her picture taken.

Tinling said he is still asked about "Gorgeous Gussie" and thinks of her often.

"Tell Gussie when you see her that I love her dearly," he said several weeks ago. "One can never forget what we went through. We're both probably a little scarred, but we're much wiser people, I believe."

Wiser, perhaps. Hardened, certainly. Most definitely shaken. But for everything Moran has been through, for everything she faces today, she is holding on. You wonder how. Moran isn't always sure herself.

"I guess you could say I'm treading water," Moran said. It was like Vietnam in 1970. I remember our chopper being hit and going down and I remember being in this cold water and being told to 'hold on.' It's sort of like treading water. You don't know where you are exactly, but you know if you hold on hard enough, you won't sink."

(June 18, 1988)

Melissa Isaacson covers the Chicago Bulls for the Chicago Tribune and is writing a book on the team for publication in the fall of 1994. A graduate of the University of Iowa, her athletic career peaked in 1979 when her high school basketball team won the Illinois state title by beating a team that starred Jackie Joyner.

NAVRATILOVA AND TENNIS: A SIMPLY PERFECT MATCH

by Sally Jenkins
Washington Post

MARTINA NAVRATILOVA DOESN'T PLAY TENNIS SO MUCH AS IT PLAYS HER. Within the vividly marked confines of the court, she has explored her character, disguised nothing and invented herself too. She has no more secrets.

For 17 years tennis has been Navratilova's chief love and endeavor, and once it was her method of escape from oppression. Before countless opponents and stadium crowds she has vented her emotions and flaws. There is very little of her that hasn't been revealed in it, whether it be her defection from Czechoslovakia at the U.S. Open in 1975, or that she cries easily, or her personal life. It gave her a Porsche and those two chunks of diamond in her ears.

"It's an extension of my being," she said. "And where else am I going to make that kind of money?"

The diamonds are ever present, cut and gleaming, and at times they are joined by a smile of surpassing largesse, white and brilliant as a third gem. It is her most attractive aspect, and when it appears, the rest of her features—the hard but fragile cheekbones, hollow and deep-set eyes—seem to suddenly settle in their rightful places. It can be brought forth by children, dogs or jewelry, but it is evoked most frequently and rewardingly when she moves around the tennis court with a little bit of heaven in her.

At 33, Navratilova is rediscovering an abiding affection for the sport. Her knees and ankles sometimes ache, she doesn't see the ball as well as she did, and all these teenagers with vacant, serial-killer expressions are milling around the locker room. But that's all right, because something very interesting is happening. In the aftermath of a painful two-year period, she has confronted the fact that she is no longer No. 1 and chased by the world, but No. 2 and chasing, with time dwindling, 20-year-old Grand Slam winner Steffi Graf of West Germany.

And she is relishing it.

"It used to be, I just wanted to be No. 1," she said. "I didn't care how. Now it's a combination of the competition, and the ability to do with a ball what I want with it. I mean exactly. To put it on a dime, with the right speed and the right spin. I love that. And giving it everything, my heart, my soul, and my body too."

There are several events on the women's tennis tour that Navratilova will attempt this season to win for the 10th time. Last week she won her 10th trophy at the Virginia Slims of Chicago, this week she is pursuing her 10th Virginia Slims of Washington title. But the magic number for Navratilova is nine. That would be the number of Wimbledon singles titles she would possess were she to win one more. She shares the All-England record at eight with Helen Wills Moody.

Graf has beaten Navratilova in the last two Wimbledon finals, and she knows that to loft the trophy again, it is inevitable that she meet the West German. That's all right too, because Navratilova has come to enjoy the mere "process" of seeking, at her relatively advanced age in tennis, to get better.

"I'm cursed by her and blessed by her at the same time," Navratilova said. "Because of her, I'm a better player and I'm still in the game. But because of her, I haven't won my ninth Wimbledon. She's faster, bigger, taller, and she hits the ball harder. If I can beat her when she's at her prime, and when I'm past mine, that would be an accomplishment."

It was a wrenching realization for Navratilova to come to, that after winning 17 Grand Slam singles titles, fourth all-time among women, and holding the longest winning streaks in tennis at 74 and 58 consecutive match victories, she was mortal. And it made her directionless and resentful and tired.

"It just wasn't easy," she said. "When I was winning all those grand slams, it was like 'Oh, another one.' I'd give anything to win one now."

At a loss, Navratilova turned to Billie Jean King, who made the Wimbledon semifinals at 39. A year ago a wretched Navratilova called King and said, "Am I too old?" King replied, "If I had your body, I'd still be playing." The result of the conversation was that King agreed to assist Craig Kardon in coaching Navratilova. They began just before Wimbledon last year, and Navratilova credits King with reawakening her game.

Navratilova still muses about what happened to her game and psyche over the last two years. Just the other day she decided it may have dated to 1986, a season in which she eventually parted with longtime coach Mike Estep. As she made up her schedule for that season, she crossed off every tournament she could until she had the bare minimum of 12. She refused interviews and public appearances. She had the flu six times, the symptoms of an ulcer, bad knees and bad ankles; she was anemic.

She did not get any happier in 1987, and in 1988 she unraveled totally, failing to reach the final of a Grand Slam event. Friend Judy Nelson told her, "Even when you're winning, you're unhappy."

Navratilova now suspects she was harboring a case of burnout. "I should have known what was going on then," she said. "My body was rebelling because I just didn't want to be out there. Billie Jean really made me take stock and decide what I wanted to do."

Accountability has been King's chief lesson to Navratilova—to admit what was wrong and fix it, rather than deny it.

"She's just accepted a lot of responsibility for herself, and she's a happier person for it," Kardon said. "In everything, not just on the court. Basically she's learned that if you look for bad things, you'll find them."

King and Kardon also discovered that Navratilova, complete as she was, had some curious technical weaknesses in her game. They went unnoticed primarily because she is so strong that she could cover them up. But in the two years without a coach after Estep left, they grew to glaring proportions. Painstakingly, she has had to relearn some things, simple things like the split step as she approaches the net. If she can move more efficiently, she can make up for the step or two of speed she has lost through age.

She also turned to other previously ignored resources like tactics. King has taught her how to look for patterns, to mix up her game more, and convinced her to try to adapt to a match, as opposed to muscling through it. "I was real stubborn," she said.

Navratilova's on-court performance can be charted by two things: her mindset and her serve. If either is out of kilter she is fretful. Experienced opponents know her various demeanors all too well. Since Chris Evert retired after the U.S. Open they have kept close company on an exhibition tour, trading confidences and opening their friendship beyond the competitive. Evert has begun telling Navratilova what she looked for, small subtle tendencies. That she frequently knew where shots were going, from certain expressions and body language.

"I always knew when I had you," she said.

"Thanks coach," Navratilova said wryly to Evert. "Why didn't you tell me before?"

Navratilova never was more readable than in the U.S. Open final last year, when for 15 games she routed Graf. Ahead by a service break and just two games from victory, she could not win them. Her serve was broken by Graf in the 16th game, when she double faulted. King has made Navratilova watch the tape of that match over and over again. Navratilova writhes in her chair as she watches, with the sure knowledge that she should have won it. "It makes her crazy," Nelson said. King's intention is to make Navratilova confront what went wrong; she retreated and gave it away.

"I pulled back," Navratilova said. "And it cost me the match."

That was especially difficult to pick up from. One facet that Navratilova never had to rely on much before, but does now, is fortitude. A perusal of her victories shows that many of them came with ease—not much was required of her when her athleticism was so surpassing. It is a quality she certainly possesses, having dealt with some lonely years after her defection, and some unpleasantly public revelations about her personal life, but she never has particularly displayed it on court.

"I knew I had a lot more than people gave me credit for," she said. "But I also know that for a long time I was depending on my athletic ability too much."

A certain perspective helps. She has allowed herself to return to her first love, skiing, with a new ranch in Aspen, Colorado. She is an insatiable reader who combs the newspapers for news of the changes in Eastern Europe, which makes her "ecstatic." She plans a trip there in May, her first since she played in the Federation Cup in 1986, which at the time was her first since she left in '75. She enjoys playing the role of the grand dame on tour, and the deeper appreciation she is beginning to receive from audiences.

There also is the lingering sense in Navratilova that she pleases the game as much as it pleases her. She loves the smooth fluidity of her play, the response of a crowd to her acrobatics. "When they go 'Woooo,'" she said. "I know sometimes when I twist and hit a shot, it can look like ballet." She is endlessly intrigued by the texture and feel of striking a ball.

"That little yellow tennis ball," she said. "I still haven't hit it perfectly yet."

(February 23, 1990)

Sally Jenkins is a senior writer for Sports Illustrated *where she covers college football and tennis. A graduate of Stanford, she previously worked at the* Washington Post, *the* San Francisco Examiner, *the* San Francisco Chronicle *and the* Los Angeles Herald Examiner. *She was nominated for a Pulitzer Prize in 1985 for her coverage of the death of Len Bias.*

Reliving the Battle of the Sexes

by Janis Carr
Orange County Register

Bras burned on street corners throughout America. Women dropped their frying pans and picked up picket signs as demonstrations hit the nation's cities.

ERA.

NOW.

Abortion rights. Equal pay for equal work. They sought it all.

In 1973, women from all walks of life were demanding equality. But the path for women to take a more active role in science, sports and politics at that time was blocked. Not until a bandy-legged bespectacled man of 55 challenged a woman to a tennis match did America finally seem to listen. Neither Gloria Steinem nor Betty Friedan sparked the women's movement more than Bobby Riggs when he played Billie Jean King in the Battle of the Sexes at the Houston Astrodome two decades ago today.

"Everyone was getting into the man versus woman thing," King, 50, said. "At that time, it was the height of the women's movement, and 1973 is when everything was changing.

"But I did think it (the match) would have an impact because of the exposure worldwide."

Said Riggs, now 75: "Billie and I did wonders for women's tennis. They owe me a piece of their checks."

Riggs was an accomplished player in the 1930s and '40s, having won both the U.S. Open and Wimbledon singles titles.   In 1939, Riggs won the triple crown at Wimbledon, taking the singles, doubles and mixed doubles titles.

But by 1973, Riggs was a self-described male-chauvinist and hustler, who told anyone who would listen that women tennis players didn't deserve equal prize money because they weren't as talented. And he was eager to prove his point. For money.

So Riggs challenged King to a $5,000 match. King refused.

King, one of the forerunners of the professional women's tour, was in the process of organizing the Women's Tennis Association, which had been formed when the U.S. Tennis Association and Virginia Slims tours merged.

"I was working so hard," King said, "working very hard constantly off the court as well as having to play on the tour, that I really didn't have time to even ponder the idea of playing Bobby Riggs."

165

So Riggs, still looking for a taker, contacted Margaret Court, one of the other top women at the time. Riggs upped the ante to $10,000 and Court jumped.

In her book, "You Have Come a Long Way," King wrote that the match, played in San Diego on Mother's Day 1973, "took on political overtones that made it bigger than any women's match had ever been."

Women all over the world now were counting on Court to win. Doctors. Lawyers. Authors. Even housewives with frying pans.

Court, rattled by the hype and Riggs's constant blathering about the 415 vitamins he chewed daily, was destroyed, 6-1, 6-2. Court called it the biggest mistake she ever made.

"If Margaret had been playing even average for herself," King said, "I felt she probably would have beaten Bobby. But she didn't; she had a bad day and that's the breaks."

King said she knew then she had to play Riggs. So the match was set for Sept. 20, 1973, at the Houston Astrodome. A winner-take-all $100,000 match. Best three-of-five. Regular court, regular rules. No handicaps. Tennis on an equal basis.

Man versus woman, straight up.

"I knew once we announced the match," King recalled, "that my life would never be the same, and it wasn't. I knew it would have a big impact one way or another."

King wrote she was so nervous she felt sick. Her mouth was dry and she was nauseated.

"A hundred thoughts flashed through my head," she wrote. "I thought about my career and my dreams as a child. I thought about women and low self-esteem, and I thought about athletics and acceptance."

She also had to keep thinking how she was going to beat this male-chauvinist, vitamin-popping, hustling old man. King decided to keep Riggs in long rallies and hopefully tire out his aging legs.

At match time King arrived on a litter, while Riggs arrived in a rickshaw. In a gesture of goodwill, she gave him a pig adorned in a pink bow. He gave her an enormous carmel sucker.

A crowd of 30,472 watched from the stands, while another estimated 40 million watched on television. For many, it was the first tennis match they had ever seen.

And what a match they saw. After struggling through the first set, King breezed in the second and third to win, 6-4, 6-3, 6-3.

King said her victory wasn't any great athletic feat. She was after all, 26 years younger than Riggs.

"But I think it helped a lot of people realize that everyone can have skills whether you are a man or a woman," King said. "That women are not always the nervous chokes of the world. That women can walk and chew gum at the same time, and that women's self-esteem went up after that day."

(September 20, 1993)

Janis Carr covers college basketball and tennis for the Orange County Register. *A graduate of Cal State Fullerton, she previously worked at the* Los Angeles Times, *the* Kansas City Star *and the* Palm Beach Post.

JENNIFER CAPRIATI'S HELPING HANDS

by Kelly Carter
Dallas Morning News

NOT SINCE CHRIS EVERT TURNED PRO IN 1972 AT AGE 18 HAS THE AMERICAN public been so smitten with a player.

As Jennifer Capriati practiced for her first U.S. Open last Wednesday in Mahwah, New Jersey, a group of fans, many of whom were adults, clung to a fence and peered through the wire at her. When she finished, the children clamored for her autograph. Although she thrives on the attention, "It's kind of weird to me that they want to see me or want my autograph," she said with a giggle.

Giggling comes with being a 14-year-old. Although she plays way beyond her years, the 5-7, 135-pound Capriati doesn't find it hard to act her age. "At home I have friends," she said. "I hang out with them, watch movies. I like to dance and listen to music."

The price of success is a stiff one, however.

"It's very tough for her because she is so outgoing and so social," said Tommy Thompson, one of her coaches and part of the broad Capriati support group. "She does know what she's missing when she sees the other kids going here or doing this and having free time and she doesn't have it."

Capriati became a household name this year, but some tennis followers had been eagerly awaiting 1990. They couldn't wait until March 28, when she turned 14.

A Women's International Professional Tennis Council rule restricting players from turning professional until they turned 14 was changed to allow them to start in the month of their 14th birthday. Another WIPTC rule was altered, allowing 14-year-olds to play in 12 major tournaments instead of 10. This was all done, some will say, for Capriati's benefit.

Her arrival has given women's tennis, especially American women's tennis, a needed shot in the arm.

She whacks the ball with more power than many adults and makes more money than most. But off the court, she still acts and is treated like the teenager she is. Since turning pro, the New York-born, Florida-based Capriati has earned $192,518 on the Kraft General Foods World Tour, a mere pittance compared with the $5.7 million her endorsements could earn her in the next five years. Yet for all the fortune and fame (she has appeared on the covers of *Sports Illustrated* and *Newsweek* and "Prime Time Live" did a piece on her), she still must be in bed no later than 10:30 p.m.

Despite the riches, her mother, Denise, controls the purse strings on shopping trips. "I don't really spend a lot," said the bubbly Capriati, who will make her U.S. Open debut Monday at Flushing Meadow. "When I go shopping, I have to go with my mom, and she still has to okay what I get."

Capriati, a ninth grader, used to attend public school but switched to the Palmer Academy on the Saddlebrook grounds last semester and made straight A's. For the 75 students who will attend this semester, education is secondary. They are there mainly to improve their tennis. Jo Palmer, who along with her husband, Norman, runs the 11-year-old academy, says it's beneficial for Capriati to be surrounded by other tennis players at school.

"They already know each other, and they know what they're doing in tennis, so they don't have to talk about tennis," said Palmer, who is an instruction supervisor. "They can talk about music and all of the other things they're interested in. That's important for Jennifer because she can't live just tennis."

When she is not at the academy, she is surrounded by her entourage. It includes her mother, a flight attendant for Pan Am who travels with her to all the tournaments. There's also her brother, Steven, 11, manager John Evert, coaches Thompson and Tom Gullikson and hitting partner Richard Ashby. Team Capriati, if you will, is run by her father, Stefano, a 55-year-old former stuntman and onetime assistant movie director who introduced his daughter to tennis 11 years ago and has continued to coach her.

"Sometimes it seems like, yeah, there are maybe too many people around or too many people involved," Ashby said. "I guess it could get out of hand if people start trying to do too much or do more than they're supposed to. But for the most part, it's worked out real well because people do what they're supposed to do. Everybody has to do what's best for Jennifer."

One of the biggest decisions was to turn pro. No one criticizes that. As a junior, she won the French Open, Wimbledon and U.S. Hardcourts 18s, U.S. Clay Courts 18s and Easter Bowl 16s and was a quarter finalist at the U.S. Open and the Orange Bowl.

"It would have been stupid for her not to (turn pro)," said Andrea Jaeger, a teenage sensation forced to retire early because of injuries. "If you can win all your junior tournaments and stay in it, you're going to regress."

Tracy Austin, who won the U.S. Open in 1979 at age 17, agreed. "She had no place else to go in juniors. There are some other cases where people turned pro too early."

It doesn't look like Capriati is about to fizzle. She made it to the finals in her first pro tournament, losing to Gabriela Sabatini. She's still in search of her first tournament victory and has yet to beat a top-five player. That's bound to change.

"My goal in life is to become No. 1," said Capriati, who figured to crack the top 30 or 20 at most, in her first year. "I just want to do the best that I can do, be the best that I can be, and whatever that is is fine because I'll know I tried my best."

Stefano said his daughter needs plenty of people involved because tennis is such an individual sport and she would become bored working with just one person. "Jennifer is the type that needs variety," said the Italian-born Stefano. "I put the puzzle together. She's young, and she doesn't know yet. I see who is the right person to be with Jennifer or not.

"I want the best for Jennifer. I give to her what she needs, and I think I have experience enough and I know what is good for her. If I were a tennis father, I would be screaming and punching her. I sometimes must be very strict as a father. I must be there. If I'm not there to protect her, who is going to protect her?"

Thompson, who coached, among others, Vitas Gerulaitis for five years, said the support system "has worked out well so far. People say, 'How does this work?' It's sort of unique, but everybody's got their place. There's been very, very, very little if any friction. Everybody understands what their role is."

Capriati has her own shoe by Diadora, which also gave her a clothing contract. She has a racket deal with Prince, and endorsements with Oil of Olay, Texaco and Gatorade.

Thompson used to coach Evert and says they are still good friends. If the pro thought the manager was stretching Capriati too thin, he wouldn't hesitate to say so.

"I know John well enough to call and say, 'Look, I know the money's good, but if she can't play six months down the road, then where are you going to be?'"

Stefano and Denise always have enjoyed tennis. When Jennifer was an infant, her parents took her on the court with them because they didn't have any place to leave her. Before she learned to walk, Capriati was able to hold a racket. By the age of 3, she was getting lessons from her father. A year and a half later, she had her first hitting machine.

When she was 5, Stefano enlisted the help of Jimmy Evert, who had coached his daughter, Chris. Stefano makes it clear that he always has been his daughter's coach and said he went to Jimmy Evert because of his experience with Chris and the proximity in Florida. "It was easy for me, and he knew a lot and was a nice person to the kids," Stefano said. "If I make a mistake, four eyes see much better than two eyes."

When Jennifer was 7, she played her first tournament. Winning didn't come immediately, but that didn't bother her father. "She was stroking the ball well, so I was very happy," he said.

After a few years, Jennifer ended up at the Rick Macci International Tennis Academy at the Grenelefe Resort in Florida. Stefano said he sought an academy not for coaching but for training.

For the past year, Jennifer has trained at Harry Hopman School, an academy at Saddlebrook Golf & Tennis resort near Tampa. Although nothing has been decided yet, Stefano said, there's a possibility she might go to Broken Sound, in Boca Raton, before the year is up.

"Big" starring Tom Hanks, was a box-office hit about a 12-year-old who was granted his wish of being an adult. "Look Who's Talking" was another success about a baby with the voice of 35-year-old Bruce Willis. Both movies are favorites of Jennifer Capriati's. It's no wonder. Her life lies somewhere between the two movies.

(August 26, 1990)

Kelly Carter, who covers the Los Angeles Lakers for the Orange County Register, *received a degree in journalism from the University of Southern California in 1985. She has worked in Iowa City, Pittsburgh and Dallas.*

FOUR

COACH, TEACHER, ZEN MASTER, BOSS

Driving Force

by Jackie MacMullan
Boston Globe

"I am Somebody. I may not be rich, but I am Somebody."
—Quotation posted at Shelburne Recreation Center

Alfreda Harris drives a Mercedes. Cars and jewelry, those are her weaknesses.

It took some doing to get the car paid off, especially on her modest salary as director of the Shelburne Recreation Center. But now it belongs to her, and she proudly parks it on Washington Street, so the kids can look at it, envy it, touch it, dream about it.

"There's nothing wrong with wanting a Mercedes," said Harris, who has worked for the city of Boston for 26 years. "But it's a matter of how did I get mine, and how did you get yours?

"I got all the black policemen and firemen in town together. I had them bring all their nice cars up to the Shelburne and we parked them out front. BMWs, Cadillacs, Mercedes.

"Then I had the policemen and firemen explain how they got their cars. How they took their paycheck down to the bank and had some money taken out each week.

"When they drive their cars, they don't have to look over their shoulders. They don't have to risk the lives of themselves or their families.

"I don't sell drugs to get my car. I don't sell guns to get my car. You might get your Mercedes quicker than me, but you may never live long enough to enjoy it."

Why should these kids listen to Alfreda Harris, a lifelong resident of Boston, a basketball legend in this city? Should they care she was the first and only woman to coach in the Boston Shootout? Should they be impressed with the countless citations, commendations, plaques, awards, ribbons, statues (okay, okay, no statues yet) that clutter her office at the center? Alfreda is so bogged down with AAU basketball trophies, she started giving them to the young kids who have not yet won their own.

"Our motto is education through recreation," she said. "We happen to have a lot of talented [basketball] kids here. But we started to realize that it was no good if they didn't finish college. It's fine to win all those trophies, but nobody was doing anything past high school."

175

Harris doesn't like excuses. Her athletes have many; she accepts none. You want respect? Earn it. You want a Mercedes? Earn it.

They have seen her earn it a thousand times over. They come to the center in the morning, and she's already there. They leave the center at night, and she still hasn't locked up.

Her time is their time. Ask Alfreda about the last movie she saw, and she'll tell you it was *Cornbread, Earl and Me*. The movie came out in 1975.

Why do these kids listen? Because Alfreda is Somebody. She may not be rich, but she is definitely Somebody.

Michelle Edwards was still a Nobody when she dribbled up the floor and a defender cut in front, sending her sprawling.

"I flipped over twice," she said. "I skinned my knees really bad, so I sat on the floor and cried."

No one offered to help the young girl up, not even the coach who terrified her. In fact, "Miss Harris" glared at Edwards in disgust.

"I got the word: no babies on the team," said Edwards. "She told me to come back tomorrow, and to come back tougher."

Edwards did. She became so tough she went to Iowa on a full basketball scholarship, where she earned All-America honors. She graduated, played professionally in Italy and is currently training with the U.S. Pan American team.

"I never would have made it without Miss Harris," she said.

Then again, who would? asks Robin Christian, a former Jamaica Plain star who followed Edwards to Iowa.

"You learn what discipline means here, and it's something you don't soon forget," she said.

The discipline is pounded home through an aggressive, no-nonsense approach, through a voice that is both booming and unmistakable, through a mix of intimidation and love that's invaluable.

"You don't see guys with hats on, you don't see graffiti, and it's always 'Miss Harris,'" said her long-time friend, UMass-Boston athletic director Charlie Titus. "The respect is always there."

Titus knows firsthand. He remembers hanging down by the park as a teen-ager, flirting with the girls and cussing with the guys.

"All of a sudden, this lady comes over and tells me in no uncertain terms that my kind of language would not be tolerated," he said. "Believe me, I didn't question her."

There are no questions about Alfreda's rules, because even if you can't shoot a basketball, she will get you back in school, bail you out of jail, help you care for your children. She is tough because the world is tough.

"Kids like to be disciplined," she said. "They want direction. They like to be taught."

Harris understands the pitfalls. She is the first to admit drugs are a problem, the dropout rate is too high, and too many children grow up without parental supervision.

She has tried to make the center an escape from all that. Sports are the enticement that draws them to the Shelburne, but once there, she convinces them to utilize the afterschool study programs, the SAT preparation courses, the counseling sessions.

"We never say, 'If you don't come to Shelburne every day, we won't help you,'" Harris explained. "Everyone in life is allowed one mistake. We have kids who are incarcerated. I believe in most cases it's the result of peer pressure.

"If a kid comes in here and my staff sees a knife, we don't throw him out. We find out why he has it. We find out why he thinks he needs it.

"People don't take the time to talk to kids anymore. They are smart, and funny, and even the kids you think are really bad are really just confused, or pressured."

Harris said the thing that disturbs her most is how quickly young people resort to violence. She has held meetings with local gangs at the Shelburne through two federally funded programs—HIP (Hope in Progress) and Winner's Circle—and has been encouraged by the results.

In fact, it was through those meetings she met Kevin Devonish and John Blake, two talented basketball players who were mixed up in gangs, but are now attending Kilgore Junior College in Texas and are hoping to transfer to a four-year university next season.

"I don't believe the theory that says if you are black and from Roxbury, Mattapan or Dorchester, and you have a single-parent family, you are doomed to failure," she said. "I was brought up in a single-parent home. My husband died when my son was 17 years old. That's a critical age, but my son grew up to be a fine young man."

Harris feels the media perpetuates negativism about young blacks by reporting on drugs and violence, yet virtually ignoring students who are accomplishing good things in the community. As a result, she says, people think the worst first.

"I'll never forget Robin Christian's guidance counselor telling her college was hard," said Harris. "Well, life is hard. Robin graduated from Iowa. She works here at the center, helping kids. Her guidance counselor wanted her to sign up for the Army."

The Shelburne Center has produced some of the top women's basketball talent in the country, including Edwards, Christian, former Old Dominion star Medina Dixon, Tonya Cardoza of Virginia, who made a trip to the Final Four last season, and Averill Roberts, who just finished her sophomore season at Ohio State.

There are many, many other women as well, yet the men's pool in Boston has never been as fruitful or successful.

Why?

"Alfreda Harris," answered Titus. "She has taught those girls discipline, responsibility, and regardless of what happens in basketball, she has told them she expects them to finish school. The boys simply have not had the same guidance." Dixon, who has played professionally in Japan the past few years and is also a member of the Pan Am team, has one semester left at Old Dominion. The school would like to retire her number; Miss Harris would like Medina to finish school before she accepts the honor.

"I'm going to do it," says Dixon, "but not because Miss Harris or my mother or anyone else wants me to. It's because I want to.

"I can take responsibility for myself. And that's what maturing is all about. That's what Miss Harris is trying to teach the kids."

The kids are not just female. More and more young men are counting on Harris to handle the recruiting process for them. When Butch Wade began looking, interested coaches—including Bill Frieder, who eventually signed him at Michigan—were expected to conduct their official home visits at the Shelburne Center.

The coaching staffs at Villanova, Boston College, Maryland, Connecticut, Northeastern, to name a few, have been through the center.

BC head coach Jim O'Brien has not yet landed a Shelburne alumnus (Jesse Martin chose Maryland over the Heights), but he continues to come, and is determined to convince "Miss Harris" he can be trusted with the future of a Shelburne prospect.

"She is very, very tough—in a positive sense," said O'Brien. "But I understand why she's that way. Her No. 1 priority is to make sure kids do the right thing.

"A lot of it boils down to familiarity. If a stranger comes in trying to sell a school, he's going to have a difficult time. She's not going to be too quick to give up her kids to people she doesn't trust."

One coach who requested anonymity said Harris has been a source of frustration to his program.

"I wish she would let the kids make up their own minds," said the coach. "She's calling too many of the shots."

Harris says that's not so, and it's clear such implications upset her. She doesn't get paid much to work at the Shelburne, and the time she donates takes away from her two grown children and her five grandchildren. She has literally devoted her life to the youth of Roxbury, and 90 percent of the time, it's a thankless job.

"I get nothing out of this," she said. "No money, no nothing. What I do get is the satisfaction of these young folks coming up through our community and prospering in life."

There have been heartaches, of course. She has watched young boys die, and others rot in prison. She has seen young women fall prey to crack cocaine.

Each time one of those kids slips away from her grasp, there is an inevitable wave of sadness and disappointment. But, not long after, that voice is booming out instructions again, because there are still plenty of kids who are willing to listen.

"I know it's hard for her," said Dixon. "But she has to learn to let go. Sooner or later, we all have to learn to take care of business."

There are many who return to Shelburne to share the lessons they've learned. One such woman is Cheri Cope, who played for Harris when she was coach at Roxbury Community College. Those close to the Shelburne believe Harris is grooming Cope to be her successor. That day, concedes Alfreda, may not be far off.

"I'm thinking of retiring," she said. "I'm tired. They think I'm joking, but in the human service field, there is no such thing as time to yourself. Your time is never your own, not if you are doing it the right way."

The right way means fielding hundreds of recruiting calls at home so your player doesn't have to deal with the aggravation. The right way means taking a youngster to court to plead his case, because the parents are working or busy of just don't care.

The right way is remembering that after all the yelling and coaching and lecturing, what kids need most is to understand you care.

"The first time I came back to the Shelburne after college," said Edwards, "I saw Miss Harris, and she said to me, 'Where's my hug?' I was looking all around, making sure she meant me. I never will forget that."

Edwards has been trying to milk that show of affection ever since. She tried to call Alfreda by her childhood nickname of "Bootsie" the other day, but permission has not yet been granted to cease the "Miss Harris" salutation.

That doesn't mean they can't poke fun at their mentor, whose tattered uniform from her days as a forward for Girls High in Roxbury hangs behind her office door.

"She says she's played," said Edwards, laughing. "I'd like to see the video."

What none of them would like to see is the day Alfreda takes down the uniform, gives away the last of the trophies and finally takes that long vacation in the tropics she's been talking about.

Some people can be replaced. Alfreda Harris, whose weaknesses are cars, jewelry and kids, isn't one of them.

(July 14, 1991)

Jackie MacMullan covers the NBA for the Boston Globe. A graduate of the University of New Hampshire, she previously covered college football and basketball for the Globe as well as the Red Sox. Her greatest accomplishment, she says, is Alyson Boyle, born March 23, 1992.

Inside Baseball:
The Passion of Sharon Jones

by Ann Killion
San Jose Mercury News

THE LETTER IS ADDRESSED:
  Sharon NIGGER Jones
  Mills College
  Oakland, California

Dear Professor Jones,
  When people see that Mills College has small-brained niggers like you, they will stop paying to send their children there and it will go out of business.

Signed by name and completed with a return address, this is one of the more formal pieces of correspondence Sharon Jones has received recently. Others are profane and threatening.

The letters have flown in from across the country and from places close to home, postmarked Hayward, Castro Valley, Ohio, Florida. They have landed on Jones's Julia Morgan desk in the hushed offices of the College Relations department at Mills College. There they are stacked up and handed over to the FBI.

Sharon Jones is a soft-spoken administrator at a private women's college who has unnerved the national pastime. By speaking out against racial slurs, she has drawn a verbal assault down upon herself and rocked baseball's front offices and fan base.

"I think she's had a big impact on the way the average American views baseball ownership," says Joe Morgan, a Hall of Fame player and baseball broadcaster. "It's like the Rodney King beating. A lot of people believe these things happen but they've never had the evidence."

Jones, 47, broke out of her private, comfortable world in December with allegations about what had passed for acceptable behavior among billionaire baseball owners. The implications of Jones's charges have shaken the owners' private and considerably more comfortable world, and have irrevocably damaged at least one of them—Marge Schott of the Cincinnati Reds. Schott now says baseball ownership may be over for her.

Some see Jones as a heroine, a modern-day Rosa Parks. Not weary from standing at the back of the bus, but from battling racism on a daily basis.

Previously, this tall, dignified woman's accomplishments included being the highest-ranking black woman in baseball and having an outstanding collection of African-American art.

"I'm proud of her," says Alameda County supervisor Mary King. "She did not wear the banner of activism, but she came forward."

Others question Jones's memory and credibility. Some denounce her as a whistle-blower and a trouble maker.

"I think the real question is how good Sharon Jones's memory is," says Jerry Reinsdorf, owner of the Chicago White Sox and co-chair of baseball's equal opportunity committee, hastily formed last winter in response to the uproar over Schott's comments about blacks, Jews and the Japanese. Schott was fined $25,000 and suspended from baseball for a season.

Reinsdorf concedes that Jones has forced baseball to re-examine itself. "She called attention to Marge Schott's actions," he says. "She helped us focus attention on that . . . . And that incident caused us to take another look at where we are."

The result is an extensive minority involvement program, unveiled in March, baseball's most aggressive effort yet to diversify the ranks.

"She brought a lot of visibility to the situation," says Giants' owner Peter Magowan, a member of the newly formed equal opportunity committee. "I don't think we're going to drop this issue. I'd like to think we don't need Sharon Jones to remind us what's right."

Sharon Jones's family has been in the Bay Area for five generations. The youngest of 10 children, she was raised in South Berkeley and attended Berkeley High. Her oldest brother played baseball for the San Francisco Sea Lions of the Negro League, but she only vaguely remembers that. She does recall meeting Jackie Robinson when he was having dinner at a neighbor's house. And as an adolescent she wrote a love letter to Minnesota player Tony Oliva.

Otherwise, baseball meant little to Sharon Richardson growing up. She wanted to be an artist.

"But my family felt that wasn't a stable job for a black person," she says. "They discouraged me."

So she went the stable route, taking a series of behind-the-scenes jobs that tapped her abilities to organize and support others.

She met Terry Jones, who had played basketball at Idaho State, when he was playing in an "old guys" basketball game in Berkeley. They married and Terry, then a probation officer, decided to get his master's in social work at UC Berkeley. Sharon worked as a receptionist and administrative assistant at Kaiser Industries. She took night business courses and attended Contra Costa College part-time.

Terry Jones earned a doctorate in 1972 and eventually went to work at Cal State Hayward. The next year their son was born, and a year or so later Sharon Jones began studying full-time at Mills College. In 1976, at age 30 and pregnant with her second child, she earned a teaching credential.

Jones credits her friend Bonnie Guiton, former assistant U.S. Secretary of Education and now dean of the University of Virginia business school, with inspiring her to improve herself.

"She had lots of ambition, and she encouraged me to strive for more," Jones says.

In the fall of 1976, Terry Jones took a leave to teach at the University of Pennsylvania, and Sharon worked at the Wharton School of Business. After two years in the East, Terry returned to Cal State Hayward, where he has worked ever since.

Sharon Jones got a job, through Guiton, as an assistant to Oakland Symphony conductor Calvin Simmons. She went on to work for the Institute for Journalism Education—a non-profit group at UC Berkeley designed to train minority journalists—founded by Oakland Tribune publisher Bob Maynard and run by his wife, Nancy Hicks.

In 1980, when the Oakland A's changed owners, she wrote the Haas family asking for a job.

"I didn't have too much interest in baseball, but I was interested in business," she says. "It sounded like it would be something fun to do. I went to a liberal arts college where I was taught I can do anything."

Jones had attended only one A's game, but it was memorable. Owner Charlie Finley was fond of promotional events, and this was Hot Pants Day. She wore hot pants to get into the game free and in the seventh inning paraded around the field with the other hot pants-wearers.

"That was before I got some social conscience," she says.

By the time Walter Haas Jr. and family bought the A's Jones had both a social conscience and ambition. She knew the San Francisco-based Haas family would need a liaison with Oakland's community. She campaigned for the job, encouraging friends and community leaders to write letters on her behalf. In September 1980, she became the new owners' first hire, an executive assistant to team president Roy Eisenhardt, sharing an office with Eisenhardt and Walter J. Haas, the executive vice president.

She ran their office, coordinated meetings and social functions, interviewed prospective employees, signed on major accounts and was a liaison between the team and major league baseball and the community.

"I thought we had a good relationship," she says. "It was a family-oriented business. I thought they wanted to help make the organization responsive to community needs, and part of my job was to be the eyes and ears in the community."

Jones eventually became the outreach director. She developed educational and community programs involving baseball, started a program to recognize Negro League players, and coordinated players' community involvement. She was a rarity—a black woman in baseball's white male hierarchy.

"It was lots of fun," she says. "I enjoyed every minute of it."

Except for a few minutes in 1987.

On Opening Day 1987, the 40th anniversary of Jackie Robinson's breaking the color barrier on the field, Al Campanis—a front office executive of the Dodgers, the team Robinson had played for—was speaking about minorities in baseball on ABC-TV's "Nightline."

Campanis said that he believed that blacks "lacked some of the necessities" to be field managers. Given the opportunity to back off the statement, Campanis stuck with it, astonishing a national audience.

The flood of negative reaction washed up to the offices of baseball commissioner Peter Ueberroth.

This is Sharon Jones's story: In the wake of Campanis, conference calls between the commissioner's office and all 26 owners were made on a regular, and often spontaneous, basis.

The call that turned baseball upside down came in May or June—Jones doesn't remember the exact date. Because it took several minutes to get 26 people onto the same conference call, Jones was holding on the phone for her boss, Eisenhardt, who had stepped out of the office.

A roll call was taken by the operator. Jones responded by saying who she was and that she was holding for Eisenhardt.

"Everyone on the line knew that I was on the line and that I wasn't one of the good old boys," she says. "Marge Schott wanted to break the ice, I guess. She said, 'I wonder what this call is about today.' So evidently it was a spontaneous call and no agenda went out. And people said, 'I don't know.' And she said, 'I guess it must be about the black thing. I'm damn sick and tired of black thing.'"

Jones adds that Schott, the owner of the Cincinnati Reds went on to say that she "had a nigger that worked for her once."

Upon hearing the word "nigger" Jones said, "This is Sharon Jones. I'm still holding for Roy Eisenhardt."

But, Jones says, Schott continued her story, saying the person she hired didn't work out because he could neither read nor write and before she "would hire another nigger to work for her she would rather hire a trained monkey."

At that point, Jones says, there was dead silence.

"I felt violated and embarrassed," Jones says. "All these people knew me. I was sharing an office with the family. If they came in, they saw me. If they called, they had to speak with me. My picture was in the yearbooks. I had reason to believe they knew who I was."

Jones says Eisenhardt came back and she told him she needed to speak to him after the conference call. Then she went and talked to Haas.

"I told him what happened, that I was upset and hurt and embarrassed and I asked him what he was going to do," she says. "He said, 'When Roy gets off the phone let's talk to him about it.'"

Jones said after her conversation with Eisenhardt, "He pretty much wanted to apologize on behalf of major league baseball right then and there. I told him it wasn't enough and I wanted him to do something about it.

"But nothing was ever done about it."

And nothing would be done for more than five years. Jones continued to work for the A's. Marge Schott continued to run the Cincinnati Reds in eccentric fashion. Each team won a World Series, the Reds earning their rings by sweeping the A's in four games.

In those five years, the status of minorities in baseball improved significantly. After the Campanis incident, minority hiring was stepped up, although the urgency abated after a season or two. The Oakland A's continued to be held up as a model organization for both their hiring practices and their community involvement.

Jones was left alone to ponder Schott's comments and the A's lack of action.

Immediately after the incident, Jones called her friend and spiritual adviser, John Collins, a minister with the Seventh-day Adventist Church.

"She told me what she heard," says Collins, now retired and living in Madera, California. "She never mentioned Marge Schott or any owners by name. I think you have to be black to understand exactly what she was feeling. She just needed to talk to someone for some type of confirmation, to help uplift her spirits."

"It's quite vivid in my mind," says Terry Jones. "It wasn't the most egregious act by a baseball person. It was one in a stack. But she did what she could about it at the time."

Jones mentioned the conversation to Al Williams, a member of the baseball commissioner's security staff, on July 11, 1987, the Saturday before the All-Star game in Oakland.

Williams's attorney has advised him not to comment now. In December Williams told the *New York Times*: "In general conversation she told me about her conversation with Marge Schott. It wasn't expressed to me as though she wanted me to look into it or anything like that. She was just making me aware of people around me, it appeared."

In the fall of 1987, Martin Wyatt, a sportscaster for a Baltimore TV station, came to Oakland to interview Jones for his series, "Shut Out," on the lack of minorities in the front offices of sports franchises. Jones told him about the Schott incident then, though she identified Schott only as "an owner."

Wyatt, now a sports anchor at KGTV in San Francisco, still has the tape. There is the younger Jones, with a softer hairstyle, telling Wyatt, "Yes, there is still racism in baseball. I want to see some action."

"I sent the piece to the NAACP but never got any response," Wyatt says. "I was surprised they didn't do anything about it then."

Jones also told *USA Today* which came to the A's offices to interview her. In a story dated Dec. 4, 1987, the incident is recounted, though—again—Schott is not identified and the word "nigger" is replaced with "black."

Jones told her employers about both interviews. Eisenhardt told her he didn't know what good it would do for her to keep talking about it, Jones says. "I got the word out as best I could, but I enjoyed working there and it wasn't like I was going to quit. I was by myself and I had a choice to make. That was my career. I had seven years in when that thing came up. I did everything that I thought I could do in good conscience so that I could look at myself in the mirror and be happy."

In late November 1992, Jones had to take another look at herself. By now she was the executive director of college relations at her alma mater, Mills, overseeing university publications and acting as a spokeswoman. After 12 years, she had parted amicably with the A's in February 1992.

"This was a better job," she says. "It was more money. And I had pretty much done all that I could do with the A's. I had reached that glass ceiling."

Janet McKay, the new president of Mills, knew Jones through her alumni work. Jones was on the school's board of governors and had been a graduation speaker in 1990.

Jones wasn't looking for a job. "I had to lure her away from the A's," McKay says. Jones called Haas, who was vacationing in Florida, and told him of her decision to leave. He wished her well.

Then, in November, accusations began to fly about Schott's usage of racial and ethnic slurs, emanating from a deposition taken in a lawsuit brought by Tim Sabo, a business manager Schott had fired. Charges and denials filled the nation's sports pages for days. Sabo's credibility was questioned.

"I had a decision to make," Jones says. "My husband pushed me a bit. He brought it to my attention and asked 'What are you going to do about it?'"

Baseball was behind her, Jones at first told her husband. But he felt that she could help someone else who needed support.

"I thought she should let what she knew be heard," Terry Jones says. "I thought it might have some impact . . . .People can't always be silent."

Jones weighed the issue and its possible consequences.

"I thought I'd already come forward," she says. "I didn't want to be hurt anymore. But I knew it was the right thing to do. And from a woman's point of view, I felt kind of mad that when a white male brought it up, it got national attention . . . .And I didn't want to have the double burden of not coming forward. I already felt bad enough when the A's had swept it under the carpet."

So the woman who had always worked behind the scenes decided to step up to the microphone. As she says, "Someone had finally yanked my chain enough."

In the six months since Jones called the *New York Times* to report the Schott incident, no one has publicly corroborated her story. But neither has anyone, aside from Marge Schott, denied it.

Sharon Jones's account of what happened in 1987 has fallen into a gray area of vague memories and skimpy records.

Baseball conducted its own investigation into Jones's statements and other accusations made against Schott. Jones's testimony was clearly the most damning.

"Marge would never have been suspended without Sharon Jones," Joe Morgan says.

But, according to a source close to the investigation, Wally Haas and Roy Eisenhardt testified that they remembered Jones telling them about a phone call, but remembered a slightly different version of events, that it was a one-on-one conversation and not a conference call.

This could be the truth. Or it could be a convenient memory lapse that enables support of Jones without incriminating baseball's brethren.

Jones told baseball investigators that she had kept records of conference calls in a logbook left with the A's. But at the conclusion of the inquiry, officials said they could find no record of the call and did not cite Jones's remarks in their final report on Schott.

"I think the easiest thing in the world for them to do is to call me a liar," Jones says.

White Sox owner Reinsdorf said he believes Jones heard Schott make racist remarks, but says, "The conference call she claims Marge made her comments on is not a call anyone I know remembers being on. There's no question Marge made the comments and Sharon Jones heard them. But it must have been a much smaller call."

Questions about Jones's credibility may have something to do with her gender. "I think people in baseball hear a woman's voice and try to trivialize it," says Richard Lapchick, the director of Northeastern University's Center for the Study of Sport in Society.

Still, baseball owners fined Schott $25,000 and suspended her for the 1993 season, a punishment Jones thinks "is a slap on the wrist."

"That's the residuals from five innings of beer sales," Jones says.

Some believe Schott—one of the few women in baseball, and a controversial, rough-edged character—made a convenient scapegoat.

"She has her flaws," says Joe Morgan, who played the bulk of his career in Cincinnati.

A's executive vice president Haas and former president Eisenhardt were prohibited from commenting during the investigation and won't speak publicly now. Jones said Haas had assured her privately that he remembers the incident.

"I'm very supportive of Sharon," Haas says. "But what's the point of commenting?"

Eisenhardt, now the director of the California Academy of Sciences in San Francisco, says: "I want to reinforce the high degree of respect I have for Sharon. I have reasons for not discussing the incident. I've talked to Sharon about it and she understands."

But she doesn't. And she still is angry that the A's—who have capitalized on their social consciousness—never pursued the issue.

"Even if it was a one-on-one conversation, which it wasn't, what kind of supervisor allows an employee to be badgered?" Jones says. "I'm more disappointed than anything else."

Jones finally got her chance to personally address the owners in February, weeks after the group had decided Schott's penalty. Jones took a support group with her to Phoenix—Terry, Mary King, Bill Patterson of the NAACP, and Marjorie Banks, wife of former Cubs star Ernie Banks.

"I have never felt as much of an outsider," King said. "We were like the elephant in the room that everybody's trying to ignore."

When trying to enter the meeting room, Jones's party was barred by a public relations assistant. Finally Wally Haas escorted them into the room, where you could cut the discomfort with a knife.

"I felt like I got in touch with America in a way I haven't been for a long time because of the circle in which I travel and the county in which I live," said King, the Alameda County supervisor.

Jones gave a detailed speech, underscoring her belief in the institution of baseball and urging the group to take steps to erase prejudice.

"Correcting your racism now makes good business sense," Jones said. "You all knew that I was on the telephone and heard and experienced Mrs. Schott's insults, yet none of you challenged her . . . .How was I to interpret your silence then? And how am I, and the American public, to interpret your silence now?"

Jones presented a seven-point program to help eliminate prejudice in baseball. She did not name the people on the conference call.

"I truly only remember the names of six people on the call," she says. "While I don't feel Marge Schott needs to walk the plank alone, on the other hand, it shouldn't just be six people. It should be the full 26 . . . .I thought about it and I decided to take the high road. They knew and I knew they were lying."

Joe Morgan agrees.

"They know she knows who was on the call," he says. "That's enough to force their hand."

On a rainy March afternoon, Sharon Jones stands on the dais of Allen Temple Baptist Church in Oakland—a few miles from her former work-place at the Oakland Coliseum—and is embraced by the Rev. Jesse Jackson.

"We thank you, Sharon Jones, for speaking up," Jackson says.

There is a standing ovation.

"Many of us in the black middle class are silent," county supervisor Mary King says. "By speaking up, Sharon may allow a new kind of move-ment, one that says it's okay to come forward and not be afraid."

Jones says ballplayers have called her to say she has their full support. They just aren't willing to say so publicly—until their careers are over. These men are hiding behind her skirts, she says. "People want someone else to be the sacrificial lamb."

At Allen Temple, former A's pitcher Mike Norris is the only baseball player there. But he's retired, and he acknowledges his support doesn't have the same impact. "It's not going to get any better until people are willing to come forward," Norris says.

Jesse Jackson says: "At this stage, athletes would not be putting their careers on the line to stand up and let their dignity correspond with their dollars. When Marge Schott referred to niggers, she referred to niggers everywhere. We can't be niggers no more. We cannot have great abilities and millions of dollars and not say 'I am present' when men of character are asked to come forward."

But baseball players tend to be an apolitical group.

"Half of these guys probably don't know who Sharon Jones is," says Giants' manager Dusty Baker about his own team. Baker has known Jones since his playing days with the A's and describes her as a "very bright, straightforward woman."

Until others decide to come forward, Jones believes she has a responsibility to help keep up the pressure on baseball. She continues to work with Jackson and is involved in the congressional effort to remove the anti-trust designation from baseball.

"I believe anti-trust fans the fire of racism and sexism," she says. "It's like working for Prince Charles. These owners are like individual kings. There's no grievance procedure."

Though baseball owners say their minority involvement in the front office has jumped from 2 percent in 1987 to 17 percent currently, critics such as Lapchick say that figure has remained static since 1989.

To the general public, it appears baseball cares about minorities only when one of its members—Campanis or Schott or someone else—inserts foot in mouth.

"I think that's a valid perception," Peter Magowan says. "But I would like to think it's not true." A new generation of owners, such as himself and Haas, comes from the business world, and for them minority hiring is second nature. "There's no question we have to do better in this area," Magowan says.

Baseball's new minority hiring plan has its skeptics. Its sanctions require self-policing, and it does not set timetables or concrete goals for hiring more minorities at all levels, from vendors to owners.

The true test will come in the winter, at the annual owners' meetings where most of the hiring takes place. In the meantime, Jones will keep the issue alive.

"We're very proud of Sharon," says Mills College President Janet McKay, who has received her own hate mail for employing Jones. "This is individually and institutionally distracting. But in the long run this is an educational institution and this is an educational issue. The good we can do by supporting her far outweighs the distraction."

Those who know Sharon Jones find it hard to swallow the questions about her credibility.

"She is a warm, loving person, a person of great integrity and strength and a private person," Terry Jones says. "She is approaching middle age, she has never been arrested, never gotten anything but positive reviews in her jobs, never had her character questioned one bit. She has not one blemish on her record."

Still, there are whispers around baseball that Jones is enjoying her time in the spotlight—the appearances with Jesse Jackson, the interviews, the applause.

"This is not something I brought on myself," Jones says. "This ensures me that I won't be employed in certain areas. That I'll never work in baseball again. I'd prefer to just let it fade away. I'd be very happy to take a back seat, but who else is going to speak out?"

She points to an envelope full of hate mail and to the FBI agents waiting outside her office. She does not want the names of her son, 20, and daughter, 18, to be printed, nor the name of the East Bay city where they live.

"Sometimes you get comfortable as a homeowner and a member of the middle class," she says, "and then you get reminded that a lot of people still think you're just a nigger."

(June 6, 1993)

COACHING WOMEN: JUST WHOSE JOB IS IT?

by Johnette Howard
Washington Post

THE UNREST AMONG MALE COACHES IN WOMEN'S COLLEGIATE BASKETBALL hasn't reached mass movement status. Yet. And as far as anyone knows, there have been no secret gatherings in sweat lodges, nor all-male group retreats to the mountains to bang tribal drums slowly.

But today, as the women's basketball world convenes for its Final Four in Atlanta, the Women's Basketball Coaches Association has scheduled an unprecedented forum at its annual convention called "Men in Women's Basketball." And a rival "alliance" for disgruntled coaches may not be far behind.

The reason? A WBCA spokesman diplomatically says the forum will address male women's basketball coaches' "concerns" about gender equity and hiring trends. But the non-euphemistic explanation, according to Toledo women's head coach Bill Fennelly, is the "potentially explosive" issue of "whether men are welcome in women's basketball at all."

"In other words, White Male Paranoia," Vanderbilt Coach Jim Foster says only half-jokingly.

Foster, the recently elected first male president of the WBCA, says he lifted the self-mocking line from last week's cover story in *Newsweek* magazine. Indeed, upon further inspection, there is a near-perfect parallel between the current debate in women's collegiate basketball and the central question the *Newsweek* article poses: "Is the white male truly an endangered species, or is he just being a jerk?"

Even the dynamics described in the article's introductory blurb seem similar: "Beleaguered by feminism, multiculturalism, affirmative action and P.C. (political correctness) zealotry, white males are starting to fray at the seams. They still have the best jobs and the most power. So now they want underdog status, too, and the moral clout that comes with victimhood?"

That sounds like the debate in women's college basketball, all right.

The idea of men crying discrimination in athletics may sound preposterous, but neither the disgruntled male coaches nor their philosophical opponents view it as a laughing matter.

Depending upon whom you talk to, today's forum has the potential to spark an all-out gender war. (Fennelly says he's been told it was "professional suicide" to agree to moderate the discussion.) Others say the forum is

192

merely a way to let male coaches be heard, learn more from a top NCAA official about what gender equity will mean for men, and set up a WBCA committee to address the men's concerns.

But everyone agrees on this: They'd rather not have the issue detract from the crowning of the 1993 national champion and women's basketball's biggest week of the year.

Whether the wish for peace comes true remains to be seen.

As one longtime WBCA official says: "I get the feeling that people are going to flood to this meeting for the same reason people go to auto racing, or boxing matches. They know it could be volatile and they're curious. They want to see who's going to end up with the bloody nose."

The male coaches who are unhappy about trends in women's basketball say they're bumping their heads on a glass ceiling that precludes men from, say, being head coach of the women's Olympic basketball team, or holding many important committee positions, or ascending to head coaching jobs—particularly at the bigger, richer state schools.

"I'm not female bashing and I'm not just pushing guys," says Georgetown Coach Patrick Knapp. "To me, the real issues should be diversity, education, what's best for the students . . . . But yeah, I think there's a sentiment out there—and I think it's becoming a major issue among the experienced males in the women's basketball community—that there is maybe some favoritism going on when it comes to who's getting the head coaching jobs.

"Especially lately, there are a lot of qualified male assistants who are just not moving up. And everyone knows no male head coach worth his salt in this game would dare hire two or three guys for his staff. And no one would let him if he tried. But I think what you're seeing now are the extremists on both sides. Some women don't want men coaching women. And there are male coaches out there, even today, who go around saying things like 'This woman coach has this sexual persuasion,' and so on. It's underhanded. It's wrong. And it's running both ways."

Though generally sympathetic to women's past exclusion from athletics, the disgruntled male coaches think affirmative action goals aren't being used to give minorities a leg up anymore—they're being used instead to practice reverse discrimination against men.

And, say the male coaches and their supporters, that's just not fair.

But even the men's appropriation of the word "fairness" strikes a raw nerve among those who support the hiring of more women and minorities in college athletics.

They point out that by any national statistical measure there is—sports participation opportunities, scholarships, budgets, jobs—men's complaints about being discriminated against in college athletics appear groundless.

Especially when it comes to jobs in women's athletics and white men.

The passage of Title IX, the federal law that sparked the boom in women's sports participation and funding of women's programs, is the dramatic dividing line. Budgets boomed—from $57,000 then to more than $3 million today, in the case of a major women's program such as the University of Texas. And look:

When Title IX was passed in 1972, 90 percent of women's college teams were coached by women and run by women.

By 1992, only 63.5 percent of women's basketball teams had female head coaches, women ran only 16.8 percent of the women's athletic programs and 27.8 percent of the Division I programs had no women involved in the administrative structure.

"I don't think anyone wants to throw the men out," insists Ohio State Coach Nancy Darsch. "Men's advancement in women's athletics has been a sensitive issue because we still need to add opportunities for women."

What's more, a man coaching a women's Division I basketball team today is paid an average of $6,000 more than his female counterpart. While men have flooded into women's sports, there's been no counter current: Men control 99 percent of coaching positions on men's teams. And you can count the number of female (or black) Division I athletic directors on one hand.

If there is any endangered species in college athletics, it would appear to be women coaches and administrators—not men.

So why do men continue to feel threatened, even when the discordant (and well-publicized) statistics have been presented to them? And what are men really reacting to when they cry reverse discrimination?

Vivian Acosta, the Brooklyn College professor who has been tracking hiring trends in college athletics for 15 years with fellow professor Linda Carpenter, suspects what is triggering male coaches' anxiety or anger is the feeling that men are being penalized for what they are, not how well they can coach.

"In the last two years or so, something like 14 of the last 15 Division I head coaching jobs in women's basketball have gone to women," Acosta says. "But even if those are the numbers, I guess I still have to ask, 'So what's the big deal?' Ever since sports began, women have been discriminated against. No one ever complains that women still are never hired to coach men.

"If men are uncomfortable seeing only one job go to a man, they now know what women have been feeling forever. And I guess they don't like the feeling."

Foster doesn't disagree. The unhappy male coaches are right about some things: Colleges are making an admitted, concerted effort to recruit minorities and women for jobs. Men who clearly do get mistreated don't get much sympathy. And some women—given the chance—can be just as self-serving or sexist as men. Foster says one of his first moves as WBCA president was to diversify the overwhelmingly all-white, all-women committees of the WBCA because "it just wasn't representative enough."

Still, says Foster, "I guess I'm not quite as paranoid as some of the other people in this profession are—male and female. I don't think people look at the big picture often enough. There are more qualified women in sports today than there have ever been. It's a more attractive dollar now, therefore the job turnover is not what it once was. Some of these guys who complain they don't get promoted are in too much of a hurry. If you look at the average age of the men who become head coaches, a lot of them are older, even a lot older, than the women's coaches who complain they're not getting jobs.

"And honestly, sometimes too, people can rationalize about not getting a job by saying, 'See, they're not hiring men!' When, in fact, they're not hiring that man, for whatever reason . . . . Maybe your philosophy isn't in tune. Maybe you didn't interview well. Maybe they want someone with regional ties."

The NCAA's recent embrace of gender equity is making men anxious too, even though the NCAA's definition won't be laid out until the 1994 national convention. The idea is often seen as the second coming of Title IX, but with this twist: This time around, schools will finally have to comply.

As Alfreeda Goff, associate athletic director at Virginia Commonwealth, puts it: "Title IX was a good start, but we never finished it. A lot of women said, 'Oh yeah, we're just happy to be here.' A lot of men looked at women's sports as a necessary evil. Then, as things progressed, women said to themselves, 'Oh, did we blow this!' They gave us a little piece of the cake, a little taste. And for a while we were satisfied. But we never got equity. Now we've woken up and said, 'Hey—no.' We need to look at why we don't get paid the same for the same work. We need to look at why scholarships are still two to one for men. Why?" Of course, all of the disgruntled male coaches say it's not equality they oppose.

But Laurie Priest, athletic director at Mount Holyoke College in Massachusetts, wonders.

Maybe, Priest suggests, what men are now labeling "reverse discrimination" is nothing more than the odd sensation of having to share power with women.

Priest tells a story from her seven-year tenure as athletic director at Marymount College in Arlington.

"When we went from being an all-women's school to a co-ed institution, I basically had to implement Title IX in reverse for the men (in 1987) because we were adding men's programs," Priest says. "From the start, we decided that no decision we made would be gender based. We flip-flopped all the practice times, schedules, on and on, so that everything was the same. Yet over and over, the men's basketball coaches kept coming in to me and saying, 'Laurie, this is just not fair. It's not fair.'

"Well, I have to tell you, I was genuinely confused," Priest adds. "I'd say, 'Wait. We're pumping the same money in your men's programs. You've got exactly the same amount of trips, new uniforms—everything. Everything is the same.' Then I finally realized this was it: When there is a level playing field, men in athletics are not used to it. They are used to being on the absolute top rung of the ladder. What they see as 'discrimination' is simply equal opportunity being given to women as well as men. Men experience that as something not being given to them."

But is that it? Could it really be that simple?

Priest, with a laugh, says, "You've seen the numbers, right? What else could it be?"

(March 31, 1993)

Angels' Jackie Autry Increasingly Taking Reins from Cowboy

by Robyn Norwood
Los Angeles Times

Jackie Autry watched from the owner's box as her husband, the man they call the Cowboy, moved with tiny, shuffling steps toward home plate for a ceremony on the field at Anaheim Stadium.

Always a private person—"even when I was a banker," she says—she is content to remain behind, out of the public eye. During a 10-year marriage to Angels owner Gene Autry, the singing cowboy who built a fortune worth more than $300 million, she has seldom joined him on the field, making a rare exception for one of his birthday celebrations some years ago.

The birthdays have kept passing, more of them than many are blessed with. At 83, Gene Autry is defined as much by his cane as by his cowboy hat. But he still keeps score every game, and talks with club President Richard M. Brown twice daily, almost exclusively about baseball matters, Brown says.

It is Gene Autry's advancing age and the club's desire to win a World Series in his lifetime that has inspired a long list of expensive free-agent signings and other attempted quick fixes by the team. He remains the public's image of Angels ownership.

But it is Jackie Autry, 49, a former bank vice president who says she was "astounded" at the club's historic lack of profitability, who increasingly directs the operations of the club, declaring that it must stop losing money and that the free spending that has marked the fervent attempts to "Win One for the Cowboy" must end.

This season, the team has sunk into last place in the American League West despite spending between $32 million and $34 million on players' salaries. According to Brown, losses will be somewhere between $2 million and $4 million this year.

"Gene's too old to go back to work," Jackie Autry said with a smile, "and I have no desire to."

She is resolute that the team must strengthen its scouting and farm systems, resist high-priced free agents and build for the future from within. Despite three divisional championships, the Angels have not reached the World Series in their 30-year history.

"Sometimes you feel that one player might do it, and that's the temptation that you have," Jackie Autry said. "With Gene's age, there are times I get a sense of panic from our people in baseball operations that if we don't

197

do it this year, he might not be around next year. I don't think that has been beneficial to this organization."

Though Jackie Autry is her husband's staunch defender, and though she more than anyone wants to give him the World Series he has waited so long for, she is convinced that the club's methods have been counterproductive.

"Gene has always believed in the marquee value of the name, and so we found ourselves continuing to mortgage our future by trading away these young people," she said. "And they've gone on to bigger and better things. We stopped doing that in 1984, but I believe we have reverted in recent years to bad habits again in terms of free agents."

When the couple were first married, Gene Autry, whose first wife died in 1980, sometimes referred to his younger second wife as the "owner in training." She now carries the title of executive vice president and is a member of the board of directors, of which Gene Autry remains the chairman.

She has also been named to the board of directors for Major League Baseball and is the first woman to sit on its executive committee.

Jackie Autry acknowledges that while she grew up "a tomboy" in New Jersey and used to love to "hunt and fish, skate all winter and swim all summer," she did not have an extensive knowledge of baseball 10 years ago. She undertook the task of learning it.

"Gene Mauch taught me one thing," she said. "Keep your eyes open, keep your ears open, keep your mouth shut and listen. People don't listen, ever."

Jackie Autry has listened for the better part of 10 years. Mauch, the former Angel manager, has tutored her on the subtleties of the game to the level that she is confident in second-guessing manager Doug Rader on the field. She can speak the language of scouts and knows the histories and statistics of the players.

She has delved into the business of baseball with the same intelligence that propelled her from switchboard operator at a Palm Springs bank at 17 to Security Pacific's 13th female vice president at 32. It was in that job, handling the accounts of the Gene Autry Hotel in Palm Springs, that she met her husband, whose holdings also include four radio stations and five music-related businesses.

After 10 years, Jackie Autry still listens, but she is no longer silent.

"She really became a student of operations," said Brown, who became club president Nov. 1 but has been associated with the Angels since 1981. "I can tell you now she's a good baseball person and a good broadcast person. It didn't happen overnight."

Brown, a lawyer by training who acknowledges that he is not a baseball expert, says he is "trying to follow in her footsteps." His realization that she had become an expert came about four years ago, when she was pronounced knowledgeable by such men as Mauch and Preston Gomez, a member of the organization and a former major league manager.

While her role in the control of the Autrys' holdings has increased, Jackie Autry's public profile has remained low. No biography of her appears in the team media guide, despite the widespread acknowledgment of the power she wields.

Perhaps her most visible involvement with the Angels is invisible, the two or so times a year she is a guest on the Angels' radio call-in show on the Autrys' KMPC, fielding fans' questions and second-guesses about the team. The callers typically seem to express a genuine appreciation that she has taken the time to listen. But at times when the team isn't playing well, she says, they can be "hostile, to say the least." Her answers are forthright, and even incendiary. On occasion, her remarks have stirred impassioned debate.

"I try to accommodate them," she said. "I know they have concerns and feel sometimes they're not answered as straightforwardly as they'd like. I try not to deceive the listeners if I can."

Early this season, after she defended, during the pregame show, the club's decision not to re-sign 40-year-old fan favorite Brian Downing, the fans raised the topic again on "Angel Talk" after the game. The phones lit up; one of the callers was Jackie Autry, who had been listening as she drove the couple's white Mercedes on the long trip home from Anaheim to Studio City.

Angels' employees no longer are certain whether she should be called the owner's wife or the co-owner, but they are clear that the only difference is whichever term she prefers. Employees are also careful to assert that Gene Autry is still in charge and has final say on everything.

"She defers to Gene," Brown said. "I have never seen her override his decision."

But Brown's rise to the presidency from legal counsel and board member is as clear a sign as any that Jackie Autry is steering the club's future.

He was brought on, with Gene Autry's approval but at Jackie Autry's behest, as part of a commitment to curb the organization's losses and to eschew high-priced free agents in favor of strengthening the scouting and minor league organizations and relying on home-grown players.

"That was the resolve I had when I hired Rich Brown to come in as president of this company," she said.

The Angels' situation is not rosy. They face the prospect of free agent bidding after this season for several integral players. She says player salaries, not owners' greed, threaten to price some fans out of the ballpark. She also doesn't understand why players would move their families to "a lousy city" to play for some owner they don't care about, for an extra $500,000 in salary.

"What can you do with $3 million that you can't do with $2.5 million a year?" she said.

"As far as I'm concerned, the players can have all the money, all the revenues that come into this company," she said. "They can have all of them. I just don't want to lose money. It would be nice to also have some type of return on our investment."

The banker in her was astounded, she said, when the club went into the American League Championship Series in 1982, and even then barely turned a profit, making $85,000 for the year, she said.

"I was fascinated. I said, 'How does this happen? This doesn't make sense to me.' Even if the ballclub was worth $10 million, you would still expect to make more than $85,000."

Winning a World Series, she said, is not necessarily the answer to a baseball team's financial woes.

"If an owner says, 'I want to go for it all and I'm willing to lose $10 million,' and if he goes to the playoffs or World Series, what has he got? Because you still lose money—you can't make that kind of money back by going to the playoffs or the World Series."

It is suggested that many owners would gladly write a $10-million check for the experience of seeing their team in the World Series, but Jackie Autry will have none of it.

"Why? It's irresponsible," she said. "It's not the banker in me. It's irresponsible."

Baseball, she believes, is facing a financial crisis, with owners' other assets being hit by the economy as well.

"Everybody wants a winner. Everybody. I can't think of one owner that doesn't want a winner. But if winning means that the fans are going to be priced out of the ballpark, if winning means that owners are going to have to file for bankruptcy, then I don't see that there's any way."

If Gene Autry indeed refuses to raise ticket prices for the second year in a row, the club might have to choose between losing money and forfeiting short-term competitiveness.

Jackie Autry said she is willing to make a stand.

"At some point in time, the fan has to understand that if they want to continue to come to this ballpark, or any ballpark in the country, that the owners have to say, 'Enough. Had enough. Can't go this way, because now a little kid can't afford to spend $15 or $20 to get into general admission.'

"Basketball has now excluded the kids because of the ticket pricing. Football has excluded kids because of the ticket pricing, hockey the same thing. And again, this is supposed to be America's pastime."

Although her feelings toward the players' union and salary escalation are antagonistic, Jackie Autry speaks with fondness and pride of the Angels' players individually, saying, "I don't think there is a player on this team that Gene and I don't like."

But if it sounds as if the Autrys have soured on the baseball business, it is partly true. They are frequently approached with inquiries about selling the team.

"I know it has passed through Gene's mind periodically because he's very discouraged, but not because of the losing," she said. "He's very discouraged by the lack of caring or the lack of sensitivity by the ballplayers. You know, you pay a ballplayer $3 million and they don't feel like they have the time to talk to you. I mean, if you ever treated your employer that way, you'd be sitting out in the street.

"I know one year we tried to retain the services of a ballplayer, and we really wanted to keep him, and we were unsuccessful in getting him to attend any of the meetings with our general manager. So Gene left three messages at his home with his wife, and the man never had the courtesy or the decency to call back. Now here's a man who at that particular time was making a great deal of money. Gene felt very hurt by the fact that this man didn't even have the decency to pick up the phone and return his call.

"It's not only that he's Gene Autry and he deserves that courtesy just because of who he is. It's just human courtesy to say, 'Boss, I hear you called. Sorry I didn't get back with you sooner. If you want to talk about contracts, I would rather not.' From then on, I was astounded they could be so heartless."

There is also the question of whether Jackie Autry would want to continue the quest for a World Series should she inherit the club.

"I would like to if we could get salaries in line with revenues," she said. "As I say, I have no desire to go back to work at $50,000 or $60,000, or whatever they're paying bank vice presidents now."

She is in part being coy; the Autrys surely are in no danger of going under. The value of the franchise, for which he essentially paid $2.45 million in 1961, has soared, and is probably worth considerably more than the $120-million asking price for the Baltimore Orioles.

Baseball, more than many other business, draws its owners into the daily ups and downs, and Jackie Autry says that when the losses on the field mount, the couple suffers.

"I have to drive that Santa Ana Freeway every day for an hour and a half to get down here," she said. "And that drive [after a loss], instead of being 50 minutes to get back home, seems like three hours."

The Cowboy has been enjoying the victories and enduring the losses for 20 years longer than she has. But Jackie Autry said the one who agonizes most is the one in the driver's seat.

"I take it much worse than he does," she said. "I'm a very competitive person. I don't like to lose. It's not part of my emotional makeup to lose."

(August 11, 1991)

Robyn Norwood *covers the Mighty Ducks of the National Hockey League for the* Los Angeles Times. *A University of North Carolina graduate, she was the* Times' *national college basketball writer for two years and has covered major-league baseball and college football.*

A GIFT FOR VIVIAN STRINGER

by Ailene Voisin
Atlanta Journal-Constitution

THIS WORLD OF SPORTS OFTEN MAKES YOU WONDER. IT MAKES COACHES CHEAT AND players lie and perpetuates a value system too often of little value. But sometimes it bestows a most generous gift, sometimes even to the most deserving.

And Vivian Stringer deserved this.

Now in her 10th season at Iowa, Stringer has brought its women's basketball program out of oblivion and into the forefront—to the Final Four this weekend in Atlanta—and she has achieved this in a most traumatic of seasons.

Her husband, Bill, died of a heart attack on Thanksgiving. Her disabled daughter, Nina, remains hospitalized after undergoing surgery. And a youngster she was most fond of, Hawkeye junior Chris Street, was killed in an automobile accident two months ago.

Lesser women would have crumbled. Stringer is not one of them. She took a leave of absence, regrouped and returned. "Vivian is such a warm, loving person, with a real strength of character," says her mother, Thelma Stoner. "There's a toughness there. She's just . . . special."

Thelma Stoner thought so highly of her daughter that she moved to Iowa City and volunteered to assist the women's program. Soon, she was selling "goal cards," season-ticket packages that generate revenue. "I won the prize last year for selling the most," Ms. Stoner reveals, proudly.

She is a tiny woman of meticulous dress, soft-spoken, almost regal in demeanor. She is Vivian Stringer 20 years from now, the resemblance is that striking. The two also share other traits. Stringer often studies films through the night. The day of the Mideast Regional against Auburn she went to sleep at 7:30 a.m. and awakened at 8.

Much is also demanded of her players. Practices usually last 2 1/2 hours, and unlike other coaches who open their doors to all who can dribble and shoot, Stringer is extremely selective. She recruits for character as much as skill. Occasionally she judges too harshly and gets burned, but more often—it is certainly the case with her current players—her instincts are astute.

This is a splendid team, generous and caring off the court, unselfish and graceful on the court. And they, too, are grieving. They knew Chris Street well. They knew the late Bill Stringer even better. An exercise physiologist at the university, he often joked that if they weren't fit he would incur the wrath of his wife. So please avoid the junk food, he would say, and they would laugh.

Now, they try to provoke laughter from his wife, their coach, and attempt to ease her burden when possible. Sometimes they practice at 8 p.m. Other times at 8 a.m., whichever places less strain on Stringer's schedule.

Their affection for their coach is obvious. They shoot concerned, caring glances her way during practice, place an arm around her before leaving, or whisper encouragement. But in this wacky world of sports, they saved their most precious gift for Saturday.

Stringer had never reached the Final Four. This was to have been the year Iowa's team finally did it. Then Bill died. Then Nina got sick, then Chris . . . Did it matter anymore? Eventually it mattered, and the Hawkeyes made it happen.

They were simply marvelous against the feared Lady Vols. They dominated the boards, executed back-door plays to perfection, and, reflecting the street fighter within their coach, tormented the bigger, stronger opponents with hands, hands, hands, everywhere.

With two minutes left, Stringer buried her face in her hands.

With 30 seconds left, assistant Angie Lee held her clipboard in the air.

With no time left, the crowd of 12,343 erupting, Stringer embraced long-time friend and assistant Marianna Freeman, threatening to hold on forever. Tennessee coach Pat Summitt stood by patiently, waiting to congratulate her conqueror, who is also her friend. They, too, embraced.

Stringer then motioned to her sons, David, 13, and Justin, 8. The three linked arms and formed a circle. Stringer said something to David. He nodded, smiled sadly, then placed his hand on her head.

Finally Stringer was summoned to finish cutting the net. She cut one cord, then two, then the final strand. Her players surrounded the ladder, poised again in case she faltered. She didn't falter. Didn't have a chance. Reserve center Cathy Marx reached out and enveloped Stringer's tiny waist. Smiling, she lifted the coach in the air, then oh-so-gently carried her to the ground.

Later, Stringer spoke eloquently, if barely above a whisper, of how the Hawkeyes played with "such heavy hearts" and of "a moment I'll never forget."

She is truly grateful for the gift, for the Final Four.

It offers another chance to forget for awhile.

And to smile.

(March 29, 1993)

Ailene Voisin *covers the NBA for the* Atlanta Journal-Constitution. *She previously worked at the* Los Angeles Herald-Examiner *and the* San Diego Union. *A graduate of the University of San Diego School Of Law, she forsook a law career because of her even greater passion for both sports and journalism.*

The Riding Instructor

by Pohla Smith
Pittsburgh Magazine

IT'S A CRISP, CLEAR THURSDAY EVENING IN OCTOBER, AND THE INSTRUCTOR'S voice cuts through the riding arena like a church bell.

"Sean, when you get to letter 'C' I want you to go into a posting trot until you reach the letter 'A.' Kevin, when you get to the letter 'C,' I want you to go into a sitting trot. Nicholas, we're not ending at the barrel. We're going all the way around."

Embarrassment colors Nicholas's face, but it doesn't break his fierce concentration. His back and shoulders remain ramrod straight, his heels down, toes up. He is the youngest and smallest in this class, and he is trying so very hard to prove worthy of this promotion.

This is an advanced Riding for the Handicapped of Western Pennsylvania class circling the indoor arena at the S.F. Ford Farm in Indiana Township. All four students, who range from about 8 to 19, have cerebral palsy, but on horseback, their handicaps—scissor gaits and physical slowness—are invisible. They post trot and canter their horses over rails with panache.

To a stranger, the only obviously handicapped person in the group is the instructor sitting in mid-arena: Donna Zook, a tiny but commanding figure confined to, but not by, a wheelchair.

It would be a different story if one were to visit during Zook's Monday classes. All but 15 or so of those 63 students are more severely handicapped, and their classes are more therapy than lessons in basic horsemanship. There are victims of spina bifida, Down syndrome, multiple brain damage, more severe cases of cerebral palsy, and autism.

"Some of the kids we just lay across the horse on bareback pads, and let them get the movement of the horse," Zook says. "It works their muscles, loosens their muscles, stretches them out. Most of the time they're sitting in a stroller all bunched up."

Others are able to sit in the saddle while volunteers escort them—one leading, one or two walking alongside. These students also stretch muscles, and build strength. They also learn to tell their left from their right; they learn to socialize or, in the case of the autistic, at least to interact.

Zook is paralyzed from the waist down, a victim of a horrifying race-riding accident 14 years ago. But she doesn't feel handicapped when she's teaching.

"I can do anything anybody else can do," Zook says, but then, Zook rarely feels handicapped. She drives an hour and a half by herself from her home in New Cumberland, West Virginia, a tiny town near Weirton, to teach these classes as an unpaid volunteer. She has raised a 16-year-old son single-handedly. She earns her living training thoroughbreds at Mountaineer Park.

The only thing Zook can't do is walk, and she doesn't let that get in the way of her life. That attitude and a natural repartee with children, says RHWPA director Toots Abbott, make Zook such an excellent teacher.

Zook, married to another jockey and the mother of a 2½-year-old, wasn't quite 22 and "riding the best I ever had in my whole career" when her racing career came to a crashing end at old Waterford Park, now Mountaineer, on June 30, 1977.

A horse in front of Zook, aboard Grace's Ensign, broke its leg and fell. An adjacent horse fell over it, and Grace's Ensign piled into both, catapulting Zook 50 feet down the track onto her back.

"I was busted up real bad," Zook says.

It was hours before anyone knew how bad. After a long wait at the track gate for an ambulance, a trip to Weirton Hospital, and another ambulance ride to the Presbyterian Hospital in Pittsburgh, an emergency room doctor realized Zook was literally drowning in blood. The impact of her fall had broken all the capillaries leading into her lungs, and the blood was draining into her chest cavity. Zook heard one of the doctors say, "She'll never make it through the night."

But the doctors managed to stop the bleeding during emergency surgery and, after Zook had stabilized, they turned their attention to her shattered spine. Two vertebrae were crushed, "and there was other damage," Zook says. Her spine was surgically stabilized with the insertion of metal pins called Harrington Rods and bone grafts from her hip. Soon she could sit up and watch television.

Zook was doing just that one day when she heard the news her family hadn't disclosed: Two of her three brothers, Chester Shriver Jr., 32, and Floyd, 25, had been horribly burned in a freak explosion near her parents' home in Mariana, Washington County. Their pickup truck had stalled in a little valley filling with what appeared to be fog but was actually propane gas leaking from a pipeline. When her brothers tried to restart the truck, the gas ignited.

Her older brother died after 12 hours. Floyd lived 14 days.

There was one more tragedy awaiting Zook. About a year after she was released from Harmarville Rehabilitation Center, her husband left her and their son Jeff. They soon were divorced, and Zook began building a new life.

In retrospect, Zook calls the breakup a positive event. "When he finally left, it made me stand on my own two feet and then I did things I wanted to do," she says.

Zook got a job as a jockey's agent—a person who books mounts for a rider. Later, she started walking horses and acting as barn foreman for trainer Gail Morrow.

In 1986, someone sent Zook two horses of her own, and she took and passed her trainer's test. Five years later, she has a string of 18 horses, a couple of employees, three clients, and a healthy career-winning percentage of 13.

By the time she was licensed to train she was well into her work with the RHWPA.

Zook, who got back on a horse for the first time as a handicapper during a weekend pass from Harmarville Rehab, joined RHWPA as a rider in the early 1980s. When the instructor died of cancer, Zook stepped in as substitute. Later, she took a four-week teaching certification program at the Cheff Center for the Handicapped in Augusta, Michigan.

She has watched some of her first students, the same age as her son, grow into confident riders, get their driver's licenses, giggle about girlfriends. It is that sort of thing that inspires her to make that long drive to Indiana Township to work for free every Monday and Thursday, April through October.

"I feel they need me," Zook says.

(February, 1992)

Pobla Smith *covered sports for United Press International for 16 years and was national beat writer for horse racing. Now a free-lance writer, editor and part-time journalism instructor, she lives in Pittsburgh with her husband, Evan Pattak, three cats and a golden retriever, Max.*

THERESA GRENTZ AND THE SEARCH FOR OLYMPIC GOLD

by Diane Pucin
Philadelphia Inquirer

WHEN SHE WAS A KID, THERESA GRENTZ WOULD SNEAK OUT OF THE HOUSE AND around the corner to play basketball. Philly-style basketball. She played with boys, with girls, by herself. Later, she coached—in a skirt, in high heels, when she was seven months pregnant.

Now Grentz—the blond woman from a Glenolden rowhouse, the hard-headed woman from Cardinal O'Hara, the rugged woman from Immaculata—is going to Barcelona, where she will coach basketball until a gold medal is hanging around her neck, or else.

"Nobody in the world hates to lose as much as me," Grentz said. "Nobody."

Grentz, 40, the supremely successful women's basketball coach at Rutgers University since 1976, is coaching the 1992 women's Olympic basketball team.

The United States has won two straight gold medals, and so a third is expected. And if Grentz is right, if no one in the world hates to lose more than she does, if, as she said, she never, ever thinks about losing and is furious when she does, the United States should have the right coach.

"I will not let this team lose," Grentz said. "If I have to, I will will them to win."

When Grentz was Theresa Shank, the tall, strong daughter of John Shank from Glenolden, she would sneak out of the house to play basketball with the guys, away from the prying eyes of parents who asked why their daughter didn't play with dolls and wear skirts as other girls did.

Grentz doesn't know why she loved to play basketball, and just about every other sport. It was just a fact. She loved to sweat and bleed. She loved to compete. She loved to win.

The kids on her block would play games until all hours, into the dark, sometimes making it dark. "Sometimes we'd knock down the electrical wires with the basketball," Grentz said. "We'd put out the lights."

Once, when she was 9 or 10, Grentz had a bad day and came stomping home. She left her basketball in the street. "I had a temper," she said, "and I had missed some shots. So I came in and said, 'That's it. I've had it. No more basketball. The ball is gone.'"

"So my father, calm as could be, said, 'Theresa, it might be a good idea

208

to bring the ball in. You might want to play again some day.' I brought the ball in and was out playing a couple of hours later."

Remember, this was in the 1960s, when girls weren't considered athletic material. But if Grentz's family sometimes wished she'd play with dolls, they never told her she couldn't play basketball.

There is another thread in Grentz's life—her Catholic religion. She went to Our Lady of Fatima grade school, Cardinal O'Hara High School and Immaculata College.

How did she end up at Immaculata? "Providence," Grentz said.

After an outstanding high school career at O'Hara, Grentz accepted an academic scholarship to Mount St. Mary's in Maryland. She wanted to leave home, be on her own.

But in March of her senior year in high school, while the family was at Sunday Mass, the Shank home burned to the ground. "All we had left was what was on our backs," Grentz said. "I had to borrow a suit to wear to interview at Immaculata."

Grentz's family had wanted her to stay close to home anyway, so she decided that in this time of emotional upheaval, she would forget Mount St. Mary's and attend Immaculata.

It happened that Immaculata had a new coach, Cathy Rush, and a group of girls from the Philadelphia Girls' Catholic League who loved to play basketball. There was no gym. "We had a cotillion to make money," Grentz said. "We practiced at a novitiate across the street."

What the team had was spirit. And Grentz, who already in those days would tell her teammates that "losing was just the dumbest thing in the world."

After helping her team go 10-2 when she was a freshman, Grentz and Immaculata took off. The little Catholic all-female college won three straight national titles and captured the attention of the nation.

So it was a natural that Grentz, considered the best player on the team, would head into a coaching career, right?

"No way. I graduated in May, got married in June and started teaching grade school in the fall," Grentz said. "That's the way it was done." She had married Karl Grentz, a childhood friend and sometime sweetheart. She began teaching at her own grade school, Our Lady of Fatima. Her life was set. Except . . .

"One day I was approached by the president of St. Joe's," Grentz said. "He was looking for a women's coach. I thought he was nuts, but I went over after school one day for the interview. Before I knew it, I was being led out on the court, wearing a skirt and heels, and being introduced as the new coach. I had to conduct practice—that day."

Grentz said she knew nothing about coaching. She would hang around at Widener, where her husband had gone and where she had gotten to know C. Alan Rowe, the basketball coach. She would pick Rowe's brain.

She would call her friend, Howie Landa, basketball coach at Mercer Community College, and say, "What am I gonna do with this team," and Landa would say, "Don't worry, you'll run a matchup," and Grentz would say, "What's a matchup?"

Grentz would attend Landa's practices (his team has won three national junior college championships), then she would drive Landa's point guard, Joe McKuen, home. It was not an altruistic act. She would pump McKuen about the matchup until the poor guy thought maybe walking home was better. "But who better to teach me than the point guard?" was Grentz's reasoning.

In two years at St. Joe's, Grentz's teams were 27-5. She was still teaching grade school and coaching part time at St. Joe's when Rutgers called, offering a full-time position. More money. More attention.

But Grentz paused. She'd always just expected to coach at a Catholic school and in Philadelphia. Her husband had a good job with Xerox. Life was settled.

"And I took the job, anyway," she said. "The day I told my parents, my mom said I just ruined their vacation. Why did I want to move away? But I did."

Her husband stayed in Philadelphia a year while she found out whether life outside Philly was palatable. It was. In 1982, Grentz coached Rutgers to a national title.

She had her first son, Karl Justin, in 1979 and Kevin in 1987. "Being pregnant was good luck," she said.

Early on, Grentz let U.S. basketball officials know she was interested in international coaching. In 1981 she coached the U.S. Junior National team, in 1989 she coached the World University Games team, and in 1990 she won a gold medal while coaching the U.S. World championship team. That qualified the United States for the 1992 Olympics and landed Grentz the Olympic head coaching job.

The decision to accept was not automatic. "It was a family decision," she said. "Karl and the boys and I sat down together. I told them that if I was going to do this, I had to do it all the way. It would be a lot of work and time away, and if they didn't want to make that sacrifice, great, fine, I understood and I wouldn't do it."

The decision was unanimous. It hasn't been easy.

Grentz missed her son Kevin's graduation from kindergarten while she was conducting the Olympic trials in Colorado Springs in May. "Man, do you know how that tears at you, when your little boy tells you he wishes you could come?"

But the family support has been non-stop, and now the time has come to win.

Grentz said she feels no extra pressure to live up to the high standards set by the previous two Olympic women's teams. "I don't think about what's happened in the past," she said. "I don't think about anything."

Anything?

"Well, winning of course," she says. And then she hurried off to a golf game.

(July 11, 1992)
Diane Pucin, *a columnist for the* Philadelphia Inquirer, *has worked for the* Columbus *(GA)* Enquirer, *the* Cincinnati Post *and the* Louisville Courier-Journal. *A graduate of Marquette the year it won the NCAA basketball championship, her work at the Barcelona Olympics was nominated for a Pulitzer Prize.*

MIKE BOYD'S FIELD OF DREAMERS

by Elizabeth M. Cosin
Los Angeles *Daily News*

MIKE BOYD PREACHES BASEBALL LIKE A RELIGION. THERE IS NO MIDDLE GROUND in this diamond-shaped temple—either you believe or you don't.

But this kind of faith isn't grounded in athletic endurance. The roots go deeper. It's not whether you win or lose, it's whether you played the right way. And to Boyd and his disciples, doing it right means discarding everything you ever learned about baseball, really breaking the game down to its purest forms.

This isn't green grass and apple pie, this is grace and style and skill.

"It's kind of like yoga, the way I teach it," said Boyd, whose brother, Dennis "Oil Can" Boyd, is the former Boston Red Sox and Montreal Expos pitcher. "The idea is to emphasize technique and skills, not strength and speed and aggressiveness."

Call it Zen baseball or call it out in left field, but this one-time minor-league prospect who was drafted second overall by the Dodgers in 1973, and who now calls himself "the minister of baseball," has quietly found a loyal following to his baseball teachings and preachings. Many are women and he is trying to start up a league for them, in part because Boyd believes anybody can play this game.

But make no mistake, these players are learning more than just baseball.

"This isn't just about baseball," said Shauna Oetting, a 22-year-old former set designer from Burbank. "There's just so much more to Mike than that. He doesn't only teach us how to play better, he teaches us that baseball is a game that involves working together, that it's a very positive game. That you can teach people to be good to each other through the game of baseball. When Mike tells you that, you believe him."

Added 25-year-old Georgia Quesnell of Arleta: "This isn't just an opportunity for us to play professionally, it proves that you don't have to be big and strong to play. Just getting the opportunity is amazing."

It is more than that. It is unthinkable for many of the 25 women between 19 and 40 who earned spots on one of Boyd's two local teams. In a real sense, Boyd has widened the field of dreams to include even those who weren't supposed to dream in the first place.

"All I wanted to do was play baseball when I was younger," said Sandra Zerner, a 31-year-old who helps teach disabled students at L.A. Valley College. "I couldn't play on any teams, so I only played in the park with the

212

neighborhood boys. My neighbor used to make me walk 20 feet behind him on the way to and from the park because he didn't want the other guys to know he hung out with me."

Like many of the other players, Zerner was approached by Boyd during one of her Burbank softball league games. It was like getting a call from Tommy Lasorda.

"I'd say it's fulfilling a lifelong dream, but dreams sometimes come true," she said. "It's actually fulfilling a lifelong fantasy. I never thought in a million years I'd be playing baseball as an adult."

It even could get better. Boyd's ultimate goal is to start a series of teams around the country, win sponsorship and actually pay the women to play professionally. A real League of Their Own.

Boyd says he came up with the idea eight months before the release of the movie about a professional women's league during World War II. Even though Boyd's vision is not even close to becoming a reality, these women have already gone too far to think about failure. Right now, they believe it's as possible, and perhaps eventually profitable, as a winning season on opening day.

They spend three hours a day working on their skills, and many spend more time at home improving their fundamentals. There is plenty of room for fun at these practices, but beneath the laughter is a determination you wouldn't see on the faces of Little Leaguers. There's a lot at stake here.

"Maybe little girls will learn how to play baseball instead of softball," Quesnell says.

A familiar lament is that even the youngest players didn't have an opportunity to play baseball as children. Many are playing the game for the first time.

"I've played softball all my life because they wouldn't let me play on my brother's baseball team when I was younger," said Margaret Christopher, a 25-year-old florist for Hughes Markets and one of several single mothers who play for Boyd.

"Softball is much more difficult than baseball," she said. "But most of us never got the chance to play. That we might get paid—that's really something. It would be wonderful if that's where this ended up."

It's difficult to say if Boyd's league will ever be a reality, but, according to his players, the experience has been worth it even before one game is played.

At a recent practice in Burbank, Boyd ran his players through warmups, infield practice and a practice game. Most seem comfortable on a diamond, if not so much with the smaller, lighter baseball. But there is something else here as well.

When one woman cleanly fields a grounder after several unsuccessful tries, Boyd stops the practice, runs onto the field and embraces her—to the cheers of teammates.

"I want to grow up to be just like him," says Oetting, who is expected to be one of the starting pitchers when the two teams play their first game Aug. 22.

"I'd like to make money doing this. That would be terrific," she said, holding a baseball she never seems to put down. "But beyond that, I hope we can be ambassadors to children and bring the game to them. Women are nurturers by nature and that's what we can bring to baseball. That's the spirit behind what we are trying to accomplish."

(August 12, 1992)

Elizabeth M. Cosin is a sportswriter for the Los Angeles Daily News. A graduate of George Washington University, she previously worked at the Washington Times where she covered University of Maryland sports. She was one of the first girls to play Little League baseball in her hometown of Ossining, New York. In high school, a gym teacher told her girls shouldn't play baseball because sliding causes breast cancer.

Lynette Woodard: From Blacktop to Desktop

by Jo-Ann Barnas
Kansas City Star

The bushy, 7-foot tree in the corner of Lynette Woodard's office doesn't belong to her.

Neither does the row of old metal trophies on the windowsill or the computer that doesn't work because the screen is burned out.

The white walls are barren of any personal touches. There are no team pictures or awards. No autographed basketballs. No photos of any of the four U.S. presidents she has met.

Office decor clearly isn't a priority for Woodard, who is about to start her first full school year as director of athletic activities for the Kansas City School District.

"So, here it is, my office," Woodard said, as if she's still getting used to the idea herself.

For as long as she can remember, her office was anywhere a basketball could be bounced—in the back yard of her family's house in Wichita; the blacktop across the street at Piatt Park where she challenged her brother's friends; the hard court at Kansas's Allen Field House where her retired jersey hangs near Wilt Chamberlain's and Danny Manning's.

There's more to the Woodard legacy: college basketball's all-time leading women's scorer with 3,649 points . . . two-time Olympian . . . first female member of the Harlem Globetrotters . . . pro playing careers in Italy and Japan . . .

But here, in her office, eight floors above 12th and McGee in downtown Kansas City, none of the souvenirs or treasures of her basketball past are on display.

The reason is as clear as the date circled on her calendar. Classes start Tuesday.

For now, nothing else matters.

She was only a month into retirement from pro basketball last spring when the school district called with a job offer that sounded more like a plea for help.

Woodard is aware of the urban problems facing high school athletic programs around the country. Lack of participation is chief among them.

School officials told her they needed a leader, a motivator who could start an intramural program in the middle schools and help raise funds along the way.

215

Woodard, 34, didn't need much persuading. She put her plans to study for a master's degree in psychology on hold and signed a one-year contract with the district for $67,117.

"Attendance problems, dropping out—kids start those sort of patterns before they reach high school," said Craig Cook, the district's assistant superintendent for business and finance who recruited Woodard for the job. "Coming from an urban environment, she knew what was happening here. Lynette can get people fired up in a positive way."

Of the 37,000 students projected to be enrolled in the school district this fall, 7,634 are in the middle schools. Woodard's pilot sports program is to involve three of the 12 middle schools this year: Bingham, Southeast and Nowlin.

Sports scheduled this fall are boys flag football, girls softball and boys and girls soccer.

All activities will be held after school and on school grounds. In addition, each child willing to participate will be on a team. There will be no tryouts, no cuts.

"The only way to go is intramural," said Claire Julian, coordinator of athletics for the Interscholastic League. "Interscholastic teams are too limiting for these middle school kids. Not everyone develops at the same time, so why not teach the sports to everyone and let it be enjoyable instead of telling someone they can't play? In some schools, 150 kids try out for basketball but only a handful make the team. That doesn't seem right to me."

But getting students involved is the first step and, quite possibly, Woodard's toughest challenge. That was the reason for her two-week "Slammin' Jammin' Basketball Camp" last month at Central High School. The camp involved not only basketball, but tennis, volleyball and golf. Woodard discovered that many children were learning how to play these sports for the first time.

"It was kind of funny watching the kids," Woodard said. "They weren't too sure if they wanted to participate. But by the time the morning was over, they were loving it."

She thinks it's harder being a kid today compared with 20 years ago. When she was 13, Woodard remembers a summer filled with basketball and bike riding. There were no VCRs, Nintendo or gang problems.

"There are so many distractions today," Woodard said. "I was never afraid to go outside when I was a kid. I probably would be today. It's not a joke. Things that were considered 'big' when I was growing up were on television, and they seemed so very far away. Now it's right here.

"People are angry. They don't understand their feelings. It's whatever goes, goes. Life is difficult today for so many kids. Many come from single-parent homes; some don't even have parents.

"I'll always believe in what sports has done for me. You learn discipline and hard work and teamwork. All of these things—winning and losing—can carry over to anything you do in life.

"But I guess sports was my thing. Someone involved in, say, music, goes through the same thing. It still comes down to a discipline, making yourself do things at an appointed time and looking for results.

"You didn't do so well today? That's okay. Don't worry about it. Go back, practice, come back tomorrow and try again. If you do get over the hump and reach your goal, then victory is sweeter, isn't it?"

The door to her office is closed, but Woodard can still hear the phones ringing outside. She spied the stacks of phone messages neatly arranged on her desk. The piles are prioritized.

"Those who probably will get called today, and those who probably won't," she said.

Julian remembers the mountain of messages covering Woodard's desk when she first came aboard last April.

"I think the first few days were pretty overwhelming for her," Julian said. "Everybody kept coming by to see her. Many were welcoming her, but others were coming by to say they met Lynette Woodard.

"She was very nice, but after a couple of weeks she said, 'I have a job to do,' and began turning down invitations. Lynette kept saying, 'I have to start taking care of these kids.'"

Every morning during the week, Woodard is up at 5:30. Out the door of her Lawrence house about 7 a.m., a 40-mile drive awaits her.

If the 80-mile daily commute is growing tiresome, Woodard doesn't show it. Athletic secretary Linda Gray observes that Woodard always leaves the office with the same bright smile she wore when she first traipsed through the door at 8:15 a.m.

Besides, her work schedule hardly matches the rigorous training routine Woodard kept when she was playing.

It still seems odd to her that the basketball part of her life is over. More than the competition, Woodard said she misses "the workout"—the six-plus hours a day of running hills, doing drills, lifting weights, swimming laps, playing basketball, teaching basketball—whatever it required to make her one of the best players of all time.

"Basketball, the game, is just a show," Woodard said. "I never saw anybody out there when I was running another hill. That's the best part, when I'm out there working out all day, trying to get one more step in, trying to do that rope, trying to lift that weight. You have to love the workout. That's the part I miss the most. I'd rather work out than eat."

* * *

Asked to reminisce about her early years, Woodard brings up her first instructor, older brother Darrell, now 35 and living in South Carolina.

Lynette was about 9 when the two would roll up a pair of socks and toss them over a door—their make-believe goal—in spirited and sometimes feisty games of one-on-one. From "sockball," Woodard's fascination with basketball grew. So did the number of broken windows.

"It was always the window in the girls room, so I knew it was her," said Dorothy Woodard, Lynette's mother. "I had to get an iron or two replaced, too."

By her sophomore year at Wichita North, the word on Woodard already was out. Kansas Coach Marian Washington remembers driving down to watch her play.

"It was the first time I had seen anyone like her," Washington said. "She had unbelievable ball-handling skills. I saw this sophomore girl running down the court faster with the ball than the other players chasing alongside her. I always described her as a ballet dancer because she was so graceful."

Once she signed with Kansas in 1978, her playing career took off. She has literally hundreds of highlights but mentions in detail only three incidents that seem to be defining moments of her life.

The first event came early, and it begins with the revelation that Woodard was a trophy monger when she was a kid. She even opted not to join the freshman team in high school because she could bring home her own trophy every weekend playing with the local youth team.

Then came her sophomore year at Kansas and the Hanes All-Star Game in Greensboro, North Carolina. She saw the tall shiny trophy that went to the game's most valuable player, and she wanted it.

"I had an excellent game," Woodard remembered. "I led in every statistic. People knew me from the last year, and they were all saying, 'Oh, you've got it this year.' I was all ready to accept it, but then they called someone else's name. Some player out of Texas who had sprained her ankle and didn't even play the second half. And my team won. She didn't even perform, and she got it. I was blown away."

Woodard paused, shaking her head.

"It was then when I said, 'Never, never again will I let something like a trophy be dangled in front of me like that. I'll never again play for anything other than just wanting to play.'"

Then there were the three years she recently spent in Tokyo, an experience Woodard says was definitely enlightening.

"There are so many things I like about their culture," Woodard said of the Japanese. "I like the way the younger people would be riding a train and when someone older got on, they'd give up their seat. Very polite. They never want to invade your privacy. People went out of their way to make you feel comfortable.

"And it wasn't because I was this basketball star. They didn't know who I was."

Finally, there was the tragedy involving her best friend, Jackie Martin, a former KU player who died of leukemia in April 1992 at age 26.

Woodard recruited Martin from Dublin, Georgia, when Woodard was working part time with the women's team. Martin's high school coach told Woodard that Martin probably wouldn't make it through college because she was a marginal student.

Oddly, Woodard was told the same thing by a counselor at Wichita North. Last year, Woodard was inducted into the GTE Academic Hall of Fame. Martin, too, earned her degree.

"I'm just starting to get over it; I mean, truly feel myself again," Woodard said of Martin's death. "She was always so proud of everything I did, so I could share with her and there was no envy, no jealousy at all. I hadn't experienced that before. I could tell her everything, and she'd be so happy."

Woodard was at Martin's bedside when she died.

"I ran into the room, and she had this smile on her face, this most beautiful smile, and it just stopped me," Woodard said.

"She was my best friend. I miss her too much."

There are times when Woodard feels overwhelmed with the work that needs to be done to solve the district's problems. She compared her first few months to a snowstorm, wondering "which snowflake is going to cause the avalanche."

But during her camp last month, Woodard saw hope in the faces of her middle school campers.

About 80 kids climbed into the bleachers one morning after Woodard blew her whistle. She wanted to teach them the trick shot she was famous for with the Globetrotters: a back-to-the-basket, half-court hook.

"No way!" a youngster yelled from the stands.

Woodard moved in from half-court and stood under the goal. In a sweeping motion with her right arm, Woodard lifted the ball into the basket. She took another step further out, and made the shot again. Then another step.

"This is how you do it," Woodard said. "You keep going. Inch by inch, day by day . . . "

(September 5, 1993)
Jo-Ann Barnas, *who has worked at the* Kansas City Star *since 1984, has a journalism degree from Michigan State. She won first place in the competition for best news story at the 1990 Associated Press Sports Editors convention. She is married to Jeff Taylor, a national correspondent at the* Star *who won a Pulitzer Prize in 1992.*

FIVE

YES I CAN

OUT OF AMERICA

by Linda Robertson
Miami Herald

ROBIN HARMONY LIVED THE GLAMOUR LIFE OF A PROFESSIONAL BASKETBALL player. She was a boarder in the Northampton, England flat of a kindly, 4-foot-3, 80-year-old lady. Harmony's teeth used to chatter in the cold room because she never had enough 50-pence coins for the pay heater.

Harmony earned a five-figure weekly paycheck: $150.00.

And the perks of being the Michael Jordan of England? Free Avon cosmetics from the team sponsor, use of a Ford Escort (plastered with Avon stickers), and $6 a day in meal money.

"The strangest thing was going to the pubs with the fans and your coach," Harmony said. "I said, 'Coach, you're really going to buy me a beer?'"

Harmony was a star in England, but in the United States, her career slipped into obscurity when her college days at the University of Miami ended.

"What happens to the best American women basketball players? They go to the glue factory," joked sports lawyer Sally Sullivan.

Actually, they go overseas. More than a century after basketball was invented in the U.S., the top American women are basketball expatriates. While the men's version of the pro game, the NBA, continues to grow in popularity and wealth—with a salary cap of $14 million per team—fledgling American women's leagues bloom and wilt in near-empty arenas.

To continue playing the game she loves, former University of Miami All-American Frances Savage was a basketball nomad, playing in Chile and Italy.

"The language barrier can be a problem," Savage said. "I wasn't always sure whether my coach was chewing me out or praising me."

Valerie Still, former Kentucky star, plays in Italy, where she cut a pop record and modeled clothes. Olympian Teresa Edwards was one of a handful of Americans who earned $200,000 in the lucrative Japanese league. Ruthie Bolton became the first American to play in the growing Eastern European leagues, on a Hungarian team.

"When I watch the NBA and see these guys making millions it makes me mad," said former Tennessee star and De Land native Bridgette Gordon, who plays for Italy's best pro team, Comense 1872. "Women do the same things the guys do, except dunk."

223

Four women's pro leagues have crashed in the U.S. since 1979. The first, the Women's Professional Basketball League, offered charm school and makeup sessions for the players. The most recent was the Liberty Basketball Association which featured skin-tight, body-suit uniforms, lower goals and a smaller ball.

"It's obvious why we can't get a pro league going," University of Texas coach Jody Conradt said. "Fan interest is the bottom line. Ridiculous costumes won't do it. I think we still have a ways to go. It doesn't help us to keep starting and failing."

Agent Bruce Levy, who represents most of the American pros, said a U.S. League would need corporate backing and TV exposure. "ESPN will take anything as long as you sell the time," Levy said. "The mistake these women's leagues have made is putting teams in big cities where there's so much competition for the entertainment dollar. They need to start where they can get grass-roots support."

Although viewership of the women's NCAA Final Four has increased 41 percent over the past five years, the road ends there for most women. Trailblazers such as Ann Meyers, Nancy Lieberman-Cline and Lynette Woodard got the most publicity of their careers during brief stints with men's teams. Carol Blazejowski is director of licensing for the NBA. Cheryl Miller is a TV commentator. The U.S. Olympic team veterans have to earn a living overseas where some also are in demand for endorsement deals.

"I don't think people fully support the idea of women in sports in this country," said Sullivan, a lawyer in Seattle. "If we could just get one or two women over the top, get them a major Nike commercial, we might start a trend."

Sheryl Swoopes of Texas Tech, star of this year's Final Four, has attracted interest from some companies, but she'll soon be out of sight, out of mind, playing in Europe.

About 100 American women are competing in leagues abroad. Levy estimates only about 30 players make more than $50,000 a year. The very best—such as Edwards—earn $200,000.

Japan—which craves tall players—and Italy have the highest-paying leagues, although Japanese team sponsors plan to eliminate foreigners next season. Most players in Spain and Scandinavia earn less than $20,000.

Leagues allow only two foreigners per team. Some invent creative ways to get around the citizenship issue.

"Two teams in Greece called us and said they wanted American players and could arrange for them to be married within two days of arrival," Levy said. "I said, 'No thanks.'"

* * *

Wherever they play, Americans face culture shock.

"We tell our players that in certain countries they should be prepared to hear the word nigger. In Japan, players get nicknames like Chocolate Milkshake—but it's meant as an affectionate thing," Levy said. "The coaches can be dictatorial and insulting. Players are always referred to as girls, not women. We explain that they can't change the culture of the country they're playing in."

At a typical game in Ancona, Italy, a crowd of 3,000 showed up to watch the local team play. They made Boston Garden seem like a library in comparison: There was the usual yelling, singing and spitting—lots of spitting. The fans also heat coins with lighters and throw them at referees or players. The benches are protected by Plexiglas barriers.

"The Italian fans are crazy," Katrina McClain said. "At the buzzer we had to run into the locker room. I just wanted to get out of there. We had a police escort to and from the arenas."

McClain, a former All-American at Georgia who now plays in Spain, played two seasons in Italy after several in Japan. She embraced Japanese culture, attending sumo wrestling matches, learning the characters of two alphabets, eating shabu-shabu ("Never got into the raw stuff, though," she said.)

The three-a-day practices in Japan could be brutal, however. It is acceptable for male coaches to hit the Japanese players, who are employees of the team's sponsor.

"I'm not talking about a slap on the arm," McClain said. "They kick the women, they punch them in the stomach. Then the women run after the coach, apologizing. Women are really looked down upon in Japan." McClain had a clause added to her contract: Physical and mental abuse prohibited.

Medina Dixon, a 6-3 black woman, was such a rare sight in Japan that she needed bodyguards. "We'd travel to small towns where the people had never seen a black person and I'd have a mob of kids trying to touch me to see if the black would rub off," said Dixon whose six-figure contract and an endorsement deal with Mizuno enabled her to buy condos in Virginia and Florida. Dixon took showers because she didn't fit in her apartment's bathtub.

Gordon, a guard on Tennessee's national champion team in 1989, plays in Como, Italy, where she has developed a passion for fungi and Fendi. She lives five minutes from Switzerland, where she buys gas—because it's cheaper there—for the BMW 520 provided by the team. She also lives in a rent-free apartment.

"The Italians consider Americans to be spoiled," she said.

Lynette Woodard, former player for Kansas and the Harlem Globetrotters, said Americans are the stars of the teams—or else.

"You come in as the savior and they expect you to carry the team," said Woodard who has played in Italy and Japan. "If you score 100 points and you lose, they think you should have scored 103."

The quality of play in the Italian league is the best in the world, but still only comparable to that of the top U.S. college teams, she said.

"It's a more physical game," she said. "The lane is wider, and you're allowed three steps instead of two."

Despite the perks of being a star in a postcard setting, life far from home has its disadvantages. Loneliness is the main complaint. Former Drake player Wanda Ford plays in Visby, Sweden, an island accessible only by plane. Gordon knows a few useful Italian phrases but refuses to learn the language because "I don't ever want to sit in another classroom." She hangs out with the other Americans in the league.

"I've been all over the world, but nothing prepared me for living abroad eight months of the year," Woodard said. "I remember crying until there were no more tears. The pay is great, but you miss your family."

Beth Hunt, former South Carolina star, played in France and enjoyed the French way of life.

"I guess I'm pretty French now. I buy fresh bread every day, I clean my plate with it, I pick up my soup bowl and I like my French wine. I only drink Pepsi when I'm alone, because it's considered tacky," Hunt said by phone before she moved to a new team in Japan. "You know, they kiss you when they see you in France. They have culture."

There are some things she may never get used to. The players smoke at practice. The coaches smoke during games.

"The players can be dirty—they'll take you out on layups," she said, tripping over her English pronunciations because she usually speaks French—with a Southern accent. "Mysterious stuff happens with the game clock. The coaches and fans get into it; you see a lot of fingers poking into chests."

Hunt lived in Mirande (pop. 4,000), near Toulouse, four hours from the Riviera. Games sold out at the 6,000-seat arena and were on TV. Players' pictures were posted in all the stores.

Hunt is not bitter that she had to go overseas to earn her $85,000 salary.

"Americans are not going to settle for second best and the women's game is second best," she said. "Women are not going to come down and make awesome pivot moves and dunk. If I had my choice, I'd go see a men's game. I'm just glad they have women's pro basketball somewhere."

(July 6, 1993)

THE PRIDE OF EAST ST. LOUIS

by Toni Ginnetti
Chicago Sun-Times

NONE OF THIS MAKES SENSE.

The streets leading to the home of champions are supposed to be lined with gold—not the blank stares of jobless men sitting on the steps of boarded-up buildings.

Shiny plaques and boastful emblems are supposed to line the school walls—not chipped paint and graffiti.

Fancy Nautilus machines, aerobic exercise programs and the newest equipment are supposed to be in the gym—not five-year-old uniforms and sole-worn cleats and patched-up benches in an unheated, unventilated weight room.

Emerald green grass is supposed to cover the home turf and cheering throngs are supposed to fill the stands. So why is a grass-worn, 50-year-old park, hidden between railroad tracks and factory smoke stacks, the sacred home field?

And where are all the fans?

It doesn't make sense at all—unless you consider the program, the people and their pride.

That's why the phenomenal winning record of the East St. Louis High School football team makes all the sense in the world.

This city's biography may be a tale of woe, but the East St. Louis Flyers have managed to author a chapter on excellence.

They are the twice-defending State High School Class 6-A football champions. They have steamrolled their way to an 8-0 mark so far this year, including a 58-3 demolition Oct. 11 of a solid Alton High School team ranked No. 6 in the state. The Flyers seem destined for a third straight state title.

So good are they that *USA Today* calls East St. Louis the best high school football team in the nation.

In their community of have-nots, this team has worked hard to have it all.

The pep assembly starts for the school's 2,256 pupils with the same admonishment that has started every high school pep assembly in history: Get rowdy and there'll be no more pep assemblies.

Still, after more than an hour of the pompom girls' performing to Prince's "I Would Die For You," students lip-synching soul tunes and a student's funky rap routine, things have degenerated into a free-for-all.

So much for another pep assembly before the big game against crosstown rival Lincoln High School.

Student throngs file out of the gym, and athletic director Walter Hood retreats to his office until the kids finally disperse for home.

Things have changed since the 1960s when Hood went to school at East Side High, as it's called here. There was a gang shooting a few blocks from the school recently, he says. There are vandalism problems and kids aren't intimidated anymore by a trip to the principal's office or the threat of expulsion.

One thing hasn't changed, though: the school's football tradition.

"You hear all the time that we're good because we have black kids," Hood said. "That's totally false. This school was the all-white school in town until the 1960s—and we were winning football even then," he said.

East St. Louis is all black now, but East Side doesn't get all of the good athletes in town. Under the local school district's open boundary policy, students can choose between East Side or Lincoln High.

Both schools have consistently good track teams—they've had a monopoly on the state track title for the past nine years. And when it comes to football, the record speaks for itself.

In the past 50 years, East Side has had only four head football coaches, whose combined records boast 378 wins against a measly 68 losses. East Side also has produced pros in San Diego Charger tight end Kellen Winslow, New York Jet cornerback Kerry Glenn and Dallas Cowboy safety Victor Scott.

"What you have is a good, solid football program," Hood said. "We've had only four coaches since 1939 and they all took the job seriously. It's good coaching and good talent."

It's had to be, because in the meager economy of East St. Louis, there aren't enough dollars to buy success.

"We don't have a budget," Hood said. "The way we get things is we have to requisition for it and if the school board decides we need it, we'll get it. Anything that involves safety, like helmets and pads, we have no problem with. But your traveling white jerseys are a little weathered and we haven't had new uniforms in any sport in five years. We've requisitioned for them, but we haven't gotten them.

"We have a weight training program, but our weight room is probably not the quality of many. But it gets the job done. We've been fortunate to have great coaches who have been really dedicated, and a big part of their job is motivation."

Motivation is vital on and off the field for these kids, Hood and principal Samuel Morgan say. Morgan personally monitors the work of the players through weekly grade reports sent to his office. The Illinois High School Association only requires that a player get passing grades, but Morgan and head football coach Bob Shannon try to set a higher standard. And when a student doesn't start improving Fs and Ds, he gets benched.

"Sometimes I have to sit hard on a boy for one game," Morgan said. "I have to tell him football's only a minute part of his life. Sometimes you have to show a kid that you must do things sometimes in life. It hurts me sometimes to do this, but I will always do this. I feel a commitment to this. And when we sit them on the pines, it works.

"I'm from a poor background. There were 10 children in my family and I was born and raised in East St. Louis. I feel I owe these kids something, so that's why I'm committed to things here, and I think I understand their problems."

Morgan tries to give the students educational support, and he admits it's "frustrating" that the team doesn't get the same kind of fan support from the student body and the community. "They're complacent until the playoffs," he said.

But the real problems he faces aren't inside school.

"My real problems here are the influences outside the school I can't control," he said. "But sometimes being deprived gives you the will to fight—especially on the football field."

You can spare the Flyers any Knute Rockne speeches. Senior defensive end Bryan Cox and his teammates know all there is to know about winning—and what it really means for them.

"Football means getting out of East St. Louis," Cox said without hesitation. "With a winning team, you have a better chance at college. There are more colleges looking at you. I'm looking at college and an education, and if pro football comes, it comes."

His thoughts are echoed by his cousin, Michael Cox, the senior star running back, junior quarterback Kerwin Price, senior co-captains Arthur Sargent and Jeffery Patterson, senior right guard David Lee and just about every other Flyer.

"Football is a way to get out," Lee said. "A lot of people look at football players and think they're dumb. That's not true. You can be an athlete and a student."

"Football means a way out and I want a better education, too," Patterson said. "I'd like to play pro, but it's a long shot.

"There's good and bad anywhere. When people think about the bad here, at least this [football team] is something good. The only way we can express ourselves well is through sports.

"This team brings pride to East St. Louis. It shows that not all the people are in gangs. It shows there are people here who want to do something with their lives."

These kids have attended two schools all their lives—the kind lined with blackboards and the kind lined with curbs. Most of them understand why making the grade in the classroom is more important than making it on the street.

"That's the first and bottom line," Michael Cox said. "When you have your priorities straight, schoolwork isn't a problem."

They don't resent the school's policy of benching players who are failing academically. "If they didn't do that and played us for three years, they'd just be using us and not be concerned about us," sophomore running back Marvin Lampkin said.

All of them know one man is always concerned about them—and not just as football players.

Somewhere in coach Bob Shannon's little office, hidden behind the papers and shelves, there has to be a magic wand.

How else does a guy with aging equipment, lackluster surroundings and no budget consistently turn a bunch of poor inner city high school kids into the nation's best football team.

His co-workers call Shannon an outstanding teacher and coach. Shannon just calls himself a hard worker.

"I guess the coaching philosophy I use is my philosophy on life itself. I think if you work hard and try to do things well, things will work out in the end. I believe that. I've tried to be the best I could.

"I believe you get an edge when others are doing leisure-time activities and you stick to working. I always say I don't like to hunt or fish. I like to coach football and I spend my time trying to get better at it.

"I knew what I wanted and I knew what I had to do to get it. I wanted this football program to be good every year. When you have good talent you shouldn't just win, you should dominate—and that's what we try to achieve.

"I know all work and no play makes Jack a dull boy, but I try not to leave any stone unturned."

He starts turning stones at 7 a.m. each day at school and doesn't stop until about 7:30 p.m. "I don't have much time to rake the leaves in the yard," he said with a smile.

But the grass is not growing around him.

Shannon, 41, came here 14 years ago after getting his teaching degree from Tennessee State University, where he played quarterback. Before East Side came a tryout with the Washington Redskins, who drafted him in the 12th round.

He didn't make the team but counts the experience as invaluable.

"It was Vince Lombardi's first year there. Just being there, I picked up things about doing things the right way, and I think those things have stuck with me.

"I tell our players, 'Coach Lombardi used to say there are usually five plays in a football game that can change winners to losers and losers to winners. You never know when those plays are going to occur, so you have to be alert on every play.'"

Shannon is East Side's Lombardi, voted the city's man of the year last year after taking his team to its second consecutive state championship and its third since 1979. He is quick to give credit to his coaching staff, including assistants Marion Stallings (an East Side alum), Kenneth Goss, Arthur Robinson, John Vinson, Curt Watters and volunteer Orlando Pope.

Together, they have formulated a success equation that doesn't rely on superstars.

"People think that we have a great football player at every position, but we don't. To be successful, you have to get the average player to play above his level. That's the guy I usually target, the average player. But I tell them all, 'You have to earn the right to play here.'

"I think one of the things that has made us successful is we're refraining from wringing our hands and using the crying towel. That's a cop-out. Those things we do, we have to do. We've try to motivate the kids not to be concerned about the things we can't control.

"I had kids practicing in shoes with the cleats coming through the bottoms. But what can you do? I coach and we do the best we can with what we have. We don't do a lot of boasting. We just do on the field what we practice every day. I tell the kids, 'We don't practice fumbles and interceptions so we shouldn't do them in a game.'"

The Kangaroo shoe company helped Shannon and the team this year by donating 25 pairs of shoes. But Shannon doesn't dwell on what the team doesn't have. "I always tell the kids the progr: in comes first. I got a good program when I came here and I'm going to try to leave a good one behind."

Shannon knows, too, that the program is the kids, and his concern for them goes far beyond the playing field.

"I get them to try to understand the meaning of self-esteem. I tell them that regardless of what goes on out there [in the streets], we're trying not to let that get to us in here. These kids come from low income homes, but that's not an excuse. I did, too. I came out of Mississippi and we were raised in poverty. It's not a crime to be poor. That doesn't have anything to do with integrity, honesty and virtue."

Shannon, who is married but has no children, says he tries not to get too close to his players "because I'm the guy who will have to crack the whip on them. But I like to think we have a close relationship, and I like to think it's because they know I'm the authority. I want to be a role model for these kids. I tell them we want to keep things good in here."

His players know what Shannon expects their priorities to be—and they start with academics.

"I'm sincere about that," he said. "I tell them the reason I did well was there were people concerned about me academically. The older I got, I realized they had given me sound, solid advice. It helped me later on. I tell the kids all the time, 'If you're not concerned about yourself, you're not the person we want. You can get injured and never play football again, but knowledge is something that can't be taken from you.'

"I know everybody isn't of the same ability, but I always want to know, 'Number one, are you going to class, and number two, are you trying?' In every inner city, kids are not challenged, so they're not used to buckling down, but if he's trying, we try to encourage him.

"But a lot of our kids have trouble adjusting when they get out of here, and that's why I try to take them out of East St. Louis when we can. I tell them, 'This is probably the last all-black situation you'll encounter in life, so you want to be able to adjust and adapt and not come fleeing back here as if this is some kind of sanctuary.'

"If I get on them, I ask them to consider three things: Am I doing it to make you a better person, a better athlete, a better student? If the answer is 'yes' to those questions, then I'm on the same level as your parents."

"You have to be a jack-of-all-trades," Shannon said. "But you know, when you get a good kid out of an inner city environment, you know you have a good kid. You have to have a lot of respect for a kid who can say 'no' to the things out there."

Even more than winning, that is what Shannon counts as his team's best achievement.

"That's one of the things that's been rewarding about teaching and coaching," he added, "because I see a lot of good kids."

(November 4, 1985)

Toni Ginnetti covers baseball and college basketball for the Chicago Sun-Times. *A graduate of Northwestern, she began her career at the* Sun-Times *in 1981 as a general assignment reporter. She has covered the Olympics and worked on such special projects as a series on organized crime's control of sports betting in America.*

BEATING THE ODDS AND FOE AFTER FOE

by Cindy Martinez Rhodes
Riverside Press-Enterprise

IT WOULD HAVE BEEN SO EASY FOR SISTERS DARLENE WILSON AND AISHA DENNIS TO let circumstances dictate their lives.

They live in an area where gangs often replace family, and family is one thing they have found in short supply.

Their mother died, their grandmother died, they were bounced between relatives and foster homes, separated and finally reunited. All before they became teen-agers. And it never seems to end. There's been teenage pregnancy and open-heart surgery. And just three months ago, Wilson was the victim of a drive-by shooting three blocks away from home.

Because their childhood was so full of loss and despair, they were content to block out the past and hide from their futures.

But it's tough to hide when you're 6-foot-5 or 6- foot-7-inches tall.

Try as they might, Rubidoux High School girls' basketball coach John Hill wouldn't let them hide.

Hill saw beyond the fear and mistrust and convinced them that athletics could change their lives.

This season, the Falcons are 19-0 and ranked second in the state by Cal-Hi Sports. Much of Rubidoux's success is due to Wilson and Dennis. Wilson, a 6-5 senior forward, said she likely will accept an athletic scholarship to Grambling State University in Louisiana. Dennis, a 6-7 junior center, hopes to follow her next year.

"When I first met them, they never spoke a word," Hill said. "They were so withdrawn, and they were turning off fast to school. I think they thought they were freaks because they were both at least 6 feet tall in junior high. They had no self-esteem or self-worth and got teased a lot. They had no guidance—they were just there."

Both girls said that had it not been for Hill, they'd be on the street somewhere. But they didn't warm up to him immediately.

Hill's first contact with Wilson and Dennis was as a substitute teacher at Mission Junior High School. He was also coaching the boys' freshman basketball team at Rubidoux at the time, and he tried to get the girls involved in sports.

But they had no use for Hill or his ideas. And they let him know it, which, incidentally, got them detention that day.

Hill didn't see them again until Wilson walked on the Rubidoux campus as a freshman. By that time, Hill was coaching the girls' varsity, and he renewed his acquaintance with her.

She still resisted his efforts to get her to play basketball. Finally, Hill told her he was planning a trip for some of the girls on his team to attend a Cal Poly Pomona women's basketball game to watch his sister, Yvette. He invited Wilson and Dennis, and they accepted . . . grudgingly.

"That night he came over to take us to the basketball game, we ran and hid in our bedroom, and he came in our room and got us," Wilson said. When they returned home that night the two sisters wanted to play basketball so badly they couldn't sleep.

"I told them that I was going to take them to a place where they would fit in," Hill said. "I told them that they would see other girls their size, and they would see what they could become. They were so excited that it was easy to motivate them from there."

Wilson's career never got started that season. When she took the physical examination required for athletic competition, she found she was pregnant. That spring, Wilson gave birth to a son, James Thomas Harris.

Wilson and Dennis laughed when they looked back on that summer, which they spent learning the fundamentals of basketball in the high school gym.

"We'd put him (the baby) in his walker and tie it to the bleachers to keep an eye on him," Wilson said. "I want him to have the best of everything—things I didn't have. I have to do well in school for him."

The one thing the girls did have in their early years was plenty of love. Although neither girl knew her father, their mother and grandmother provided a happy, stable home.

Their lives began to unravel at the ages of 7 and 6. Their mother, Valerie, died on the operating table during open-heart surgery. The girls said Valerie was diagnosed as having Marfan Syndrome, a hereditary disorder that affects the elastic tissue in the body. It is characterized by abnormally elongated bones, especially in fingers and toes, and circulatory and eye abnormalities.

Four years later, just as their lives had taken on some degree of normalcy, their grandmother died of a massive heart attack.

"We had been in bed, but when we heard the ambulance, we automatically started crying because we knew something was wrong," Dennis said. "We couldn't sleep, we were shaking so bad. We just started praying."

From the day of their grandmother's funeral, they were passed around between relatives. They stayed with an aunt for a time, but she became ill and could not care for them. They were sent to a shelter home in Riverside and farmed out to separate foster homes.

"They tried to tell us we were crazy, but I was so unhappy that I wouldn't eat or talk or go to school," Dennis said. "It got so bad that when my aunt got sick, I wanted to die, too. I figured if everyone is leaving us, then let us go with them."

Their mother's sister, Robbie Overton, recovered and took both girls back, and they have lived with her since. Recently, they all moved in with Overton's brother, Willy Adams. Overton and Adams take pride in trying to give their nieces the chance they wish they'd had.

"Basketball is finally their good break and more than that, it will give them a chance to get an education," Adams said. "A lot of us (African Americans) don't have a chance to get educated because of the way our parents lived. We don't always want to admit that. Darlene and Aisha have a chance not to let history repeat itself."

Through the turmoil, both girls began to excel on the basketball court. Wilson averaged 20 points and 24 rebounds her junior year and is averaging 22.4 points per game this season. Hill said Wilson, for just having picked up a ball three years ago, is nearly a complete player.

"Darlene is in the position to be one of the top players in America," Hill said. "She is able to run the court well and rebound. All she needs is a little more confidence in her jump shot."

"I think they both have more potential than what we've seen," said Temecula Valley coach Chris O'Sullivan, whose team lost to Rubidoux in the Riverside County tournament. "Especially Darlene—she's a good ballplayer, I'd take her in a second."

Dennis would have started for the Falcons last season, too, but doctors detected a heart murmur during a routine athletic physical. Two days later, Dennis was admitted to Loma Linda Medical Center for emergency open-heart surgery. Dennis said goodbye to her sister because she believed she was going to die, just like her mom.

"I didn't want her to see me cry, but I didn't leave her room. I slept on the floor and in chairs until I knew she was okay," Wilson said.

Dennis recovered fully but sat in the stands last season with tears rolling down her cheeks because she figured playing basketball was out of the question.

But with permission from her doctors and encouragement from Hill, Wilson and her Rubidoux teammates, Dennis has made a complete comeback. She is averaging 13.5 points and double figures in rebounding. Some defenses, though, are hard to let down. Wilson still has a quick temper, and Dennis is still introverted at times.

"Aisha is a sweet girl, but I misunderstood Darlene at first," Hill said. "With all that adversity she was withdrawn. I took that as arrogance. She still has that tough image—it's part of what makes her so fiercely competitive. She is truly a survivor."

While they have both made great strides, there are still reminders that theirs is a volatile world full of harsh reality.

Just three months ago, on their way home from a party in their neighborhood, Wilson was the victim of a drive-by shooting. A bullet from a pellet gun remains in her hip, but she was back on the court within three days.

Again, Hill was there for them.

"We never had a father, so I guess coach Hill is the closest thing," Dennis said. "He's strict, but he's always there for us. Darlene even calls him dad sometimes."

Hill, who is just 11 years older than Wilson, said many times he feels like their father. And like any parent, Hill is preparing for the day when Wilson will leave for college.

"Basketball has really changed their lives," Hill said. "When Darlene leaves, I'll be waving. Waving and crying at the same time. I do love them."

(February 4, 1992)

Cindy Martinez Rhodes covers high school sports and writes features for the Riverside (CA) Press Enterprise. *A 1987 graduate of Cal State Long Beach, she previously worked at the* Long Beach Press Telegram *and the* Orange County Register.

Why Aren't Women Racing at Indy? Janet Guthrie Knows

by Tracy Dodds
Los Angeles Times

IT WAS 10 YEARS AGO, IN 1977, THAT JANET GUTHRIE BECAME THE FIRST woman to drive in the Indianapolis 500. She's proud that she has the distinction of being the first. But she's piqued that she still has the distinction of being the only.

Why is Guthrie no longer driving Indy cars? And why have no other women followed her lead to Indy?

"The stick-and-ball sports editors who suggested that you ask me that question are probably the same guys who are still puzzling over the question of why there are no black managers in baseball," Guthrie said.

Guthrie keeps answering the question, though. She's been doing it for years. And every time she does, she suffers the consequences.

She explains about the high cost of racing, the dependency on multi-million-dollar corporate sponsorship, the good ol' boy network that keeps racing very male—and then the good ol' boys explain that women can't race.

It's kind of like saying that women don't have the "necessities" for racing.

"Get ready for the knee-jerk reaction," Guthrie said. "I'll talk to you about this, and I'll guarantee what the reaction will be because I've been through this 14 dozen times. It will be written off by men who will say that women can't compete and more specifically, that Janet Guthrie wasn't competitive.

"I know that that is not true. I stand on my record . . . . But it's hard to have your reputation kicked around again and again."

Guthrie, 49, lives in Aspen, Colorado, and is busy working on an autobiography that she hopes will show the "passion and complexity" of the world of auto racing. She is engaged to Warren Levine, a United Airlines pilot. And she still does a lot of traveling and speaking.

Guthrie would be in Indianapolis racing today if she could get the sponsorship. "Obviously there is money available to sponsor racing because the race fields remain full of sponsored men," Guthrie said. "Sponsors supposedly put up that money because they want to sell products, but a lot of those products are used by both men and women—beer, for example. But what I especially notice are the sponsors like Tide, Crisco, Folgers and Haines pantyhose who are putting their money behind men.

"Men are getting sponsorship and women can't. That sounds unfair. But who cares about unfair? What counts is the bottom line. Sponsors want the publicity that racing brings. But a successful woman driver will get 10 times the attention that a man will get. So now what really is important?

"It keeps coming back to the good ol' boy network. A lot of corporations are spending a lot of tax deductible dollars to sponsor male racing drivers."

And the only way to justify passing over a driver like Guthrie is to say that she can't drive.

"I would like to point out that when I was racing, there were some very good teams that would have had me, and that I would have given my eye teeth to work with—Bignotti for example, McLaren for example—but I had to bring the sponsorship with me, and I was being told that there was no sponsorship available," Guthrie said.

The way it's retold in Gasoline Alley, she didn't really merit sponsorship.

A quick review:

Janet Guthrie did not show up at Indy in 1976 as a publicity stunt. She was a 38-year-old woman who had a degree in physics and had worked as an engineer for Republic Aviation.

She learned to fly planes when she was 13. She had been racing sports cars for more than 10 years and was able to take the engine of her Jaguar XK-120 apart and put it back together.

Guthrie was quite serious about wanting to race cars.

She conducted herself in a calm professional manner at all times, enduring constant scrutiny as she went through some frustrating setbacks with her cars and some cutting remarks from other drivers.

She failed to qualify her first year at Indy because her car was not fast enough. A.J. Foyt was curious enough about her ability to let her take his backup Coyote out to see if she could get a good car up to qualifying speed. She could. But he couldn't afford to go handing out his backup car, so she ended up driving in the World 600 stock car race on the day of the Indy 500.

In 1976 she was in the running for rookie of the year on the NASCAR circuit.

In 1977 she was back at Indy with a car that was good enough to make the field—barely. She qualified 26th and finished 29th after spending more time in the pit than on the track.

After taking on a full load of fuel, the heat of the day and the heat of the car caused the fuel to expand and spill over into her lap. She wore that methanol fuel-soaked suit for hours before she was able to get it off and find some water to rinse away the burning chemical. There was then just one shower in Gasoline Alley, so she had to have her crew construct a makeshift shower stall for her.

She commented to the reporters shadowing her and recording her every word that one shower was hardly adequate.

In 1978, she qualified 15th and finished 9th. Not bad at all for a second try. And, she points out that she did that with a budget that was about five percent of what the top teams were spending that year. She had $120,000 while the Penske team had about $2.3 million.

So did her cohorts herald her arrival and proclaim her worthy of promotion? No, but they couldn't say that she was scared or dangerous or didn't know the sport or didn't know cars. So they said that she ran just to finish. That she didn't challenge the leaders.

To that, she says, "Horsefeathers."

In 1979 she was back in a car that lasted just three laps. It was the car that didn't want to challenge the leaders. And she hasn't been back in the race since.

She would still like to race with a top team so that she would have the wherewithal to challenge.

There were, in her early days in Indy cars, some drivers who showed her respect. Foyt, for one, was willing to give her a chance. After a race at Trenton, Johnny Rutherford acknowledged that she had made a quick transition from sports cars and said, "It's a shame she didn't have a better car." Tom Sneva said, "She ran as fast as the car would run."

But others continued to say that she was just trying to finish, not trying to win.

She's heard it all over the years, about how women don't have the strength, endurance or courage for this sport.

Ever the intellectual, Guthrie counters each point with evidence: "Okay, let's talk about strength. How about the 115-pound woman power lifter who [can] lift 352 pounds? Endurance? What about the ultra-marathon runners and triathletes? The record for the English Channel swim is held by a woman. Courage? Downhill skiers risk terrible injury. A gymnast doing a triple back flip on a balance beam constantly risks breaking her neck. How about Betty Cook, a world champion in power boat racing?

"How about all of those things and more, all in one? The Iditarod [a dogsled race of more than 1,000 miles in Alaska]. In each of the last three years, that's been won by a woman. I have a T-shirt that says, 'Alaska. Where men are men and women win the Iditarod.'

"Women just can't do it? Horsefeathers. I find that highly offensive."

Guthrie is convinced that it's the system that is keeping women from developing into top drivers. She cites examples dating back to the early 1900s in which women of independent wealth successfully ran sports cars.

And she cites the WASPs as examples of how men will strive to deny the history of women who succeed on their turf. The Women Air Force Service Pilots flew planes to and from the war theaters. Thirty-nine were killed in the line of duty during World War II. But they didn't win veterans benefits until 1977 because the military was so determined to keep them classified as civilians.

"We can go all the way back to hot air balloonists in the 1700s to find examples of how women's history has been deliberately suppressed or denied."

So Guthrie is not at all surprised that her efforts of 10 years ago not only have failed to lead to greater opportunities for women, but are shrugged off as an experiment by someone who was not competitive.

"Am I surprised that there haven't been other women at Indy in the last few years?" Guthrie asked. "I'm distressed.

"There have been some great natural talents emerge, like Kathy Rude [who survived a terrible racing accident four years ago] and there will be others. Whether they get the chance to drive at Indy is a matter of funding.

"Me? I keep hoping that one of these days, somewhere in Aspen, I'll run into a multi-zillionaire who wants to go racing.

"I'd love to have the money behind me for the car, the team, the testing program that it takes to be competitive."

(May 24, 1987)

Tracy Dodds is sports editor of the Austin American-Statesman. *She previously worked at the* Los Angeles Times *where she covered UCLA sports and the 1984 and 1988 Olympics. A graduate of Indiana University, she has also worked at the* Milwaukee Journal *and the* Houston Post.

SCOUTS' HONOR

by Amy Niedzielka
Miami Herald

THE MANAGER WITH THE STRAGGLY BEARD WAS GNAWING ON A WAD OF TOBACCO when J.D. Patton approached him in the dugout. She told him she was a scout with the White Sox. He looked at her. She asked for a roster.

"You know," he said, "I've been in baseball for 20 years and I've never met a woman who knew a thing about it. Why should I think that you do?"

Patton was in her first year as a major-league baseball scout. Having previously coached boys' Little League in Tennessee, she had already met plenty of people like this manager. Many times she had reminded herself of an uncle's words: "If you just do your job, and do it in a professional manner, ignorance changes."

Patton seemed to be a magnet for ignorance. She shook it off, again.

"As long as the people who hire me know that I know what I'm doing," she said to the manager, "I don't give a damn what you think."

Jennie Diane Patton is one of just five women scouts in the four major professional sports in the United States. History books tell us about one other, Edith Houghton with the Phillies in 1946, a woman softball star.

Since then, however, Patton, Susan Epps of Fort Lauderdale, Florida, Deborah Wright of Montreal, Dorothy Fox of Rochester, New York, and Linda Bogdan of Buffalo, New York, have been the beginning and the middle (they hope not the end) of women's sports scouting history.

Five women with five immensely different backgrounds, they have little in common besides a love of scouting and first names that are often confused with "honey," "gal," and "sweetheart."

But they say they are scouts to stay.

"I can't not do it," Epps said during a high school baseball game in Fort Lauderdale. "Whether I have a contract with a club, or not, I'm going to go to games and I'm going to scout."

The others agree. Introductions are in order:

Epps, 44, an associate (unpaid) scout with the Astros, began scouting in 1988 not long after having a late-night conversation in a Denny's restaurant with two Royals' scouts.

The two men and Epps began talking about the Louisiana State University-Tulane baseball game they had just attended. After a while, one of the scouts—Kenny Gonzales—asked Epps if she would like to scout college baseball in Louisiana.

"This is my boss," Gonzales said at the time. "We've been interviewing you for the past two hours."

Several weeks later Epps was invited to scout in the Fort Lauderdale area.

Epps said she would love to scout the Mexican League for a major-league baseball team, but she does not aspire to a full-time scouting position. A neck injury—a herniated disk suffered in a car accident about eight years ago—prevents her from working long days.

The accident, incidentally, got Epps into baseball.

She had never played the sport and knew little about it. But after the accident and surgery, Epps was bedridden for several months and began watching game after game on television. When she attended her first major-league game at the Houston Astrodome in 1985, she said, "I didn't even know what a scout was."

She has learned.

Patton, 36, an administrative assistant/part-time scout with the Milwaukee Brewers who aspires to be a full-time scout, was a boys' baseball manager for 11 years before being offered an associate scouting position in 1988 by the White Sox.

Patton, then working as a lifeguard in Sarasota, was grilled for three hours by White Sox owner Jerry Reinsdorf and a number of coaches in the stands during the winter instructional league. The interview had been arranged by an Illinois congressman.

After a year, she was promoted to part-time scout, which meant she received a salary of about $1,000 a year plus expenses. Devoting herself full time to her part-time job, Patton lived on that income until she no longer could. Nearly broke, she quit after last season and was hired this summer by the Brewers.

"I've lived on peanut butter sandwiches for a long time," she said. "I know what it is to be hungry."

She still drives the same 1981 Ford Fairmont (168,000 miles) because she hasn't gotten used to the idea that she can afford a new car. Her dream is to become a full-time scout, but not until she gets a few more years' experience and deserves the title. "I haven't been a token woman to this point; I don't want to start now," she said.

Dorothy Fox, 69, an associate scout for the Brewers who scouts Triple-A games, mostly in Rochester, New York, grew up playing baseball. About 20 years ago, tired of her 9-to-5 job in marketing at Eastman Kodak, she asked Harry Dalton, then the Baltimore general manager, for a job. He didn't think she was capable of evaluating players. She said she would work for nothing—not even expense money—for the season. "At the end of the year, you're welcome to call me and tell me I'm no good," she said.

She never received a call. She received a letter the following February offering her an associate position.

Linda Bogdan, who will not disclose her age, corporate vice president/part-time scout for the Buffalo Bills and the daughter of Bills' owner Ralph Wilson, asked her father for a scouting position in 1986 because she "got tired of too many 2-14 seasons." Her position quickly earned her the unwanted double label: "I'm not only not 'one of the boys,'" Bogdan said, "but I'm also 'the owner's daughter.'" She splits her time now between her love—scouting college games—and her duties as vice president.

Deborah Wright, 26, a part-time scout for the San Jose Sharks who scouts junior-league and college games in Canada and the northeastern United States, became obsessed with junior-league hockey when she was in college. She saw game after game, jotting down observations about teams and players. She attended about 350 games in 10 months last year, and her interest led her to apply to the Sharks for a scouting position. Report-filled binders now occupy eight bookcases in her apartment.

She also subscribes to a number of equine publications and often studies, rates and ranks the horses. "I've always been analytical," she said.

All these women know they are being scrutinized by fans and fellow scouts, and all sort of enjoy it. All have been tested, and are tougher for it.

"It's not a question of anybody lowering standards just because you're a woman," Fox said. "You have to raise yourself up to their level. You always have to show a little more than the average guy does."

That becomes obvious from the first day on the job.

"Other scouts will say, 'Oh, you don't understand this,' or 'What pitch was that?'" Fox said. "After a while, when they realized they couldn't get your goat, they were willing to share."

Said Patton: "I have run into a lot of discrimination, but I've also met some awfully decent people."

Wright's biggest problem is that she looks young—the age of many of the players—and does not wear a wedding band. "Some people might accept me more if I were married," she said. "But if I was in this to meet hockey players I wouldn't be working so hard." All the women work hard. They have to.

"There is a heavy price for this," Patton said. "You don't always have time for friends and family. You are alone a lot of the time. You have to like yourself, because it can be a very lonely business."

Epps remembers going into the office of Coconut Creek Athletic Director Ron Hamilton on her first assignment. She needed a schedule, but thought Hamilton would not believe she was a scout. So she fibbed.

"I told him I had a friend who was a scout who needed a schedule," Epps said. "He told me, 'When your friend gets into town he can get it.'"

Epps fessed up, won an instant friend, and never again tried to pretend she wasn't somebody she was.

"Mothers of ballplayers relate to her very well," Indians scout Phil Zelman said. "She can get information, and that's very important. You can't get enough information about a ballplayer. She loves what she's doing and she's good at it."

If there is a common core, this is it.

"As far as I'm concerned," Dalton said, "judgment is genderless."

Before Patton was hired by the White Sox, she became friends with a now-retired Dodgers scout. When he would come to town for games, Patton would drive to the ballpark and sit with him, talking baseball. "You know, it's a shame you're a girl," he told Patton in 1981. "You'd make a good scout."

Patton agreed, sort of. Yes, she certainly would make a good scout.

Soon after being hired by the Sox eight years later, Patton sent the man her new business card with a short note.

It read: Guess what? Times have changed. J.D.

(October 18, 1992)

Amy Niedzielka covers the Florida Marlins for the Miami Herald. *She graduated from Princeton University in 1991 with a degree in electrical engineering that she finds utterly useless in her chosen career.*

Memories of Iowa's Cherished Six-Girl Game

by Jane Burns
Des Moines Register

"Gentlemen of the Association, if you attempt to do away with girls' bas-ketball in Iowa, you will be standing in the center of the track when it runs over you."

—John Agans
Superintendent, Mystic schools, 1925

THE BIRTH OF IOWA GIRLS' BASKETBALL COULD BE TRACED TO 1898 WHEN Marshalltown and Ames sent their first teams out to play. Or it could have officially started when Muscatine claimed the state title in 1904, although there is no record of the tournament they won. Or perhaps it began the first day a farmer put up a rim beside a barn—for his daughter.

There is no doubt about when the state's special contribution to girls' basketball ended, though. That happened Wednesday when the Iowa Girls High School Athletic Union voted to switch exclusively to five-player basketball after next season.

That vote wrote the last chapter in the six-player game that has made Iowa girls' basketball unique. What made the state unique in 1926 was that it offered girls' basketball at all.

When basketball was invented by Dr. James Naismith in 1892, the game quickly spread across the country. Men and women both partici-pated without a second thought. But in the years that followed, a change in philosophy had a strong effect on girls sports around the country. *Competition* for boys was good, physical education theorists surmised, but *participation* was what was important for girls. Girls' ath-letics nationwide was soon relegated to physical education classes.

"They really pushed that and that was a big reason basketball disap-peared from most schools," said Janice Beran, professor emeritus of sports history at Iowa State.

Lillian Schoedlr of the women's division of the National Amateur Athletic Federation roamed the country in the 1920s preaching the new theory and much of the United States listened. They listened in Des Moines and it was not long until girls' basketball disappeared from the capital city's schools.

246

The Iowa High School Athletic Association also listened and decided only boys should get the gym after school. After all, the girls really didn't need it anymore since competition was bad.

That's when Mystic Superintendent John Agans and his colleagues put their feet down. They refused to accept the philosophy that basketball was bad for girls. If it was so good for their communities, how could it be harmful? So in 1926, those administrators split from the athletic union and founded the Iowa Girls High School Athletic Union. It is uncertain whether the towns that joined had not heard the new competition-is-bad-for-girls philosophy or just chose to ignore it. But whatever the reason, they refused to give up basketball.

Most of the schools in the new association were from rural areas. They played in church basements, in opera houses and above stores. Anywhere open enough was fine for many of the teams. In 1926 Hampton beat Audubon, Ida Grove and Mystic in the first state tournament to be sanctioned by the girls' union.

"Rural Iowans were looking for a way to make life in the country more enjoyable, and basketball fit in very well with that," Beran said. "It brought excitement. It brought something for the high school girls to do. There was some concern about the rough play, and there really was quite a bit of that. But it was hardly rough compared to the work they had to do on the farm. It was a game compared to that. It was more of an escape."

The six-player game that is being phased out today looks hip and funky compared to the one those administrators fought to keep. The girls got three dribbles—one more than current rules—but the ball had to bounce higher than the knees. The court was split into three courts, not two. The center section featured the jumping center and the side center. The jumping center tapped it to the side center who would get the ball to her teammates in the forward court.

"I think they stood still when they bounced it," Beran said. "A jump ball after every score slowed down the scoring. When a ball rolled out of bounds, the first girl to get to it was awarded possession. That was a main reason folks thought the game was a little rough."

By the 1950s and '60s, the larger Iowa towns were playing the six-girl game, too, but the small schools had consistently better teams until 1973. Then, with the passage of Title IX, the larger schools slowly began to work their way into the tournament. What Iowans had always understood to be just—that girls could play, too—was now federal law. Big school or small, everybody now had girls' basketball.

"It's somewhat amazing," Beran said of Iowa's lead in the female athletic realm, "but the more I read about Iowa women, it isn't so surprising. The women here were strong and independent. It doesn't surprise me that the men who worked and lived alongside them thought they were capable of doing it."

(February 7, 1993)

Jane Burns, a native of Mount Horeb, WI, is a graduate of Drake University and has been with the Des Moines Register *since 1993. She was the 1993 winner of the Mel Greenberg Award for her coverage of women's collegiate basketball.*

PAM MINICK: INEXORABLY TIED TO ROPING

by Cathy Harasta
Dallas Morning News

PAM MINICK TENDERLY CLEANED THE CLODS FROM HER HORSE'S FEET. BYRON, her horse for the past 15 years, had just carried her to a $300 payday at the Windy Ryon Memorial Roping.

Her horse needed her first. Then came the deluge. The people needed her help.

The sound of her name rang along a row of booths selling saddles and sterling silver spurs, belt buckles almost as big as encyclopedias and hamburgers the heft of manhole covers. Someone shouted, "Pam!" from the dark interior of a barn. Her name echoed behind her as she slipped inside a trailer near the stock pens.

Minick, co-chairing this elite fund-raiser for the first time, exchanged her cowgirl hat for the bare-headed business of bookkeeping. She did not even get a chance to watch Troy Aikman's turn at the Celebrity Washer Pitch.

Cowgirls entered Minick's trailer to collect their winnings. Debbie Garrison, one of Minick's team-roping protegees, proudly brandished the jeweled bracelet she won for her finesse with a 35-foot nylon rope.

Cowboys filed into the trailer to hand their entry fees to Minick, a former Miss Rodeo America and Nevada high school rodeo champion. They asked her for draw sheets, safety pins and advice.

An exultant young cowboy unfurled his fingers to reveal a silver earring. He extended his palm to Minick, who had lost the earring while on the heels of a charging steer. She did not discover the earring's loss until after she washed her horse's feet. Byron always came first.

Minick had ridden Byron in hundreds of team-roping competitions like this one, about 40 miles northwest of Dallas. When it was over, Byron knew what to expect—clean feet and an occasional ham sandwich. Always, the clean feet.

"Animals know two things," Minick said. "Fear and repetition."

Minick, 38, conquered the first and learned to prize the second in her many-faceted rodeo career. She overcame fear of the unknown in childhood, when she taught herself to ride a horse. In sewing her ornate rodeo costumes, she learned that repetition fosters keenness and confidence. And that rhinestones and ribbons mesh with the gritty chores of tending livestock in rodeo's alluring paradox.

"It was all kind of a fate thing," said Minick, who recently won her second consecutive team-roping championship at the annual Walt Garrison Multiple Sclerosis Rodeo in Mesquite. "I'd do it all over again the same way. I learned by the seat of my pants."

Minick turned pro as a high school senior in 1971. She spent 16 years barrel racing before limiting herself to competitive team-roping, mostly at events in Texas and Oklahoma.

She ropes about twice a month as a sideline to her broadcasting and advertising jobs. But she says her roping is important beyond the money she routinely wins: "The biggest thing is the challenge," she said, "and the best thing is the camaraderie."

Roping connects her to the years she spent hauling a horse trailer to rodeos around the West. Sometimes, she would be on the road for six months: Arizona to California to Nevada to Oregon, then on to Washington and Wyoming.

"It wasn't easy to stop going down the road," said Minick, who lives in Roanoke. "But it also wasn't easy being on the road. Roping is a little more forgiving than barrel racing, which is like a kamikaze thing."

Minick's broadcasting work gives her visibility. Her role as the interviewer for The Nashville Network's cablecasts of the Mesquite Championship Rodeo has made her friends and fans from New Jersey to Nepal.

"Nobody explains it like Pam," said Gary Leffew, a former world champion bull rider. "Everybody knows her."

Minick's job as promotions and advertising manager for Billy Bob's Texas, the landmark Fort Worth nightclub, rewards her with security. She and her husband, Bill Minick, a former bull rider and rodeo producer, are part-owners of Billy Bob's Texas.

Her work as vice president of the Women's Professional Rodeo Association allows her to help direct her sport's progress.

But roping fills the void left when she stopped living the all-out rodeo life.

"We've never been able to make a good living at rodeo as contestants," Bill Minick said. "But that's where our roots are."

Those who rope with and against Pam Minick say she is a much-feared contestant. In team-roping, a pair of riders works together. The "header" ropes the steer's horns. Then the "heeler" finishes the job with a burst of speed and a precisely timed fling. The heeler's rope must capture the steer's back feet while they are extended straight out and parallel to the ground.

Danger lurks in the process of tightening the rope after the catch. The steer's weight creates tension, making the taut nylon blade-stiff. Debbie Garrison, who is married to former Dallas Cowboys football star Walt

Garrison, held up her finger, which had been severed in a roping accident. Surgeons re-attached the finger after it was found in her roping glove.

"Pam is very consistent," said Debbie Garrison, who frequently teams with Minick. "She gets to pick and choose her partners. Everybody helps each other. The girls in team-roping are a little older. There is not so much petty jealousy. Pam has the respect of all the men. This is really a macho type deal."

It began for Minick in her native Las Vegas with a homeless horse. Minick was 9 when she and her sister, Lynn, acquired a pair of horses displaced when plans for a theme park dissolved.

Minick, whose family knew nothing about horses, taught herself the basics of riding aboard Rebel, her palomino. She laughs now about the connection between a Vegas amusement park that never got off the ground and her career, which did.

Eventually, her mother, Edith Martin, traded an old Studebaker pickup to a neighbor on the condition he give the girls riding lessons. Minick started competing in a variety of events for young rodeo aspirants. She entered competitions including barrel racing, pole bending and even a novelty called the potato race, a speed event that required riders to spear potatoes at various points.

"I could have been a lot more successful at an earlier age if I had more training," Minick said. "But kids who had that professional training seemed to lose interest. We entered every event. It didn't matter whether we knew how to do it."

During her high school years, she borrowed a horse trailer and drove to rodeos in Nevada each weekend. She'd get her rest in a sleeping bag under the stars.

"There was not much time for movies," she said. "I never went to a high school football game."

Minick said she did not groom herself to become a rodeo queen, but her Miss Rodeo America title in 1973 was pivotal in her career. The crown required her to do some modeling and spend a year on what she called the "rubber chicken circuit" appearing at luncheons and fund-raisers.

She said the title led to broadcasting opportunities that began in 1976, when she was married to an Arizona auto dealer and traveling on the pro circuit. She has had steady work on equine sports programs. CBS, NBC, ESPN and TNN have tapped Minick's expertise.

Her experience and familiarity with rodeo technicalities help her to get the often shy cowboys to open up in an interview.

"I don't want to sound like a dumb blonde," she said. "That's important to them and that's important to me."

During a recent TNN taping at the Mesquite Arena, Minick interviewed Clemson football coach Ken Hatfield and his wife, Sandy, a barrel racer.

"Pam brings rodeo into people's living rooms around the world," Ken Hatfield said. "The support Pam has given rodeo has helped its exposure."

Kay Young, a former National Finals Rodeo barrel racer who traveled with Minick, said perseverance was Pam's trademark.

"Pam was one of the few Miss Rodeo Americas to really make a career out of it and have broadcasting longevity," Young said. "She earned everything she got. Her only fault is that she can't say 'No.'"

Young said Minick sometimes competed with less than first-rate horses, a hindrance for a barrel racer. "Pam was a good competitor," Young said. "But you get a horse that can take you to the National Finals Rodeo about as often as a trainer gets a Kentucky Derby winner."

Minick's best year was 1978, when she just missed a top-15 finish. She said she regrets never having won a barrel racing world championship. As the 1980s approached, she realized her broadcasting was taking more time. She cut back on her barrel racing. Roping helped take up the slack as she eased up on competition.

Her career pursuits often took her away from her Chandler, Arizona, home. Minick said she is not sure what role her absences played in the breakup of her first marriage. Perhaps that union lasted longer because she was not home much, Minick said.

Brandy Minick, 22, snickered as she viewed the old photographs of Pam with her rodeo trophies. Pictures covered the big dining room table in Pam and Bill Minick's two-story log house on an unpaved road in Roanoke.

"It's not nice to make fun of your stepmother," Pam said to Brandy with a laugh.

On a rare weekday at home, Pam got out her sewing things to mend a beige skirt for Brandy, Bill Minick's daughter by a previous marriage.

"Brandy is truly my best friend," said Pam, who married Bill almost nine years ago. "I think I've always been more of a sister figure than a stepmother figure to her."

In the summer, Pam and Bill Minick wait until the cool of evening. Then they turn on the lights of their 10-acre ranch's arena. They saddle a pair of horses and move their small herd of Mexican steers to the arena pens. Then they practice roping.

Pam persuaded Brandy to take up roping. Brandy got her boyfriend hooked on the sport.

"It's addictive," Brandy said. "You have to be very flexible when you're dealing with a partner, a steer, a horse and a rope."

She did not mention that a roper also must be precise. That went without saying. Pam was looking at the beige skirt and deciding exactly how to fix it.

(June 28, 1992)

Cathy Harasta, *a sports columnist for the* Dallas Morning News, *has covered such events as the Super Bowl, World Series, America's Cup and the Olympics. A native of Glens Falls, NY, she has a masters in English literature from the State University of New York in Binghamton. She and her husband, Joe, have two daughters.*

LIFE ON THE FLY

by Laura Vecsey
Albany Times Union

THIS IS THE LIFE, BONNY WARNER, ISN'T IT? STANDING ON TOP OF SOME GOD-forsaken mountain in Igls, Austria, with a cold, driving rain pelting down on your 29-year-old body, a body you concede might be getting a little old for this nonsense.

There you are, on the wintry, weather-beaten face of a mountain, thousands of miles from home in sunny California, waiting for your turn to practice your trade, which is sledding, also known as "sliding"—riding reclined, feet first, on your back, on the luge.

"This is not all a bed of roses," Warner will admit. "Just yesterday, when it was absolutely pouring rain, coming down so hard you can't see, I'm thinking, 'Here I am on some stupid mountain, on this stupid sled, what the hell am I doing here?'"

What she was doing was listening to that little voice in her head, the one that utters the words: Faster, faster. Higher, higher.

For the past decade, the sport of luge has been Bonny Warner's major preoccupation. By now, she's quite comfortable hurling her body down ice-slicked tracks at speeds most normal people would find . . . well, quite frankly, a bit nauseating.

The funny thing is, this flirtation with life in the fast and furious lane does not end with the luge.

Nope.

This articulate woman, who slid into prominence in the 1988 Winter Games in Calgary when her sixth-place finish was the best ever by an American in Olympic luge competition, now straps herself into the cockpit of jet airplanes and helps fly them.

"Ever since I was a little, tiny kid, I've been infatuated with flying," Warner said. "My goal, besides wanting to be in the Olympics, was that I wanted to be a pilot."

One year ago this past week, Bonny Warner received her pilot's license from United Airlines, where she now serves as a 2nd officer on 727 flights, acting as flight engineer by controlling fuel, pressurization, monitoring the engines. By next summer, she'll be a bona fide pilot.

It's an achievement she relishes.

"When I got hired, it was more exciting than going to the Olympics," Warner said. "The competition is so stiff. It's that competitive, and it takes that much time and energy. For me, it was a lot easier to make the Olympic team."

Since the beginning of this month, Warner has been on leave from United, her flying commitments temporarily put aside as she trains in Europe for World Cup competitions and the 1992 Winter Olympics in Albertville, France, where she wants to win a medal.

This endeavor does not stop her from training in her other chosen field. On the way to a luge training site in Latvia, Warner turned the flight into an on-board tutorial on piloting.

"I was jump-seating with the captain of this Aeroflot plane because it's the Russian equivalent to the 727," Warner said. "Pilots are pretty friendly folks, quite fraternal."

This is a typical Bonny Warner-ism, knowing how to extract the most from each experience; knowing how to seize the moment, see the future in everything she does.

In the long run, Warner knows her future's up there in the friendly skies. She takes great comfort in this. It's as if the course of her life is now charted, she says. Flying has ensured that the world of speed and travel is not stripped from her once she's finished with the glorious life of riding sleds through snow and rain.

For Bonny Warner, there's nothing alarming or dangerous or daredevilish about riding a sled 80 mph down a mountain. Likewise, there's nothing dangerous or daredevilish about piloting a huge airplane full of human passengers.

"The only thing that's common is the perception of being dangerous or daredevilish," she said. "Actually, you wouldn't be a good luger if you were a daredevil. You wouldn't be precise enough. And you certainly would not make it as an airline pilot. There's no room for error there."

There's a definite connection between sliding and flying, Warner says. "There are similarities, I think, in some respects because both are challenging," she said. "There's never a perfect luge run. There's always something you can do better. Same is true with flying. There's always a bigger airplane. There's always a goal you can attain. You're never perfect. It's a never-ending cycle. You can always be better, so you can never become complacent."

This word "complacent" would never describe Warner, a woman who was turned on to the little-known sport of luge during the 1980 Winter Games in Lake Placid. Warner was 17 at the time, arriving at the tiny Adirondack village as an Olympic torch bearer. Before the Games were done, she took a slide down the Mt. Van Hoevenberg luge track and found herself hooked on sledding, and the idea of competing for an Olympic medal.

The success came quickly, although Warner's involvement in the sport turned her college career at Stanford University into a marathon before she finally earned a degree in journalism seven years later.

By 1981, Warner was a member of the U.S. National Luge Team and in 1984 she went to Sarajevo for the Winter Games, where she crashed and finished way out. In 1987, she finished fifth at the World Luge Championships, tying for the highest U.S. finish ever in that event.

In Calgary, Warner made a tremendous impression on followers of those Olympics by her incredible sixth-place finish. She took the notoriety and ran with it, transforming herself into the unofficial U.S. spokeswoman for the sport of luge, determined to enlist the youth and enlighten the masses.

"I have gotten so much out of this sport, and when you get something out, you should return it," she said. "I think I'm going to be returning for rest of my life."

Warner's main thrust in promoting luge, she said, has been to quash the misconceptions, the myths.

"It's a lot safer than people think and it's not something that crazy daredevils are compelled to do," she said. "I've felt my job has been to dispel the image of lugers as a bunch of insane lunatics. I think that we're making headway."

Because of luge, Warner said, she will always "look at the world differently."

"I've seen Europe change. Over the last 10 years, what has happened is incredible. Seeing that has been very important to me."

In facing her future, it was crucial for Warner to stay in touch, to have this access to the world.

"I wonder what my life would have been if I hadn't gotten involved in luge, because that turned into flying," she said. "For years, I've had this. I know Europe like the back of my hand and I want to see more, South America, travel and see the world."

The security of her future in the sky has given Warner a renewed enthusiasm for and focus on this year's competition. She feels, after 10 years of sliding, that she's on top of her game. It's tinged with a sense that this may be the last time she'll slide around the world.

"When we arrived in Latvia for the first training session, I wanted it to be good because perhaps it might be my last time there," Warner said. "I have gone to that track and been in that town 30 times over the past 10 years. I found that on my last day, I was pushing to do my best. It was that important to me."

(Noember 10, 1991)

Laura Vecsey is a columnist at the Albany Times Union *where she began as general news reporter covering dying cities and growing suburbs. A graduate of Sarah Lawrence College and the mother of a five-year-old boy, she is the co-owner of a small cafe in Schenectady that specializes in vegetarian food and gourmet sandwiches.*

RICHLY REWARDED

by Barbara Barker
Bergen *Record*

A WOMAN IN A WOOL CAP CROUCHED NEXT TO A CHAIN-LINK FENCE ON WEST 106th and picked at her bare feet. Several yards away, two tired-looking men poked through the remains of a motor.

There was garbage and graffiti everywhere. There also were television cameras and reporters and a bunch of important-looking people in expensive suits.

They did not come to talk to the woman. Nor the two men. The object of their attention was a ceremony on the other side of the fence, where a 21-year-old basketball player officially became a millionaire Thursday.

Jamal Mashburn, who has yet to play a professional basketball game, announced a multi-million-dollar endorsement deal with Fila, a sportswear manufacturer, on the playground behind Booker T. Washington Junior High School. As a signing bonus, Mashburn received a 1993 Ferrari Spyder, which was driven onto the playground for all to admire.

His mother and father and college coach at Kentucky, Rick Pitino, were there to witness this rite of passage. So was a small group of Booker T. Washington students. This was their reward for making the honor roll.

Each student got a pair of sneakers at the end of the presentation. Some got to shoot baskets with Mashburn and received his autograph. Weaved in with the million-dollar contract and fancy sports car and talk of being a role model, however, the students also got a somewhat disconcerting lesson on the meaning of success.

The students were told that Mashburn, a University of Kentucky star who will almost certainly be among the first three players chosen in the June 30 National Basketball Association draft, grew up on 159th Street and Eighth Avenue, not far from their school. Corporate type after corporate type walked to a podium to extol the virtues of the young man who came from their neighborhood.

"We're here to show hard work gets rewarded. That's why today is special," Jack Steinweiss, vice president of sales, told the students. "Today a young man from New York City who has given it his all and has carried himself with grace and dignity has grown from humble beginnings and become a millionaire.

"You couldn't have picked a more deserving person."

There is little doubt Mashburn is a deserving role model. Asked by one of

258

the students who his heroes were when he was growing up, Mashburn gestured at his parents.

This was obviously a very big day for Mashburn's father, Bobby. A former heavyweight fighter, the elder Mashburn never achieved the financial success his son has now. Bobby Mashburn mugged for photographers and signed autographs.

He said he soon would quit his job with the New York City police to spend time with his son.

Helen Mashburn, who had most of the responsibility for raising Jamal after divorcing Bobby eight years ago, did not seem to share the rest of her family's love for the limelight.

Helen works as a bookkeeper and still lives in the Harlem apartment where she raised her only son. She said she might move, but likes her job and probably will keep it.

"I guess I have some decisions to make," she said.

She wanted to keep her son busy when he was growing up. She took him to movies and museums and ballgames, hoping to find something that would interest him. Basketball is simply what took.

"I guess the secret is that I always kept communication open," she said. "I wanted Jamal to know he could talk to me about anything, even if it was something I really didn't want to hear. We talked."

It's too bad they don't make shoe commercials about middle-aged bookkeepers.

They also don't make commercials about junior high students in the ghetto. And they don't give them cars. This was a point not lost on one young student, who asked Mashburn how important it was that he was making a lot of money.

"I had a dream fulfilled, and everything else comes along with it," he said. "The important thing is to be in school and be humble and respect your parents and everything will fall in place.

"I just think being happy is the key. Money isn't everything, but it helps."

A bell rang inside the school, meaning the news conference would soon end. The television cameras would leave. So would the men in suits.

The graffiti and garbage and the woman and the two men on the street would remain. The children passed them on the way home.

(June 11, 1993)
Barbara Barker *covers the National Football League and other sports for the Bergen* Record *in New Jersey. She has degrees from the University of Michigan and the graduate school of journalism at Northwestern and is indebted to her parents for sharing their love of sports and good writing.*

Peggy Schlater's Foreign Policy

by Cathy Breitenbucher
Milwaukee Sentinel

As a metaphor for life, there's no better sport for Peggy Schlater than figure skating.

Schlater has seen her 15 years on the ice go by in a blur, as if she's performing one of those dizzying flying camel spins that leave her stomach someplace last Tuesday when today is Friday.

She's had to pick herself up from many a fall, brush the snow off her rear end and get back on her feet.

And Schlater has had to smile bravely while wondering why she's trying so hard but not getting ahead. Tears and rhinestones are a terrible combination.

"Sometimes I wish, why couldn't I have been a runner? You cross the finish line and you know where you've finished," said Schlater.

Ever since blade first touched ice, figure skating has been encumbered by politics, petty jealousies and accusations of deal-cutting.

Judging controversies have provided some of the sport's most vivid pictures in recent years—from Dorothy Hamill tearfully circling the ice at the 1974 world championships while the crowd booed the previous skater's scores to Alex McGowan holding his nose in protest at the '88 Olympics over the numbers posted for his pupil, Debi Thomas.

Schlater says politics have been part of her skating career, keeping her from ascending to the upper echelon of the U.S. rankings. But now Schlater has turned the politics of international sport to her advantage.

Schlater—born, raised and trained in Wisconsin—competes for Italy. In October, she won the first of four meets that will determine the Italian national champion. And waiting for her at rinkside when she completed her routines was Carlo Fassi, perhaps the world's most respected coach.

"I think he's really good politically for me, standing at the door," Schlater said. "The judges are afraid to place his kids where they don't belong."

Besides being blessed with the talent it takes to succeed in figure skating, Schlater was born with something else—a claim on Italian citizenship. Her mother, Lena, was born in Rende in southern Italy.

"I moved to Kenosha in 1955 when I was 7 years old," Lena Schlater said recently at the State Fair Park indoor ice arena, where Peggy trains when she is in this country. "I never thought this would open up the doors for her to skate."

But skate she has, starting at age 4 at the Kenosha County Ice Arena. "She was the only one, and I wanted her to learn to play the piano, swim, things like that," Lena Schlater said. "Little did I know it would go this far."

Just how far Schlater ultimately will go in figure skating will depend on many factors: how consistently she can land those crucial triple jumps, how quickly she can build a reputation with the judges, how well other Italian skaters perform. Much of it is out of her hands.

At the first meet of the Italian nationals, reigning champion Sabine Contini, 22, placed third. Schlater stood on the top step of the medalists' podium.

"I thought it was a big win, not just because I beat her (Contini), but because in the last two (Italian) competitions I got third," said Schlater. "Now they have to think about sending me to Europeans or Worlds. They have to stop and think, 'Oh, she's skating really well.'"

Note that Schlater doesn't talk about the 1992 Olympics. Even if she did win the two phases of the Italian championship that precede the Olympics, the national skating federation would be under no obligation to name her to the team for Albertville. And because Italy is not a traditional power in figure skating—only four times in all Olympic history has an Italian woman placed in the top eight—that country gets only one entrant in the Games.

No, Schlater is pointing for 1994, when the Winter Games move to their new schedule and will be held in Lillehammer, Norway.

"That would be the perfect age for me," said Schlater, who turned 19 on Oct. 21. "I'd like to start school, but I've worked so hard to get here I'd be thinking about what I could have done."

No regrets. That's the philosophy Peggy Schlater has built her skating career on. Rather than leaving home at the age of 10 or 12 to train, as many skaters do, Schlater stayed introverted at home in Kenosha.

"This way, she had a real normal upbringing," said Lena Schlater. "She was able to go to the prom, be in plays."

However, by declining to move to a major skating center to work with a big-name coach, Schlater probably sacrificed her opportunity for success in the U.S. figure skating system. Only when she had graduated from St. Joseph High School was Schlater ready to commit her all to skating. On Sept. 30, 1990, when she didn't speak a word of Italian, Schlater left to train in Milan.

"I had never even flown by myself," she said.

Now Schlater flies regularly—from Wisconsin to Italy, and between ice rinks on two continents. In the past year, she's added two triples to her repertoire, bringing to five the gravity-defying three-revolution jumps she performs.

"She's very striking when you see her out on the ice," said Sue Susic Ervin of New Berlin, who has been Schlater's primary coach for four years. "She has great natural speed and she doesn't show any fear in going for these more difficult jumps at a high rate of speed. That impresses you."

The jumps come at a price, measured both in time and dollars. Schlater is on the ice three hours a day, and coaching and ice time in Italy are double or triple the cost in Wisconsin. Then there are the five flights—so far—Schlater has taken to Milan. Because she represents Italy, Schlater isn't eligible for financial aid from the U.S. Olympic Committee or the U.S. Figure Skating Association.

Further complicating the situation is the fact that Schlater's father, Fred, has lived in Raleigh, North Carolina, since his 1990 transfer by Massey-Ferguson. Lena Schlater is staying in Wisconsin until their Kenosha house sells.

So how does the family manage to pay the bills?

"I don't know," Schlater said, rolling her eyes. "We haven't had a new car in a while."

What the Schlaters do have is a dream.

"I've worked so hard for this," Peggy said. "It's what I've always dreamed of. Going to the Olympics would be the ultimate."

(November 15, 1991)

Cathy Breitenbucher spent 10 years as a sportswriter for the Milwaukee Sentinel *where she covered the 1984 and 1988 Olympics. Now a Milwaukee-based free-lance writer and editor, her specialties are Olympic sports—particularly speed skating—and hockey.*

Joyner-Kersee Beat a Tough Start

by Miki Turner
Oakland Tribune

THERE ARE MANY THINGS THAT SET JACKIE JOYNER-KERSEE APART FROM OTHER world-class athletes.

You may start with her consecutive Olympic gold medals in the heptathlon, her World Championship wins in the long jump and heptathlon, her Sullivan Award as America's top amateur athlete and her many world records. It is a list of accomplishments that allow her to be considered among the greatest female athletes in history.

Then there are the things that aren't measured by minutes and seconds, by distance and height. The things that make her a great person.

To fully understand what motivates this champion, it is necessary to journey to a place most natives are loath to call home, much less to want to return after escaping.

The place is East St. Louis, Illinois. It's a dreadfully ugly, perpetually impoverished and crime-ridden industrial city nestled on the banks of the muddy Mississippi.

This is the place Jackie Joyner-Kersee calls home.

It is where she witnessed a murder at age 11. It is where she ate mayonnaise sandwiches for dinner. It is where she was teased for wearing the same outfit on consecutive days. It is where her grandfather was shot to death by a murderer under the influence of drugs and alcohol.

It is where she dreamed. And it is a place she never really left.

Despite her riches, her lucrative endorsement contracts, her big house in the San Fernando Valley and her worldwide fame, Joyner-Kersee has remained a simple East St. Louis homegirl—a purist.

"It's important to me to stay close to home both physically and mentally," she said during a recent Bay Area visit. "The people at home are always on my mind and in my heart."

With that in mind, she established the Jackie Joyner-Kersee Foundation in 1988. It is an organization, located just blocks from what's left of her old family home, that provides financial assistance to young aspiring inner-city athletes.

"It's important to me that the kids there see that their dreams too can become reality," she said. "I tell the kids who come to the center not to aspire to be like me. I tell them to aspire to be the best they can be and to work

263

hard."

Perhaps no one has worked harder or had to work harder than Joyner-Kersee. She is finally reaping the rewards and gaining the respect an athlete of her caliber should have realized long ago.

She says Barcelona was her proudest moment as an athlete because winning back-to-back heptathlons was no easy task. She considers herself blessed to have done it. Her only regret is that her mother, who died when Joyner-Kersee was a freshman at UCLA in 1980, didn't live to see it.

Mom would have been very proud. So extraordinary was her performance that former Olympic decathlete Bruce Jenner proclaimed her the greatest athlete ever. It's a crown she wears with both pride and her own unique brand of modesty.

"I take all that stuff in stride because I know where I come from and I know what it took to get where I am," she said. "I also realize that in years to come there's going to be someone else. Plus, I feel that my existence as a person is more to me than the things I have accomplished athletically."

Nonetheless, 30-year-old Joyner-Kersee has turned a deaf ear to those who feel she should retire now while she's at the top. The tough little girl from East St. Louis has never backed down from a challenge. Nor has she ever lost sight of her goals.

"My goal is to go to Atlanta in 1996," she said. "The temptation of competing on American soil is just too great. My first Olympic experience was Los Angeles, and if I could finish my athletic career on American soil, then, God willing, I'm going to do it."

There are few athletes who can walk comfortably alongside Joyner-Kersee. Hers is a huge shadow. It takes a special kind of person to do what she has done, to go where she has gone, and still remain only a heartbeat from home.

It is said that great athletes are born out of struggle. If that's the case, then Joyner-Kersee must surely be the greatest of them all.

(August 14, 1992)

Miki Turner, who covers colleges and writes an occasional column for the Orange County Register, *was the first African-American woman to write a regularly featured sports column at a major metropolitan newspaper, the* Oakland Tribune. *She also hosts a television sports talk show.*

SIX

PLAYING GAMES

THE MOST INTIMIDATING GAME OF ALL

by Lesley Visser
Golf Digest

I SHOULD SAY RIGHT UP FRONT THAT I'VE NEVER BEEN TO THE CATHEDRAL IN ST. Andrews, never been to Carnoustie or Troon, and the only time I've seen the wild, open spaces of Royal Birkdale, I was more thrilled to learn Liverpool was only 35 miles away, where the Beatles first sang "Twist and Shout." I guess that makes me a heathen. But I'm also a struggling golfer, a Johnette-come-lately who now wishes her childhood fantasies weren't of shagging balls off "the Wall" at Fenway Park but of passing down Augusta's Magnolia Lane with a swagger and a 6-handicap . . .

That is, if they decided to allow women through Augusta's Magnolia Lane. And I don't mean legally, I mean psychologically. Now, don't make that face, because you know who you are. And so do we. I've dated them, I've worked with them, I might even be married to one of them. I'll give you an example.

Two winters ago, some very nice people from the Doral Ryder Open invited me to play in their pro-am, which had never invited a woman before.

Well, judging from the reaction of my colleagues, you'd think I'd been called to plan strategy for the next Desert Storm. John Madden—a man who loves teaching football to women—was horrified. "You can't play in the Doral pro-am," he sputtered. "What if you hit someone in the gallery?" Terry Bradshaw, my friend and teammate on "NFL Today," was even worse. "There are thousands, I mean thousands, of people watching," he said, his Louisiana accent in full bloom. "What if you whiff?"

So, completely intimidated, I asked the nice people from Doral if they'd call again later, after I'd entered some priesthood of golf and perfected my game.

Intimidating women through golf is nothing new. In fact, it should be one of those courses they teach at the Harvard Business School. I'm sure that back around the 15th century, when the game was first played on the moors of Scotland, the men would unfasten their armor, remove their sweat-soaked clothes and the game would be on. The women, meanwhile, would wait in the clubhouse—assuming they could get in, and that's a big leap in historical logic—dressed in their fine brocade, hoping only to be noticed at the end of the day. Since then, of course, outstanding women golfers have made tremendous progress, but the average Jo and those of us with certifiable 28-handicaps face social and psychological terrors every time we tee up.

I remember the day novelist John Spooner took me to the hallowed grounds of The Country Club in Brookline, Massachusetts, for a round in the early spring. It was 1979, and I'd played golf maybe four or five times in my life (up to 30 times as I write this). I'll never forget the sickening look on his face when he realized I would be taking my pitiful game around the institution that had been home to Francis Ouimet and Julius Boros.

Okay, I was no Curtis Strange, but in fairness, he'd been warned. I told him that my two favorite clubs were the sand wedge and the rake. By the time we faced the interminable 11th hole, the one that stretches on for a mile with what seems like the Atlantic Ocean in the middle, Spooner was praying for rain. I'll never forget the 18th, either. My fifth shot went over the green, my wedge rolled past the pin and I three-putted to finish the day. I was ecstatic. Spooner ran to the clubhouse and ordered a double Manhattan. He never invited me back.

Other women have similar tales. Cindy Shmerler, a friend of mine and an accomplished writer, once invited Ivan Lendl to play with her at Fairview Country Club in Greenwich, Connecticut. Lendl, a gracious and easygoing golfer, decided to work on his comic routine. When the gallery had filled to 30 or 40 people, he went for his best stuff. "I'm going to stand in front of Cindy," he announced to the crowd as she prepared to swing. "It's obviously the safest place."

At least Shmerler was allowed to play without feeling she'd violated someone's Constitutional rights. Another friend of mine, Judy Carlough, the former general manager of radio station XTRA in San Diego, used to play occasionally at Charles River near Boston. Now Charles River is one of those clubs where the people are very nice, as long as a woman isn't trying to do something unseemly, like eat a hamburger in the men's grill.

"It's a wonderful place," said Carlough, "but a woman definitely feels like an Indian strolling through the army camp." And forget being single. Carlough considered joining Charles River until she was made to feel "as if I were an untouchable wearing a sign—LOSER. CAN'T FIND A HUSBAND."

Why is it that otherwise courtly and considerate men become such terrorists when we take to the tee? We can get up and down out of a sand trap with the same bad swing and same bad judgment that most men have. I know the perception is that most women golfers are slow, uncoordinated and have never sunk a putt that mattered. But some of the men I see are pretty lousy, too, and they aren't hurried off the course. They even have a tournament to celebrate how bad they are. I remember reading about that guy, Angelo Spagnolo, a grocer from Pennsylvania, who shot a 257 for 18 holes and was invited on the "Today" show. A woman would have been run out of town.

At least we don't blame the equipment. Every man I know changes his clubs about every 10 minutes. They all think that some dazzling new combination of manganese, graphite and copper will make them the next Greg Norman. And a woman would never confuse the issue by calling a piece of equipment a "metal wood."

I'll admit it, maybe we don't look so good playing golf. It's an awkward sport and, hey, a lot of men don't look that great either. We can hack our way through the sawgrass, humbly communing with nature's flora and fauna, and still walk the final fairway in shame the same as a man can. And it's not like basketball, where the move counts almost as much as the bucket. They say golf can't be mastered. Why should we be excluded from trying?

I should tell you about my marriage. When I first met Dick Stockton, I thought I'd been blessed. This was a man who knew every starter of every Final Four team and could play Gershwin on the piano. For a woman who covered sports and loved "Porgy and Bess," I thought I'd won the Stanley Cup. For the first six or seven years, all was bliss. We'd take our tennis racquets everywhere from Portofino to Glasgow. We went to shows and museums and saw strange animals in the Galapagos Islands and the San Diego Zoo.

I blame Bill Russell for what happened next. Dick's former broadcasting partner—the NBA Hall of Famer who symbolized strength and independence—reduced my husband to a winged foot who actually talks about clubhead speed. He sent Dick a new set of golf clubs (okay, in truth, he sent me a set, too) and Dick's never been the same. Three years ago, we went to Kenya on a safari with Vince Doria, who had been my sports editor at the *Boston Globe*, and his wife, Suzanne. On the third day—and I am not making this up—Dick and Vince found a nine-hole course on the outskirts of Nairobi. They had to tee off next to a watering hole and drive around some kudus and a wildebeest. To this day, I don't think they've ever talked about the breathtaking wildlife of the Serengeti or the glory of Mount Kilimanjaro, but they revel in that par 3 by the natural salt lick.

Five years ago, we bought a home in Boca Raton, Florida, where we overlook the 14th tee. There are already 15,000 golf courses in this country and I expect the Japanese to be adding another 20,000 or 30,000 in the next few months. All these will simply offer more opportunities for women to be intimidated. We will be plunking down thousands of dollars for the right to eat by ourselves in a quarantined room, to be hurried off the course (after noon, when we're finally allowed to play) and to have men roll their eyes at us from yards away.

At Boca West, where we live, there is at least a shred of decency. As

Gerry Witt, one longtime addict, said the other day, "When I go out to play at 7 in the morning, which my wife thinks is crazy, I get dressed in the kitchen." Seven a.m.? While the course is still wet? I know about this first-hand. Dick has a group of guys who are finished playing by 9:30 in the morning. They call it "fast-break" golf. One man, Bud Seretean, is in a particular hurry. He will be ready to play at 7:01, have hit both his drive and his mulligan by 7:02 and be driving down the cartpath at breakneck speed by 7:03. Of course, at that hour, they can't even see the ball. They have to judge where it landed by the sound, or follow the wet trail in the grass. Bud tells the story that one time, when he agreed to play at 11 in the morning, he got stuck behind a foursome of women. "They begin hitting their shots quickly and running up to the ball. It was sad," he says.

Oh really?

The most intimidating experience I've ever had, in or out of golf, was the time CBS took a group of football directors, producers and announcers to Pebble Beach for a three-day seminar. I was the only woman invited and easily the worst golfer. For years, having read almost all of John Steinbeck, I'd wanted to see this part of the country. And having watched Jack Lemmon a few times in the Crosby, I drew strength from the fact that not everyone in the Monterey Peninsula had a 3-handicap. The first night was fabulous. We stayed at the Inn at Spanish Bay, traded stories and laughs and set our alarms to get up early with the mist.

Cypress Point was inspirational, with those rolling hills, the wild deer and the headland that juts into the Pacific. Some have even referred to it as the Sistine Chapel of Golf, and that about sums it up. At 8 a.m., we all went over to the club, dividing into foursomes by the modest wooden golf shop. I was having a great time. Then I saw the first hole—421 yards, downhill, and slightly more difficult than climbing Mount Everest. Randy Cross, one of our announcers and the former All-Pro center for San Francisco, drove the ball 250 yards. Dan Jiggetts, the offensive lineman with the Chicago Bears, nailed his down the fairway.

I thought I was melting. By the time I approached the tee, I'd completely forgotten the majestic beauty of the cypress trees and was concentrating on avoiding a panic attack. Why did the hole have to curve to the right? Why was I left-handed? Why didn't my father take me to a golf course when I was old enough to walk? I hit the ball about 60 yards and people clapped as if I'd won the Pulitzer Prize. The next few holes, thank God, were in the forest, where no one could see me except my own supportive group. There, in the solitude, I shot 10s and 11s on those endless par 5s. The short seventh was actually fun and I even hit enough straight drives to look forward to the back nine.

Or so I thought, until everything led out to sea for all to see. I know that everyone who has ever played or watched the game of golf has an image of the magnificent 16th hole at Cypress Point. Inspiring wonder and reverence, you have to drive across the ocean to a promontory 233 yards away where the green sits like an angel on the head of a pin. As Dave Marr once said, "You twist in the wind all day, waiting for the 16th to appear." To the right is nothing but ocean, to the left a tiny sliver of peninsula and in front of the green is a beach full of ice plant. For a rookie golfer, a woman, and someone playing with the likes of Randy Cross, it was an accident waiting to happen.

Okay, I said to myself, it's only a par 3. Sure, and the Olympic 100-meter is only a sprint. Optimistically, I put only four balls in my pocket and thanked the gods of golf that there wasn't a 40 m.p.h. gale. Wishing to spare you the discouraging details, suffice it to say that I made it to the green in 9 and got down in 3. My memory is that such a challenging hole, with the target so close and yet so threatening, surely must have been designed by a man. A woman would have made it equally dramatic, but left something to save the ego.

All of this isn't to imply that women should give up on golf—or on men. I'd love to learn the game and I've accepted the fact that our vacations now include a Nicklaus course or two. Last summer we headed for Mauna Lani on the Big Island, and I was just as excited about seeing the lava along the fairways as I was about witnessing the Kohala coast.

I've never been to the Masters, but, like most sports fans, it's on my list— even though when it comes to women and golf, Augusta is the mother of all intimidators. Frank Chirkinian, the legendary CBS producer, once said with a straight face, "There is nothing humorous at the Masters. Small dogs do not bark and babies do not cry." Women, apparently a cut below, do not even rate a mention. But there is hope. More women are taking up the game and more are getting better at it. Maybe one day, we'll be heading membership drives and organizing tee times. Of course, the real breakthrough will occur when Frank begs me to handle the commentary from "Amen Corner."

(April, 1992)
Lesley Visser, a sports broadcaster for CBS, became the first female beat writer in the National Football League in 1976 when she covered the New England Patriots for the Boston Globe. *A cum laude graduate of Boston College in 1975 with a degree in English, she is particularly proud of having been named one of* Esquire *magazine's "women we love" in 1990.*

MY GOLFER, MY SELF

by Christine Brennan
Washington Post

WE TRUDGED TOWARD THE 18TH GREEN, MY GOLFER AND I, OUR THREE-DAY, 11-MILE journey over the emerald hills and valleys of Hershey, Pennsylvania, all but a few yards from being over. People in lawn chairs were waiting for us around the green. There were several hundred in the gallery and they were applauding, which I thought was nice. The cheering wasn't for the person loaded down with the bag, of course. It was for the woman carrying the putter I had just handed her.

The 18th is the place where dreams come true, or where they just get strung along for another week. It's where one pro golfer wins the tournament on Sunday afternoon when the shadows get long. And where all the others pick up their balls and walk off, dreaming about the day they will be in her place.

"Someday," said Tracy Kerdyk, the 24-year-old LPGA golfer I've known for eight years. "Someday, I'll walk up 18 and everyone will be standing there, cheering for me. I have tears in my eyes right now, just thinking about it."

This day, we arrived at 18 two hours too early. Tracy was not among the leaders.

Her name never made the big board that flanks the green. She was one of those also-rans whose names appear down the list in the agate type Monday morning in the sports section. She was going to finish tied for 54th, earn $679 for the week and move on to the next stop on the tour.

Tracy and the two other members of the Ladies Professional Golf Association she was playing with waved to the people surrounding the green and disappeared into a tent to add up their scores. A par on 18, a three-over 75 for the round, a week's work completed on a sun-splashed Sunday afternoon. We went back to the hotel, changed, packed, checked out and still made it back to 18 in time to watch a woman named Cathy Gerring take that same walk and win the tournament.

Tracy has never won on the LPGA tour, but she's in just her second year and she will win, because she is very good. Gerring is in her sixth year and until Hershey, she had never won. Leading on Saturday and tempting fate, Gerring asked her husband to fly in from Columbus, Ohio, for the final round. He almost flew to the wrong city.

And when tournament officials told Gerring right after she signed her score card that it was time for her victory ceremony on the 18th green, she said she couldn't go out there. They told her to come along. Thousands of people were waiting. A high school band had just marched in.

Still she resisted. It turned out that she too had dreamt of this moment as she walked up six years' worth of 18th fairways.

"I'll be there in a few minutes," she said. "I've got to go call my dad."

I have a few disclaimers to issue right off the bat. I took lessons as a kid, but I don't play golf now. I don't know golf. I don't watch golf. And I don't do sand traps. Or, at least, I didn't until this spring.

I'm a sportswriter at the *Washington Post*. I play lots of sports for fun, but I observe for a living. I don't cheer when the Redskins score a touchdown. I write it down. In my job, I'm on the outside, looking in.

Nearly a year ago, Tracy, then in the midst of a satisfying run that ended with her being runner-up LPGA Rookie of the Year, asked me if I wanted to caddie for her someday. Tracy is like a little sister to me. When she was in high school and I was beginning my career as a sportswriter at the *Miami Herald*, she'd come by the University of Miami press box to find me and talk. One day she was depressed and thinking of giving up golf. I told her to give it a few more weeks before she made up her mind. That was six years ago. So she trusted me to carry her bag and play amateur psychologist for the week.

"As long as you don't mind that your caddie gives you absolutely no help," I said.

No problem, she said. I remembered that George Plimpton couldn't skate and still played goaltender for the Boston Bruins. He became my inspiration.

Tracy and I picked Hershey because the purse of $300,000 wasn't the tour's largest. Tracy did warn me that the hills of Hershey were murder. I bought a Lifecycle and started working out.

I liked the idea of caddying for her. I'm never going to be allowed to stand in a Redskins huddle. I can't listen to Georgetown basketball coach John Thompson during a timeout. But here was a professional golfer inviting me to spend a week as her caddie, to carry her bag, to clean her clubs, to listen to her, to laugh with her.

Another enticement was the opportunity to write a story about someone I first wrote about eight years ago. I deal with all kinds of professional athletes now, but I wasn't there when they were kids. I didn't get to ask them what they were thinking, what they were dreaming.

With Tracy, whom I had written about when she was 16 years old and beating the boys, I did.

* * *

"Let's give a warm Chocolate Town welcome to a graduate and two-time all-American from the University of Miami, a member of the 1988 U.S. Curtis Cup team and the 1988 collegiate player of the year, Tracy Kerdyk."

It was Friday afternoon, and the announcer was introducing one of the final threesomes at the start of the three-day, 54-hole Lady Keystone Open. I stood beside one of the tee markers—which are shaped like big Hershey Kisses—with my hands on Tracy's upright blue and white Mizuno bag, watching Tracy tee it up.

She hit her drive. Her Titleist 8 landed in the fairway, and we both breathed a sigh of relief. She pulled her tee out of the ground as I gathered up the bag and scurried over to her. "I was so worried about you, I thought I might duff it off the tee," she said.

As Tracy and I were embarking on our adventure, I imagined the worst things that could happen: that I would step on someone's ball, walk in a player's putting line on the green, sneeze during someone's shot, yank the entire cup out as I pulled the pin from the hole or get fired.

We had been practicing since Monday at the site of the tournament—the Hershey Country Club West Course—so that I wouldn't make a fool of myself or, worse, of Tracy. That first day Tracy had tossed two balls on the first green and told me to tend the pin. I knew what this meant: I had to stand beside the pin, grab hold of the flag and pin with one hand and pull it out of its tight hole when she hit the putt. Months earlier, over the phone from a tournament in Hawaii, she had issued her first warning to me: If the ball hits the pin while you're holding it, it's a two-stroke penalty. Two strokes at the top of the Hershey money list ended up meaning the difference between $45,000 and $14,250.

So she stroked the putt and I pulled the pin. As I brought it out, I put a nick in the grass above the hole. No, Tracy said, you can't do that. That little mark might change the way a ball rolls around the hole. If another golfer sees a caddie do that, it's big trouble. And the player is responsible for the caddie. So Tracy started getting nervous. I didn't blame her.

The rest of the day, I learned to stand with my feet together, shoulders thrown back, my free arm behind my back, perfectly motionless, as I held onto that pin. I pulled it out without hitting anything. I felt better, but I needed more practice.

My next work came Wednesday, the day of the pro-am. Pro-ams are silly but necessary. Tracy played with four amateurs, men of varying ability. The worst but most lovable was Sid, a county official from Harrisburg. He told Tracy that he wanted a kiss for every birdie putt he made. Tracy seemed safe—until Sid sank two birdie putts in a row. Joyous, he amended the rule to include the caddie.

Tracy returned the favor by telling Sid that if any of his drives didn't make it past the ladies' tees, he'd have to play strip golf. One look at Sid, an older gentleman with an ample belly, had everyone rooting strongly for him to hit towering drives. On the first hole, it was a close call. The rest of the way, Sid—and all of us—were safe.

The pro-am was fun and games for the golfers but I still had duties—like cleaning golf balls, tending the pin and carrying Tracy's bag, of course. Thank God for the evolution of shoulder pads in women's clothing. My shoulder never ached, not even after five trips around the 6,300-yard course. I gave full credit to Liz Claiborne.

Several holes into the pro-am round, I was struggling to keep my head above water. Tracy was pulling clubs, using them and handing them back to me, and I was trying to clean them with my omnipresent white towel—half-wet, half-dry—and put them back in the right place as I walked with the bag over my shoulder. I was failing, miserably. Half a dozen clubs were out of place. I set down the bag for Tracy's next shot, and she looked at it. Startled, she looked up at me.

"This cannot happen during the tournament."

There was no laughter in her voice. I was in trouble.

Thursday night, on the eve of the first round, I met in the hotel bar with Tommy Grogan, a 38-year-old former Wall Street sales rep who has caddied on the LPGA tour for five years for various players, including Cathy Gerring and Tracy. Tommy caddied for Tracy a month before I did, and he became my coach. His first piece of advice to me was simple: "Don't fall down."

I told him about my lack of organizational skills with Tracy's clubs. He said not to worry about it, and that if things got a little tense, I could even use the incident to loosen Tracy up. He said, "Tomorrow, a few holes into the round, even if every club is in the right place, I want you to mess a few up, put down the bag, look her right in the eye and say, 'It's happening!'"

My opportunity came early in the first round of the tournament. We had gone through a few holes and Tracy had parred every one, but when I set down the bag in the fairway, I noticed the 9-iron was where the 5-iron should have been, and vice versa. I hoped Tracy wasn't looking as I pulled the two clubs out to make a fast switch. She was looking. I shrugged and said my lines: "It's happening!"

Tracy smiled. A few holes later, when she was four over par, she wouldn't have laughed. Jokes only work at even-par or better.

Another trick of the trade Tracy wanted me to learn was to immediately hand over her putter after a shot to the green. It was an exchange, really;

she would hand me the club she had just hit, and I would give her the putter. It took me a couple holes to pick this up. Then, I got good at it. So good,
in fact, that in the pro-am alone, I twice handed her the putter when her
approach shot was not on the green. Sheepishly, I put the putter back in the
bag and trudged on, waiting to see what disaster awaited us.

Tommy gave me one other tip. If my player was in a bunker by the green,
I should have the putter ready to hand her when she hit out of the trap. On
the 12th hole of our first day of the tournament, I had a chance to practice
this little maneuver.

Tracy was in the sand trap; I stood beside it, holding the rake in one hand
and keeping the bag still with my other hand. I leaned the bag against my
leg and reached in for the putter as she dug her feet into the sand. Tracy has
a very consistent game around the greens, but, for some reason, she hit a terrible shot out of the trap. I watched it pop up and settle into the rough well
short of the green.

"Set down the rake," she said sharply. "Come with me."

Before I could move, she eyed the putter in my hand. I wished it could
have turned invisible at that moment. And me with it. She had just hit her
worst shot of the day, and there I was rubbing it in by foolishly holding the
club she could not yet use.

Tracy bogeyed the hole, saving herself the ignominy of a double bogey
with a wonderful putt, an eight-footer downhill sliding to the right. I breathed
hard.

"I feel so stupid," I told her.

"Don't worry about it," she said, handing me her putter.

The next hole, No. 13, she three-putted to go four over par and walking
up the fairway on 14 I told Tracy I didn't know what to say. I couldn't help
her with yardage or club selection or the wind or reading greens, but at least
I thought I could keep her loose. But that wasn't happening. I had told her
the day before that, when the tournament started, we were both going to be
confident and have fun.

"I have no confidence and I'm not having fun," Tracy told me.

Great, I thought. I had given up on the jokes I memorized for the occasion. I was stumped. How do things start unraveling in sports? Does poor
playing lead to a bad mood? Or vice versa? It's like momentum in a football
or basketball game. One moment a team can't be stopped, the next it can't
do anything right.

But coming up were the 15th and 16th holes, both par 5s, both birdie
opportunities. Thank goodness. And sure enough, Tracy ended up with a
three-foot putt for birdie on 15 and a seven-footer for birdie on 16. She made
them both and finished the round with pars on 17 and 18 for a two-over 74.

I'll personally take credit for both birdies. I figured it was time to get silly on the 15th green when she gave me her ball to clean with my towel. I was a big Detroit Tigers fan in 1976 when pitcher Mark "The Bird" Fidrych was talking to the baseball. So I talked to Tracy's golf ball before handing it back to her. I held it close to my mouth and said, "You're in the hole. Go in the hole. In the hole."

Tracy raised her eyebrows, amused.

"You're talking to the ball," she said.

"It worked for Mark Fidrych," I said.

"Who's Mark Fidrych?" she asked.

After being interviewed by a local radio station, Tracy told me to meet her at the driving range. For half an hour, I cleaned balls and she hit them. Rather than boring, I found this time delightful—we had finished a round, I had had a good time, and we were still friends.

We walked to the putting green, where fans always gather. A fat guy in a black T-shirt critiqued Tracy's putting and drove her nuts, but he did buy her a Diet Coke.

Across the green, I spotted a little girl who was on the other side of the yellow rope separating us from the fans. Her father told me her name was Laura. She was 6 and wanted to be a professional soccer player when she grew up.

I didn't realize Tracy was listening. She stopped putting for a moment and walked toward her bag, which was lying nearby. She pulled out a red Magic Marker, took out a ball and signed her name on it, then walked over and handed it to Laura. She then went back to her putting.

"We're going to go home and put that in your dresser drawer," the father said to Laura. "We'll take it out in five years, and when we look at the name, it will be like looking at Nancy Lopez's name now."

In her room in her parents' house in Coral Gables, Tracy has a collection of souvenirs from her junior golf career. One of her prized possessions is a golf ball autographed by Nancy Lopez.

When Tracy came out of the University of Miami, having won more tournaments than any other collegiate woman golfer in history, there was no doubt she was headed for greatness. International Management Group, the sports management firm headed by author and entrepreneur Mark McCormack, signed her up. She appeared on a calendar in Japan with Curtis Strange and played in corporate pro-ams. Last year, as a rookie, she finished 51st on the money list, officially earning $64,644. She made an additional $35,000 in the JC Penney Classic in December in which she and PGA player Jay Don Blake finished tied for third.

Tracy figures it costs about $45,000 a year—for airfare, hotels, rental cars, meals, caddie fees, etc.—to live on the tour. It's a popular misconception that sponsors and tournaments always pick up the tab. Certainly, there are deals for clothing; Tracy gets paid to wear clothes made by Aurea. She also is paid to use clubs, bags and shoes by Mizuno, and Titleist gives her golf balls. Endorsement money is pretty good at the entry level, but the really big bucks come later. If you last.

Tracy teed off early Saturday morning, the second day of the tournament. She bogeyed the first hole, but she still was happy. We had come up with some new ground rules for the second round. Because I wasn't advising her on club selection as other caddies do, I was to make her feel as comfortable as possible when she pulled the club from the bag.

"That's the club," I'd say. "You've got the right club."

I had no idea if she had the right club. But I began to realize that positive vibes are everything in golf. That little white ball just sits there until you hit it. It doesn't move as it does in other sports. Not this sport. It's incredibly mental, which meant I now was heavily into lying.

Five-iron? Six-iron? Who knew? Not me. But I knew my lines.

"Yes, Tracy, that's the right club."

Tracy knew I didn't know. I told her I felt really stupid saying those things. "That's what I want to hear, though," she told me.

It began to work. Tracy birdied No. 3 and parred No. 6 after hitting the ball behind a big willow tree. I reminded her that in addition to the fact that she had the right club, she was great at the tough shots, the trick shots, because her pro down in Miami, Charley DeLucca, spent hours teaching her how to hit balls from behind trees, out of water hazards, left-handed and even on her knees.

By late morning, the wind was blowing toward us from the chocolate factory, and the air smelled like brownies. Life was good. Tracy birdied No. 9 to make the turn at one-under for the day. She had bogeys on 11 and 12 and a birdie on 13.

She birdied 16, parred 17 and was one hole away from a one-under 71 when she stepped up to 18 and hit her drive into the trees right of the fairway, forcing two marshals to take a dive. Jeez, I thought. I reached her ball well before she did, to find it in the high rough beneath an evergreen. A bogey, at least. Shoot.

"I hate it when that happens," I told her as she came up to the ball. That brought a slight smile.

With a branch of the evergreen pressing on her hair, Tracy chipped the ball out onto the fairway, 20 yards from where it had been. This was not good. From there, she hit a 6-iron—"That's the perfect club," I said—and put her ball 45 feet from the pin. She needed that putt to save par.

"Well, we just made bogey," she said as we walked to the 18th green.

"What kind of attitude is that?"

"I hate this hole," she said. "No way am I going to make it."

I knew she was just talking, just blowing off steam.

Tracy had me tend the pin because her ball was so far from the hole she couldn't see where it was. I had done this a few times now and felt good about it. Tracy told me I was batting a thousand today, no mistakes. So I wedged my feet between the putting lines of the other two golfers, held the pin with my left hand and waited for Tracy to hit the ball. She had told me to walk completely away from the hole once I pulled the pin, so the ball couldn't possibly hit me and cause a two-stroke penalty.

She hit the putt, hard. It was coming fast. I took a few quick steps, reached the fringe of the green and turned around to watch that little white ball travel its last 10 feet and then drop off the face of the earth into that beautiful little hole.

The gallery cheered wildly. Still holding the flag, I raised my arms and pumped my fists. Tracy had her arms raised and was smiling one of the biggest smiles I'd ever seen. It was a tremendous par, Tracy ended the day one-under, she had most definitely made the cut to play the final day, and I was one happy caddie.

One of the first things I did to prepare for Hershey was to read the LPGA caddie guidelines. No. 5 threw me: "Act like a gentleman at all times."

There are half a dozen or so women who caddie on the tour. Tracy introduced me to one of them, Chris Lebiedz, the caddie for Sherri Turner. Chris, who is 31, had hopes of being a pro golfer herself and played the mini-tour—a minor-league version of the LPGA tour—until she went broke.

As I got to know some of my fellow caddies—or "loopers" as they are called because they make the 18-hole loop again and again—I realized I was a bit envious of them, and a little sorry for them too. Envious because they work outside all day under the sun in some of the most glorious settings imaginable. Sorry because they aren't treated right.

For starters, they are fourth-class citizens, below even journalists. "I can't walk in that dining room right there," Chris told me, pointing to the next room. She didn't have the proper pass.

They don't make much money either. The going rate is $250 to $450 a week, paid by the player whether or not she makes the cut. If the golfer makes the cut, then the caddie receives a percentage of the earnings. The usual breakdown is 10 percent for the caddie if the player wins the tournament, 7 percent if the player finishes in the top five and 5 percent if she makes the cut.

Most of the caddies cut expenses by staying with friends at tour stops or sharing motel rooms. Tommy Grogan had booked rooms for the next 10 weeks for himself and another caddie for $40 a night. "We do a lot of Super Savers with Days Inns," he said.

They live week to week. There are no benefits for the caddies, no security blankets.

"You're only as successful as your player," Chris said. "If she's not making cuts and making money, you're not making money either."

Caddies are coaches, friends, teachers, spies. They've been known to go out before or after their player's round and hide behind trees to scout opponents. They know everything. In that bag, they carry all that's important to a player: money, car keys, aspirin, tampons. Sometimes, when you see a score in the high 70s, it had nothing to do with the wind or course conditions. The caddie knows. It was just that time of the month.

Despite my perception that caddies are the kind of people who couldn't hold down 9-to-5 jobs, most of those I met were intelligent and highly capable; they'd just rather be on the tour.

"This is my Walter Mitty thing," Tommy said. "We're all a family. Just don't loan anybody money."

The LPGA is 40 years old this year. Gone are the days of Patty Berg and Babe Didrikson Zaharias, who won 31 tournaments before her death in 1956. She earned about as much for those 31 victories—$66,237—as Tracy did last year.

There are 144 women, including Tracy, playing on the tour with exempt status, meaning they don't have to qualify for events. Other, non-exempt players fit in where they can.

Tour members can play up to 39 events this year, although no one golfer plays them all. Total prize money is $18 million, $4 million above last year, nearly $17 million above 1975. Betsy King, the tour's latest star, earned a record $650,000 last year. Twenty women have become millionaires playing golf.

But all is not completely well with the LPGA.

The LPGA has an identity crisis. It has tried to showcase its prettiest players as pinup girls, and has taken some heat for that. It has focused on the increasing number of mothers and children on the tour, but that's not particularly appetizing to network executives trying to sell women's golf to male viewers. And it now seems to have settled on women as athletes.

"These are athletes who are women, and it's very popular to sweat," said Bill Blue, a polished former liqueur executive, who took over what some called "the worst job in golf" when he became commissioner of the LPGA 18 months ago.

Why was his job perceived this way? First of all, women's sports have always been perceived as second-class. Then there were the constant comparisons with the PGA tour, and the emergence of the tremendously popular senior men's tour. For example, the reason the LPGA Championship is being held in Washington is that its old site, in Cincinnati, decided to go with a seniors tour event.

The LPGA is so concerned with marketing itself that it has brought in a consultant named Beverley Willey to do the players' hair, advise them on their makeup, touch them up before TV interviews and even take them shopping.

"The girls are very visible," Willey said. "We're marketing this tour all the time. You would think that just because they're the best golfers in the world that that should market itself. But it doesn't. So we have to go beyond that. The general public expects a little bit more of lady athletes. I don't think it's fair that they expect to see a perfect woman playing golf, but that's a fact of life."

Sex appeal sells. Bill Russell, when he was a commentator on NBA games years ago, said the shorts and sleeveless uniforms were one of the draws of his sport.

Spend a few hours in an LPGA gallery and there can be no doubt about it. I once watched Cathy Reynolds, a very attractive LPGA veteran, hit a tee shot into the rough, and heard a man tell his buddies, "She's still the prettiest girl out here."

This preoccupation is shared by a majority of women on the tour. Tracy and I talked about which outfits looked best on her, her earrings, her nails, her shoes, you name it. Tall socks are preferable to footies because they look softer, consultant Willey says. Golfers don't wear sunglasses because, in addition to depth perception problems, they hide their faces. Tracy wears a sun visor because it bears the name of her sponsor, but it also keeps her hair out of her face. (That works for caddies too.) And, in boring moments on the course, we even discussed the way certain golfers walked, which ones carried themselves well, which ones did not.

"People are watching how you dress and how you act," said Lori Garbacz, the class clown of the tour, who once had her caddie carry a lawn chair so she could sit in the fairway and read the Sunday paper between shots. The LPGA is trying to market itself as a sport to be watched by the emerging female golfing population (four out of every 10 new golfers are women, Blue said) and by men who can identify more with the LPGA game. Unlike the PGA, women pros play a brand of golf that some men could hope to match.

"It's been such a male-dominated sport," Willey said. "Look at the clothing. The shirts. All they did was take a man's shirt and put a ladies label in it and sell it in the ladies side of the store."

Even on the tour, there is a lack of respect. The small towns love the LPGA, but in Hershey one day, a local kids' driving competition was being held on the range as the pros tried to practice. In Atlantic City a couple of weeks later, the players had to tee off early and clear out of the locker room by mid-afternoon Saturday so the country club could host a wedding reception. It's impossible to imagine those things happening on the PGA tour.

Still, the women of the tour persevere. And thrive, mostly.

"A lot of us have come from modest means, some have come from the country club atmosphere," Lori said. "But the one bonding thing, I think, is we're all in this together. We're women. We're a minority in sports, and we're building something. I think we're very aware that we're judged by a different standard than men athletes are. We're under more scrutiny. For 150-some women together, we get along remarkably well in a competitive environment. We're pretty much a big family. We try to take care of our own."

We started our final day in Hershey the way all the others began: Tracy got up and turned on the Weather Channel, the official television station of the LPGA. Hang around LPGA people for a while and they'll talk about what was on the Weather Channel the way non-golfers talk about "L.A. Law."

This morning, the predictions were for rain at the tournament, so we packed the necessary gear. The umbrella always is with us, but the bag gained a few pounds with the other stuff. Tracy said it would be "a clown act," with the juggling of umbrella, clubs and clothes. (The Weather Channel was totally wrong. We had sunshine all day. So I got to carry the gear for nothing.)

In the room, Tracy was busy getting the bag ready for the final day, making sure her caddie hadn't lost one of her 14 clubs and getting her things together for the trip to Wilmington, Delaware, site of the next tour stop. She travels for three or four weeks at a time, then goes home to take a week off, see her family, work with Charley and do laundry before going back on the road. During this stretch, she went from Miami to Hershey to Wilmington to Atlantic City to Providence to Miami, in three weeks.

She spends hours a day on the phone in her room, making plane, hotel and car reservations and talking to family and friends. When we'd come back from dinner or playing tennis, there would always be another message to call her boyfriend, her parents or her management group.

On Sunday, we went to the course an hour before her tee time, as usual. Tracy began the third round at one over par, eight shots behind Gerring. We teed off at 10:40. The leaders weren't going to arrive at the course for another hour, at least. They teed off at 1.

Just as we did Saturday, we began with another bogey. But it was a significant bogey. I helped Tracy make a decision on a club.

Tracy drove into the left rough. We walked to the ball. She told me her choice was either hitting a 4-wood, which she would have to coax around a bunker to get to the green, or hitting a 4-iron to lay up in front of the bunker. The safe choice was the 4-iron, she said.

"Nuts to that," I said. "It's the final day. Go for it."

She hit a wonderful shot just off the green and chipped on, but two-putted. The putter didn't feel quite right because her stomach was upset. Now her hands were shaking slightly. She also told me this couldn't be used as an excuse.

Although she didn't feel great, Tracy hung in there nicely. She remained one-over for the day through the seventh hole. It was then that I thought it was time to liven things up a bit and once again offered some financial incentives on her putts.

On the par-3 eighth, I offered $30 if she made a 15-foot putt for birdie. She did.

On nine, she faced a 36-foot putt, breaking hard to the right, for birdie. I put up $30 again. She knocked it in.

"I'm a money player," she said joyously.

This, by the way, was legit. We didn't exchange any money because I didn't carry any during the round. Caddies are known to bet with their players on important shots. Most of the time, however, they're playing for drinks.

Now Tracy was one-under for the day, even par for the tournament. After parring 10, Tracy ran into disaster. Bogey, bogey, bogey. The wind changed, but something else did too. How does a happy camper, with birdies on eight and nine, suddenly lose it? I was befuddled.

"It really doesn't matter anymore," Tracy said as we walked up 14, now two-over for the day. "I have nothing to lose."

I looked toward the sky. There must have been a thousand ideas floating around up there of things I could say. Again, I knew she didn't really mean what she was saying, but I wanted to throw something back at her, something that might help. I told myself that Tracy plays better when she's on edge, when she's in trouble, when she's angry. So, I thought to myself, here goes, and I tried to sound as furious as possible.

"So you're looking for something to play for, huh? Try this. My story. You're ruining my story by the way you're playing."

Tracy turned sharply to look me right in the eye.

"Damn you!" she said.

"Damn you!" I shot back.

We didn't say anything to each other until she chipped onto the green and waited for Myra Blackwelder, one of the women she was playing with, to putt.

Tracy leaned over as I stood next to her on the fringe of the green, a couple of feet from the gallery.

"You really hurt me with that comment," she said, the words piercing the air.

I started to smile.

"You believed that?" I said. "I just wanted to get you going. The story's all set. Come on, I was just joking."

If it was possible, Tracy got even angrier. She made her putt for par, slid the putter into my hand, yanked her driver out of the bag and stormed off.

I didn't mind. At least we'd stopped that string of bogeys.

Ah, but 15. The great thing about golf is that every hole is a new beginning. Unless you're in a funk. Tracy hit her drive so far to the right, it was almost in the 16th fairway. As I followed her into the rough, she stepped on the restraining rope to get over it. Every other time she did this, she didn't move until I stepped on the rope and went by too. But this time, she charged on, leaving me to nearly trip over the snapping, knee-high rope.

Tracy next hit a 4-iron across the fairway and into an almost impossible position, in the rough, in a rut, on the side of a hill, heading down, 122 yards from the pin. It wasn't hard to imagine her next shot going about 70 yards straight down to the bottom of the hill. Can you say double bogey?

We arrived at the ball. We were speaking again.

"I think I'm going to hit an 8-iron here," she said.

"What other club can you hit?" I asked.

"I think this is it," she said.

An idea came to me. One of the all-time great motivational lines was said by Herb Brooks, the coach of the 1980 U.S. Olympic hockey team, as he sent his players out to face the Soviets:

"You were born to be a player. You were meant to be here. This moment is yours."

So, just before Tracy stepped up to the ball, I tried a variation:

"You've practiced this shot a thousand times for this moment."

It wasn't the Soviets against the United States, but we amateur psychologists have to use our good lines anytime we can.

Tracy hit the ball as well as she possibly could have; it bounced onto the green, rolled past the pin and even earned her a little applause from the gallery. If I hadn't been holding the bag, I would have applauded too. She didn't sink that putt, but she did make her putt for par. Other than her putt on 18 the second day, that 8-iron was her finest shot of the tournament.

On 16, I said I'd give her $100 if she made an eagle and she said she'd give me back my $60 if she didn't birdie the hole. Unfortunately, I got my money back.

She bogeyed 17 to go three-over for the day and four-over for the tournament. She missed a 16-footer for birdie on 18 and tapped in for par.

I caught up with her at the edge of the green, before she went in to add up her score and sign the card.

"Am I fired?" I asked, laughing.

"Heck, no," she said, breaking into a smile. "You can do this for me any day."

Perhaps someday I will. But I'd rather be standing in the gallery on 18, applauding as she walks in with the last group and turns around to see one name, her name, on top of the leader board.

This day, that seemed so far away. She and I sat at the edge of the green watching Cathy Gerring putt out to score 208 and win the Lady Keystone Open and $45,000. Tracy ended with at 220 and wouldn't have made expenses if I hadn't been working for free and picking up some of the costs.

"It's hard to sit here watching this," Tracy said to me. "I want to be her."

That's something Cathy Gerring understands. A week later, reflecting on her victory, she said, "I always wanted to be the winner too. I don't know. Maybe I wanted it too much. I wasn't ready to win. And you know what? I finally realized how you get ready to win. By simply playing week after week. Oh, and one other thing. By watching other people win."

(July 22, 1990)

Christine Brennan covers the Olympics and international sports and writes a weekly column for the Washington Post. *A native of Toledo, OH, she received her undergraduate and graduate degrees from Northwestern. She began her career at the* Miami Herald *and was president of the Association for Women in Sports Media from 1988-90.*

My Mother, My Rival

by Mariah Burton Nelson
Ms.

THE FIRST TIME MY MOTHER AND I COMPETED AGAINST EACH OTHER SHE WAS 37 and I was five. We swam one lap of our neighbor's pool. She won.

As a five-year old I didn't realize—and I don't think my mother realized—that she was teaching me about love. We thought we were just fooling around.

Later we had diving competitions, which she also won, though I would argue, and she would concede, that I deserved higher marks for versatility. For my jackknife, I would boing into the air, desperately grab my toes, then splash down on all fours. For my back dive, I would reach my hands meekly overhead, then fall into the water as if I'd been shot. Mom had only one dive—the swan dive—but if you do only one dive you can learn to do it very well. She'd fly skyward, arch like a ship's proud figurehead, then streamline toward the water and quietly, tapered toes last, disappear.

Eventually I gave up diving—pointing my toes always seemed so unnatural—but I joined a swim team, and by the time I was 10, I could outswim Mom. ("Oh, I don't know about that," responds my mother now. "I think you were eleven.")

Mom was my fan, too, when I would race against Jean and Joan Spinelli the indomitable twins at Cedarbrook Country Club in our mini-town of Blue Bell, Pennsylvania. Jean had skinny arms as sharp and swift as Osterizer blades; Joan had furious legs that started kicking in mid-racing dive, like a windup bathtub toy. I didn't stand a chance.

But Mom would root for me anyway, yelling from the sidelines as if I could hear her underwater. She'd transport my friends and me to swimming meets all over the county (she liked to drive fast over the hilly, back-country roads so we'd fly up out of our seats and scream), and she even arranged practice time for me during family vacations to the New Jersey shore. It made me feel important to skip deep-sea fishing trips with my dad and siblings to work out at a pool.

Mom was also my teammate; the two of us ganged up on the Spinelli twins in the mother-daughter relay races at Cedarbrook's year-end championships. Mrs. Spinelli, a lounge lizard of sorts, had a great tan but no speed, so Mom and I were undefeated for six years until adolescence caught up with me and I left swimming for more important things like basketball.

So when I think about competition I also remember the Spinelli twins, who

286

would join me in the showers after the meets, the three of us giggling and whispering until all the hot water ran out. I think about Gordon, whom I later met on the basketball court; he would guard me by pushing on my waist with one hand and I still remember that push, and how much more honest it felt than my boyfriend's gropings. I remember 6-foot-3-inch Heidi, my teammate, who would rebound the ball viciously, sharp elbows out; I hated her elbows but loved her audacity and her long strong hands, mirrors of my own. When I think about competition I realize that beginning with my fiercely, playfully competitive mother—who at 55 took up tennis and at 60 tried downhill skiing—athletes have taught me most of what I know about love.

Competition is about passion for perfection, and passion for other people who join in this impossible quest. What better way to get to know someone than to test your abilities together, to be daring and sweaty and exhausted together.

"If you compare yourself with others," a line in the inspirational prose poem "Desiderata" warns, "you may become vain and bitter, for always there will be greater and lesser persons than yourself." Yet I find that by comparing myself to other athletes, I become both self-confident and humble. Through competition, I have learned to acknowledge my failures and make allowances for the failures of others. Isn't that what intimacy is about?

But competition is not all fun and games. Like families, competitors can bring out the worst as well as the best in each other. Like romance, competition has many faces, some of them ugly. In addition to showing me my grace and graciousness, the mirror of sports has reflected back to me my jealousy, pettiness, and arrogance.

For instance: I have taken a friend to a tennis court, and said, "Let's just hit a few," then fired the ball down her throat. I have, during a recreational, two-on-two volleyball game, refused to pass to my partner so we could win.

Believing that "competitive" was a dirty word, I used to say, "I'm not competitive, I just happen to be the best." My teammate Heidi and I had a tearful yelling match one night after a basketball game, and I accused her of not passing me the ball. "How am I supposed to score more than 19 points if you won't even look in my direction?" I screamed. "Why are you so competitive with me?"

"Look who's being competitive!" she countered. "Since when is 19 points something to be ashamed of? Only when it's compared to my 29, right?"

Later I told friends, "I've realized that I am in fact very competitive."

"No!" they said sarcastically. "You?"

I guess I was the last to notice.

But despite such humiliations, Heidi and I are good friends, and because we have played basketball together, she knows me better than friends who only chat with me over lunch. I am never more naked than in the heat of competition. I never feel more vulnerable than after flubbing a catch in the ninth inning, or rolling a bowling ball into the gutter.

In sports, as in love, one can never pretend.

For this reason some women avoid sports altogether; they choose not to unveil themselves in that way. In a society in which women's attractiveness is of utmost importance, why get muddy and sweaty and exhausted? Why risk anger, frustration, aggression, and other unseemly emotions. It is far safer to stay seated demurely in a cafe.

"I hate competition!" some friends have said to me. These are the women who were never taught how to throw or catch a ball, and I don't blame them. As an untrained musician, I know that if my childhood had been filled with music competitions, and I were chosen last for music teams and humiliated in front of other great musicians, I would resent both music and competition. Who enjoys doing things poorly?

A third reason many women have an ambivalent, if not downright hostile attitude toward sports—and why others embrace sports—is that team sports are an intense, physical activity. To play sports with women is to love women, to be passionate about women, to be intimate with women. How scary. Or, depending on your point of view, how thrilling.

So competition is about love, I noticed early, and, I noticed later, about fear. That's why I like to remember my childhood, when the love part was relatively pure, untainted by fear of failure, fear of looking like a fool, or fear of loving women. I feel blessed to have had a big brother who taught me how to throw, and a mother who never let me win. Even today, when I compete at water polo, bad-knee tennis, Nerf basketball, Ping-Pong, billiards—whatever I can persuade someone else to play with me—my favorite competitor is my mom. She is 69 now, I am 37, and when I visit her in Phoenix, we still race. "Give me a head start," she'll suggest, "or better yet, I'll do freestyle and you swim backstroke, just kicking, okay?" If she wins, she smacks her hand against the wall, jerks her head up, and yells, "Ha! Beat you!"

I complain that she must have cheated. She splashes me. I dunk her. We laugh a lot. And I think, yes, this must be love.

(May, 1988)

Mariah Burton Nelson's book, Are We Winning Yet? *(Random House) received the Amateur Athletic Foundation's Book Award in 1992. Her second book,* The Stronger Women Get, The More Men Love Football, *has been published by Harcourt Brace. One of her rebounding records at Stanford still stands.*

Girls Basketball:
The Tears of Grief and Pride

By Jacqui Banaszynski
St. Paul Pioneer Press

Tears will be shed at the Met Center this weekend. Some of them will be mine.

It has become a ritual of mine, since moving to Minnesota six years ago, to watch the state high school girls basketball tournament and, briefly, to cry.

I don't cry for a particular girl or for a favorite team, or even from the vicarious passion of winning and losing.

My tears are more selfish. As I watch today's young athletes, I am reminded of myself half-a-lifetime ago—a gangly teen-ager with a decent jump shot but no right to play the game.

Back then I shed tears of frustration and anger. Now I shed tears of grief for what I was never allowed to be, and tears of pride for what these girls have become.

You see, I could have been a player too.

I was born with all the right features—height, heft, heritage and heart. My father was a formidable athlete who dabbled in semi-pro baseball before detouring through World War II and the raising of five children. My mother was a farmgirl who believed it was okay to sweat. My four brothers were big and brutal under the boards. They taught me to fake with my eyes and to make space with my elbows.

Often I was the first one out on the driveway court after supper. We played through the seasons, shoveling the snow off the cement in the winter for games of H-O-R-S-E and 21, playing late into the night under floodlights and stereo speakers. Basketball was a family tradition, a neighborhood social event, a reprieve from homework, a physical outlet for the emotional intensity of adolescence.

But that's all basketball ever was for me, and my game never left the driveway. Because I was born female, and I was born too soon.

I graduated from high school in northeastern Wisconsin in 1970—two years before Title IX required public schools across the nation to provide equal athletic opportunities to girls. For me and my peers, sports meant the now-antiquated Girls Athletics Association, and that usually meant bowling.

Minnesota, typically progressive, established girls basketball by state decree in 1969. The first state tournament was in 1976—just 11 years ago on the calendar but an age ago in attitude. A now semi-retired columnist for a now-merged Minneapolis newspaper covered that tournament and compared the girls' game—unfavorably—to loaded skunk wrestling.

I wonder what he expected. To be good, you have to play the game. And to play the game, you have to spend time in the gym. You need equipment and coaches and encouragement.

You also need a history. Until recently, girls had none of that. The young women who will take the floor in today's tournament are the first generation who have had unquestioned access to basketball since infancy.

When I was their age, there were about 10 of us from my hometown who played outlaw ball—playing in my driveway, sneaking gym time between the boys' team practices, coaxing a sympathetic priest to let us into the church gym on Sundays. We were a coach's dream without a coach. My cousin and I each stood 5-foot-10 and could handle the ball. My best friend was 6-foot-3; she seldom had to jump. Our shortest starter was 5-foot-7 and had a deadly outside shot. We all played for keeps—when we were allowed to play at all.

Even at that, we were terrible. The only coaching we ever had was in physical education class, and then it was under old-fashioned girls rules: six to a team with only two running guards playing full court; a forced pass-off after three dribbles; rarely allowed a free throw after a foul.

You don't learn to dribble if you aren't allowed to dribble. You don't get fast or strong if you're not allowed to run. You don't learn to take the pressure unless you stand at the line.

But the game has changed dramatically since then, and continues to improve each year. The girls move like the athletes they are. They pass hard and on the run, dribble on the pivot and shoot on the jump. They maneuver with their elbows, shoulders and hips. They bruise and they get bruised.

It's still a different game than the boys play. It's slower, and it's played below the rim. It's a game of precision, teamwork and finesse rather than power, height and flash. But it's hearty basketball nonetheless, with scores often in the 70s, aggressive rebounding, minimal mistakes and patient play-making.

Advances in the game are reflected in the stands. The state tournament now draws more than 50,000 fans, up from 34,000 in 1976. The fans aren't just parents or girlfriends, but full-fledged cheerleading squads, pep bands and boyfriends—the future fathers of daughters who might play basketball.

An ironic, but perhaps more significant, sign of progress is that girls basketball now is taken for granted. Today's players, even the lanky stars like Hill-Murray High School's Mya Whitmore, are blissfully unaware of the limitations they would have faced in the not-so-distant past.

Whitmore didn't set out to be a basketball player. She had no older brothers dragging her onto the driveway court for some token guard duty, no professional role models to emulate, no sports career to work towards. But she was tall, and because she was tall she was asked to play on her school's seventh grade team. She discovered she was good and, more importantly, that she was having fun.

Her story disappointed me at first. I wanted to hear about a little girl who shot buckets in the cold January darkness, dreaming of the day she would be on the court. I wanted her to be more like me.

I spoke briefly to Whitmore of history, of those who came before and opened the gymnasium doors. Of Dorothy McIntyre, the associate director of the Minnesota High School League who, 20 years ago, learned to drive a school bus on her lunch hour so she could chauffeur girls to underground basketball games. Of Janet Karvonen, the New York Mills, Minnesota, phenomenon who, 12 years ago, dragged her father to the gym to demand playing time for his daughter. Of my high school days—not so long ago—when being female and an athlete meant being a cheerleader.

Whitmore's interest was polite, but not passionate. She did not have to fight the fight; she got to play the game.

That is as it should be.

I couldn't resist the urge to ask Whitmore if she had ever heard of Title IX. She's a bright young woman, obviously used to knowing the answers. She shook her head with a sheepish, almost apologetic giggle, as if she were caught unprepared in class.

I hadn't heard of Title IX when I was 17 either. It didn't exist for me to hear of.

But that was half-a-lifetime ago. And in that time, a revolution took place.

(March 19, 1987)

Jacqui Banaszynski, an assistant managing editor of the St. Paul Pioneer-Press, *won the 1988 Pulitzer Prize for feature writing for her series, "AIDS in the Heartland." A 1974 graduate of Marquette, she covered the 1988 and 1992 Olympics and has reported from Turkey, Northern Iraq and Antarctica.*

THE LADY BUFFS ARE FINALLY GETTING THEIR DUE

by Donna Carter
Denver Post

THE LADY BUFFS ARE ON THE FRONT PAGE!

That's the thought that struck me last month when I gazed at the *Post* sports section and saw an action photograph of University of Colorado woman basketball player Jamillah Lang.

A slow smile spread across my face.

It was not the usual flavorless lines from a wire service on a back page, but a picture and a full-length story. It's not every day I can see women basketball players on the sports page. Truth be told, it rarely happens.

The Lady Buffs elbowed their way onto the front page with their meteoric rise from No. 25 to No. 4 in the Associated Press national poll and their Big Eight championship.

It's a development that warms the cockles of every woman who ever laced up high tops, went down to a playground and listened to some guy say, "Why don't you go skins?" when teams divided into shirts and skins.

The front page means respectability, sanction or, at the very least, grudging recognition of women's basketball.

It's been a long time coming.

It took a federal law, the Education Amendment's Title IX passed in 1972, before schools were compelled to offer women athletic programs.

But Title IX opened the door to more equal athletic opportunity and college scholarships. And a few bold souls, who knew the joy of making the perfect pass to a teammate, begged their mothers and fathers for leather high tops.

I was one of them. I wasn't inspired so much by women basketball pioneers, but by the serenity of exhausted limbs and the glory of a perfect jump shot.

I never got my leather high tops. My parents didn't want me to get hurt or compromise my education. And they thought boys wouldn't like me if I played sports.

So I made do with Chuck Taylor canvas Converse, an old ball and a bent rim at a junior high. I apprenticed on playgrounds where I was the lone girl, initially overmatched and unaccepted. But I never quit. And there was a feeling of pride when guys said, "You've got the girl. Play her. She can shoot."

I earned a scholarship to the University of Southern California, where I led the Women of Troy to the second of their back-to-back national championships in 1984.

Okay, the truth is Cheryl Miller, 6-foot-2 twin-towers Pam and Paula McGee, two-time Olympian Cynthia Cooper and Rhonda Windham did most of the work winning the basketball championship.

But I won a scholarship, played basketball and ran track and cross-country for the university. I was a part of it, and my life was profoundly enriched.

When the Lady Buffs played the final home game against Nebraska, many in the crowd were young girls, with the Lady Buffs as role models.

Even if these girls don't play college or professional basketball, they will know the joy of stretching their bodies in daily exercise, the camaraderie and ideals of sportsmanship.

And they may go on to consider careers in sport, from sportswriting to athletic training or orthopedic surgery.

One thing is for sure: Those little girls who watch the Lady Buffs in the NCAA playoffs or catch them reflected in a newspaper photo will know it's all right to be whatever they want, even the shirt who runs the fast break in the lunch-time game at the local YMCA.

(March 14, 1993)
Donna Carter *covers the Denver Nuggets of the NBA for the* Denver Post. *A broadcast journalism major at the University of Southern California, she has worked for the* Los Angeles Times, *the* Long Beach Press Telegram *and the* Orange County Register.

TRYING OUT

by Michele Himmelberg
Fort Myers News-Press

A NEW KID HAS MOVED INTO THE TAMPA BAY PROFESSIONAL SPORTS NEIGHBOR-hood, but neither the Buccaneer football team nor the Rowdie soccer club is expecting a surge of competition. Instead, they and most of the community's fans are wondering if the Tampa Bay Sun, the latest addition to the Women's Pro Basketball League, will ever rise into being.

The team's owner, Bill Byrne, has issued hints about the Sun's creation for months, but vital life signs have been hidden under dark shadows of financial instability and vague promises. The only indication that this team existed was a coach without a firm contract, a general manager who was camping out in the coach's apartment "temporarily," four of 10 draft picks who expressed a willingness to play—and lots of talk.

Similar image problems plague the entire league, which now consists of 13 teams after one folded and two others relocated last year. Skepticism still abounds despite two full seasons of play, in which the women have followed all the NBA rules but one (they use a ball which is about one inch smaller in circumference). Several teams had television contracts last year, but clubs are still losing money. Faith in the league's survival dissipated further when its greatest publicity device—the Olympics—was boycotted in the U.S., thus denying the WBL's future stars a chance to impress the American public via television.

These ominous signals failed to put off Byrne, who is also serving as the league's commissioner until he can find a replacement. He vowed to install a team in Tampa.

The Sun's first official public appearance was to be a free-agent tryout over Labor Day weekend. It seemed the perfect opportunity to explore this team's viability, and that is why I decided to join 41 other women at the MacDill Air Force Base gymnasium to try out for the Tampa Bay Sun.

The bump-bump-bump-bump of my heartbeat was keeping pace with the thump-thump-thump-thump staccato of bouncing basketballs emanating from the large white gymnasium, and both grew louder as I got closer. But as I filed through the doors at 8:30 a.m., I was comforted by the familiar sights of two glass backboards, rims, nets, a polished floor and a score of leather balls.

Already a group of women were hovering under the backboards, trying to wake up their bodies as they warmed up their shots. But before I could join them, a form releasing the Tampa Bay Sun of any responsibility for injuries was handed to me with the order: "Sign this." The long brown brace on my right knee must have been more obvious than I thought.

After stretching carefully, I grabbed a loose ball and ambled toward a basket, trying to appear confident. The first few shots careened off the rim, but once I got a rhythm going they started to fall.

But a Southern drawl jolted my concentration: "Jes' look at all these girls," it muttered close to my ear.

I did look. Scattered about the gym were 41 other women, some smaller and some taller than me; about half were black and half white; some with two-handed set shots, one with a smooth one-handed jumper; some leaping an arm's length off the floor for rebounds and some dribbling, scooting around the floor like giant bugs.

That's when the question hit me again: "What am I doing here?" I had asked myself that at least 50 times the night before while tossing and turning in my hotel bed.

Okay, so I'm gathering information for a story, but I still want to play well. Oh, admit it, Michele. You'd risk cracking your nose for the third time and breaking four more fingers (all former basketball injuries) to play on a professional team. Who *wouldn't* want to get paid for playing a game they love?

But how realistic is this? I'm nearly 24 years old and far from being in the best shape of my life, with a wobbly knee and ankles weakened by the sloppy pick-up and recreation league games I've played since my last college competition at Southern Cal two-and-a-half years ago. My subconscious kept screaming at me: "You're a washed-up, frustrated athlete who refuses to realize you were born about five years too late to take advantage of the boom in women's sports." But I was going to try, anyway.

At least I wasn't the only one worrying and sleeping fitfully. In the bed next to me was my roommate whom I had met at the hotel where the Sun arranged for discounts on rooms. We were splitting the hotel bill 50-50 as the team provided no money for transportation, meals or lodging—nothing.

Cathy was equally nervous, though for different reasons. She is 22, recently graduated from Atlantic Christian, a small North Carolina college where she set numerous records and became the first woman to have her jersey number retired. She was anxious to impress the coach with her "undeveloped potential."

Cathy envied my 5-foot-11 stature. She stood barely 5-6 with her Afro fluffed out. I coveted her youth and experience. She, like many of the women who tried out in Tampa, had been to another WBL tryout. Earlier this summer she tried out for the Dallas Diamonds, but was cut.

The expenses for that tryout came out of her own pocket too. But money—$10,000 a year if you're lucky in this league—is not one of her considerations.

"Basketball's been a big part of my life for a long, long time," she said.

Sports have been a big part of my life too, but my basketball experience has been sporadic. I played in junior high—in a dress-like uniform with matching bloomers that were always too big—under the old-fashioned six-player "girls" rules. In high school I opted for a cheerleading skirt, but I did play on the basketball team my senior year.

Then I spent two years on a lousy junior college team and learned most of what I know about the game from a summer school class taught by the men's coach. I also played one year, 1977 at Southern Cal, when its young program could absorb an interested but inexperienced player like myself.

The Southern Cal experience had provided me with an item valuable at this tryout: a T-shirt that said "USC." It was impressive, and it helped me in the psyche-out game we were all playing during warm-ups. We were all trying to impress each other: hitting 25-footers, burning opponents one-on-one, or just loafing, ogling and grinning smugly.

Their T-shirts represented the East and the South—Maine, Maryland, New Jersey, Louisiana, Tampa and others. Snatches of conversation revealed that many were college stars who had graduated anywhere from 1975 to 1980. Many had jobs secured for the year and were at the tryout on a once-in-a-lifetime whim. The typical profession was teacher/coach, but there were recreation coordinators, a secretary, a retail clothing manager and five former WBL players. Some were married such as a former Delta State star who had her husband feeding her passes during the warmup.

Finally, at 9:05 a.m., a shrill whistle sounded.

"All right ladies, gather up over here," a deep voice hollered. It was coming from a tan-faced, burly man, about 5-9. A yellow T-shirt stretched over his barrel chest, blending into gold shorts that clung to thick, stumpy legs. This was the coach: Tom Mosca, formerly head coach of one of the most successful girls' high school programs in the area, Tampa Robinson.

"We're going to run through a few drills to see what kind of fundamentals you have," he announced. "I want to see not only how you shoot, but how you handle the ball, rebound, pass and play defense."

We began with a fast-break drill, then went to a 3-on-2 that emphasized the transition game and later worked a 4-on-4 exercise. Laps around the gym were required after your turn in each drill.

The drills were sloppy at first, but passing and shooting grew sharper as nervous fingers began to relax. Adrenaline was finally being checked as, unconsciously, the quiet tension in the sticky gym was being broken with clapping and yelling that acknowledged sharp plays. The quick-paced drills consumed a solid hour in the stifling heat, as eyes kept drifting to the overhead fans that curiously were not turning.

After a short water break the whistle blew again, beckoning the workers to the crucial labor of the day: full-court, 5-on-5 scrimmaging. Shirts and skins being impractical, we were issued T-shirts bearing a large sun and the words "Tampa Bay Basketball" on the front and, appropriately, "Sun Bank" (donators of the T-shirts) on the back. The blue and yellow shirts made it easy to identify the unfamiliar teammates who ranged in appearance from 5-2 to 6-3, 16 years of age to 28.

My team consisted of three of the shortest but sharper guards in the gym, a slick 5-9 forward and another girl about my height. We played 10-minute running games with Mosca serving as a lenient referee. The first game was spent testing each other's moves and trying to work together, though some players seemed more interested in their own 1-on-5 game. But by the second game picks were being recognized and more shots were sinking.

We alternated playing these games until nearly 11:30 a.m.—lunch time. By now, many of us felt more like sleeping than eating but we grabbed something light and rested until 2 p.m. before heading back to the gym.

The afternoon session—from 2:30 p.m. until 5 p.m.—was almost entirely scrimmaging, under the scrupulous eye of Mosca and Steve Brown, the general manager. The quick friendships begun over the breaks became meaningless on the court, with each player fully aware of the short time she had to prove her worth. The games became more intense, with bodies hurdling after loose balls, elbows flying under the boards and legs plowing through the key on a drive. The defense was strictly man-to-man, without the slightest quibble (among the women) over the misnomer.

The court noise was familiar: "Ball, ball, take ball! Pick up your man. Switch! Go out on her! Behind you, watch behind. Shot! Same team. Shot! (swish) Damn!"

As the afternoon wore on, bodies began to slow down and fast breaks became less common. My right hamstring was sore from the previous week's sprint to work and each jump or lunge coiled the muscle tighter. Salty sweat was dripping into my stinging eyes. My ankles were tender from the cutting and sudden stopping and starting.

"Push," I kept telling myself. "Push-push. Shot's up, crash the boards. Block out. Move. Stay with her. Deny the pass. Push."

It didn't get any easier when our other tall forward hurt her leg and I ended up playing center against the 6-2 and 6-3 players—two of whom made the final cut. I felt like Jamaal Wilkes trying to outmuscle Darryl Dawkins.

During the short periods our team sat out, I watched the other players critically. The few who had been terribly out of place were gone, failing to make it to the second session. The few who stood out were either consistent outside shooters or floor-burn hustlers. A college scout might have drooled over the talent here and wished more of the women were still eligible, but Brown and Mosca were dealing on the pro level and sadly admitted only two or perhaps three of these women would ever make the Sun's roster.

The buzzer ending the final scrimmage sounded and Mosca again gathered his flock.

"I want to thank all of you for attending and I hope you all understand our situation. We only have so many openings," he said. "There is a list with the names of people we want to come back on the ladies room door. Further cuts will be made tomorrow. Be here at 8 a.m. sharp."

Some ran toward the door and the notebook sheet of paper with 21 names scrawled on it. Some strolled coolly. There were whoops of delight, bursts of cursing and a few long faces, but tears were rare. I searched for my obtrusively long name. It was not on the list.

For an instant I was disappointed—then relieved. It was satisfying to know people like me—pick-up players without finely tuned skills—are not filling the rosters of the WBL: That people are paying money to see a truly professional team. Yet, the experience had been encouraging, proving that more women are participating and excelling in athletics. Only once before had I seen so many women drawn together just to play basketball, and my only regret was that more of them didn't live in my neighborhood. It would be fun to play with them for a change, rather than with the hundreds of men who haunt gyms and dominate pick-up games.

(September 4, 1980)

Michele Himmelberg is a general assignment reporter and part-time columnist for the Orange County Register. *A graduate of the University of Southern California, she previously worked at the* Sacramento Bee *and the* Fort Myers News-Press. *She won the 1991 California Newspaper Publishers Association award for sportswriting.*

SEVEN

BOYS AND GIRLS TOGETHER

The Lady Who Rode Like a Man

by Maryjean Wall
The Horsemen's Journal

The sad part of the story is that they never gave her a sporting chance. Time and again she struggled to convince them she could ride a race as well as any man. She dreamed, she hoped, she argued; she went all the way to the House of Representatives in Illinois.

But race-riding was a man's world then, and Lillian Jenkinson had come along 40 years too soon. Even when the courts eventually did clear the way for women to ride, she would still hear her request denied. By then, in 1969, the reason given was her age. Sixty, said the Illinois authorities, was too old for anyone to ride a race.

Too old for most, maybe, but not for the jockey they called Lady Jenkinson. Each day she rose at dawn to gallop up to 20 horses at Cahokia, a small pari-mutuel track in East St. Louis, Illinois. Two doctors there informed the racing authorities that Jenkinson was in excellent physical condition and fit to ride a race. Forty-six owners and trainers held the same belief and signed a petition asking the Cahokia stewards to give her a license. The jockeys even gave her an endorsement—perhaps the best recommendation of all—but the system would not bend.

So, in the end, Jenkinson felt she had no choice. She could remain the rest of her active years at pari-mutuel tracks like Cahokia, riding a decent class of horses but confined to exercising them in the mornings. Or she could push aside her pride and go back to where she began, to those hole-in-the-wall, unlicensed county fairs and half-mile tracks where anybody is allowed to ride a race. Jenkinson had been a jockey at these dusty little bush tracks from the time she was 17. At 60 she saw no reason to quit doing what she liked best.

Jenkinson had ridden upwards of 3,000 winners at these little tracks in about 10,000 races dating to 1926. The totals are approximations, suggested by those who knew her well, for no one really knows how many races she won or rode. Her scrapbooks were burned in a fire, and her name is not to be found in any of the record books. But it is almost certain that few jockeys in history raced more than the Lady Jenkinson. And while she never had the opportunity to ride in a Kentucky Derby, she is remembered throughout far flung corners of the midwest for winning all the big $500 derbies at places like Shawneetown and Greenup and Sedalia.

* * *

301

Lady Jenkinson was a wonder to behold. Not only was she unique as a daring woman jockey in times when women did not set foot outside their kitchens but she was also a darned good rider. In the 1920s and 1930s she rode as the crowd favorite in Kansas, Oklahoma, Nebraska, Iowa, Minnesota and Missouri. In the 1940s she moved to Illinois and Ohio, where she remained until her competitive days were through.

Day and night she competed fearlessly against the men, sometimes riding at two county fairs in one day. As late as the age of 59 she achieved the distinction of riding five winners in a single afternoon. She was still riding five or six races every day—unknown beyond the ferris wheels and cotton candy booths, yet one of the greatest, toughest riding jockeys of our time—when she went down in a spill at the McLeansboro (Illinois) Fair in 1969.

The spill occurred a few months after she was turned down for a jockey's license at Cahokia. The accident ended her career. At age 60 she was too far along in years to mend.

"Whenever anybody gets hurt like that, you'd better just let 'em die and be done with it," Jenkinson reminisced recently. She didn't care much for life without racing, and sometimes she said she wished they'd left her on the track to die. In that one spill she broke ten ribs, punctured a lung and suffered numerous other multiple fractures and abrasions.

"I was hamburger ground up with bone," she said. "That's the way it felt.

"Hurts? Why, it still hurts all the time."

It was late in the summer of 1976. Seven years had passed since the wreck at McLeansboro. Jenkinson and her husband, Chick Holder, were sitting outside their house trailer parked on the fairgrounds at Pinckneyville in southern Illinois. They no longer raced, for Lillian's back hurt too much to handle a horse well. But they lived not 20 yards from the track's first turn because they couldn't entirely let go of the life.

The day was hot; the air thick and stifling. Lillian, small, thin and somewhat gray and stringy-haired, stooped to shoo away a billy goat who nibbled too close to her chair. "I'll tell you something about that spill," she said. "It was the worst in all the years I ever got hurt."

She believes the horse suffered a heart attack. Jenkinson was on the lead, turning for home, when the horse suddenly bore out and all her strength could not pull it back in. At the head of the stretch, on the outside fence, there were three iron bar gates. Lillian remembers thinking, just before they hit, "Oh, no; he's headed there. This is it."

"There was a terrific crowd that night and they were parked right outside those gates. He never tried to jump the gate. He was already dead. He just crashed through it. That's all I remember. Someone told me later they pulled me out from under a car.

"They said I rode the horse over the first car, and that I went over it clean. Then he hit a second car and that's when I went off, smack against the windshield. Then the horse hit another car after that before he was stopped, cold. There was three cars wrecked."

The place was a bloody mess. But wrecks at these tracks were a common sight. Besides, Lillian had been hurt plenty of times before, though never seriously enough to find herself slowed down for long.

Injuries were simply part of racing at the half-mile tracks, where most of the horses were cripples or outlaws and where riders had little protection. The fairs were the end of the line. You had to be desperate to ride there. When it came to safety, Jenkinson took her chances and hoped for a run of good luck.

"It was dog-eat-dog out there," explained her husband, Chick, who traveled with her everywhere through the 20 years of their marriage. "The horses, some was doped and some wasn't. Some of the jocks was drunk and some was sober, but you still had to ride with a bunch of drunks."

"You had to have nerve," Jenkinson agreed.

Lillian was game. She also was the proud possessor of a stubborn streak. Chick had watched her insist on riding with two broken ankles propped in the irons. He'd had to help her on and off the horse. Another time he'd seen her tape her broken ribs and go right back out to ride the next race. One night found him slipping out in the darkness to search the depths of the race track for Lillian's false teeth. She'd lost them in a fall earlier in the day, but had felt too embarrassed to retrieve them in public.

"She won one race and never even knew she won it," Chick recalled. "She was unconscious when she rode it from the spill she'd had in the race before. But this was her horse, and she wasn't going to let anybody else ride it, so she insisted on going back out. She didn't come to till an hour or so after the race when the horse had won and cooled out."

Two considerations kept Jenkinson away from riding at the recognized tracks. They told her women were ineligible because no dressing room was available. Any chance of beating down the dressing room argument was killed by the 1939 ruling.

Jenkinson was suspended from the pari-mutuel tracks indefinitely in 1939 when a horse she co-owned with her father was caught running on caffeine at Sportsman's Park in Chicago. Most of her friends thought the suspension exceedingly harsh, especially since they believed she was taking the blame for what appeared to be her father's actions.

"All I fed the horse was apples," Lillian insisted. "Sure, sometimes out on the bush tracks we'd stimulate him. We'd give him a spoonful of caffeine and a couple of ounces of whiskey if we were going to sprint him. But we wouldn't do that at a Chicago track."

Nonetheless, the suspension remained in effect for the next quarter century. Lillian was not returned to good standing until 1964, when she became a licensed owner, trainer and exercise rider in the months she wasn't riding races in the bushes.

One of her friends, a part-time announcer and fair official named Dean Bartle, has always suspected the suspension stayed in force so long because Jenkinson was a woman rider. "At that time they didn't want any part of women around the race track," he declared. "Had she been a man, and no more involved than she was, I'm sure they would have opened it up sooner, because they've reinstated a lot worse ones. But they wouldn't even consider her."

"They was prejudiced, very much so," Jenkinson agrees. Chick said she never lost her bitterness over the preferential treatment given men at the race track.

Jenkinson believes she would have been rich if the men had let her ride recognized races. As it was, she usually was paid $5 if she lost and $10 if she won.

Chick and Lillian formed an inseparable couple, traveling from fair to fair in a Chevy truck that hauled six horses, sometimes seven if you squeezed them in real tight. Many times their home was little more than a cot set up in an empty stall. They owned a farm house in Nebraska, but while on the road they knew few luxuries.

They met at the races, and their marriage raised something of a curious commotion. One friend remarked he was surprised, for he'd never seen Lillian keep company with any man. No one recalled seeing her in a dress. Chick was a musician who played banjo and saxophone for a living. He was a few years younger than Lillian.

They married in Perry, Oklahoma, while on their way home to Nebraska from Hot Springs, Arkansas. The marryin' judge was occupied when they showed up, presiding at the trial of an Indian accused of slaying one of his tribesmen from the reservation. But the judge bowed most graciously to the racetrackers' request, and called for an immediate recess. Participants in the trial were called forth to serve as witnesses, and Lillian and Chick were promptly joined in matrimony.

Jenkinson was a farm girl raised near Monroe, Nebraska. She fell in love with horses when her father bought a pony from a band of traveling horse traders. She rode her first race as a child, finishing second in a quarter-mile dash at a town picnic. Before she finished high school she had ridden races at two county fairs.

"I could tell you the history of my life from A to Z and you wouldn't believe it," Jenkinson declares. "Why, I rode races in places in Nebraska where they'd have the rodeos, the buckin' horses going on in the centerfield chutes, while the races was going on around the track. Didn't have a starting gate. They'd just line 'em up across the track."

Her specialty in those days was the relay race. This was a contest requiring riders to change horses several times before the finish line was reached.

"You rode a horse into the station on a dead run," Jenkinson explained, "and you was reaching for that saddle horn on the next horse while the man holding that horse had ear rings on it or tongs on its nose. He'd cut that horse loose before you ever got on him. You'd flip off one of them horses, you hit the ground and be on the next one in full flight. You changed horses every half-mile, and you went one and one-half miles."

Some of the men didn't like it when Jenkinson started riding on the bull ring tracks. But she took her lumps and never complained. "I've ridden in many a race where every jockey was out to get me," she says. "Sometimes 26 horses on a half-mile track. That can get rough. A lot of them hated me because I was a woman; others because I wouldn't have anything to do with their fixed races. The odds would be against you. The starter would be against you. Everybody would be against you. You just had to outsmart the whole works."

Jenkinson was known for her honesty. The fair officials and horse owners alike knew she would never, under any circumstances, pull a horse.

Other riders would. All kinds of little games went on at the bull rings, for the riders were often people who had been ruled off the recognized tracks. They fixed races. Many of them used machines. Even Jenkinson admitted to carrying a battery now and then.

"Aw, the judges didn't care too much," she said. "Why, heck, the big part of them boys down here for years and years rode with them taped onto their bats."

Betting at the fairs was sometimes done through pari-mutuel machines, but more often it was accomplished man-to-man, through bookmakers or through an auction or Calcutta pools. Lillian recalled one little track in Missouri where betting money was accepted under a most interesting guise.

"Instead of pari-mutuel betting they called it donations," she said. "You donated $2 towards paying the purses and if that horse you donated on won, why, you got paid back.

"Out there they didn't have jocks' rooms," she added. "They kept the riders together where they saddled the horses. You just wore the same colors all day. I had my own. Every once in a while somebody would give you a set and you'd run to the barn and change."

There were a million tales about Lady Jenkinson. She in turn could tell a million stories about racing on the leaky roof circuit.

"I'll tell you who raced more good horses in the bushes than anybody," she says, "and that was Two-Gun Charlie Irwin, a dentist in Cheyenne. He used to run 50 or 60 head around those fairs and rodeos. He'd keep them all in a tent.

"He was a great, big, fat guy, and when he came to the races he stayed in the car. He wouldn't even try to get out. In Cheyenne he had a great big chair, and he'd set that at the paddock gate at the head of the stretch and that's where he sat all afternoon.

"Now, in Cheyenne, you didn't enter horses, you entered riders, and you entered up at the Chamber of Commerce. Well, everybody would be leading their horses into the paddock for a race, and here'd be a horse Charlie Irwin didn't think his could outrun. So he'd send his horse back to the tent and get another. He did that all the time, because the horses weren't entered, the riders were. It was more interesting that way, when you didn't know who you was going to ride."

Then there is the story about the bookie at the McLeansboro Fair.

"They had an airplane in the center ring one day, and there was a bookie who used to operate on top of a mound in the center ring. Well, one day when the airplane was there, and the horses were going to the gate, the bookie had everybody's money and he went over and got in that airplane. Everybody saw him. They all charged over there and tried to catch him, but the airplane took off. The bookie waved to them all, got up in the air and circled around, then came back down and got out of the plane and asked, 'Now, where's all the Doubting Thomases?'"

There are those who say Lady Jenkinson was a rough rider, that she put the whip to as many jockeys as she did to horses. But she and her friends insisted that she always rode clean . . . unless she had to reciprocate.

"Lillian was never vicious," according to her friend, Bartle. "But when a rider came up alongside and whipped her horse in the face, she knew how to take care of herself. Those riders knew that if they crowded Lillian, she'd whack them right across the top of the head with that bat."

"Roughest I ever was on anybody was on another woman," Jenkinson said. "I was riding this one-eyed mare, and this old gal was hitting her in the bad eye with her bat. Well, that made me mad and I worked her over. I really worked her over. She knew I had a bat before it was over with."

Bartle said Jenkinson never was a problem to have around the track. "She was an asset. You'd never see Lillian drinking and carousing around. And the crowd was always for her. They'd always stand up and really yell."

Lillian remembered how 100,000 people showed up one day at the Van Wert Fair in Ohio to see her ride. She required a police escort to get safely to and from the track.

Before Jenkinson married Chick she traveled the circuit of summer fairs with her father and her sister. The family raised its own stock on the farm in Nebraska, then toured the countryside all summer long to run their horses. Some of their best thoroughbreds were the famous Beans horses: Runners with names like Just Beans, More Beans and Beans Again. The names came from an old racetrack philosophy: "It was Just Beans for breakfast, More Beans for dinner and Beans Again for supper."

Bartle remembered Jenkinson and her sister, Babe, as "peculiar people." When Lillian and her sister came into town for the races, Bartle said, "the first thing they'd do was go get their hair fixed. Ha. You'd think that would be the last thing Lillian would ever do."

Bartle thought her "peculiar" in other ways, too, for Jenkinson didn't fit the standardized image of that day's woman. "She had a single-mindedness about her," he said. "Maybe peculiar is not the right word, but she was unusual because not many women would be content to spend their lives right around the barn, to just live and breathe and think horses.

"But she was a pretty fair horsewoman. She just had what it takes, that's all. I know a race rider when I see one."

One of Jenkinson's assets was her ability to break quickly from the gate. Chick maintained this was possible because she would let a horse have its head when it broke. Only when it settled in stride would she take up on it.

"Well, you can beat any starter's gate," Lillian insists. "They all make some motion with their lips or their hand or something and you know they're going to pull it. And when there's a hometown horse in a race, you know the starter's figuring on getting that horse off on top, so you watch the rider on the hometown horse. When it looks like the boy's going to make a move on him, you break in front of him and you'll beat him out of the gate."

One of the earliest gates Jenkinson saw was made out of chicken wire they once used at Pinckneyville. The starter there invented the gate, which had big springs. Jenkinson remembered that, "when they'd release those springs the whole thing would fly up in front of you. But it wouldn't fly up fast enough. You'd tear your clothes off trying to come out of that gate."

Thirty-six years before Kathy Kusner and Penny Ann Early tried to break the all-male jockeys' ranks, Lady Jenkinson made her initial application at the recognized race tracks—and was turned down. When girls began riding and winning at race tracks she tried again in 1969, and sought help from various politicians.

One of those who came to her aid was William J. Cunningham, a Republican who went before the House of Representatives in Illinois to plead the female jockey's case. The assembly adopted a resolution urging the Illinois Racing Board, which had backed up the Cahokia stewards' decision, to "reconsider its arbitrary refusal" in denying her a license because of her age. But not even the influence of the assemblymen could get Lillian Jenkinson to the races.

She's old now, old beyond her years because of her racing injuries. Lillian never really recovered from the spill at McLeansboro in the late 1960s. Last fall, while exercising a horse at Pinckneyville, she took another spill. The combined injuries keep her confined to bed and in continual pain.

Chick and Lillian still occupy the house trailer parked near the first turn at Pinckneyville, but racing at the fairs and bull ring tracks goes on without them. Sometimes Lillian will look out the window to watch a horse galloping along the track, but the calcification in her neck begins hurting and she'll concede she could never ride a horse like that. Other times she'll long to get outside and ride. "If I didn't have a horse, I'd be lost."

Chick says only two things could make Lillian happy now: "One would be to get back on a horse. The other would be the satisfaction of saying she'd ridden races at a real race track."

(October, 1981)

Maryjean Wall, a staff writer for the Lexington (KY) Herald-Leader, *was the first women sportswriter admitted to the National Turf Writers Association and has won numerous awards, including an Eclipse, the Oscar of thoroughbred racing. A lifelong horsewoman, she trains and shows her own Arabian in dressage.*

THE JERSEY BELLES

By Jenny Kellner
New York Post

IT IS A RAINY AFTERNOON AT MONMOUTH PARK. THE SADDLING AREA, USUALLY ringed with racing fans, is empty. On the other side of the tall, wooden fence, the jockeys' swimming pool (the only one in the country) is filled to overflowing.

To get from the women's jockey quarters to the saddling area, you have to walk through the pool area—which is awash with puddles—and through a gate, the lower few inches of which are underwater.

After the third race, a maintenance man shows up with three eight-foot-long wooden planks, which he lays down over the puddles. "You see," he says with a twinkle in his eye, "chivalry isn't quite dead."

It is a small gesture, but one that is typical of this seaside racetrack, which venerates its small and unique colony of women riders . . . not as curiosities or novelties, but as winners.

For the third straight year, the irrepressible Julie Krone stands atop the rider standings, having ridden 50 winners. Joining her in the top 10 are the tall, elegant Diane Nelson—who is familiar to Meadowlands and Aqueduct patrons—and Maryann Alligood, long a fixture on the Philadelphia area racing scene.

Going into yesterday's action, the three had combined for 78 winners. On a recent Saturday, the talented trio won seven of the 10 races, and rarely a race goes by without at least one of them riding in it . . . and, more often than not, winning.

"It's not unusual to have three girls riding at one major track," said Alligood, noting that Nelson, Krone and Karen Rogers all rode at Aqueduct through the winter. "But to have three girls riding every day and winning every day . . . that's different."

At the smaller tracks around the country, especially in New England and throughout West Virginia, women riders are the rule rather than the exception. Nelson recalls an afternoon at Rockingham where in one race all the riders except one were women. But in the big leagues, or even the Triple A tracks such as Monmouth, that has not been the case.

Until now.

"In New York this past winter, we were thought of as unusual," Nelson said. "We weren't expected to do well.

"Here, it's every day," added Nelson, 23, who has signed on with the Ford Modeling Agency and recently appeared in a feature on unusual occupations in Woman's Day. "They expect us to win here. Everybody asks, 'How many races are the girls going to win today?' It's different than in New York. From day to day, I'm not worrying about how many I'm going to ride, or how few. I'm not sweating it out."

Monmouth's three leading ladies are vastly different in temperament and personality but, aside from the usual vagaries of professional competition, they seem to get along extraordinarily well.

"We really do," said Krone, 25, the winningest female jockey of all time. "I'm a people person, and I've known Maryann for 10 years. And Diane is so easy to get along with. The atmosphere here also makes it easy. When I'm off for two races, I go lay by the pool and sing, 'I love Monmouth Park, I love Monmouth Park.' And now, Maryann, when she's galloping horses in the morning past the honeysuckle, which grows all over the track, she's singing the same song too."

If Krone is at the zenith of her profession, and the youthful Nelson is steadily scaling her way upward, then Alligood, at 33 is making her first major stab at success.

"Actually, I came to the meet thinking that if I could win 20 and change a few people's minds, I'd be doing well," said Alligood, who, in her nine-year career, has seen her mounts earn more than $6 million in purses. "I do well in the Philadelphia area, but it's the same people, the same outfits, over and over again. I figure, it's now or never. I know I'm not going to ride forever, so I'll try to go on to bigger things the last five years of my career."

Without benefit of Krone's long-established clients or Nelson's four-week head start on the backstretch prior to the meet's opening, Alligood, who has first call on Danny Hasbany's 25-horse outfit, is not above, well, begging for a mount. Last week, for example, when trainer Sonny Hines blew up after discovering in the paddock his chosen rider was four pounds overweight, Alligood pounced on the opportunity.

"I said, 'Please, please, please can I ride him?'" recalled Alligood, a smile creasing her suntanned features. "He said, 'Can you sit chilly?' I said, 'Like an ice cube.' We came in third in the stake. When I stopped by the barn, he said, 'Well, looks like we'll have to find you something else to ride.'"

Alligood also recalls happily what brought her to the racetrack back in the late 70's. She had never even seen a horse in the flesh until she was 22.

"I was working in a 7-11 and in a factory, and I knew they weren't the right jobs for me," said Alligood, who moved to Philadelphia from Stuttgart, West Germany, with her mother after her father was killed in an auto crash. "Rochelle Lee was riding at that time, and she was like a magnet for me. I knew, when I saw what she did, that that's what I wanted to do."

Befriended by a parking lot attendant who also trained six horses, Alligood started off as a hotwalker, then graduated to rubbing horses. In the meantime, she was learning how to ride at a nearby farm.

"I learned how to ride on a pony who threw me, and then walked over me," Alligood said. "But I learned how to gallop horses on the racetrack. It took a lot of getting dropped and run off with—a lot of embarrassing moments—but it was worth it."

Alligood began riding the last day of February, 1980, and was the leading rider at the Philadelphia Park winter/fall meet that year. Along the way to winning millions of dollars in purses she has weathered several major spills as well as the barbs of jealous male riders, but can't envision doing anything else.

"The harder I work, the luckier I get," said Alligood, whose workaholic attitude mirrors that of Nelson and Krone, both of whom, despite their success, still hit the barns every day at 6 a.m. and work straight through the end of the card.

That kind of devotion, as well as the development of a thick skin to block out the stinging remarks from the less-secure of their male counterparts, are necessities for women riders.

"Jockeys are fiercely competitive—that's the nature of the game," Alligood said. "But in order to be successful as a woman jockey, you can't just be as good as a guy—you've got to be twice as good . . . and work twice as hard."

And just keep winning.

(July 12, 1989)

Jenny Kellner covers horse racing for various New York publications. A graduate of Hofstra, she has worked at the New York Daily News, *the* New York Post, *the* Miami Daily News, *the Associated Press and United Press International. She has two children, David and Erica.*

A Team Player

by Patricia Rodriguez
Fort Worth Star-Telegram

ASSISTANT FOOTBALL COACH TIM WRIGHT STANDS PROTECTIVELY IN FRONT OF the girls' restroom in the Sabine High School gym, his arm stretched across the door.

"Tammie's in there changing," he says, "and she told me not to let any of y'all in."

Not the four-person crew from Channel One, the national TV news program aimed at high school students. Not the cameraman from the Tyler TV station. No reporters, even though they've been coming from Dallas and Longview and Shreveport, just to get a look at Tammie Overstreet, one of the eight girls to make Texas history this fall by playing varsity football.

This night's game in Sabine was the season opener for the Pittsburg Pirates, for which she plays third-string offensive guard, and the reporters want to get the story.

Overstreet just wants to play the game.

"I just love it. I've always wanted to play football, ever since seventh grade," says the 17-year-old senior. "When I went out for the team, I didn't think nothing about it. It wasn't a big deal to me."

But in Texas, where everything about high school football is a big deal, the lifting of the ban against girls has become the biggest deal of all.

Reporters have called the University Interscholastic League, the agency that recommended letting girls play, from as far away as New York City, Washington, DC, and even Tokyo, says Peter Contreras, media director for the UIL. The story made *USA Today*. And only a week into the season, Tammie Overstreet—who didn't even play in the first varsity game—already has endured nearly a dozen interviews.

All this despite more than 40 other states already having allowed girls to play football.

"I've had calls from most of the 50 states, and I've asked them all what is the big deal. It wasn't a big deal when (girls) played in Wyoming, was it?" says Eddie Joseph, executive vice president of the Texas High School Coaches Association.

"I guess maybe it's that we in Texas held out so very long. Most people probably thought we would hold out forever."

They have been holding out, in fact, since 1947. That year, a 120-pound junior named Frankie Groves made national headlines by playing a few downs for the Stinnett Rattlers. The day after she took the field, girls were banned from the game.

No girls played again until this year, adding to the mystique already attached to Texas high school football.

"Texas has a reputation of playing the best high school football in the country, and when this was first announced, the reaction was, 'Oh, my God, now you're going to let girls play,'" Contreras says.

"But in all honesty, once the initial shock wore off, people realized that the rule just says that a girl has the opportunity to play, just like a boy . . . Our contention is that the impact girls will have on high school football will be minimal."

In general terms, that appears to be true. Only eight Texas high school girls made their school football team this fall, according to the UIL, compared to about 130,000 high school boys.

But in small towns like Pittsburg (population 4,561), where Tammie Overstreet has gone to school since kindergarten, the effect promises to be much greater.

"She's become a celebrity," says Susan Taft, editor of the weekly *Pittsburg Gazette*.

"This is the most attention we've gotten since we won state in 1980," says senior English instructor Diana Hicks. "Anything that brings success to the school is good."

"She's helped put this town on the map," says Calvin Hill, head football coach at Pittsburg High School and the school's athletic director. "And we enjoy the attention, believe it or not."

Speak for yourself, coach.

The object of all the attention—an honor student and gifted athlete who hopes to attend college on a softball scholarship—would prefer to practice in anonymity, to just be part of the team.

This is no publicity stunt.

"I think the only one tired of y'all (reporters) is her," says junior Pymetheus Grant, pointing to the field where Overstreet is practicing with her teammates in preparation for the next night's game.

Indeed, her teammates cheerfully offer opinions on everything from the team's chances this year (all right, they decide) to Overstreet's performance as a player (good—for a girl, most agree).

"I'm proud of her, wanting to get out here and play with us guys," says junior defensive end Kennie Allen.

But Overstreet prefers to stay on the field, practicing her blocking and studiously watching plays. Listed at 5-foot-3 and 221 pounds, though she seems a few inches taller and a few pounds lighter, she is as sturdy as most of the boys on the field, but not as seasoned. She needs every bit of practice to try to keep up.

The natural athletic ability, however, is there.

"She's been a tomboy all her life," says her father, Bruce Overstreet, an antiques dealer who also owns the local livestock sale barn. "She's been playing with these boys since kindergarten, so I don't think any of them were surprised when she wanted to play this year."

Her mother, Margie Overstreet, who manages the family's 19-unit motel, adds, "She doesn't care about all the publicity. We do."

"What father wouldn't?" interjects Bruce.

But it was Dad's rules—not the state's—that prevented her from playing football even earlier.

As far back as the seventh grade, local school coaches had given her the okay to try out for the team, she says. Her parents, however, said no, so she contented herself with volleyball, softball, track and other sports.

Last summer, after the state's rule reversal, and with her senior year approaching, Overstreet decided to take one more run at football. First she approached Coach Hill to find out what she needed to do to prepare for the season and make the team. Then she went to her father.

"He wasn't going to let me, but then I cried," she admits. "So he finally said, 'Okay, get out there and get your neck broken.' But now he's proud of me, he really is. I think he's regretting he didn't let me play earlier."

Indeed, the acceptance of Tammie onto the team has been amazingly easy, say teammates, coaches and school officials.

At "Meet the Pirates Night" at the Pittsburg stadium a few weeks ago, Overstreet got the only standing ovation, Coach Hill says. At the pep rally the day of the season opener, the students gave her the loudest round of applause, and friends reached out to give her high-fives as she walked with the rest of the team around the gym floor. When the end of the Sabine game loomed and it looked like she wouldn't play, the band started a cheer begging the coach to put her in.

And teammates are still bragging about her performance at a junior varsity scrimmage a few weeks ago. Two players rushed her, and they couldn't knock her down. Upset, the opponents later tried to intimidate her on the field.

"One of the guys swung at her—and she swung back," Coach Hill says. "She doesn't back away from anything."

That determination was what convinced Hill that Overstreet could make the team. At first, he acknowledges, he wondered if she could take the intense physical demands of the sport—the running, the weight-training, the two-a-day practices in the hot Texas sun.

But one day before practices even started he looked out his window and saw her starting a dreaded training ritual called pulling crossties. In this exercise, the player is harnessed to a railroad crosstie and runs while pulling it. Some boys walk with the tie, but Overstreet was running, and at an uphill angle to boot.

"When practice started and those boys saw Tammie pulling those crossties, she gained their respect," Hill says. "They knew how tough that is. I never had to say anything to anybody. If anything, having her helped motivate the team. If they saw Tammie doing it, it would be an embarrassment for them to quit."

Hill's remaining doubts ended the day team members put on pads and started contact work.

"Right off the bat, she started hitting folks," he says. "She doesn't have the upper body strength, but she doesn't mind tackling folks and giving it everything she's got."

Overstreet knew that if she got to play, she'd never quit. She's not a quitter.

She rises at 4:30 a.m. every day to care for her animals, including some 25 rabbits, 100 goats and 30 or more hogs. Then it's on to school, where she has a full schedule of seven classes, including pre-calculus, anatomy and physiology. After school she practices football. (She is also a member of the volleyball team and worked out a deal to miss football practice on volleyball game nights.)

Then it's back to care for the animals. After dinner at 8 or 9 p.m., she does homework until she finally falls asleep sometime before midnight.

Though some might balk at such a schedule, Overstreet says she loves it. And she especially loves playing football.

"Softball has always been big on my list, but football is right up under it. I love it," she says. "It's so physical. You can get out there and hit somebody and you don't get thrown out of the game."

The few annoyances have been minor.

At the Sabine game, dozens of students, and a few of their parents, lined up as the team trotted onto the field, trying to spot Overstreet, looking for her as if she were an oddity. But if Overstreet even noticed, she didn't show it, although she did keep her blond French braid tucked inside her uniform, perhaps making it harder for opponents to detect her.

A few people have warned her and her parents that she'll get hurt playing with all those boys, she says. One school patron, it is rumored, was telling people he'd refuse to buy his season tickets because the team had a girl playing.

And Coach Hill laughs when he recalls that soon after practice started, Overstreet complained about the odor in the boys' locker rooms. At school practices, Overstreet dresses alone in the freshman locker room because the freshmen practice at a different time.

"I think she went out and bought one of those air fresheners and put it on her locker," Hill says, laughing. "But other than that, there have been no problems."

As a first-year player, Overstreet will get limited playing time, Coach Hill concedes. She didn't play in the Sabine game, which ended in an 8-8 tie. That game was too close to use the more inexperienced players, which disappointed but did not surprise her.

Her greater long-range impact may well be in changing the way girls in Pittsburg think about football.

"I think everyone's behind her," says senior Ebony Hill, the coach's daughter and a friend of Overstreet. "I think everyone admires her for doing this, especially the girls. I know I do, because I couldn't do it."

Karen Weathers, a special education aide at the school, says her 11-year-old daughter admires Tammie Overstreet's achievements and hopes to follow her onto the football field one day.

"Tammie's the reason we went to the scrimmage last week," Weathers says. "There were more girls than I've ever seen at a scrimmage. I think they're proud of her."

And she already may have changed the way some coaches think of female athletes.

"If I had a vote, I would have voted no. I just figure there's a time and a place for everything, and girls playing football is one of those things," says offensive coordinator Tim Wright. "But Tammie's special. It takes a special kind of girl to play any kind of contact sport, and Tammie's that kind of girl."

His own two daughters will never play football, Wright vows. But Overstreet—well, she's okay.

Before the game at Sabine, Overstreet trudges through the gym with her bag full of equipment, a couple of coaches trailing her, as she tries to find a place to dress. After discovering the girls' locker room locked, she goes back to the restroom, dragging the gear a little lower this time.

"You know, Tammie, I'd carry that for you, but I know you don't want anybody doing anything for you," assistant coach Lawrence Cleveland calls after her.

Overstreet laughs, and turns around and tells him she'd make an exception this one time, but she never does hand over the bag. The coach is right. She wants to do it herself.

(September 12, 1993)

Patricia Rodriguez, a feature reporter for the Fort Worth Star-Telegram, *has also written features for the* Dallas Times Herald, *the* Cincinnati Enquirer *and* USA Weekend Magazine. *She has a journalism degree from the University of Missouri.*

LIEBERMAN LOVES GAME IN SPITE OF ALL THE PAIN

by Melissa Isaacson
Orlando Sentinel

YOU LOOK DOWN AND SHAKE YOUR HEAD. YOUR SHORTS ARE DROOPING, AND you feel you're getting sick. Surely there are better things for a 27-year-old millionaire to be doing on a Friday night than standing in a strange locker room, tugging at her shorts and sniffling. There have to be.

But rundown or not, you have a job to do this evening, and you don't let a little discomfort interfere when you're Nancy Lieberman, the first woman to play professional basketball in a men's league. You pull on your shorts and sign autographs and give interviews. It's only the USBL—not the NBA—but these guys are just as big and maybe more physical, and you do not want to look stupid.

You want to help draw fans to see you and your team, the Springfield Fame, because that is your job.

You know you're there for the publicity. They told you as much, and you're no dummy, but you also happen to love basketball. You're certainly not doing it for the money, $10,000 for the season. So you shoot 200 foul shots every day, and you stay after practice to shoot some more. Then you go home and run, because you have your pride and you want to show people that you're the best woman basketball player ever. That's important to you.

You also happen to love the team atmosphere, the camaraderie you don't get traveling around the country attending to roughly a dozen charities, sporting goods stores, real estate ventures and a budding movie career. Mostly, you feel lonely when you do that.

You also happen to love these guys on your team, a mix of NBA has-beens and promising up-and-comers, and people who just love the game and don't want to quit. Like you. You counsel them on business and dealing with the media, and you encourage the ones who think they have a shot at the NBA. You don't mind, because you think you have a lot to offer. In turn they look to you like a big sister and not some dumb girl taking up a place on the roster.

They even slap your hands when the coach, former Philadelphia 76er Henry Bibby, sends you into the game for them. On this night, you play for 4 minutes and 45 seconds. You come in toward the end of the first quarter and make a nice assist to Baskerville Holmes, and settle back in a zone defense they use only when you're in the game.

The opposing team's point guard tries to draw you out of the zone, wants desperately to burn you, but you don't bite and he ends up launching an errant shot well out of his range. He doesn't score while you're in the game, and you're satisfied because the score varies little from when you came in.

After the game, you remember how exhausted you are. But you put on makeup and a skirt because you want to look nice representing the team. You half-hobble out of the locker room because your knee has been giving you some problems and you ignore the other team's cheerleaders, who whisper and giggle and mimic your walk as you go past.

You talk to more reporters and answer more questions you've answered before, and you try to be patient when one of them asks what you would do if one of your teammates got into a fight. You explain that you would be right in the middle, trying to stop it if you could, because these guys are your teammates, and that's what you do. You ignore his astonished look and his chuckle.

Finally, you go back to your hotel and sit in the bar, where it's at least 110 degrees because the air conditioning has broken down, and you talk to a teammate who is depressed about his game.

Later, you go get a pizza and bring it back to your room. You watch David Letterman and kill a foot-long cockroach and laugh about Florida being the bug capital of the world. You talk about what you've accomplished in your 27 years, playing on a silver-medal team in the Olympics and two national championship teams in college, the two years in two women's pro leagues. You talk about how much fun it will be telling your grandchildren about how lucky you've been.

And you look ahead to tomorrow, where it will be a 4-hour bus ride to West Palm and your next game. You joke about how easy it would be to hop a plane there and skip the misery. But you know you won't because you love this.

(June 19, 1986)

ALL DRESSED UP AND NOWHERE TO GOALIE

by Rosie DiManno
Toronto Star

A DOZEN NEW GOALIE STICKS ARE LINED UP AGAINST THE WALL, BITS OF TWISTED hockey tape are strewn about the room, and a discarded jock strap lies in the middle of the floor.

Make that a jill strap.

There are other odd touches in this dressing room. Like the eyeliner on the vanity table, and the dainty suede pumps that are tucked underneath. At the moment the occupant of this mini-clubhouse-for-one is just down the hall, lying prostrate on a table, while a trainer rubs oil on her skin and massages her aching muscles.

A curtain has been drawn around this makeshift cubicle deep in the bowels of the Lakeland Civic Arena, but there are gaps in the fabric enclosure where sly photographers try nonchalantly to slide in their cameras. Meanwhile, other players in various stages of undress pad by in their bare feet, steadfastly averting their eyes.

In this novel situation, nobody really knows the rules. Everybody is learning as they go along.

The young woman getting the rubdown is Manon Rheaume, the first female ever to participate in a National Hockey League training camp. And this arena, 35 miles east of Tampa, is the rehearsal hall for the Tampa Bay Lightning, Florida's spanking new entry into the professional shinny wars. There are few recognizable faces in camp, this being a motley team of unknowns, has-beens and never-wases. But Rheaume's is one face here that is quickly becoming familiar, even to a populace that doesn't know a hip-check from a hat-check.

The 20-year-old goaltender from Quebec city, who stands 5 feet 6 inches when she's not on skates, has become an instant celebrity since camp opened just over a week ago. The national media has descended on this strip-mall community to record every nuance and every awkward circumstance of this beauty among the beasts. And it does help that Rheaume is a comely nubile with hazel eyes, a glowing complexion, and a decidedly feminine grace. There is no hint of testosterone in her nature.

Every day, reporters and photographers trail her movements. So far, she has attracted the attention of *People* magazine, *USA Today*, CNN, ESPN, "The Today Show," "Good Morning America" and "Entertainment Tonight."

"The other guys get to play golf and lie in the sun when they leave the rink," sighs Rheaume. "I'm always doing interviews."

This, of course, was precisely the plan as hatched by club president and cosmic publicity force Phil Esposito. A showman as a player, he recognized a promotional windfall when he saw one as a ticket-boosting administrator. And bringing a girl to a fledgling hockey franchise's debut training camp ranks right up there with Bill Veeck sending a midget to bat for the St. Louis Browns. It's pure hucksterism on a club where the advertising slogan is: Kick Ice.

"I'd be an absolute blatant liar if I said that wasn't part of it," Esposito was saying the other day, between fielding umpteen calls on his cellular phone. "But, hey, this is entertainment and any athlete who doesn't believe he's an entertainer should get out of the goddamn business."

It's a symbiotic relationship, he argues, between a player and a team both trying to make names for themselves in a competitive business.

"She knew what the deal was. This has been very beneficial for her. But let's not forget one thing—she has not gotten any special treatment, except for having her own dressing room. And let me tell you, the guys really complained about that."

He roars with laughter. This is a joke, one presumes.

"But seriously, she's actually quite good. Better than any of us had expected. I had two general managers call me last night and ask if I'd trade her. Really. One guy offered me a lot, I couldn't believe it, a goalie in return. I said no way. She's ours."

Several months ago, after originally gaining notoriety when she played 17 minutes of a Major Junior A game with the Trois Rivieres Draveurs— another first for a female—Rheaume was offered $75,000 to pose in the buff for a skin magazine. She turned it down.

"Not interested," she sniffed. "At the very least, I should be able to control what magazines I appear in."

Make no mistake, Manon Rheaume is very much in control of her destiny. There may be exploitation at work here, but it's a two-way relationship. She decides when she will give interviews, to whom, and how long they will last.

"Five minutes," she tells one reporter. "I'm busy."

Mostly she has been busy on the ice, which is what this is ostensibly all about. There are seven goaltenders in camp and Rheaume has faced her share of slapshots. The players, if you buy the company line, haven't shown her any tender mercies during shooting drills and scrimmages.

"I was very nervous coming into camp," she admitted yesterday morning while tucking into a breakfast of strawberries, toast and chocolate milk. "I've never faced shots this hard before. I didn't want to make a fool of myself."

To her credit, she hasn't. Rheaume performed well during a four-day intrasquad tournament earlier this week. She played the entire second half of one game, holding the opposition scoreless including a penalty shot. She has a quick glove hand and doesn't flop in the crease, although her puck-handling ability leaves much to be desired. But some days have been better than others.

"There's a lot of pressure on me every time I go on the ice," she says. "I'm only human, and I will have some bad performances. When camp started, the other players didn't know what I could do. I had to prove myself to them and I think I've accomplished that. That game where I didn't allow any goals gave me a lot of confidence and I think the guys took me more seriously after that."

Rheaume has been playing hockey since she was 5 years old. Her father was a peewee coach, her two brothers both played on teams, and she wanted in.

"I used to skate in the backyard with my brothers. I didn't want to just watch. I wanted to play. I became a goalie because that's where my brothers put me, it's the only position they would let me play."

"I never stopped loving hockey," says Rheaume, who also back-stopped the Canadian women's national team that successfully defended its world championship title in Finland. "I mean, there are other things I enjoy doing. I love to shop, but I am good at this and I wanted to see how far I can go. That is why I am here, to see what more I can learn. I am not a fool, I do not expect to make the NHL. But how could I have said no to this opportunity? I may try and fail, but if I didn't try I would spend the rest of my life wondering—how would I have done?"

On the ice, during hockey tutorials from the coaching staff, she usually stands alone and apart from the group.

"If she had asked me for any tips, I would have been happy to give them," says fellow goalie J.C. Bergeron, "but she's never asked."

It has been awkward for these guys, most of whom have never played hockey with a female before, not even in their peewee days. Esposito claims his main worry once the experiment began was that "they would hit on her." The team has no anti-fraternization rules. "She's a grown woman," says Esposito. "She can do what she likes."

Rheaume has survived the first round of cuts in camp. She was not among the casualties sent home a few days ago. There was some talk of her dressing for tonight's exhibition game against the Minnesota North

Stars. But Esposito, shrewdly playing out the string, now says Rheaume's debut will be delayed until at least the end of the week.

(September 9, 1992)

Rosie DiManno *is the city columnist for the* Toronto Star. *She began her career as a sportswriter in 1975 and has also been an entertainment writer and feature writer. She has done the play-by-play of a dozen tours of the Royal Family to Canada and the United States.*

THIS FAIRY TALE ENDS 1-16

by Cindy Martinez Rhodes
Riverside Press-Enterprise

THEY PREFER TO BE THOUGHT OF AS JUST ANOTHER BASEBALL TEAM, NOT A curiosity or a joke or a charity case.

But it's hard to ignore the modern-day fairy tale the Perris Temple Christian baseball team has become. This is a story where the girls rescue the boys.

Allowing the girls to play on the baseball team, Coach Jeff Bell acknowledged, had nothing to do with chivalry or progressive thinking or Title IX requirements—he simply wanted to field a team.

The student body totals 63. Not enough girls showed up to field a softball team, and just enough boys, nine, attended the season's first baseball practice. To senior pitcher Bill Neal, the solution was obvious.

"The girls had no alternative, so a couple of us guys asked some of them if they wanted to come and try out for the baseball team," Neal said. "They honestly wanted to play and saw that we really wanted a team. They really helped us out—the girls kind of came to our rescue."

Principal Dan Kitabjian said he made the offer for purely practical reasons. And being the former softball coach, he knew that many of his girls were physically and athletically capable of making the transition.

"I think the girls clung to the fact that they wanted to be part of a team," Kitabjian said. "They had enough guts and courage to compete against the guys and try out for the team."

Three girls started this season—Julie Splain at shortstop, Jennifer Reno at first base and Lori Ecker in right field. Kristen Sissung and Renee Trujillo also were on the team. Bell apologized for not being a more diligent statistician but said none of the girls went hitless.

As many would expect, there were taunts, but they fell on deaf ears. And nothing stopped hecklers quicker than a solid base hit from one of the girls.

All the girls had at least six years of softball experience and said the two games are similar in many ways. Reno was the only one who had baseball experience. She played Little League in Hawaii before moving to Perris last year.

"I'm a little intimidated sometimes, but the guys are great. They treat us like one of the guys, but they're protective of us too," Reno said. "And the other teams—at first they're really shocked, but I think they respect us for trying so hard."

Neal said the guys on the team walk a fine line in not trying to be too protective.

"At first we heard some rude comments from the stands and it makes you angry and you want to say something," Neal said. "And when they get hurt, it's hard not to run over and see if they're okay. But they take care of themselves. They're tough. We see it in practice every day."

Kitabjian is pleased with the results but said he wasn't sure what others in the Victory League think. There are concerns, and Riverside Bethel Christian Coach Kevin Leatherman reluctantly raised a few.

"I have some pretty big hitters in my lineup, and I would hate to see a girl try to field a shot hit hard right at her and get really hurt," Leatherman said. "My wife says I sound like a true chauvinist pig, but I have to say my first thought was concern that one of them would get hurt."

Looking for a happy ending? It didn't come in Temple Christian's record. The Swordsmen finished 1-16, and 0-12 in league.

But if you talk to the 15 players, 10 boys and 5 girls, they'll tell you winning is not the issue.

"We have a lot of fun and try to set a good example for the other schools," Splain said. "We try hard and it would be nice to win, but it doesn't really matter."

"Winning isn't the purpose," Bell said. "We're here to try to be a good witness. We're a Christian school, and we do things differently. We need to teach these kids to be good to each other—to let people know there is a God."

(May 28, 1992)

EIGHT

PIECES OF OUR MINDS

A Damnable Defense

by Sonja Steptoe
Sports Illustrated

In the aftermath of Mike Tyson's conviction last week for rape, I am left with a particularly troubling image: Tyson sitting at the defense table, listening impassively as his attorney Vincent Fuller pressed beauty pageant contestants for testimony providing every last unsavory detail of the fighter's marauding behavior during that fateful July weekend in Indianapolis. As I heard the accounts of the boxer's groping, fondling and sexually explicit, expletive-riddled remarks to the women, I shook my head.

Now, I know that even before he raped Desiree Washington, an 18-year-old contestant in the Miss Black America pageant, Tyson had a well-deserved reputation for horrific behavior. And the press reports of his coarse conduct toward other contestants in the pageant only reinforced that image. But a court of law is a very different forum from your morning newspaper. One would have expected the prosecution to cast a harsh light on Tyson's most objectionable actions, and the defense to try to put the best face on them. After all, anybody charged with a crime is entitled to a vigorous defense, which ordinarily involves an effort by his counsel to find the humanity that lies in even the worst of us.

Instead, quite the opposite happened in the Marion County courthouse. In prosecutor Greg Garrison's successful presentation of the facts, Tyson was a deceiver, a slick operator who used his wiles to lure Washington into his hotel room, where he proceeded to rape her. Yes, Garrison developed the idea that Tyson had engaged in brutality, but he also showed him to be a crafty individual capable of a wicked sort of charm. Consistent with this theory of the case, Garrison portrayed Tyson as being almost playful toward the contestants. The prosecutor did not seem eager to dwell unduly on Tyson's boorishness toward them.

It was left, jarringly, for Fuller to do that. In his opening statement, Fuller told the jury that Tyson "is not a high school graduate. He's never been trained in public speaking. He's never been trained in the skills of projecting himself . . . . He's been trained to do one thing, to defend himself in a ring and to go to battle in a ring." And so, Fuller said, when Tyson came to Indianapolis after having just won a bout with Razor Ruddock, he was anxious to "relax for the first time in weeks" and went on a sex-crazed rampage at a pageant rehearsal, uttering obscenities and making offensive overtures to the contestants. During the trial Fuller went to great lengths to elicit testimony about that conduct. In effect Fuller was saying to the jury: Tyson is your worst nightmare—a vulgar, socially inept, sex-obsessed black athlete. And any woman who would voluntarily enter a hotel suite with him must have known what she was getting into. In other words, both principals were animals—the black man for the crudity of his sexual demands, the black woman for eagerly acceding to them.

I understand that it was Fuller's job to adopt whatever strategy he felt gave him the best shot at winning the case. But the suspicion is inescapable that in choosing the course he did, he was pandering to bigoted perceptions about blacks, apparently hoping that the jurors would buy into those perceptions and vote to acquit Tyson. In another example of the same mind-set, Fuller's defense team tried unsuccessfully before the trial began to introduce expert testimony about the size of Tyson's genitals as an explanation for the vaginal abrasions Washington suffered, a tack that inevitably became the basis for a spoof on NBC's "Saturday Night Live."

That this strategy didn't fly is a credit to the jury of 10 whites and two blacks, who saw it for the cynical business that it was. What concerns me, though, is that there was a far wider audience for Fuller's presentation: the public at large. And to this audience the defense sent disturbing messages, some of which transcend this trial. One of those messages, the idea that star athletes can play by different rules than the rest of us, was, blessedly, shot down by the jury's verdict. The other message. however, endures. It was bad enough that Tyson had raped a woman. But he was even more than a rapist; he was the stereotypical savage black man run amok, this by the characterization of *his own lawyer*. The stud defense is a Faustian bargain if ever there was one. In Fuller's effort to win his client an acquittal, the defendant was affixed with a label: BEWARE— DANGEROUS SEXUAL ANIMAL. Which only reinforced a stereotype of black men in general.

I am baffled as to why Tyson's black supporters overlooked this travesty when they held prayer vigils in Indianapolis for him during which they raged about the perceived racial injustices committed by the prosecution. These apologists for Tyson said the rape charges were racially motivated, even though Washington also is black. Just as many blacks attacked Anita Hill for the allegations she leveled at Clarence Thomas during his Supreme Court nomination process, so did they excoriate Washington for pressing charges that put this black man in a jam. The way they saw it, Tyson now joins Thomas and former Washington, DC, mayor Marion Barry as high-profile black martyrs persecuted for behavior that white men get away with.

But it wasn't the prosecution that perpetrated an injustice in the Indianapolis case, and it wasn't Desiree Washington. The wrongdoers were Tyson, for committing rape, and his own legal team, whose misguided and contemptible defense fanned the fires of racism by perpetuating the worst kind of racial stereotypes.

(February 24, 1992)
Sonja Steptoe *writes golf and does investigative reporting for* Sports Illustrated. *A graduate of the University of Missouri and Duke Law School, she previously worked at the* Wall Street Journal *where she wrote about insurance, pharmaceutical companies and the stock market.*

No News Is Bad News

by Shelley Smith
San Francisco Examiner

MOST NEWSPAPERS IN THE BAY AREA DON'T PRINT WOMEN'S COLLEGE SPORTS stories because they either don't have the space or their readers aren't interested, sports editors say. But the reason readers aren't interested, counter women's sports officials, is that the newspapers won't make the space to print the stories.

"It's the age-old problem of which comes first," said John Rawlings of the *San Jose Mercury News*. "People have to show there's an interest there for us to commit the manpower."

Not many people attend women's sports events at Bay Area colleges. An average of 100 people attend volleyball games, with basketball drawing slightly higher.

"Every decision we make is based on what is of interest to our readers," said Dan McGrath of the *San Francisco Chronicle*. "I can't see us doing much more unless we are shown there is more interest out there."

Charles Cooper of the *Examiner* said that except for major college football and basketball games, he uses the same criteria to determine whether to cover a women's event as that of a men's event.

"If we have the resources and the space we put it in," he said. "It's the same test for youth soccer or anything else."

But, he said, he doesn't think the *Examiner* covers women's sports as much as it should. "I don't think any newspaper is satisfied with the amount of women's sports it covers," he said.

Cooper said he believes there is a definite interest in women's athletics, but says it's difficult to gauge whether there is interest in reading about women's sports. And most of the editors agreed that it is not the newspaper's responsibility to create that interest.

"We're there to report, to analyze, to provide information," McGrath said. "In terms of creating interest, the problem is with them. I sympathize with them. It really is a Catch 22."

Most of the newspapers send reporters to women's sports events if they are significant—like a major tournament or a regional championship—and most will follow a local athlete who is competing for one of the colleges. However, most print short stories called in by each college after the game.

Bob Valli of the *Oakland Tribune* said he tries to send reporters to as many women's events as possible. "We started that four or five years ago," he said. "We thought it was something we couldn't ignore, but it's hard to tell if the interest is there."

Most of the editors said they would add coverage if they got more complaints, but until the events start showing good attendance figures, they don't see their policies changing.

Rawlings said he heard 12,000 people attended a women's gymnastics meet at UCLA last winter. "I told (San Jose State's) Mary Zimmerman that when she can put that many people in the stands, we'll get there."

Zimmerman said she felt helpless. "What am I supposed to do to let people know that we have a game that night? Get a sound truck and a bull horn and drive around the streets yelling, 'Game tonight at State?'"

Chuck Dybdal of the *Contra Costa Times* said that if the schools would start playing powerhouses like USC, he would send reporters to the games. "But when they play these run-of-the-mill colleges, we'll just take the calls from them and take it from there," he said.

Jay Clapper of the *Hayward Review* said his paper will follow the local athletes that play in Bay Area colleges by writing feature stories and updates, but conceded that game coverage is almost non-existent.

"As women's sports get better, though," Clapper said, "newspapers can't ignore them anymore. We're not trying to ignore them, but there's a limit to what you can cover."

(November 29, 1984)

Shelley Smith *is a special correspondent for* Sports Illustrated. *She previously worked at the* San Francisco Examiner, *the* Associated Press *and as a free-lance sportswriter in Japan. A graduate of the University of Nebraska, she is also covers the NBA for the ESPN television network.*

No Super Sunday for Battered Women

by Joan Ryan
San Francisco Examiner

WENNY KUSUMA WALKED LAST SUNDAY AFTERNOON THROUGH DOWNTOWN San Francisco, which was quiet and nearly empty. So many people were home watching the 49ers-Cowboys NFC Championship Game.

"I had this feeling of dread: Before the night's over we'll have more battered women in either Dallas or San Francisco. The phones will be ringing in one place or the other," she said.

Kusuma works at Women Inc., which refers battered women to counselors and shelters in the Bay Area. Football Sundays are heavy workdays for battered women's shelters. Not that most other days aren't.

A woman is battered by a husband or lover every 15 seconds of every day. The U.S. Surgeon General reports that violence is the leading cause of injury to women between the ages of 15 and 44. One-third to one-half of all female murder victims die at the hands of their spouses or lovers.

For all the high-octane anti-drug campaigns, domestic violence is a more pervasive problem. A person is five times more likely to be involved in a violent relationship than to use drugs on a regular basis.

Next week's Super Bowl Sunday could be the worst day of the year for battered women. It usually is.

"It's sort of a violent man's weekend," said Allan Shore of the Oakland Men's Project.

A wife or girlfriend steps in front of the television. She doesn't fetch his beer quickly enough. She can't keep the children quiet. She contradicts him in front of his buddies. Anything can trigger the beating. But it's the beer, the betting, the bruising and banging of players on TV that lead the way. The athletes on the screen—men often admired to the point of reverence—reaffirm the batterer's belief of what it means to be a man: aggressive, dominant, physical.

So who better than the athletes to take up the campaign against domestic violence? Who better to counter sports' unspoken message of brutality by denouncing brutality in the home?

Responding to a request by a coalition of domestic violence groups, NBC has agreed to air a public service announcement during the Super Bowl broadcast. It is an unprecedented step. Up to now, the sports community has met the issue with silence and avoidance. Even Mike Tyson's rape conviction last year turned into a racial issue rather than a violence issue.

332

But by airing a PSA during the Super Bowl, the sports world finally has pulled back the curtain, however slightly. It raises hope that sports might recognize its unique position of strength in the war on domestic violence.

"(A campaign by athletes) would be more effective than any other program we could have," Shore said.

Leagues and teams took up the anti-drug campaign in response to their own athletes' drug problems. Domestic violence is no less a problem. Every week some athlete or other is charged with assaulting a woman. Rather than denouncing the behavior, the sports community has tended to reinforce it, wittingly or unwittingly.

When Craig "Ironhead" Heyward was suspended from the New Orleans Saints at the end of last season, coach Jim Mora made it clear the player was not being punished for charges of assaulting two women. Rather it was for abandoning his training regimen and for other violations of club policy. Assault and battery isn't enough to be suspended, but gaining weight is.

Players in all sports are suspended and banned for using drugs, but to my knowledge no one has ever been penalized for beating up women. Former Dallas Mavericks center Roy Tarpley was kicked out of the NBA when he tested positive for drugs three times. Meanwhile, he had been charged four times with assault, the last one landing his girlfriend in the hospital with a dislocated shoulder.

Even those who would never raise a hand to their wives or girlfriends can become part of the problem. When a respected coach, such as Joe Paterno of Penn State, jokes after a tough loss (as he did in September 1991), "I'm going to go home and beat my wife," he puts battering women on the same level as kicking dogs or smashing chairs—unattractive but not unacceptable outlets for anger.

Men joke easily about smacking a woman around. Most don't mean it, but too many do. A 1992 Judiciary Committee report on Violence Against Women revealed 1.1 million reported assaults, murders and rapes against women in 1991. The same report found that more than half of all homeless women are on the street because they are escaping domestic violence.

Yet last July the national domestic-violence hot line—which handled as many as 10,000 calls a month—was disconnected for lack of money. Shelters, strapped for funds, can't keep up with the demand. San Francisco's three battered women's shelters turn away five women for every one they can house. Incredibly, nationwide there are more shelters for abused animals than for abused women.

The United Way is the NFL's primary charity, as one can tell by the advertisements during every NFL game. Some of United Way's money goes to women's crisis agencies. So the NFL is helping. But the NFL and other pro leagues have an opportunity to contribute something money can't buy. A message. A message that to be a man is to be strong enough to control one's temper, to be strong enough to seek help. The 30-second spot during the Super Bowl raises hope that the message might finally be delivered.

(January 24, 1993)

I'VE SEEN MORE FLESH ON THE M1 ROADWORKS!

by Liz Kahn
The Mail on Sunday

I WAS RIDING HIGH ON A BUGGY, A GOLFING SUFFRAGETTE ON MY WAY TO A small slice of history.

Sitting next to Michael Bonallack, secretary of the Royal and Ancient Golf Club, we were heading for the locker room at the exclusively male club of Muirfield.

Host for this weekend's Open championship, this men's enclave, properly entitled The Honourable Company of Edinburgh Golfers, sent Tom Watson packing from the course after he won on it in 1980, and denied Payne Stewart permission to play during his reign as U.S. Open champion.

Intimidating stuff and I felt apprehensive. It is one thing to struggle for equality in a man's world, quite another to cross the threshold that for so many years has remained forbidden territory.

My small step for womankind took me into the intimidating inner sanctum of the men's locker room—nowhere near the urinals, you must understand.

What did I find? Well, I've seen more bare flesh on the M1 roadworks. The most any professional golfer might rip off is a left-hand glove.

Bonallack is the enlightened man who has changed the face of entrenched chauvinism in golf. He was sympathetic to women journalists having equal opportunity and access to the locker room to work alongside their male colleagues at an Open.

Only two years ago, I was bodily evicted from the locker room at St. Andrews in Open championship week. To some, it may seem a joke; for me, it was an upsetting and demeaning experience to add to so many others.

In 1970, the first Open I attended at St. Andrews, when my male colleagues trooped into the clubhouse for a drink in the historic Trophy Room, I attempted to accompany them.

I made it through the front entrance, but at the next door I was stopped by an attendant. "Ladies are not allowed in here," he told me.

"How extraordinary," I muttered.

"No, madam, not even the Queen," he replied, over-stretching the point.

335

At the next St. Andrews Open in 1978, the former, now deceased, secretary of the R and A, Keith Mackenzie, roared at me to get out of the clubhouse when he saw me step just inside the door.

Inevitably, when I walked into the locker room there were cries of "What's a bloody woman doing in the locker room?" jokingly on the part of Ronan Rafferty and Gordon Brand Jr, who have been staunch supporters of my quest.

"Hello, love," Lee Trevino said cheerily, as I collected him in the locker room for an interview. Gary Player was equally welcoming, and we arranged a later working meeting.

Traditional locker room design is preserved at Muirfield with the warmth of seasoned wood for benches and stacked lockers that line the walls, each with a brass style name-plate.

Friendly attendants Jimmy and Tom not only dispense coffee, dishes of fruit and pretzels, clean shoes and deliver letters, they also provide a sympathetic ear when a professional unwinds with a boring shot-by-shot account of his last round.

The atmosphere is hospitable. Overall it's a place of calm. There are obvious underlying tensions and a special camaraderie between players, who banter, congratulate, commiserate, exchange gossip and are sensitive to hopes realised or shattered.

Walk through the first sizable room and you reach a small inner sanctum where lockers for the week belong to an elite group of past champions.

After two rounds, the casualty list of the privileged sanctum was a roll call of historic golfing glory. Jack Nicklaus, Tom Watson, Gary Player, Seve Ballesteros and Tom Weiskopf sadly cleared their lockers and buried their dreams.

The novelty of a woman appearing in a men's locker room in Britain—in America it is commonplace—prompted a steady flow of humourous comment.

"Are you a fixture here?" Trevino demanded, seeing me for the second day. And then he launched forth.

"You know what really bothered me yesterday? I read an article talking about the golf gods having been against Tony Jacklin at Muirfield when I chipped in here in 1972 and won the Championship. Then it said he got his dues back when we were both Ryder Cup captains in 1985 and Tony's team beat mine.

"Tony said I wouldn't shake hands when we came face to face. Well that's absolutely ridiculous. When Sammy Torrance holed that putt, I was the first to congratulate Tony.

"I'm going to ask him about it when I see him. I can't believe he said that."

Now, I'd never have found THAT out if I had still been standing outside in the rain. Opening the closet door has certainly been a revelation.

(July 19, 1992)
Liz Kahn, a London-based journalist for more than 20 years, has written for the Daily Telegraph, *the* Guardian, *the* Independent *and* The Mail on Sunday. *She was the first woman journalist to become a member of the Press Golf Society in its 80-year history. In 1993, she became its first woman captain.*

Two Bitter Slices of Life

by Mary Barker
Monterey Herald

Less than 24 hours.

That's all it took to change my sports world.

To turn everything I had trusted topsy-turvy.

In my 11 years or so as a sportswriter, there have been plentiful servings of perspective, convincing doses of disillusionment, handfuls of humility.

But after Wednesday night and Thursday afternoon, this job will never be quite the same.

Martina and Magic.

I suppose I could blame them. But blame really doesn't seem to fit here.

Maybe it was just bad timing. Perhaps it was simply inevitable.

Sports, after all, is merely life inside painted white lines.

The players are people, too. Sometimes, though, it's so nice when they don't seem like it.

I had never seen Martina Navratilova in person until Wednesday night at the Virginia Slims tournament at the Oakland Coliseum.

But I had wanted to since she beat Chris Evert for the first time.

As a kid, I spent as much time as I could hitting make-believe home runs and as little time as possible on my hair and clothes. I couldn't help but side with Martina.

I've seen almost every one of her nine Wimbledon victories. After each one, I worried that she would retire before I saw the serve-and-volley face-to-face.

But there she was Wednesday night so much smaller than I had imagined. So much thinner. So much more tainted. So much more affected.

She made fun of the ball boys and girls, she was rude to the chair umpire, she barely signed autographs, she begged for attention. She left me empty.

I still greatly respect her for her courage, honesty and overwhelming talent and dedication.

But my hero turned human. Then, less than 24 hours later, everybody else's hero did, too.

Magic Johnson of the Los Angeles Lakers has tested positive for the AIDS virus. He will announce his retirement from professional basketball. He is the first prominent sports figure to go public with the disclosure.

The message on the electronic ticker-tape at the BART station in Oakland ran over and over. I could only read it once.

My arms and legs felt heavy. As the train pulled up, I welcomed the chance to sit down somewhere. Dumbfounded, I stared out the window and wondered why? And how?

I thought about Magic's new bride. I remembered his smile. I envied his courage. I hoped he was doing okay. I prayed he would help bring positive attention to this cruel disease. I wondered who deals the cards and why they get shuffled the way they do.

And I realized that I, too, thought people like Magic and Martina were somehow untouchable.

I mean, come on. Magic Johnson retiring because of AIDS instead of bad knees or something?

Mr. Assist maybe someday needing help simply to stay alive?

Still four days later, it almost doesn't seem real. It certainly doesn't seem fair.

But Magic would probably tell you himself that even in every full-court press, there's somebody open. Somebody who can make a difference.

Magic can do that now, just not in the way anyone imagined or hoped.

He won't be junior-skyhooking or behind-the-backing while looking the other way.

He'll be telling kids and teaching people that no matter how high you can jump, or how fast you can run, you can't get away from life.

He'll be telling them how you can be a hero and still be human.

(November 10, 1991)

Mary Barker, *a columnist for the* Monterey (CA) Herald, *wrote her first story when she was eight years old—a rewrite of a broadcast about the assassination of Robert Kennedy. She has since covered professional football, U.S. Open golf, Indy car races, Grand Prix motorcycles and, inevitably, high school football.*

OH, NO! NOT ANOTHER BORING INTERVIEW WITH STEVE CARLTON

by Diane K. Shah
Los Angeles Herald-Examiner

HAVING RECENTLY PASSED A STATISTICAL BENCHMARK, THAT IS, HAVING JUST written my 300th column, I find I am besieged by athletes begging me to interview them. I know that only 15 other sports columnists in the history of journalism have reached this plateau, but I must say this constant round of interviews does grow wearisome. Every time a new team comes to town it's the same thing. You'd think all the athletes could just get together and agree to one mass interview.

To make matters worse, I once again find myself covering the playoffs. So now the requests for interviews have intensified all the more. Yesterday morning, no sooner had I reached my office when the phone rang.

"Yeah," I said.

"Er, Miss Shah? This is Steve Carlton with the Philadelphia Phillies. I was wondering . . ."

"I haven't even had my coffee yet," I grumbled. "Don't you guys ever sleep?"

"I'm sorry," said Carlton. "It's just that I was, er, wondering if you would have time today to interview me."

"What team did you say you were from?"

"The Phillies. I'm a pitcher."

"Oh, right, I remember. But haven't I interviewed you before? When the Phillies won the 1980 World Series or after you got your 300th win? I'm sure I did."

"Actually, you didn't," Carlton said. "I was rather hoping you would, but you always walk right past me. I've even sent you notes requesting interviews, but you never reply."

"You know how many games there are in a season?" I said.

"Yes," said Carlton meekly. "But I felt I had to give it a shot."

"So what is it you want me to interview you about?" I said, trying not to sound bored.

"Well you could ask me about my tough conditioning program," he said. "The Kung Fu and pushing my arm into a tub of rice. Or how many more years I'm going to pitch. Or what I think about the playoffs."

340

"Same old stuff," I said, stifling a yawn. "You'd think occasionally one of you guys would come up with something new to say."

"Perhaps you could ask me about being an oenophile," Carlton suggested.

"Don't try to impress me with big words," I snapped. "I hate looking things up in the dictionary."

"Oh," said Carlton deflatedly. "Well, er, I did lead the league in strikeouts. With 275."

"Are you a Cy Young candidate then?"

"No," he said sadly. "That would be John Denny. He pitches Wednesday night."

"Don't take this personally," I said, "but readers would probably be more interested in finding out what he has to say."

"I wouldn't need much time," Carlton pleaded. "Although I usually like as much time with the writer as possible."

"I've heard that before," I sighed. "You athletes think the longer the interview the better the story. Only I'm not getting paid to shoot the breeze with you guys. I get paid to write a column. I know it's important to your line of work to get interviewed, so I try to accommodate you when I can. But it's not in my contract here at the paper to just sit around doing interviews all day."

"I'll try to be as brief as possible," said Carlton. "Perhaps we could have lunch or a cup of coffee before the game."

"Absolutely not," I screamed. "You want me to talk to you, we'll talk at the ballpark. I hate when athletes try to interfere with my private life."

"Fine," said Carlton. "What time should I meet you?"

"Well, let's see. I'll get out to Dodger Stadium about two-and-a-half hours before game time. Then I have to go up to the press box and set up my word processing machine. I have to find a plug and take the machine out of its case and make sure it works. This is a special time for me. I don't like to be rushed."

"How about after you finish word processing practice?"

"No, 'Cause then I like to stroll around the batting cage chatting with my colleagues from the other papers. It's really annoying when an athlete comes over and interrupts. Some of the best jokes I hear are said at the batting cage."

"After that?" said Carlton hopefully.

"No," I went on. "Next I have to stop in Tom Lasorda's office. I need to check out the food and which celebrities have come by. And then I have to run through the Dodger clubhouse and say hello to everyone 'cause they expect hometown writers to be friendly to them."

"Gee," said Carlton. "This is really important to me. It's the playoffs."

"Tell you what," I said. "I'll send an intermediary. I'll get Vin Scully to interview you. He'll give the tape to Steve Brener, the Dodger publicist, and he'll screen the best answers out."

"I really appreciate this," said Carlton.

"Sure," I said. "By the way, what did you say your name was?"

(October 4, 1983)

Diane K. Shah *became the first woman in America to write a sports column—for the* Los Angeles Herald Examiner—*in 1981. She has written non-sports articles for GQ, the* New York Times Magazine *and* Esquire, *and two mystery novels set in 1947 Los Angeles. She is co-author of* Chief: My Life in the LAPD, *with Daryl Gates.*

Hey Guys, How about Just Saying No?

by Susan Fornoff
Sacramento Bee

THE PREVAILING ATTITUDES ON A COUPLE OF RECENT "SPORTS" ISSUES HAVE ME really steamed. The sexual double standard—man as conqueror, woman as Kleenex—has surfaced in the sports pages once again in a format written by men about men and for men. They may want to turn this page, because I don't think too many of them are going to like what I have to say.

Let's take things in chronological order, beginning with Wilt Chamberlain's impressive estimate of having had sexual encounters with 20,000 women. Impressive it is, apparently, to men, whose prevailing comments have been, "How did he find the time?" and "What kind of line did he use?" Some of them at least had the decency to wonder if he used 20,000 condoms. That was really big, really conscientious of them.

I wasn't one of Wilt's 20,000 victims, I'm happy to say. But I feel sorry for every one of them. Some of them, poor things, probably thought love had something to do with it. Others might have thought they were something more than a chalk mark on Wilt's blackboard. And I'm sure most of them are feeling pretty humiliated and degraded by the whole business.

"But that's just because you're a woman," a reporter friend of mine said. "Women look at it differently."

No kidding. A woman who had had sex with 20,000 men would probably be in intensive therapy, if not a psychiatric ward. She would feel far too sick, embarrassed and ashamed to boast in print and chat with Arsenio. Conducting intimate relations in Xerox machine fashion is not something to brag about.

But that's what Wilt was doing before Magic Johnson went public with his AIDS revelation. Bragging. Now he's a little more humble. That's really big, really conscientious, of him.

Then Magic's plight brought us another by-men about-men for-men theme. It has nothing to do with fidelity or discretion or, no, never, abstinence. It is this:

"Those poor athletes. They're so good-looking and rich. Everywhere they go, women want them. They have no choice but to be promiscuous."

Women, I ask you, is promiscuity the only option upon being pursued for sexual favors? Didn't we learn, somewhere along the way, to say, "NO!" Is it possible that we've misdirected the "Just say no" slogan for anti-drug propaganda when we ought to be educating men about their right to decline sex?

(Guys, the answers are: No, yes and yes.)

I do not dispute the fact that women chase athletes. I've seen the photos falling out of the mail that goes into the baseball clubhouses. I've been shown some of the letters. I've seen flowers showing up, not usually from wives. And the phones ring constantly.

What I don't understand is the athlete's reciprocity. What I don't understand is why a man who has so much going for him would be more careful about the foods he eats than the women he sleeps with. And what I really don't understand is the prevailing male attitude out there that all of this is okay—even enviable!—as long as the guy wears a condom.

One athlete told me a story not long ago about being out with three teammates and encountering a woman who, it turned out, had had sex with each of these four men when they had been with four different teams. I have no doubt that they discovered this because each of them had to take his turn to brag. Athletes don't announce, "Wow, man, I've now been faithful to my wife for 1,346 days." Fidelity is not fair game for locker-room banter.

There was, though, a married athlete who told me on the last weekend of a baseball season several years ago, "I've been true all year—first time."

(You ask: "Why would he tell you that?" It's one of the pluses of being a woman sports journalist: Athletes tell women things they can't tell men.)

It occurred to me to tell this guy that I had thought "forsaking all others" to be a standard clause in the marriage contract. But I could have been mistaken—and, anyway, he seemed so proud of himself that I went along with him.

"So," I asked, "how did you do it? What was your secret?"

"Fear of AIDS," he replied.

It was a funny story for the last few years, not so funny anymore. And if we're going to have to read about AIDS in the sports pages—yes, we will, until we find a cure—then that is the message I would like to find, somewhere, amid the male locker-room braggadocio and the myth of the athlete as sex god.

Women learn to say no. Men can, too. And maybe Wilt Chamberlain and Magic Johnson can help erase that dumb, old, double standard.

(November 18, 1991)

Susan Fornoff, *a co-founder of the Association for Women in Sports Media, has covered sports for the* Baltimore News American, USA Today *and the* Sacramento Bee. *Her first book* Lady in the Locker Room, *was an account of her experiences covering the Oakland A's. She is presently at work on* Who's the Gipper?, *a sportstalk guide for women.*

NINE

SOME OF THE MEN WE LOVE

THE LITHUANIAN LEGEND

by Jackie Krentzman
Santa Rosa Press Democrat

ALL SARUNAS MARCIULIONIS WANTED TO DO WAS PLAY BASKETBALL. HE DIDN'T want to be pulled into politics. Especially when they weren't his politics.

But there he was, a trembling 22-year-old university student, standing behind a podium, speech in hand. The language was Russian. The words, which everyone would think were his, were those of a Communist Party ghostwriter whose job was to write paeans to communism and the Soviet Union, to be read by local heroes throughout the various republics.

Marciulionis was chosen because he had just been named Lithuania's athlete of the year. The basketball star for Vilnius's Statyba team was to read this propaganda sheet and pretend he revered the communist ideals it extolled.

Standing before him were his countrymen who, like Marciulionis, didn't feel the USSR was their country, or that communism was their philosophy. But Marciulionis had no choice. This was 1986, Lithuania was still under Soviet rule, and communism had yet to be discredited.

"It was a farce," recalled Marciulionis, the Golden State Warriors guard and star of the Lithuanian Olympic team. "People from the factories and all over the city were forced to come and listen. I was told if I didn't read it, I would be failed in all my final exams, and I wouldn't get an apartment. The speech was putting down the Lithuanian independence. It was all about how freedom was bad, and how the Soviet system was good.

"I read it, and it was the most embarrassing moment in my life. It was the worst thing that ever happened to me. I try not to think or talk about it anymore, it brings such bad memories."

Since then, Marciulionis has shied away from politics. His country declared its independence in February 1991, the first Soviet republic to do so. Later that year Soviet tanks rolled into the country's capital but were turned back. Scattered across Lithuania are large cement bases with gray marks on top, where statues of Bolshevik heroes once stood. Lithuanians toppled them in the frenzy of newly discovered freedom.

Lithuania now is following a democratic course and freedom of expression is permitted. No one is forced to deliver speeches denouncing communism. Even so, with the memory of political manipulation burning a hole in what has otherwise been a successful and independent life, Marciulionis does not trust politicians or governments.

347

* * *

What he does trust is himself. And basketball. And his ability to transcend all the sadness and evil of the world with basketball.

Friday night, Marciulionis led the Lithuanian Olympic basketball team to a stinging 116-79 victory against the Commonwealth of Independent States team in the Olympic European qualifying tournament in Spain.

Four years ago in Seoul, Marciulionis and three other members of the current Lithuanian team were the starters for the USSR team that defeated the United States in a semifinal game and eventually captured the Olympic gold medal. Marciulionis is proud of that as an individual accomplishment only.

Now, he can reunite the personal and the political. This year, Lithuania was not only expected to beat the CIS team, but is one of the favorites to win an Olympic medal.

But while the country eagerly anticipated Friday's showdown with the CIS—the president of the Lithuanian basketball federation declared the game was more important than the Olympics itself—Marciulionis was calling it just another game. He has friends on the CIS team, including Alexander Volkov of the Atlanta Hawks. While his teammates and countrymen were looking forward to a victory as payback, a symbolic step toward asserting Lithuanian manhood, Marciulionis was taking pains to compartmentalize. Sports equal pleasure. Politics equal pain.

"Even now, six years later, I don't like to talk about politics," he said. "It's a good government when the people have enough to eat and they can express their opinions. Even though I like the political system here now much better, I don't want to be used by them either."

That isn't to say Marciulionis is apolitical. In Lithuania, everyday life is political. When you're growing up, and you go to the bakery and there's no bread, it isn't because there are no farmers growing wheat. It's because politicians have decided the grain this week should go to Moscow instead.

Politics permeate everything. Marciulionis has plenty of opinions that are political in nature. He is critical of his country, because he doesn't like seeing his best friend earn $20 a month as a doctor while politicians grow rich because of alleged Mafia ties. He wants to help his country, and he is in a position to do so. He probably is the richest man in Lithuania (his Warriors salary of $2 million a year can certainly buy more in Lithuania than Patrick Ewing's $7 million a year can buy him in New York), and arguably is more influential than all of the politicians squabbling for a piece of the pie.

To that end, Marciulionis is building two basketball schools for the young. Children will go there to play basketball and other games after school. He will train future Olympians and keep troubled kids off the streets. He figures if he can't put food in people's stomachs, he at least can fill their souls with happiness for a few hours a day.

"Sarunas believes the future of Lithuania is in its children," said Donnie Nelson, Marciulionis's close friend and assistant coach of both the Warriors and the Lithuanian national team. "He knows if he wasn't lucky he'd be in their shoes. It's his way of giving back to his country."

Marciulionis also has knowledge. Not only has he seen how things operate in the West, he lives there. After three years in California, he is appalled by what he calls the "anti-logic" of the Lithuanian way of doing things.

"Life has no value here," he said. "Doctors here make less than cab drivers or someone selling ice cream in the street. We have what people in the United States want—universal health care. But what good is free medical care if the care is terrible? There is no budget for medicine, so if you get a headache you can't find aspirin. The hospitals are overcrowded. There aren't enough beds, so they use car doors instead. But people are just glad to get into the hospitals.

"But how can people put value on human life, when for years their government didn't? After World War II, 500,000 or more Lithuanians (including his uncle) were deported to Siberia. That sent a message that our life had no value."

With independence and the switch to a market economy, prices soared and salaries sank. The average salary fell from more than $100 a month to $20. Physicists are now selling books to tourists because they can earn four times as much money that way. Teachers are moonlighting as bartenders. A legacy of distrust and fatigue caused by a chronic shortage of goods under communism has been overlaid by a desperation and hunger generated by chronic shortages of cash.

The causes may have changed, but the net effect is the same. Distrust and jealousy color interaction. People on the street do not say hello or excuse themselves when they bump into you. Vilnius, a city of 500,000, and Klaipeda, a town of 10,000, seem like New York.

"When we first moved to Alameda (in 1989), the neighbors came over to greet us and bring us food," Marciulionis said. "That would never happen here. It can take years to build trust. In the U.S., people automatically assume you are good. It is the opposite here. I try to say nice things and smile at people on the street to set an example but they don't understand. People are too jealous of each other. Maybe with religion allowed again here, it will get better, as religion teaches you to care and respect others."

There is a Russian parable that is applicable. God granted a man two wishes. The man thought for a minute then said: "I wish for you to poke out one of my eyes. Then I want you to go next door and poke out both of my neighbor's eyes."

People don't have that have-a-nice-day attitude because a nice day here is when you go to the store and it has half of what you want for one-and-a-half times what you can afford.

"People here are suspicious and selfish because they have no faith in tomorrow," Marciulionis said. "In the U.S., you walk into Safeway one day, and you know everything you see will be there the next. Not here. If you see what you need in a store, you must hoard it, because it might not come back for months. There are more things in the stores now, but with the transition to the free market, they cost more. A Lada (Russian car) that cost 30,000 rubles last year, costs 500,000 now."

As a result of independence and the opening of trade with the West, the Mafia has moved in. People are so desperate, they will kill for $10.

"In the past, you couldn't trust anybody because they may turn you in for saying the wrong thing." Marciulionis said. "Now, it's fear of crime. I feel safer in the States. The crime is much worse here."

Marciulionis, like many successful Lithuanians, says that people here are lazy. The implication is that it is a national character trait, similar to how the French are considered rude and arrogant. But to Marciulionis it is an example of "anti-logic" for people to still work half-heartedly, even though there is an open market system and much money to be made.

Marciulionis always has been driven and a hard worker. He was the exception here. Until independence in 1991, it didn't matter how hard you worked, the government would still pay you the same wage. Incentive was not part of the vocabulary.

So when Marciulionis inveighs against his country, he is really railing against the discarded Soviet system that has permeated everything here. Lithuania may have thrown off the political yoke, but it is more difficult to overthrow 70 years of brainwashing.

This is not to say that Marciulionis has rejected his country. He has a dual residence, a home in Lafayette and an apartment in Vilnius. He loves his country and feels more at home here than in California. He may sound bitter, but his criticisms are intended as constructive.

"I have some ideas I could give the politicians here, but I won't until they ask me," he said. "They are too busy fighting each other in Parliament to ask. But I can tell them how life is in the West and how they can use that as a model for improvement. I want to help, but this is not the right time."

* * *

Marciulionis grew up in Kaunas, a city of 400,000 about 100 kilometers from Vilnius, the capital. His parents still live in the same faceless apartment building in which he grew up with his sister, Zita, 34, who works with computers.

The apartment building looks like a project in the slums of America: huge, gray, dirty, with each cubicle exactly like the next. Even on an 80-degree, sunny summer day, the monolith does not exude warmth.

Marciulionis shared a bedroom with his grandmother until he was 18 and left for college. His father, Juozas, a retired engineer, and his mother, Laima, a retired geography teacher, chose not to move when their son struck it rich in America. They have new furniture, including a large TV and VCR, as well as a second door for protection. But a split-level ranch house is not their style.

"They felt comfortable here," Marciulionis said. "People are conservative in Lithuania; they don't like change. And people here are very jealous. They didn't want to set themselves higher than everyone else. You have to be smaller than you are here. In America, when athletes get that first big contract, they buy a big house and car. That is not the mind-set here."

There is another reason Marciulionis's parents did not move. It's the same reason Sarunas drives a Russian Lada (which makes a Ford Pinto seem like a BMW) instead of the cherry-red Trans Am he brought back with him. The Lithuanian Mafia has as much or more power than the police. Within a week, his Trans Am would be stolen, he said. It stays in a garage. And his parents are easy marks because everyone knows their son.

A visit to the apartment has his parents serving tea and an array of cookies. Out come the photo albums of Sarunas's childhood. Marciulionis initially is embarrassed, wailing the equivalent of "Oh, Mom!" in Lithuanian, but soon is engrossed in his past.

Walking outside brings another jolt from the past. Behind the apartment is a small basketball court. The ground is cement blocks. The backboard is 10 pieces of plywood nailed together. Marciulionis did the nailing some 15 years ago. This is where his signature bullish drive to the hoop was formulated. He walks around the court, remembering its contours, then begins shooting, the first time he's done so here in years.

"Sarunas was always ultracompetitive," his sister, Zita, said. "When he was young I would take him to play basketball with the older boys. He didn't like the game at first, because he would lose. He had to win at everything."

He beats a reporter in a game of HORSE, then imitates a Chris Mullin dunk. His usual reserve dissipates on the court. His smile stands in stark contrast to the miles of projects stretching out behind him, the only color coming from the wash hanging on symmetric rows of clotheslines.

But Marciulionis is used to all the sameness. It is familiar to him, just like the landscape of Lithuania—miles of farmland and thin pine trees, similar to southern Ohio or Indiana, another pretty good basketball state.

"When I drive to the Oakland Coliseum on Highway 24 and go through the Caldecott Tunnel, and see that enormous panoramic view of San Francisco and the bay, it is beautiful," Marciulionis said. "But it's like a picture to me. It's not real, because it's not mine. I don't feel I belong to that city. But here, when I drive and see something beautiful, it may not be as spectacular, but it is mine.

"My first time in the U.S., in 1983 with the Soviet junior team, I felt uncomfortable," he continued. "All those huge buildings, trees, cars and stores. Everything seemed too big, out of proportion. I'm more used to it now, but it still feels a little strange."

Maybe the sprawl and bravado of America is so odd to Marciulionis because blending in is important to him. It's not easy when you're a 6-foot-5 basketball star, but he tries. In California he drives a Mercedes, lives in a large home and shops at Safeway and the ultrachic specialty store in his Oakland suburb. He eats Chinese food out of the container with chopsticks when he's in a rush and shops at malls. In Lithuania he drives a Lada, eats borscht and drinks beer the morning after a party to get rid of his hangover. And only in Lithuania would he reveal that he used to play the accordion.

"I'm comfortable in both places," he said. "I adjust quickly. I remember when I first came back here, I got into a Lada, and I laughed at this cheap Russian car everyone drives. But by the next day it felt natural and I was happy to be driving it."

Marciulionis's friends and teammates say he hasn't changed. A teammate on both the 1988 and 1992 Olympic teams, Valdemeras Khomicius, said that Marciulionis hasn't rejected his Lithuanian roots.

"He is still as Lithuanian as all of us," Khomicius said. "He could come back here and drive a fancy car and wear expensive clothes and act like we're not worthy of him. But he hasn't done that."

That's because this is his home. Marciulionis looks healthier and happier here than in Oakland. This is natural. He knows his country like we know our own bedrooms in the dark. He can move around Lithuania with his eyes closed, bumping into nothing.

* * *

Perhaps Marciulionis can adapt so well to two very different cultures because he has a strong sense of self and is not afraid of being subsumed by either. He has a streak of independence, a trait the Lithuanians say is the most important of the many that set them apart from the ethnic Russians.

When Marciulionis was drafted into the Soviet army after his third year at the University of Vilnius, he went to officers' camp. Because he was a basketball star, he was required to serve just a few months instead of the mandatory two years. He lasted just a few days.

"We had to go simulate an attack and shoot bazookas," he recalled. "Well, I shot too low over the heads of the instructors and set the grass right behind them on fire. They dismissed me right away.

"That was the idea. I wasn't built for the army. When someone gave a command, I would ask why. I questioned everything. That's my nature. In the army, you have to do as you're told, but that is against my principles."

Marciulionis, like most Lithuanians, is very nationalistic. When Warriors assistant coach Gregg Popovich, who can speak Russian, met Marciulionis in Europe several years ago, Marciulionis refused to speak with him in Russian, saying "I am not a Russian."

Most Lithuanians never bought into the Marxist ideology. The bookshelf at Marciulionis's parents' apartment was filled with Stendhal, Remarque, Dreiser, even Tolstoy. From an early age, he rebelled against the Marxist tracts force-fed him at school.

"We had to read Lenin, but to me it was like reading a play on words," Marciulionis said. "It was so far from the reality of how we lived and thought. But on the other hand, the lies were so natural, so much part of our life. My friends and I would laugh about it, quietly. I remember near the end of Brezhnev's life, he could hardly walk or talk. But we still had to listen to him and pretend he was making sense. But it made no sense."

Now life is making more sense for both Lithuania and Marciulionis. The country is struggling, but it is its own struggle. And Marciulionis has success, his own success. He no longer must pretend to believe someone else's beliefs or play on some other nation's basketball team. Now, he is setting the parameters.

Marciulionis is a folk hero here, and along with teammate Arvidas Sabonis, is the most famous Lithuanian. "He's Lithuania's version of Elvis."

But being Elvis is a tremendous responsibility. Marciulionis's friends worry that sometimes he carries too much weight on his shoulders. He is separated from his wife, Inga, because he had no time to give to his family. Besides being expected to lead his country past the Russians and to an Olympic medal, besides raising the bulk of the money for the team, besides starting up two basketball schools, he also has opened a hotel and sports bar in Vilnius: Hotel Sarunas and the Rooney Cafe.

The immaculate 26 room hotel is probably the best in Lithuania. It has a faux marble staircase and fresh pinewood furniture. Rooney (Sarunas's nickname) was involved every step of the way, from choosing the blueprint to picking out the shoeshine machine in the foyer.

The bar is an American-style sports bar. There are framed posters of Mullin, Michael Jordan, Magic Johnson and Karl Malone. There are autographed sneakers of a dozen NBA stars hanging from the ceiling. Magic's get the place of honor over the bar. There is a 4-foot long Swatch watch on the wall. The satellite TV is always tuned to MTV; that's what the teen-age boys tending bar want to watch.

There is the basketball the Warriors sent Marciulionis in 1989 when the team was trying to make him the first Eastern Bloc athlete to play for an American sports league. "Sharunas (sic)—Hope you can be with us," it reads. Corny, yet heartfelt.

Otherwise there is no mention of Marciulionis in the bar. No sneakers, no jerseys, no pictures. He is a shy man who only named the hotel after himself to attract business.

The night before the Olympic team left for Greece to play in a tournament, Marciulionis threw a party for his staff. He wanted everybody to have some fun and get to know and trust one another before they began working together. The party started at 9 p.m. and lasted all night.

At the party, the Lithuanian Sarunas emerged and the American Sarunas faded. He drank vodka, he danced, he sang national folk songs, and he tossed off toasts all night. Never in America would you see a party like this, he said proudly. This is how we do it in Lithuania.

His message: Life may not always be good, but you can always have a good time.

Rooney had come home.

(June 28, 1992)

Jackie Krentzman is a sportswriter for the Santa Rosa *(CA)* Press Democrat. *She has covered the Golden State Warriors, the San Francisco Giants, Oakland A's and San Francisco 49ers.*

AWOL Tackle Puts Family First

by Melanie Hauser
Houston Post

Seeing Scot Cooper Williams take his first breath and let out his first cry was worth the $125,000 paycheck it cost dear old dad.

But was it also worth the possible suspension offensive tackle David Williams faces for missing the Oilers' game in New England Sunday? As the proud father said from his home in The Woodlands Sunday night, nothing was going to keep him from seeing his first child born Saturday night. Nothing.

"I don't regret what I've done," Williams said. "I wanted to be there for my child to be born and I was going to stay there until he was. We lost one last year (his wife, Debi, had a tubal pregnancy in August 1992). I didn't want anything to happen. That's the way I felt about it. I'm sorry they can't accept that. I'm sorry they don't understand it."

Because the baby—9 pounds, 15 ounces—was born at 6:25 p.m., Williams missed the team's mid-day charter flight and the final flight of the day from Houston (6:54 p.m.) to Boston. Williams said he looked into possibly chartering a plane, but Boston's Logan Airport was fogged in.

General manager Mike Holovak, offensive coordinator Kevin Gilbride and offensive line coach Bob Young were all upset with Williams's decision because none thought he made any effort to get to Boston.

"He doesn't make $125,000 a week to stay home and watch television," Young said. "They ought to suspend him for a week, maybe two. Everybody wants to be with his wife, but that's like if World War II was going on and you said, 'I can't go fly. My wife's having a baby.' You have to go to work—especially when you get paid like that." Williams was replaced in the lineup by Kevin Donnalley.

Holovak confirmed that Williams would lose this week's paycheck ($125,000) and face a fine and possible suspension.

"All I can tell you is he will be fined, but I don't know how much because I have to check the rules," Holovak said.

As for a possible suspension?

"I have to check the rules specifically," Holovak said.

Added Gilbride: "I don't think I can put into words how disappointed I am. I understand the support of your family—that always has to come No. 1—but there's a judgment, too. He fulfilled his commitment to his family. His place had to be with us with our backs up to the wall."

Although Young said Williams let his teammates down, none of them agreed. Both center Bruce Matthews, whose four children were all born during off-seasons, and backup guard Erik Norgard, whose wife is due with their first child Nov. 18, said Williams's decision was "a tough call."

Guard Mike Munchak, a father of two, said, "David did what he had to do," while Donnalley admitted it was a tough choice.

"His wife was probably saying, 'Dave, I need you here,'" Donnalley said. "He made a lifelong commitment to her, but football's his job. I didn't envy his situation."

Williams said no matter what happens when he reports to practice today, he'll be ready.

"I did what I had to do," he said. "They'll do what they have to do."

(October 18, 1993)

Melanie Hauser covers golf and the Houston Oilers for the Houston Post. *A graduate of the University of Texas, she previously worked at the* Austin American-Statesman. *She is a member of the board of directors of both the Golf Writers Association of America and the Professional Football Writers Association.*

An Emotional Goodbye to Chucky

by Lynn Zinser
Memphis Commercial-Appeal

WHITE BLOSSOMS TUMBLED FROM A MAGNOLIA TREE ONTO THE TATTERED house and yard where Chucky Mullins grew up. Rain rolled off the leaves like teardrops.

Clouds of sadness blanketed Russellville as Chucky came home for the last time Saturday. The town that raised him lowered him into the ground and covered him in sorrow. It said goodbye to a man who was its hero long before his death and long before a crippling injury on Ole Miss's football field made him a national figure.

To the people of Russellville he was just Chucky. And he was theirs.

"He's coming back home," said Don Cox, Russellville High's football coach. "He'll always be in the hearts of Ole Miss people and they had a wonderful memorial service for him Wednesday, but this is more like his funeral. Here he was loved and here he will be laid to rest. We're more emotional. We're closer to him. He was with us a lot longer."

The world came to know Chucky on Oct. 28, 1989. Then playing freshman defensive back for Ole Miss, Chucky lunged to tackle a touchdown-bound receiver. The hit left Chucky slumped on the ground, his neck broken, his body paralyzed. He fought to rebuild his shattered life until a blood clot in his lungs cut short that fight last Monday. He died in Memphis's Baptist Memorial Hospital. He was 21.

In the 19 months following the injury, Chucky touched people nationwide and money poured in for his care from around the nation. The outburst of love from Ole Miss to a poor, black Alabama athlete was stunning.

The people of Russellville, though, had long been familiar with the traits a nation has just begun to know. The determination with which Chucky fought paralysis had lifted him from a destitute background. The smile millions would see on television had lit a town since he was a child.

"He's been fighting his whole life," said Wayne Ray, Russellville High's principal. "The fact that he fought paralysis so much didn't surprise anybody here."

Thousands, black and white, filed by Chucky's coffin Saturday. Hundreds drove the twisting narrow road to the cemetery. Tree branches seemed to hang lower over the roadway as they passed.

Chucky's funeral, like his life, drew a small Southern town together.

People say racial strife does not divide their town, but tradition does. Chucky was buried in the "black" area of the cemetery. Most blacks go home to the withering houses and narrow streets of Reedtown, the markedly poorer neighborhoods.

Russellville's 7,800 people reside in the northwest corner of Alabama, but they are very much part of the Old South. The closest thing to racial harmony was Chucky.

"People rallied around Chucky," said Carver Phillips, Chucky's guardian. "He had more white friends than black ones. We called it our big happy family. Color didn't matter. That's the way it should be all across America."

Blacks make up 12 percent of Russellville's population, but Chucky's appeal permeated the town.

"They all loved him, especially the white kids," said Bobby Brown, a local minister. "One white kid would pick him up and drive him to school every day. The kids would always rally around him. It was like there was no color. It was just good old Chucky.

"When his injury happened, there was a gloom over this town. Everybody called to see how he was. It wasn't black and white people. It was just people."

Those people remember Chucky for his smile, a constant fixture on his face. In his worst moments, they say, he could always muster a smile for you.

His friends don't spend much time explaining his downtrodden beginnings. They simply point to the house on Madison Street, the one with the flaking green paint and lopsided porch. It leans toward the railroad tracks that run alongside as if too tired to hold itself straight.

Chucky's father had never been a part of his home, and his mother died when he was 12. He moved in with Phillips, but he was Russellville's son. Townspeople say several white families offered to take Chucky in when his mother died. The town continued to watch over him, gathering money to send him to summer football camps and to Ole Miss when Phillips couldn't afford the trip.

"I think people wanted to do everything they could to make sure he made it," said Jerry Groce, a city councilman and a longtime friend of Chucky's. "Everybody in Russellville knew Chucky's circumstances. They just wanted to help."

The overwhelming determination a nation saw when Chucky was paralyzed had its roots in his earliest days. He lived in desperate poverty until Phillips gave him a better home. People here say they admire Chucky because he had every reason to go bad, but didn't.

He could have turned out like his brother Horace, Chucky's antithesis. Government officials agreed to let Horace out of the Alabama State penitentiary Saturday to attend Chucky's funeral. But Horace, imprisoned for several drug-related crimes, arrived shackled and under guard.

"Not one time was there a discipline problem with Chucky," Ray said. "He helped put down a lot of discipline problems. He had to work hard to make it through, but here he was, every day at school."

Nearly everyone can share their favorite football story about Chucky, who seemed always to make the big catch at receiver and make the big hit at defensive back. They called him the best ever to play at Russellville, a rare Golden Tiger to play major college football.

"He made the big play all the time," Ray said. "There was one state playoff game where there was no score and we had the ball with about a minute to play. The quarterback is scrambling and finally he just throws it toward the end zone. There are about four or five defenders there, but there's Chucky. He jumps about six inches higher than anybody else and pulls down the ball."

Chucky's personality transcended football. He drew a crowd wherever he went. After his injury, he would return to Russellville often, impressing even those who knew him with his resilience.

"When he came home the first time, I was on the committee to welcome him," Brown said. "We were waiting at Carver's house. It was so cold. When the van pulled up, Chucky got out and he was just smiling to beat the band. You could see he had a problem, but it was like he didn't. He looked at us like, 'Why are you looking at me? There's nothing wrong with me.' I'll never forget that day.

"Being a minister, there are things I preach about, faith and overcoming obstacles. You could see everything I've taught come alive in him."

When his life ended, a quiet town grew quieter. To his last days, Chucky was telling people he'd make it out of his wheelchair. And they believed him.

Cox said he shared so much with Chucky that he often felt like he was Chucky's daddy. Cox was proud that Chucky wanted to be a coach and told him he would hire him as an assistant the minute he returned to Russellville.

"He didn't come back the way I wanted him to," Cox said, fighting back tears. "I wanted him to come back as a coach, someone for others in his situation to look up to. And he wanted to be that person.

"I don't know. Maybe he's been more successful than I could ever dream for him.

"He shows it's possible to rise from a small, poor town in northwest Alabama to everyone in the country knowing him by his first name."

(May 12, 1991)

Lynn Zinser, who covers the Atlantic Coast Conference for the Charlotte Observer, *has gone from her home town of Rochester, NY, to Syracuse, Washington, DC, Memphis and Raleigh, NC. Her goal is to visit all 50 states, although perhaps not live in them.*

A.C. Green and the Abstinence Rap

by Helene Elliott
Los Angeles Times

WHEN HE WAS A ROOKIE, AND OTHER PLAYERS MOCKED HIS DEVOUT CHRISTIANITY and his decision to abstain from sex until marriage, A.C. Green's steadfast faith helped him silence his doubters.

Eight seasons into a distinguished career as power forward for the Lakers, when he was asked to play shooting guard while Byron Scott was idled by a sprained foot, that same faith sustained Green through another trying time.

"I said whatever it takes to equal victories and good, solid play, I was willing to try it. If that even meant trying to play point guard, I'll shake my head and rub my face and we can talk about that a little bit longer, but if that's what you want me to do, coach, it's okay, I'll try it," said Green, who hadn't played guard since a brief try in college, at Oregon State.

"It was really, really new. But one thing about me is I don't feel I have many limitations. I feel I can do just about anything. The Bible tells me—and I really believe in the Bible—Philipians 4:13 says, 'I can do all things through Christ, who strengthens me,' and this is scripture that I take to heart and really try to apply to my life. So there's not a lot of things I really feel I can't do."

He has lived those words as a starter and a reserve through 527 consecutive regular-season games, the longest streak in team history and the 11th-longest in NBA records. This season, at age 29, he tested and proved his faith yet again when he replaced Scott, averaging 12.7 points and 10.9 rebounds over nine games. The team's top rebounder in five of the last six seasons, Green has been the leading rebounder in 13 games this season, including seven while playing the off-guard spot. Overall, he's averaging 10.1 points and 7.6 rebounds per game and shooting a career-high .517 from the floor.

"What he is in terms of his convictions and religious beliefs, he brings to the workplace in terms of working hard and being competitive," Laker coach Randy Pfund said. "He's the type of player a coach really loves. He's exactly the kind of guy you love to have as a player, a son, a neighbor, the whole package."

Green brings that same conviction to his mission to help youngsters build moral strength in a society he feels fails to teach them that "you need to have some form of self control and respect for yourself. If you can't respect yourself you won't know how to respect others."

Through the 3-year-old foundation that bears his name, Green runs a summer camp for children, and he hopes to create job internships for youngsters in

Los Angeles-area businesses. To warn about the danger of promiscuity, his Athletes for Abstinence program made a rap song and a video called "It ain't worth it," which is scheduled for release in a month. Green hopes to distribute it to schools and TV networks such as MTV and BET.

That's not all he plans. With two business partners, Green plans to open a bottling plant that will provide jobs and hope in areas of the city ravaged by last year's riots. Someday, he'd like to establish a home for unwed mothers.

"There has to be more emphasis put on self control and responsibility. If there's so much sex education going on in schools, why are teenage birth rates and abortion rates on the increase?" said Green, who has no marriage plans and for now dotes on his nine nieces and nephews and two godchildren.

"I really want kids to think about what they're doing. I don't want them to give in to peer pressure and half-truths. I don't want to scare kids. I don't tell them, 'You're going to get a disease if you have sex.' I'm more concerned with what kids have to go through in terms of emotional hurts and scars . . . They hear those stories about entertainers and athletes [being promiscuous] and they don't know what commitment is. They think you're a piece of property. They lack respect for the human body and for human beings. I'm concerned with young people not having a chance to grow up happily. There's enough problems trying to economically survive. You see a lot of single-parent homes and that's enough of a burden in itself.

"There's just a lot of things that weigh on my heart. Someone has to try and communicate with young people and not be a talking head."

Green long ago communicated his sincerity to his teammates, earning respect even from those who urged him to tone down his sermonizing and others who tried to set him up with women and bet he'd succumb to temptation.

"He brings a lot of qualities to this ballclub, a lot of inspiration and a lot of leadership, being a [lay] minister and having a lot of principles in life in general. He applies those to every aspect in his life," James Worthy said. "People listen to his word and value what he says. His attitude is probably the best and his work ethic is even better . . .

"I think only people who are ignorant make fun of him. People respect him. It's not easy to walk that road, and a lot of guys that joked about him and gave him a hard time probably wanted to be like him but couldn't."

Said James Edwards: "He reminds me of a Dennis Rodman-type player. He's always hustling, always working hard on the floor and trying to make things happen. He's always attacking the boards and just by doing that, it helps out the young guys. He's an ideal player for a rookie to watch."

It's likely the Lakers are years away from recapturing their old distinction. And when they do, Green might not be with them because he's finishing a four-year, $6-million contract and will be an unrestricted free agent after the season.

His future, he says, "is the furthest thing from my mind. My main concern is trying to get this team to play up to the potential and capability I know we can. The contract next year, the Lord will take care of that. In that sense, it's all in good hands. I'm more concerned with the here and now and what's in my face every single day."

His parents, however, are campaigning for him to come home to Portland and they keep him posted about what the Trail Blazers are doing.

"The talk of possibly going home to Portland comes up every year because people know how much I love it. It's my home. All my family is there and I was born and raised there," he said. "The team is good, very competitive. The attraction of Portland will always be in my heart and mind and to really have a good feeling for them. So I will never rule them out.

"But I've really enjoyed my stay here. I've really enjoyed my experience. The Lakers are great. The whole organization is great, from the general managers to the secretaries. Everybody has been like a family and money can't buy that. To get that feeling, to capture that and sense that, it's one of those indescribable things, an intangible, and you can't place a price tag on that."

(February 2, 1993)

Helene Elliott *is the national hockey columnist for the* Los Angeles Times *and previously worked at* Newsday *and the* Chicago Sun-Times. *She has covered the last four Winter Olympics. Her high school guidance counselor told her "women can't be sportswriters," but she never wanted to be anything else.*

COACH DAD

by Sally Ann Michalov
Cardinal Side Lines

A STORY IN A NATIONAL SPORTS MAGAZINE ONCE REFERRED TO HIM AS A GUY with white hair and a pink face.

Joe and Molly know him as Grandpa and Phoenix Cardinals' fans will know him soon as their new defensive coordinator, Fritz Shurmur.

One thing about Fritz Shurmur is that with him there is only black and white, no grayish hues anywhere to confuse anything.

You're either loyal or you're not, hardworking or you're not, unselfish or you're not, intense or you're not, conservative or you're not.

Fritz Shurmur may have invented the Eagle defense, the Big Nickel and the Hawk, but there are other things that you might like to know as well.

He still is married to Peggy Jane Tisot, that gal from his math class at Roosevelt High School in Wyandotte, Michigan. They are, to put it simply, soulmates of the most intense fashion.

He is the father of three children, all college graduates, a fact that makes him intensely proud.

He is the grandfather of two and he is the mushiest, roll-on-the-floor, kissy, huggy kind of grandfather you'd ever want to see.

In between the marriage 37 years ago and the newest grandchild six months ago has been a series of events, trivial in nature to most, that give glimpses of his past.

In 1962, he took his pregnant wife and two small children away from their beloved family in Michigan to far-off Wyoming, a place so foreign his mother-in-law thought they were moving to Oklahoma.

He built Wyoming's defense into the best in the nation, trekking back to Michigan at every opportunity to convince inner-city kids that Wyoming was paradise, a notion he still firmly believes.

After a debilitating racial incident involving players' rights versus the head coach's edict, he took the head coaching job at Wyoming and left as he had entered four years earlier, proud of how he had tried to rebuild a slumping program.

Since then, he has been the defensive coordinator for the Detroit Lions, the New England Patriots and the Los Angeles Rams, and each time he has given the job his all from the first day to the last.

Fritz is furious when people make a big deal of his work habits because he thinks he works the way everyone should—full-speed ahead, taking no shortcuts.

The only concessions to his age of 58 are half-glasses for reading, caffeine-free diet Coke instead of regular diet Coke and decaffeinated coffee.

He jogged around Disneyland's parking lot at noon for nine years when he worked for the Rams and probably by now has a similar place scoped out in the desert.

He loves his family, his work, his country and fishing—always in that order.

Politically, he's more conservative than Ronald Reagan and Dwight D. Eisenhower combined.

But the hard as rock exterior turns to mush quickly when he calls his children frequently on the phone, making sure there is enough money in the checking accounts and that vehicles are working properly.

The children are 34, 32, and 28.

Basically, you fans are in for a helluva treat.

And I've got one helluva dad.

(February-March, 1991)

Sally Ann Michalov, a graduate of the University of Wyoming, covers high schools for the Casper Star-Tribune, *Wyoming's largest daily. She and her husband Scott have two children, Joe and Molly. This article appeared in the official newsletter of the Phoenix Cardinals. In 1994, Shurmer was named defensive coordinator of the Green Bay Packers.*

THE CANNON IS QUIET

by Maryann Hudson
Los Angeles Times

THE COLORS OF THEIR CHILDHOOD ARE STILL BLACK AND RED, INTENSIFIED through images of flashing lights in the street, and the sounds of hitting and screaming. For Lyle and Peter Alzado, it was like growing up in a horror movie.

After a time, when Lyle and his older brother were big enough, they would run downstairs to protect their mother from their alcoholic father while the three younger children hid in the closet, holding each other, terrified.

They watched as their father, enraged, pulled the phones out of the wall, or purposely broke the heater in the midst of a bitter Brooklyn winter. They can still feel the hurt from the physical abuse their beloved mother suffered. They too, were physically abused.

The pain is still vivid; the emotional scars forever present. As a tall, thin adolescent, Lyle Alzado was like an explosion waiting to happen. The only way he really knew to express himself was physically, so he excelled in athletics and picking fights with other kids. He was a sweet kid, but he didn't talk much. He didn't like people.

On the football field, the violence and intensity with which Lyle played seemed connected to his early years. He was able to use that negative emotion constructively. Anger worked here—on the field he could rip opponents' heads off and people cheered him for it, even paid him for it.

Off the field, he grew to like people, even to love them. He earned a degree in special education and spent nearly every weekend of his 15-year NFL career visiting sick and disabled children in hospitals, trying to make them laugh while he cried for them inside.

Now, others are crying for Lyle Alzado.

He is suffering from inoperable brain cancer, a terminal disease that eats away at all that is life-giving until it wipes away the last morsel of one's soul. Alzado at times knows this is one game he cannot dominate, one force he may be unable to stop. But he's not settling for a tie. He's still playing to win.

Since the cancer was diagnosed last April, Alzado, 42, has been in and out of the hospital. He has good and bad days, sometimes requiring assistance to walk, other times not needing it at all.

He has lost about 90 pounds and is now slender, as in the days of his youth before he began bulking up with steroids.

Alzado's cancer is a rare form of an already rare type of cancer, a primary brain lymphoma, and its track record is dismal. Treatment is a daily experiment. Cancer usually begins in the body lymph chain system, but Alzado's began in his brain.

For a few months last year, Alzado's cancer went into complete remission after radiation and monthly chemotherapy treatments. But it came back about a month ago and is now layered over nerves in his spinal column, keeping him in severe pain and making it difficult for him to swallow. His speech is raspy, and he talks with a slight lisp. Twice a week he is taken to UCLA Medical Center for chemotherapy that is injected painfully into his system.

Last week, Alzado's wife, Kathy Davis, helped him to the living room of their modest Beverlywood home for an interview. He was dressed in black, his bald head covered by a Raider cap.

His eyes filled with kindness, Alzado smiled, settled down on his couch and said to the reporter: "I can't talk too loud, so maybe you should sit here next to me."

Lyle Alzado used to like to say: "If me and King Kong went into an alley, only one of us would come out and it wouldn't be the monkey."

The first player drafted out of Yankton College in South Dakota—there were 225 students—he started in 66 of 68 games for the Denver Broncos before he suffered his first injury. A year later, he was the NFL's defensive lineman of the year and a starter in the Pro Bowl.

When he came to the Raiders in 1982, he immediately took future NFL star defensive linemen Howie Long and Greg Townsend under his wing.

"Howie wanted his own way and that way was to teach himself," Alzado said. "But before he could do that, I had to teach him a few things. I taught Howie how to knock someone's head off. I taught Howie how to step on somebody. I taught Howie how to curse at somebody. I taught Howie new curse words."

"I was in awe of the guy," said Townsend, who grew up watching Alzado play. "I saw that exhibition match Lyle fought against Muhammad Ali (in 1977) and I thought, 'This guy has his hand in everything.' Then in my rookie year, on the practice field, I was in Lyle's group. I had to pinch myself. Here he was talking to me and was so soft and gentle, and I had heard these mean things about him. He wasn't a big, mean guy. He is a big, nice guy."

It was that soft side of Alzado that touched the lives of children. Alzado was a front-office dream, a player who could be relied on to go to a charity function at the last minute when someone else canceled. Millions saw that gentleness on television in the closing minutes of the Raiders' Super Bowl victory over the Washington Redskins at Tampa in 1984, when tears streamed down Alzado's cheeks.

"I don't think people expected me to be that way," Alzado said. "I looked up at the clock and I saw we were beating Washington, 38-9. The moment when it happened was so exciting to me and so overwhelming, and when Marcus Allen came over and hugged me and said, 'Congratulations, this one's for you,' it was all so heartwarming."

After the 1985 season, Alzado, 36, retired from football. He was doing national television commercials and was a regular on "The Tonight Show" by then and movies were a natural. He even had his own short-lived television series playing a school teacher by day and a masked professional wrestler by night.

But football wasn't out of his system and in 1990, at the age of 41, Alzado tried to make a comeback with the Raiders. His strategy was intense, "revolutionary training," he called it, but it involved massive doses of steroids and human growth hormone, which Alzado believes caused his cancer.

Hobbled by injuries throughout training camp, Alzado finally accepted retirement in late August after a long meeting with Raider owner Al Davis, who was extremely saddened.

"Men can love each other, and I was sad, not that Lyle couldn't make the team, but because Lyle so much wanted to make the team," Davis said.

Alzado doesn't wear his diamond-studded Super Bowl ring as often now; it doesn't fit anymore. He is saving it for his 9-year old son, Justin, who lives in Long Island with Alzado's ex-wife.

Alzado first knew something was wrong when he and his friend, actor Nick Klar, were in a gym working out. Alzado started to lean a bit and didn't feel well. Everyone thought it was flu, except Alzado.

"I'd notice that we would be someplace and he would start to walk over to the corner and his balance would be a little off," Klar said. "He has such pride that he didn't want anyone to see that. Finally Lyle said, 'I better go to a doctor. I don't know what this is.'

"It all happened with such intensity and such speed. I hadn't talked to him or seen him for a few days and he said, 'Nick, I'm not feeling well, I'm real thin.' I was kidding and I said, 'So what are you now, 230?'"

One month after Kathy Davis, a former fashion model, married Lyle, doctors told her he had inoperable brain cancer. She broke down, but when they went in to tell Alzado, he didn't cry. Instead he said: "Let's beat this thing. What do we have to do?"

"Please excuse me if I don't listen to statistics," Kathy said. "My husband is a fighter and he is geared to beat this. He is strong. The only way I can look at it is that he's going to get better, and we are going to have a baby. I have to try and reinforce a positive attitude."

The news hit his family, friends and former teammates hard. Al Davis called Kathy every other day for an update. Alzado, home from the hospital, was arrested for allegedly assaulting a marshal who came to his house early one morning to serve him with a warrant. The case is pending.

And then rumors of Alzado being a gay, AIDS victim bannered the tabloids. Alzado says he is not gay and his doctor, Robert Huizenga, says a misunderstanding about the type of brain cancer Alzado has may have fueled the rumors.

"Primary brain lymphoma is a rare disease that has become more common in AIDS patients," Huizenga said. "AIDS patients however, have been found to have B-cell brain lymphoma whereas Lyle has yet a rarer form called T-cell brain lymphoma."

Alzado's claim that steroids caused his cancer has also created controversy. He began using steroids in college, to help bulk up his thin frame. He became so addicted to steroids that he never gave them up, even after he quit playing football.

But in research, steroids have been linked only to liver cancer, not brain cancer.

"When you eat right and drink right and you don't stay out late at night and you get sick, in my case, it was from steroids." Alzado said. "I made a big mistake, and my wife and I are trying to tell the kids of America to stay away from it because I believe wholeheartedly that it has given me cancer. I would hate for anyone else to go through this pain."

The first time in his life that Alzado had been afraid was during a stay in the hospital last year, when he nearly died.

"He said to me once, 'Peter, I'm scared,'" Alzado's brother recalls. "Lyle has a stamina and a force of character and he can bear the cross very well, with a great deal of dignity. It breaks my heart, truly."

"You can never give up. Giving up is the worst thing you can do," Alzado says.

About 10 times in his life, Alzado says, Al Davis has bailed him out financially. Last week, Alzado and Kathy drove to Davis' office in El Segundo to ask for help again. Kathy said Davis greeted them by saying, "What can I do for you? In what way can I help you?"

Davis has a difficult time talking to others about Alzado's playing days, his battles on the field. "Lyle is in the battle of his life right now," he said.

"As someone once wrote, the cannon is quiet on the battlefield. All is quiet for Lyle right now. I am saddened about where we are headed."

Recently, a highly publicized tribute to Alzado that would have raised some money fell through hours before it was to begin. Friends and family came to Los Angeles from all over the country, only to find the event canceled. At the same time, the organizer, Alzado's business manager and best friend, Greg Campbell, had a heart attack. All this occurred five days after Alzado was told his cancer had come back. He was disappointed for his friends, but the night wasn't lost.

Huizenga quickly organized a cocktail party at his house. Gene Upshaw, who had flown in from Washington, along with Franco Harris, Bob Golic and Henry Lawrence, were just some of the many friends who came. When Alzado saw Harris walk up to him, he brightened. "He used to beat the (crap) out of me," Alzado told Kathy.

Friends are planning another tribute soon and Upshaw said he would fly out again in a minute. "At the cocktail party I got to hold Lyle and tell him how much I care about him," Upshaw said. "I don't know how many more chances I'm going to get to do that."

(Jan. 26, 1992)

Maryann Hudson covers the Dodgers for the Los Angeles Times. *A graduate of the University of Southern California, she has done investigative reporting and has won awards from the Associated Press Sports Editors, the California Newspaper Publishers Association and the Greater Los Angeles Press Club. Lyle Alzado died May 14, 1992.*

A FINE WHINE

by Mary Schmitt
Milwaukee Journal

WHINERS. CRYBABIES. COMPLAINERS.

You know the type.

National Basketball Association players who've never committed a foul in their careers. Every call is a personal attack. Every penalty a production. These guys aren't nominated for sportsmanship awards. These guys are nominated for Oscars. They've made more faces than Estee Lauder and thrown more tantrums—but fewer chairs—than Bobby Knight.

So in honor of today's NBA All-Star Game in Chicago, the *Milwaukee Journal* polled a dozen NBA executives, seven top NBA reporters and half a dozen players from various teams—a league rule prohibited referees from taking part—and asked them to select the NBA's All-Whiner Team.

"I'm on it, right?" asked Detroit center Bill Laimbeer.

Bill, you're the captain.

Laimbeer received more than twice as many votes as the next closest complainers, Danny Ainge of the Boston Celtics and Moses Malone of the Washington Bullets. In fact, one player filled out his ballot for the NBA's All-Whiner team thusly: 1. Bill Laimbeer. 2. Bill Laimbeer. 3. Bill Laimbeer. 4. Bill Laimbeer. 5. Bill Laimbeer.

For his part, Laimbeer took the dubious honor graciously and with a smile, not a smirk. "I'm a smart basketball player," he said, "so I see a lot that happens on the court and I'm constantly pointing out to my teammates and the referees, 'That's the way it should have been.'"

Charles Barkley of the Philadelphia 76ers finished fourth, but he got one strong vote from a general manager who told the following story.

"Two years ago he was thrown out in between his own free throws," said the general manager, who, like most of those interviewed for the poll, requested anonymity. "He'd already gotten the call and was at the line and between the first and second free throw he got thrown out. I think that's all-world complaining. That stands out in my mind as world-class complaining."

The following players tied for fifth: Magic Johnson of the Los Angeles Lakers, Tom Chambers of the Seattle SuperSonics, Kelly Tripucka of the Utah Jazz and Isiah Thomas of the Pistons.

"I never complain," Thomas complained, smiling. "I don't know what they're talking about. I don't complain. I try to reason."

Phil Jasner of the *Philadelphia Daily News*, although probably not meaning to, came out as a champion of the whiners.

"Charles gets crazy when they get beat," Jasner said of Barkley. "He says some things that he's sorry that he said later. But 99 times out of 100 it's directly related to losing. People talk about Ainge as a whiner. I can almost see that because he's kind of an antagonistic type of player. I think he uses it to his advantage, turns it into a strength and gets people concerned either with how he behaves or what he says or what he does on the court to the point where it distracts them from what they're supposed to be doing. Anyone who can do that, God bless him."

If that's the case, the NBA has been blessed. In fact, there was some sentiment for naming any player who ever put on an NBA uniform.

One NBA official nominated "the entire Boston Celtics." And another voted for "any Celtic." After watching the constant griping by Ainge and Co. during the Bucks' playoff series with the Celtics last season, one exasperated Milwaukee fan yelled to Larry Bird, "Hey, Larry. Aren't you tired of playing with these babies?"

Although the Celtics were the only team nominated en masse, almost every team had somebody get a vote for the All-Whiner Team.

Bob Ryan of the *Boston Globe*, declaring whining at an all-time low and picking his team under duress, presented special citations to Kevin McHale of the Celtics and the Bucks' Jack Sikma, who was second in the league to Portland's Steve Johnson in fouling out of games last season.

"Jack cries a lot," said Ryan, the dean of NBA writers. "He's one of the last of the old school actors. He's one of the great floppers and actors left. It's a dying art. And Kevin mixes big-time moaning with this exaggerated approval routine. He goes out of his way to make the referee feel like he met with some great approval."

Pat Williams, general manager of the Orlando Magic, agreed with Ryan that whining was a dying art. "It seems not quite like it used to be," Williams said. "I don't know if the referees are stronger or better, but they've made it clear they won't tolerate it. It's not like it was many years ago."

Added Tommy Heinsohn, a former player and coach with the Celtics who is now a CBS announcer, "The extent of non-conformity with the referee now is to drop the ball and make the referee go get it," Heinsohn said. "That's it. It's not like the old days where players would go nose-to-nose with referees."

With that in mind, the *Journal* created a Whiners Hall of Fame, and Williams, as well as many others, had some nominations.

"Rick Barry, of course, would have to be on that team," said Williams, naming the No. 1 pick in the *Journal*'s poll for the Whiners Hall of Fame.

"Jerry Sloan and Norm Van Lier, they never fouled. Those would be the three founding members. Billy Cunningham would be one of the forwards. At center nobody comes to mind, but the forwards and guards are easy.

Hey Pat, did you forget a guy named Wilt Chamberlain? You remember, kind of a big guy, scored a lot of points?

"Probably the coach you would want on there would be Dick Motta," Williams said. "He was the guy who believed his team never committed a foul. Dick picked up this reputation as a terrible antagonist of referees. But Dick really loved those referees. He sent them cards every Christmas—in braille. He was always kind to them at Chicago Stadium. He'd help them feel their way into the gym."

Actually, Kevin Loughery headed the voters' list of former coaches considered whiners. He led the league's coaches in technical fouls last season with 20. Coming into the season, Motta led all coaches with 324 technicals during his career. Loughery was second with 320.

"Every season Kevin would make a new year's resolution to not get on the referees," said Atlanta general manager Stan Kasten. "That would last until the first quarter of the first game."

Doug Moe of the Nuggets headed the voters' list of whiny current NBA coaches. Other former NBA coaches nominated were Cunningham, the only two-way inductee, Hubie Brown, Don Nelson, Larry Brown, Red Holzman and Red Auerbach. "Red retired the trophy," Ryan said of Auerbach. He did it a long time ago with those jaw-to-jaws with Sid Borgia. Richie Powers always told the story, during a Los Angeles-Boston playoff game in the '60s, he had had enough and he took the whistle out of his mouth and he slid it across the floor, it landed at Red's feet and he said, 'You do it.'

"The great sideline artists are still in college. Cunningham covered ground. Doug Moe's a very active coach during the game. Motta was out of the Red Holzman school. He was a sniper. You wouldn't even know he was ripping the ref unless you were two seats away. When the Knicks would come to Boston, he'd tell the refs something on the order of, 'They're good enough, you don't have to help them over and over again.'

"The best line of that nature came from Red Holzman. It's a second-hand story, but I like the source. The Knicks had a road game, and he was getting what he thought was a bum deal from Don Murphy. Finally, he said, 'Hey, Murph, plan on opening a bar here after you retire?'"

Last, but certainly not least, were the other former players nominated for the Whiners Hall of Fame. Oscar Robertson finished second behind Barry, with Cunningham third. And in addition to Williams's other nominations, the following old-timers received votes: Darrall Imhoff, Jerry West, Elvin Hayes and Bob Lanier. Heinsohn nominated himself and offered a reference.

"Sid Borgia wouldn't call a foul unless you were bleeding," Heinsohn said. "Everybody tried various methods to get to him. And once I tried humor. I said, 'Sid, this game is on national TV. My mother hasn't seen me in three months. If you call a foul on this guy, she'll see me when I go to the free-throw line.' So we go down the court, the defender is four feet off me, and Sid calls a foul. I step to the line and he says to me, 'That's it for your mother.' I never got a call the rest of the season."

(February 7, 1988)

Mary Schmitt grew up in Milwaukee where she was captivated by Al McGuire's NCAA basketball team at Marquette and became the first woman sports editor of the college paper. She currently covers the Minnesota Vikings for the St. Paul Pioneer Press. *She has also worked in Milwaukee, Washington and Eugene, OR.*

AFTERWORD

WOMEN AND CHILDREN ARE
NOT ADMITTED TO THE PRESS BOX

by Mary Garber

[*Editor's Note:* In May, 1992, Mary Garber, who has been a sportswriter for the Winston-Salem *Journal-Sentinel* since 1944, spoke at the annual convention of the Association For Women In Sports Media in Minneapolis. She was introduced by veteran basketball coach Jack McCloskey.]

EONS AGO, I LEFT PENNSYLVANIA AND WENT TO WINSTON-SALEM TO COACH the Wake Forest Demon Deacons. I wasn't quite prepared for the young lady who came into my office and introduced herself as the beat writer. The first time I saw her, she was wearing a dark blue navy pea coat, gloves, a Wake Forest cap and the greatest smile you've ever seen.

I learned over the years to really appreciate this lady for her great insight into the world of basketball, her style and her tenaciousness. Her ability to analyze the game and to tell her readers about it was just amazing.

We had some interesting times together at Wake Forest, didn't we, Mary? I think I integrated the Atlantic Coast Conference. We went down to Columbia, South Carolina, to play a game and they threw black cats on the floor as our players warmed up. And Mary, through her writing, tried to educate the bigots in the South that change was necessary. I'll always appreciate her for that.

This lady, I think, is your Jackie Robinson. She set the standards, she set the principles, she set the pace for you. Mary, you are loved, respected and honored by your peers. There can only be one greater accolade and that is that you are the nicest person any human being could be or hope to be. I sincerely mean that. This is the nicest person I have ever met in my life, bar none. Ladies, the great Mary Garber.

Soon after I started writing sports, I was waiting outside the Wake Forest basketball dressing room when a little boy approached me.

"Are you Mary Garber?" he asked.

It seemed like a friendly enough question, so I admitted I was.

"I read your stuff," he said.

I never know how to answer that one.

"You write pretty good," he said, "but it sure is weird having a lady write sports."

Before you dismiss this young man as a male chauvinist, I agree with him. It is indeed weird having a lady write sports. It was weird when I began in 1944, and I feel sure there are times when it is weird for you today.

I sewed up a high school boy's basketball pants so he could play in the game. Talk about pressure. Every time that kid went up for a rebound I waited to hear my stitches rip and to see him exposed in all his glory. My stitches held.

I shared my suite with two football coaches from the University of Florida. But don't get any ideas. This was a Fellowship of Christian Athletes conference. I'm not sure that was the sort of fellowship they had in mind.

I was covering a football scrimmage at Winston-Salem State by running up and down the sidelines when I realized I was going to be run over by a 190-pound running back. But as he crossed the sideline, he dropped the ball, picked me up and set me to one side. I wasn't so fortunate at North Carolina State where John Baker, a Raleigh policeman who guarded the State football dressing room door, welcomed me one Saturday by sweeping me into his arms and giving me a bear hug. He cracked two ribs.

Yes, I have had problems. Yes, I have been frustrated and angry, and I have even shed a few tears. But I am an optimist. Many of the problems I faced were solved long ago. I believe the problems you are facing today will be solved, too.

In 1946, I was barred from the press box at Duke, even though I had credentials. While I was arguing with the sports information director, a little boy was hopping up and down the press box steps. He could sit there, but I could not. I was put in the wives' box, where I tried to cover the game as the coaches' wives gossiped and the kids beat on the table and cheered.

The next Monday, I talked with our managing editor, Leon Dure and he wrote to the athletics directors at Duke, North Carolina, North Carolina State and Wake Forest. He told them that when they turned me away they were turning away the Winston-Salem *Journal-Sentinel*. The ADs didn't want to upset one of the biggest papers in the state so I was admitted. For years after that I worked in press boxes wearing a tag which read "women and children are not admitted to the press box." The regulation which barred me and other women from the press box was from the Football Writers Association, which I was not allowed to join until 1965. I have since served two terms on the association's board of directors.

I was barred from membership in the Southern Conference Sportswriters Association and later in the Atlantic Coast Conference Sportswriters Association. I asked Leon Dure to help me with this, but he said membership in the organization was not necessary for me to do my job as a sportswriter. Organizations, he said, could leave out anyone they wished. I finally got into the Atlantic Coast Sportswriters. I served on their board for several years and I was president. Three years ago, the association established an award for the best woman athlete in the ACC. It is named the Mary Garber award.

In many ways, I was lucky. When I began, I worked for an evening paper, which meant I had no problem meeting deadlines. I could afford to wait to talk to players without being concerned about missing the first edition. I worked on a medium-sized paper with a staff of two, Carlton Byrd and me. As editor, he picked what he wanted to do and I was free to do anything left. That gave me the chance to do a variety of things.

I worked in a medium-sized community, a place where I had grown up and knew people. When my dad worried about me roaming the city at all hours of the night, he expressed his concern to the chief of police, who was a friend of his. "Don't worry," the chief said. "Mary has a department of big brothers looking after her. Every policeman keeps an eye out for her." It was a gentler time. It was safe to wander around the streets at night.

For many years, I was the only woman covering sports in the area. In one way, it was easier for me than it is for you. I made my own way. I didn't have to worry about someone else screwing up things. I did that myself. There were some lonely times. No one was ugly to me. No one called me names. They just left me alone.

It was my fault as much as theirs. I could have made the first move. But I didn't want to stir up any problems. So I stayed quiet. You must remember that in those days there was no civil rights law to require equality. Men and women moved in separate and unequal worlds. Men and women knew how to act in a social situation, but we were not used to being thrown together in a professional and competitive world.

Coaches and players accepted me early. Maybe that was because at first I dealt with small colleges and high schools. In a segregated world, I covered black high schools and colleges. They were happy to get coverage, even from a woman. In those early years, I got a lot of help from coaches. I often took high school coaches with me to games. They took my credentials and went into the dressing room to talk with the coaches when I couldn't go. They were better than I would have been. They knew more what to ask. Since I worked for an evening paper I didn't have to write an on-site story. We talked on the way home and I learned a lot. Bones McKinney, the basketball coach at Wake Forest, moved his post-game press conference outside the dressing room so I could listen. After that, all the other coaches did, too.

I don't ever remember a player giving me a hard time. Most of them went out of their way to help. Guy Rodgers of Temple played in the NCAA regionals in Greensboro. After the press conference, I asked him if I could talk with him, since I couldn't go into the dressing room. He not only talked with me, but he told the male reporters they couldn't listen in. "You can talk to me later," he said. "She can't."

I am always introduced as the first woman to go into the dressing room. Frankly, that irks me. I hope I have done something more important in 47 years than go into a dressing room. I never went into a football dressing room when the players were changing clothes. I went into the basketball dressing rooms only for the last few years I covered ACC basketball.

In a way, life was simpler for me than it is for you. I knew I couldn't go into the dressing room so every game I had to be prepared to work around it. Assistant coaches fished players out of the dressing room. Assistant sports information directors got quotes for me. But it was always nerve-wracking, time-consuming and stressful. I always asked for more players than I needed, knowing that at least one wouldn't show up. I learned to spot moms and girlfriends and stay with them. They'd make sure Johnny talked.

N.C. State football was my easiest assignment. John Baker, the policeman who cracked my ribs, made my life so simple. I would go down on the field a couple of minutes before the game ended and he would watch the game from the end zone. As soon as it ended, he would unlock the dressing room door and slip me into the coaches' office where the press conference was held. This was just off the dressing room. I would give Mr. Baker a list of players I wanted. He saw to it that no player on the list got out the door without talking to me.

Once Dave Buckey, the N.C. State quarterback, was delayed by interviews. When Mr. Baker found I was still waiting for him, he went into the dressing room and literally grabbed Buckey by the arm and dragged him in to talk to me. Poor Dave was trying to zip up his pants as he was shoved along.

When I started working for the *Journal*, which was a morning paper, Carl Tacy, the Wake Forest basketball coach, gave me a break. I had the Wake Forest dressing room for the 9 p.m. game in the ACC tournament. No way could I wait until everyone showered and dressed. I asked Carl for help. He told me to come to the dressing room just before the game ended and Dave Odom, who was then an assistant at Wake Forest, would slip me into the dressing room and I could talk to players during the cooling-off period. Yes, it was against the rules.

Dave got me inside and suggested that we step back into the shower while Carl talked to the players. That is the basis for my story that Dave Odom and I were in the shower together. Wake Forest upset Carolina for an amazing win and the dressing room was bedlam as the players hugged each other, laughed, cried and danced. No other writer saw it. Carl explained why I was there, asked the players to please talk to me quickly because I had only the cooling-off period. I got a great story, but the men were furious.

Norm Sloan, the basketball coach at State, was the person who made the first move to let women into the ACC basketball dressing rooms. I told him how hard it was to work around the dressing room and he promised that he would talk with the other coaches and see if something could be worked out. I am sure you can guess what it was: an interview room. No one would be allowed in the dressing room. Of course, the men flipped. I didn't want them mad at me. So I called Norm, told him to forget it. I'd gotten along all these years. I could still do it. But Bill Brill, who was president of the ACC sportswriters, got a committee of coaches and writers together to work out a plan. Dressing rooms were to be open to women and men after the cooling-off period. But after 15 minutes, the women were to leave. I worked under the system for several years, and I was never asked to leave.

I still don't understand the dressing room problem. Federal law says that men cannot be given any privileges that women are not. If men go into the dressing room, then women must be permitted to go in too. And, yes, if women go into the women's dressing room, so can men. I hear the tired old excuse that young players will be embarrassed if women are in the dressing room. Come now, embarrassed when these players go to schools that have co-ed dorms where men and women are in each other's rooms at all hours? And suppose they are. There are bathrobes and towels to cover their inadequacies.

So all you women writers want to go into the dressing room so you can peek at naked men, right? If you want to peek at naked men, there are a whole lot better places to do it than a dressing room. Let's face it. Dressing rooms are the pits. No one in her right mind would want to go into a dressing room. It's hot. It's crowded. If you're my size, you run a risk of getting trampled. It's hard to get near a player. Most of the time you can't hear the question or answer and you can't read your notes because your paper is wet from all the steam. And I don't believe that there are any really great stories found in dressing rooms. Sure, once in a while someone pops off. But not too often. And there's no way you're going to get an exclusive in a dressing room. Too many people are listening in.

What concerns me is that women get the blame for the dressing room flap. It's not our fault. I believe the dressing room is not about women but part of the growing adversarial relationship between writers and athletic people. When I began writing sports, writers, coaches and players had an easy-going relationship. If I wanted to talk to a coach, I dropped by his office or even his home. I never thought of making an appointment. I had every coach's home phone and they had mine. We never hesitated to call each other. If I wanted to talk to a player, I stopped him after practice or I went to the training table and chatted with him as he ate. I could usually prevail on him to swipe me a plate of cookies. Wake Forest's training table has the best cookies in the world.

Not so now. If I want to talk to a coach, I call his secretary and face an inquisition about the subject of my interview and how long it will take. The coach may or may not call me back. One coach returned a call four days later. Setting up an interview with a player, I must go through the SID office. And there are limitations on when and where we can talk. Part of this is because of the growing demands on coaches' and players' time. But more of it is because coaches and other athletic personnel see the media as a foe. Some coaches are paranoid about what their players might say. They don't trust us. More than that they don't understand us. They think our role is to promote the team, to make the players feel good about themselves, to paint a rosy picture that will sell more tickets. They do not understand that our job is neither to promote nor pan. It's to tell people who love sports the things they would like to know but cannot find out for themselves. It might be good. It might be bad. We don't make the news. We just write it.

As I see it, athletic people are using women in the dressing room as an excuse to do something they have wanted to do. This is to control our access, to put limitations on what we can do. And this is as much a problem for men as it is for women. I don't think anyone really cares about the dressing room. We must be free to decide when and where we talk to athletes and coaches. This is not a decision that should be made by someone else. True, we must be reasonable. But we must keep the freedom to move and question when we need to do so.

I am concerned about the numbers of women who come into sportswriting enthusiastic, ambitious and anxious to do a good job. But after a few years, the battle gets to be too much for them. The grind of travel wears them down. All too many of them drop out of sports. Yes, this happens to men, too. But we truly need to keep our good women writers in sports.

Most of us think that the history of women sportswriters started with World War II. I might have thought the same thing if I hadn't cleaned out my bookcase last week and found a book on news writing I had gotten in 1939. It was a collection of talks put on by the New York Newspaper Women and one of the papers was on sportswriting by Joe Williams, sports editor of the *New York World-Telegram*. In it, he said that sportswriting was a field for men and women should not be in it. Yet he admitted that a woman on his staff, Nan O'Reilly, wrote golf well. And he said that the best story on the Dempsey-Tunney fight was written by a woman, Jane Dixon. That fight was in 1926; I was 10 years old. Jeanne Hoffman was a sports cartoonist and a feature writer in 1937.

The big influx of women sportswriters came in World War II. All the men were in the armed forces and if women didn't do a job, it didn't get done. We showed then that we do a lot of things people never believed we could do. But when the war ended, most of the women dropped out of sportswriting. There were a few of us, but we didn't know about each other.

Then came the civil rights act and affirmative action and all of a sudden, women became a hot commodity. Papers scrambled to hire them and unfortunately some of them didn't care whether the writer was competent or not. One of the women hired in that period told me the sports editor didn't ask her if she knew or cared anything about sports. Some of the women who moved into the field then did us more harm than good. I was on a TV program with a woman sportswriter who said she really didn't care about sports. She much preferred the ballet to any game. Some of the women took advantage of the situation to insist that they be either columnists or feature writers. No hanging around the dressing room for them.

Obviously, the men resented this. And women got the reputation of being prima donnas. I was at a panel on women sportswriters for the American Press Institute and someone asked me if I ever had to work the desk at night. I said yes, I took my turn just like anyone else and I bitched about it just like anyone else. He didn't ask me any more questions.

I understand that Frank Deford told you that men do not accept women sportswriters and he indicated that they were not likely to. I don't believe it. Many of you have already earned acceptance. You have earned it by doing your job in a professional manner. You have paid your dues. But the job isn't complete. It is still true that if John messes up, everyone says John is a jerk. But if Mary does, they shrug and say "Women can't be sportswriters." So it's important that each of you remember that what you do reflects on all of us. Sure, there are times when it's tough. Yes, sex discrimination exists and it's not going to go away.

First, have a sense of humor. You'll need it. When the men in my department put up girlie pictures, I asked for equal time and put up bare-chested men. The girlie pictures came down. Second, don't whine over every little slight. Leon Dure advised me well. If it's your ego, forget it. If it's your career, fight for it. Third, don't look for discrimination where none is intended. I once complained to a male sportswriter friend that I felt I lost good assignments because I was a woman. "You're lucky," he told me.

"When I lose an assignment I want, I know it was just because I wasn't good enough."

I look forward to the day when little girls will ask, "Mama, what do sex discrimination and gender equity mean? I never heard of them." I look forward to the day when every sportswriting job and assignment will go to the person who does the best. Believe me, it's coming. Our publisher told me that women are going to be running the newspaper business in a few years. They are moving in to take over. I say good.

That's why it is so important that each of you accept responsibility for our profession, that each of you do your job so well that you are accepted by the people in sports, by your colleagues and your editors.

The future of sportswriters who happen to be women is in your hands.

ABOUT THE EDITOR

Ron Rapoport *is a nationally syndicated sports columnist for the Los Angeles* Daily News *and a sports commentator for National Public Radio's "Weekend Edition."*